THE MASTER BUILDERS

STRUCTURES OF EMPIRE
IN THE NEW WORLD

ALSO BY J. V. FIFER

BOLIVIA: LAND, LOCATION, AND POLITICS SINCE 1825 (Cambridge University Press)

"This is a masterly and scholarly book and, what is more, a most readable one."
— *The Geographical Journal*

"An excellent book . . . a monumental job of synthesis . . . There are few volumes that so effectively demonstrate the interrelationships of the perspectives of geography, economics, anthropology, and political science, all within a meticulously integrated historical context."
— *The Hispanic American Historical Review*

"Skillfully written . . . One of the many reasons that makes the book such an enjoyable experience for the reader is that it presents an important thesis and proceeds to demonstrate, chapter by chapter, its validity and significance . . . Here is a book that can very profitably be read for its poignant insights and clear analyses."
— *The Journal of Developing Areas*

"Dr. Fifer's book is an outstanding example of scholarship that is both intensive and extensive."
— *The Americas*

"We applaud this happy fusion of history, geography and economics, and wish we had more studies like it."
— *World Affairs Report*

AMERICAN PROGRESS: THE GROWTH OF THE TRANSPORT, TOURIST, AND INFORMATION INDUSTRIES IN THE NINETEENTH-CENTURY WEST (The Globe Pequot Press, Connecticut)

"It is refreshing these days to read a serious, scholarly work on the American West that is not, in some sense, an accusatory tract . . . Fifer's richly layered book presents a whole series of western geographies (not frontiers) that are seldom addressed by western historians. In presenting these geographies, Fifer at once clarifies the way in which we should look at the post-Turnerian West . . .

This is a very significant book, one happily dealing with the intellectual history of the West, or at least with that other progressive West of the imagination that we seldom see because it is a landscape without violence or savagery or nostalgia . . . Fifer has indeed given us many geographies to consider in this fine book."
— *American Historical Review*

UNITED STATES PERCEPTIONS OF LATIN AMERICA, 1850–1930: A 'NEW WEST' SOUTH OF CAPRICORN? (Manchester University Press)

"A carefully researched analysis, which is a valuable contribution to the literature on the history of inter-American relations."
— *Journal of Latin American Studies*

"This well-organized and thoughtful study . . ."
— *The Journal of American History*

"Stimulating, absorbing reading . . ."
— *Nyt Fra Historien, Denmark*

"Deftly argued, . . . a persuasive and intriguing study . . ."
— *The Historian*

• NEW PERSPECTIVES ON AMERICAN HISTORY •

THE MASTER BUILDERS

STRUCTURES OF EMPIRE IN THE NEW WORLD

Spanish Initiatives and United States Invention

J. V. FIFER

DURHAM ACADEMIC PRESS

© J. V. Fifer, 1996

First published in 1996 by
Durham Academic Press
South Church
Bishop Auckland
Durham

American Office and Distributor:
The Pentland Press Inc
USA Division
5124 Bur Oak Circle
Raleigh
North Carolina 27612
USA

All rights reserved; no part of this publication may be reproduced, stored in a retrieval system, or transmitted in any form or by any means, electronic, mechanical, photocopying, recording, or otherwise without the prior written permission of the publishers and the author.
ISBN 1-900838-01-X

British Library Cataloguing-in-Publication Data

A catalogue record for this book is available from the British Library

Typeset by Carnegie Publishing, 18 Maynard St, Preston
Printed and bound by Bookcraft, Bath

Contents

Figures	ix
Foreword	1

PART I
SPAIN'S COMPRESSION STRUCTURE

1 The Spanish Initiative — 5

2 Preparation for Empire: Early Construction Work on the Peninsula — 8
The Medieval Builders

3 Building the Castilian Compression Structure — 15
Strengthening the Structure
New Institutional Tie-Beams
Final Testing

4 Laying out the First Site-Lines in the New World — 29
Initial Reconnaissance: Spain's Discovery of the West Atlantic and the Caribbean, 1492–1519

5 Design Enlargement — 39
The Need for Increased Compression
The Implications of 'Scaling-Up'

6 Extending the Ground-Plan of Empire — 43
Continental Expansion: The Land and the Rivers, 1519–1543
The Problems of Co-ordinating the Ground-Plan

7 Spain crosses the Pacific: Delimiting the Western Perimeter of Empire — 58
The Insertion of a New Tie-Beam

8 Oceans Apart: Spain's Search for Certainty in the New World — 65
Weight and Mass • Prestressing • Beams and Cantilevers • Joints • Resilience and Fracture

Spain's 'Reduced Risk' Construction Policies:
1. Administration 66
2. Church 76
3. Town 84
4. Immigration 91
5. Trade 96
6. Overland Transport; Its enduring perception as 'interoceanic' travel 113

9   **The Survival of Empire**   125
New Survey Work and New Construction

PART II
THE UNITED STATES' TENSION STRUCTURE

10   **The English Initiative**   140
Laying out the first Site-Lines and Starting Construction

11   **The Failure of the First Tension Structure**   149

12   **A Newly Designed Tension Structure: The Invention of Federalism**   151
Utility • Economy • Expansion

13   **Spain's Influence on the Early U.S. Perimeter Ground-Plan: I**   161
The Mississippi 'Coast'

14   **Spain's Influence on the Early U.S. Perimeter Ground-Plan: II**   173
The development of Transoceanic Empire
New England enters the Pacific

15   **The First Phase of Land Empire**   191
Spanning the Interior: the Problems of Diverging Styles of Construction, 1800–1860
New Bridging and Trussing Skills strengthen the North and West
Pseudo-Tension and greater Compression weaken the Deep South. Echoes of Imperial Spain

16   **The Extension of Land Empire in the Trans-Mississippi West**   216
1. Structural Engineering after the Civil War: strengthening the Foundations, Supports, Spans, and Surfaces 216
2. The Structural Significance of the word 'Transcontinental' 239

17	**Afterword and Conclusions**	243
	Design and Construction in the New World	
	1. Contrasts in Interpretation: Responses to Risk	244
	2. Contrasts on the Peripheries of Empire	247
	3. Cross-bracing	250
	4. Maintaining and Strengthening the United States' Tension Structure: Structural Analysis • Critical Load • Americanization • The Language Component	255
Notes		273
Bibliography		289
Acknowledgements		311
Index		313

Figures

1	The Iberian Peninsula and the expansion of Castile	10
2	Major North–South tie-beams in Castile's compression structure	20
3	The first East–West tie-beam in Catholic Spain: the medieval pilgrimage route to Santiago de Compostela	24
4	Europe's initial survey of the New World: Spanish exploration of the Caribbean Sea and the Gulf of Mexico,1492–1519	33
5	The ground-plan of empire: Spanish exploration of the American continent, 1519–1543	46
6	Key structural components: cities, towns, and principal overland routeways in the Spanish American empire	88
7	Spain's oceanic tie-beams: the early trans-Atlantic and trans-Pacific imperial routeways	104
8	The major load-bearing compartments: Spanish viceroyalties in the New World in the late 18th century	128
9	The United States urban population, 1790	144
10	Conflicting attitudes in the United States to the proposed new Federal structure, 1787–90	154
11	Early ties across the trans-Mississippi West, 1821–1861	218
12	Strengthening the ties: the Pacific Railroad Surveys, 1853–1854	233
13	Railroad expansion in the United States, 1870–1890	236
14	Relative location in the New World: West and East America	251
A	Medieval compression structures in Castile	14
B	The United States' Federal tension structure	160
C	Economy and Adaptability: 19th-century truss bridges in the United States	204/5

Foreword

Building empires means building **structures**, and all structures are designed to support loads—the **'dead load'** of the structure's own weight, and the **'live load'** of people and goods circulating within and through the structure, together with the additional 'loading' introduced from time to time by various environmental hazards. The basic principles of structural engineering, therefore, offer a helpful analogy and fresh insights in the analysis of the theory and practice of empire, particularly the empires of Spain and the United States—the two most original imperial structures ever to be built in the New World.

Despite their differences, the Spanish and the United States empires in the Americas shared certain characteristics which were unique in the history of imperialism:

- Both were intended *from the outset* to be large-scale structures designed to bear heavy loads.

- Both had to respond to the peculiarities of the American continent, including its extreme isolation in relation to the world's other land masses, and its unbroken extent north-south.

- Both included the Atlantic and Pacific Oceans in the earliest stages of design. Indeed, there was a strong sense of continuity in the 'double ocean' concept since the rapid adjustment to the *continental* and the *global* scale of Spain's empire was a crucial factor in the primary patterns of development of the United States.

In engineering terms, however, Spain built a *compression structure*, the United States a *tension structure*. The need to reduce risks caused by tension marked every phase of the building and maintenance of Spain's imperial compression structure for more than 300 years. The United States by contrast deliberately designed for increased risk and increased tension in society. Both the Spanish and the U.S. designs were innovative and daring, each unique in scale and concept in the handling of compression and tension. There were of course variations in the timing and the technologies of the two empires, but in the final analysis these variations were not as crucial as the fundamental contrast in the approach to *risk*.

This is an interpretive study, one that sets the broad history of the Spanish and United States empires into the engineer's framework of compression and tension, push and pull, stress and strain.* Two very different building styles were extended across the Americas. But the relative strengths and stability of the two great structures would eventually depend on their relative skills in the productive management of risk, and the study concludes with the challenge that a continued mastery in the field of risk management will always present to the United States—the world's largest and most successful tension structure.

---

* Stress should not be confused with strain.
Stress is a measure of *how hard* the atoms at a particular point in the material are being pushed together (under compression) or pulled apart (under tension) as a result of external forces.
Strain is a measure of *how far* the atoms at a particular point in the material are being pushed together or pulled apart.

Part I

Spain's Compression Structure

Other ships may sail the deep.
Old bounds are moved, new city walls spring up
On distant soil, and nothing now remains
As it has been in the much-travelled world.

A time shall come, with the slow years,
When Ocean shall unloose the chains from earth,
And a vast continent be revealed;
When a pilot will discover new worlds,
And Thule no longer be the limit of this land.

>(Seneca, born in Spain at Córdoba, *c.*5 B.C.; *Medea*)

1

The Spanish Initiative

ON FRIDAY, 3rd August 1492, Columbus's flagship, the *Santa Maria*, and two caravels, *Niña* and *Pinta*, left the small Atlantic port of Palos in southern Spain:

Sunday, 7th October 1492
Continued west . . . This day, at sunrise, the caravel *Niña* went ahead . . . and they all pushed forward as quickly as possible in order to be the first to sight land, and secure the reward which the Sovereigns had promised to whomsoever should first sight it . . . A great flock of birds passed, flying from north to south-west. For this reason the Admiral resolved to abandon the westward course and to steer west-south-west, and proceed in that direction for two days . . .

Wednesday, 10th October 1492
The men could bear no more and complained of the length of the voyage. But the Admiral encouraged them as best he could, holding out to them bright hopes of the rewards they might gain from it. He added that however much they might complain, having come so far he had nothing to do but go to the Indies, and would go on until he found them, with the help of our Lord.

Thursday, 11th October 1492
The course was west-south-west . . . They had a rougher sea than they had experienced during the whole voyage. They saw petrels and a green reed near the ship, . . . and other vegetation which grows on land . . . After sunset, the Admiral steered his former course to the west, and up to two hours before midnight they had made ninety miles, which are twenty-two leagues and a half. And since the caravel *Pinta* was swifter and went ahead of the Admiral, she found the land and made the signals . . . two hours after midnight . . . a Friday.

> From the *Journal of the First Voyage of Christopher Columbus*,
> on the sighting of San Salvador (Guanahaní island, Watling Cay)
> in the Bahamas,
> 12 October 1492

So began the momentous discovery of new lands, detached and isolated from the limits of the known world. Columbus found

America for Spain, but in doing so he had also discovered the western margin of the Atlantic. Far beyond the more familiar island outposts of Madeira, the Canaries, the Cape Verde archipelago and the Azores, Columbus's four great voyages in search of Asia would reveal instead the extent of the Atlantic to an unsuspecting Europe, the boundary of a New Ocean as well as a New World.

Spain's immediate reaction to Columbus's first voyage was to repeat it, and before long to establish a proprietary system of navigation across the Atlantic, an action without precedent, and for centuries without equal. For crusaders and conquerors alike, the hazardous, 3,000-mile ocean crossing in tiny ships was an unavoidable initial test of nerve and endurance, but Spain was undeterred by the formidable physical obstacles placed by Nature across its path. The Mediterranean world in time would be challenged by the Atlantic basin, but the response was to be varied and often slow. Spain, on the other hand, needed to act quickly. The Ocean demanded a new scale of adjustment to distance and geographical isolation, a new perspective which encouraged Spain to take the American continent in its stride, and even to remain undaunted by the unbelievably greater distances involved in sailing the Pacific. Portugal went around the world; Spain went across it.

Successful trans-Atlantic passage at the end of the fifteenth century was thus the model for two new movements, one trans-oceanic, the other transcontinental. The extent to which Columbus's European discovery of the Americas was anticipated by other seamen—from Scandinavia, Lisbon, Bristol, Ireland, or elsewhere—is irrelevant here. Discovery is more than sighting or encounter; discovery puts knowledge on record and makes that knowledge available to others. Columbus the Navigator had no antecedents. He sailed into uncharted seas in search of the Great Khan, the Moluccas and the lands of India, not, as he recorded, "by going eastward as is customary, but by a westerly route, in which direction to this day we have no certain evidence that anyone has gone."[1] If the importance of historical events is judged by their consequences, then Columbus's discovery of the continent in 1492 was decisive, for it marked Europe's first permanent contact with the Americas in political and economic terms.

The Columbian achievement, and Spain's swift response to it, created new patterns and rhythms of global proportion that were to form the major geographical expression of the transition from medieval to modern times. Europe's New World, once discovered, could not be ignored, but by the same token, the Americas were to remain influenced by the Old World, by Africa as well as by Europe, across a void that three continents would in time perceive as a great central ocean. In the beginning, however, the trans-Atlantic world was a Spanish invention.

To Castile and to León, Columbus gave a New World . . .

Then went out the ships one by one crying *A dios, A dios*, and Spain replied, *Buen viaje, Buen viaje*.

2

Preparation for Empire: Early Construction Work on the Peninsula

ROME

GOTH

ISLAM

AT THE END OF THE FIFTEENTH CENTURY, Spain set out for the New World from the small Atlantic ports of Andalusia and the Canary Islands. There were other points of departure, however. Spain's mental approach to the building of an American empire had originated farther north and centuries earlier.

Widespread conquest and organization of Iberia (the Greek name for the region) were gradually achieved by Rome after 218 B.C. During the first and second centuries A.D., the Roman empire created an extensive urban and road network throughout the Peninsula, and by the fourth century Christianity had become well established. Language, law, administration, and religion in both Spain and Portugal were thus the heritage of their incorporation into Rome's Hispania—the western bastion of empire, and a major source of minerals, wheat, wine, and olive oil. With the collapse of imperial rule in the fifth century, however, the Peninsula was prey to conflict among warring tribes invading from north of the Pyrenees, and torn by bitter regional rivalries that culminated in control of most of the area by the Visigoths. The economy meanwhile declined to subsistence level, famine was widespread, rebellion persisted; Catholicism, however, survived.

The Berber and Arab invasions of the Iberian peninsula across the Tarifa-Gibraltar Strait began early in the eighth century and proceeded with such astonishing speed and intensity that within seven years (A.D. 711–18) virtually all but the most remote pockets of resistance in the far north were subdued. Behind the Cantabrian mountain wall, these isolated outposts of Christendom were always to remain beyond the limits of effective Muslim political and economic organization, whether of the powerful Emirate (after 929 the Caliphate) of Córdoba, or its smaller successor states (the *taifas*). The North African conquest of Iberia had emphasized the geographical contrasts between the coastlands and the interior, the north and the south. The massive peninsula bridging Europe and Africa, and set between the Atlantic and Mediterranean worlds, was now to become a world of its own.

It was nearly 800 years before the Moslems were finally expelled from their last stronghold in Spain, and for 500 years they ruled the southern half of the peninsula with skill and determination. Their influence was pervasive in civic and political organization, unmistakable in architecture and design. By the introduction of new techniques in metallurgy, ceramics, textiles, leather, paper and glass manufacture, as well as through other branches of the fine and applied arts, science and technology, the Moors displayed a flair and mastery which were lasting in their impact, and which tapped the combined resources of Christian, Arab and Jew. At a time when backwardness, isolation, and fragmentation characterized the 'Dark Ages' in much of Gothic and Anglo-Saxon Europe, the culture and expertise of the eastern Mediterranean, the Middle East, and the Orient were transmitted to Iberia via North Africa.

Innovation in irrigated agriculture, seed selection and stock rearing led to dramatic increases in food production. Grain and olive harvests, for example, were in regular surplus for the first time since the Roman period, while the introduction of new breeds and new crops raised standards to levels unmatched elsewhere in Europe: merino sheep, stronger breeds of horses and mules, the cultivation of cane sugar, cotton, alfalfa, rice, oranges, date palms, bananas, pomegranate, mulberry, and many other varieties of fruit, fibres, nuts and vegetables were all introduced by the Moors. Thus, important advances in the pastoral, agricultural and manufacturing economy, in civil and military administration, and in medicine, mathematics, astronomy and philosophy flowed from the Arab world into the Iberian peninsula, where al-Andalus absorbed a unique blend of European, African and Asian intellectual and technological accomplishment.

Toledo and Saragossa were the two most northerly of the major Muslim cities. Toledo on a spectacular meander core of the Tagus controlled important east-west, north-south routeways across the peninsula. Saragossa, in the middle Ebro valley, commanded the cross-routes of Aragón and the north-east, beyond which there lay the Spanish March of Catalonia, on the fringe of the Carolingian empire. Arab territorial organization, however, remained strongest and most effective in the more congenial environments of south

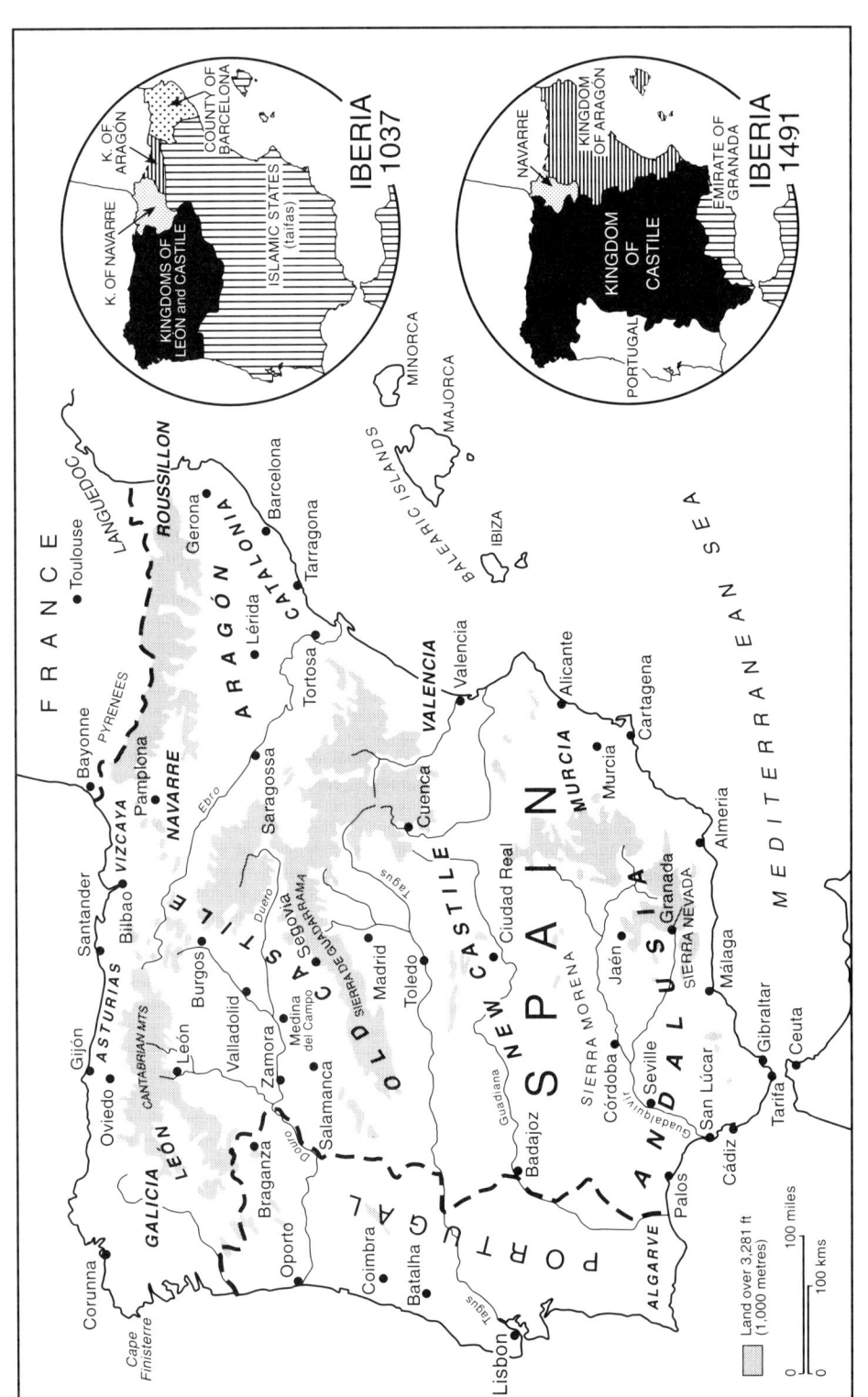

Figure 1 The Iberian Peninsula and the expansion of Castile.
(Based on H. Herring, *A History of Latin America*, Jonathan Cape, 3rd edn 1968)

and south-central Spain, sustained by large-scale grain production, an irrigated sub-tropical crop economy, and the labours of a large, compliant peasant population. At first, the northern Visigothic kingdoms behind the Cantabrian mountains were little more than scattered tribal areas claimed by various groups of shepherds and subsistence farmers, but the failure to subdue and incorporate them into Arab-Berber life had resulted in the survival of local chieftains and small Christian core areas from which *guerrilla* activity could be mounted against the Islamic state.

Northern Spain's opposition to the Moor, in consequence, developed a double-edge. Primarily, it stemmed from economic weakness since the north's backwardness and poverty contrasted sharply with the prosperity evident farther south. But northern envy also acquired strong religious overtones which demanded that the Cross be carried back into the lands of the Infidel. As a result, the fervour of Christian conviction in Spain, intensified by proximity and hostility to the Moor, had no counterpart elsewhere in Europe. The northern kingdoms mounted their own military crusade, the *Reconquista*, with a dedication that sets Iberia apart as one of the very few areas within the Muslim world ever to shake itself free from permanent Islamic occupation. Paradoxically, the dualism of approach to territorial expansion—religious and secular, Church and State—had been learned from the Arab. Christian Spain was to make it its own.

Internal changes in Islamic territorial organization of the Peninsula at the beginning of the eleventh century were to have a profound effect on the future patterns of power. The disintegration of the Córdoba Caliphate after 1031 into a mosaic of some twenty-six states (*taifas*) gave a strong stimulus to the political recovery and expansion of the northern Christian kingdoms. (Fig. 1) The *taifas*' enviable economic wealth was no longer defended by a skilled, unified military command, and now presented a unique opportunity to the poorer, increasingly bellicose Christian states. Following an initiative by Navarre, Christian leaders developed a tribute system whereby many of the Islamic states were forced to pay specific annual sums of gold to their northern neighbours in return for peace and protection. Rival Christian princes identified their own particular tributary states: the *taifa* of Saragossa for a time paid its tribute to Castile, Toledo to León, and Badajoz and Seville to Galicia, although at one stage, these four immensely important *taifas* were all paying tribute to Castile.

Gold was flooding into the north in the first half of the eleventh century, noted Gabriel Jackson, making Christian Spain one of the three European centres of financial prosperity at this time, the other two being northern Italy and Flanders . . .

> But whereas in Italy and Flanders manufactures and commerce were responsible for the flow of gold, in Spain the acquisition of precious metal resulted almost solely from the levying of tribute on the industrious south. Christian knights bought weapons, armour, equipment for their heavy cavalry, and luxury goods. Monasteries bought land, and the services of Muslim artisans and builders.
>
> In this century Christian Spain developed several of its characteristic traditions which were to affect not only the entire *Reconquista* but the later style of imperial development in America: the preference for investment in land rather than commerce and industry; the notion that manual labour was proper for Muslims, Jews or Indians, but that the function of Christian Spaniards was to rule; the idea of gaining wealth by levying tribute based upon superior military power.[2]

The mid-eleventh century dominance of al-Andalus by the northern Christian kingdoms was not to last. Although Christian forces managed to retain Toledo after capturing the city from the Moors in 1085, new Muslim invasions from Morocco between 1086 and 1110, and again in 1146, re-established unified Islamic authority throughout much of the Peninsula. Nevertheless, a significant shift in the perception of their future destiny had occurred among the Christian states that would in time encourage new alliances, new crusading fervour, and new determination to pursue a policy of direct conquest of the Moors rather than a *modus vivendi* based on tribute.

THE MEDIEVAL BUILDERS

If you go and look at a medieval cathedral you may well wonder whether you are impressed more deeply by the skill or by the faith of the people who built it . . . If you had had the chance to ask the Master Mason how it was really done and why the thing stood up at all, he might have said . . . "The building is kept up by the hand of God—always provided that, when we built it, we duly followed the traditional rules and mysteries of our craft."

Naturally, the buildings we see and admire are those which have survived . . .

(J.E. Gordon, *Structures*)

Monumental structures, centuries old, still stand as evidence of the skill and ingenuity of their designers and builders. As far as is known, they had no mathematical methods of calculating the sizes and strengths of the members of their structures. They relied upon trial and error, intuition, and craft experience and knowledge passed on from one generation to another.

(W. Morgan, *The Elements of Structure*)

Belmonte, Cuenca, La Mancha

Torrelobatón, Valladolid

MEDIEVAL CASTLES

WEIGHT AND MASS: dramatic compression structures built originally for conquest and defence.

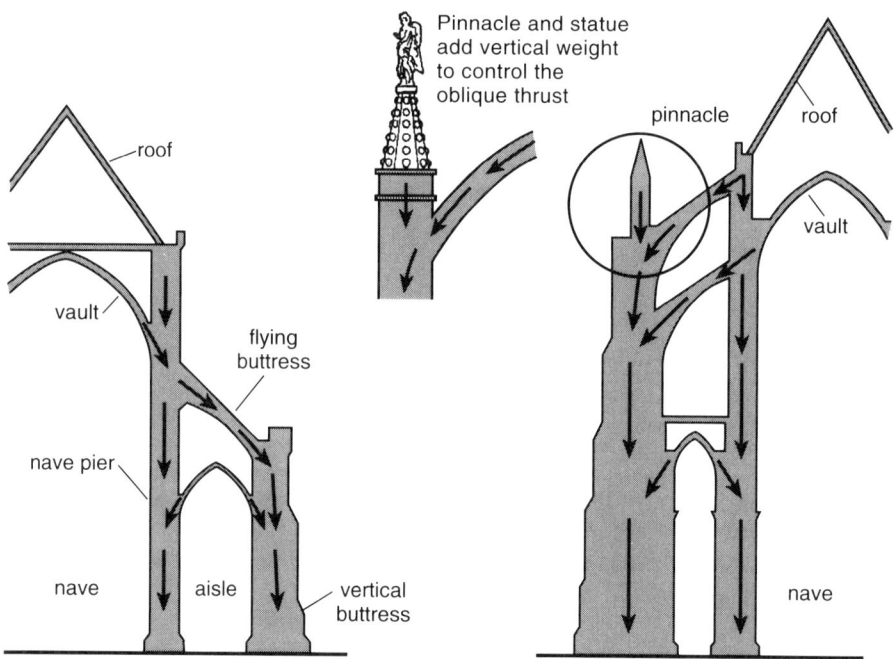

MEDIEVAL CHURCHES AND CATHEDRALS

WEIGHT AND HEIGHT: here, the compressive thrust is conducted into the ground through an elaborate architectural framework of walls, pillars, ribs, arches, buttresses, statues, pinnacles and balustrades.

Figure A.   Compression structures in Castile

3
Building the Castilian Compression Structure

> Castile's compression structure, gradually extended across the Peninsula, was medieval in design. It therefore posed the problem faced by all medieval builders in their largest structures—cathedrals, monasteries, castles, fortresses and towers—that of keeping the structure in compression at all times.
>
> Medieval builders reduced tension stresses and strains (the two main causes of collapse in the compression structure) by adding weight and height to the walls and piers, by keeping thrust lines strong and well centred, by using buttresses to help support the compressive load, and by introducing a complex pattern of arches, ribs, beams and pillars to assist in distributing it. Compression structures rarely fail by compression; they fall down by getting into tension.

Thus, *the avoidance, or reduction, of risk caused by tensile forces*, in different forms, and in scattered locations, remained Castile's structural priority.

Between the eleventh and thirteenth centuries, León, Galicia and Asturias gradually became unified behind the Christian frontier state of Castile—a hard, barren land, locked in the interior but dangerously exposed to Moorish attack from the south. The name Castile denoted a kingdom bristling with fortresses and castles (*castillos*); Castilian attitudes similarly reflected lives dogged by risk, suspicion and uncertainty. Over the years, the Reconquest suffered delays, setbacks and regional jealousies, but it was interspersed with local successes and decisive victories. Above all, progressive southward advance opened new worlds as the frontier penetrated the strikingly different geographies which band the Iberian peninsula.

The earliest stages had involved expansion from Spain's cool, wet northern fringes on to the dry, dun-coloured levels of the *meseta*. This great mountain-ribbed plateau, a little over 2,000 feet above sea level, presents a wild, almost treeless landscape unlike any other in western and central Europe. Clear skies, surface dust, shimmering summer heat, chill night temperatures, cold winters, and blistering winds from the high *sierras* harden the heart of Spain. Still farther south, the down-faulted edge of the *meseta* drops abruptly from the Sierra Morena into the Guadalquivir valley, and there the armies of north and central Spain entered the rich vine, olive, and wheat lands of al-Andalus. The impact of the Guadalquivir Depression was stunning, its size and fertility quite new to Castilian eyes. There is nothing else like it in the whole of Spain, indeed, in terms of potential, the great valley is one of the agricultural treasures of the Mediterranean world.

> The religious pray to Heaven for earth's good, but we soldiers and knights put their prayers into execution with our good right arms and at the edge of the sword . . . And we do this not under cover of a roof but under the open sky, beneath the insufferable rays of the summer sun and the biting cold of winter.
>
> (Cervantes, *Don Quixote*)

Mobility, hardship and endurance characterized life on the great sheep-grazing lands of Castile and Aragón. Bouts of summer campaigning were spurred by land hunger, pride, ambition and boredom, but fighting had to be accommodated to the annual routine of work on the range and tended, therefore, to adopt a seasonal rhythm synchronized with regional transhumance patterns. The ragged, aggressive advance towards the richer spoils of the south, with its crusading overtones, became a seasonal pursuit of strangely assorted bands of horsemen—lord and knight, drover and herder, master and man. Predatory raids from the north were invigorated by what could be regarded as the most noble justification of all for armed conflict, the sanctity of holy war. But in fact, the charms of the south needed no additional pretext to justify the steady drift of population towards the heartland of Andalusia, for in the south and south-east lay the real frontier of opportunity—the prosperous cities, the gardens of Spain, and the despised but coveted wealth of the settled agriculturalist. Never had Church teaching offered a clearer reminder of continuity and promise:

> The Lord thy God bringeth thee into a good land, a land of brooks of water, of fountains and depths that spring out of valleys and hills; A land of wheat, and barley, and vines, and fig trees, and pomegran-

ates; a land of oil olive, and honey; A land wherein thou shalt eat bread without scarceness; thou shalt lack nothing.

The recapture of the Peninsula from the Moors thus provided the framework, as well as the practical exercise of progressive re-colonization and Christian conversion. The Crown and three powerful Military orders organized the Reconquest with growing assurance. These religious societies of knights—Calatrava, Santiago and Alcántara—had been founded between 1158 and 1166 with the pledge to defend the frontiers against Islam. As the Christian forces advanced southward, there were new regions to be settled, defended and administered, a responsibility often devolved to noblemen as a reward for services rendered to the Crown. The process was known as *repartimiento* (allocation, distribution), and involved land grants, colonizing and municipal charters, royal offices, titles, and other privileges. Indeed, the Crown had to pay lavishly one way or another for the support of the nobility during the Reconquest, and the increasing territorial gains of both the Church and the secular aristocracy revealed the immense strength of their position. By the mid-thirteenth century, parts of the Mediterranean coast and most of the major urban centres had been regained. The advance of Aragonese and Catalan forces extended the frontier southward to Valencia and the Balearic Islands by 1238, while continued eastward expansion led to the conquest of Malta, Sardinaia, Sicily and southern Italy. In the southern interior, the fall of Córdoba in 1236, and particularly of the valuable river port of Seville in 1248, confirmed Castile's new mastery of the Guadalquivir valley, and opened a Castilian window on to the Atlantic Ocean. (Fig. 1)

Although still blocked in the south-east by the Moorish hold upon Granada, the mid-thirteenth century advance into the most prosperous agricultural, urban and manufacturing centres of Andalusia represented a significant breakthrough for the hitherto land-hungry and landlocked Castile. It was indeed the great turning-point in future Castilian development, both in Spain and subsequently in the Americas.

The political centre of Castile had already moved from Old into New Castile, south of the Sierra de Guadarrama. To the east lay Aragón, with its interests in the Mediterranean; to the west, expansion was curtailed by the Kingdom of Portugal, which declared its independence from Spain in the mid-twelfth century, and which by 1267 had finally freed its southern province, the Algarve, from both Muslim occupation and Castilian claims. In 1385 Portugal's independence was confirmed. Flanked, therefore, to east and west, Castile had assumed the central role in the Reconquest's great Peninsular expansion, an expansion which, despite interruptions, was progressively to link mountain and plateau, forest and steppe, valley and coast.

* * *

> **BEAMS**
>
> **One of the fundamental problems in structural engineering is the bridging of openings.**
> **The oldest solution was the HORIZONTAL BEAM, a structural element that supports a load across a gap.**
> **The TIE-BEAM however has another job to do. The function of a TIE-BEAM is to prevent two other structural elements from separating. It resists tensile forces.**
>
> (W. Morgan, *The Elements of Structure*)
>
> (A. J. Francis, *Introducing Structures*)
>
> **BEAMS AND TRUSSES of various sorts play an immensely important part in sustaining the burdens of the world. They are one of the most important devices in the world of structural engineering.**
> **Architectural trussing was a late Roman invention, although it never caught on properly until the Middle Ages.**
>
> (J. E. Gordon, *Structures*)

STRENGTHENING THE CASTILIAN COMPRESSION STRUCTURE

New Institutional Tie-beams

1. *Sheep Ranching and the Mesta*

Castile's traditional pastoral economy already depended heavily on the seasonal transhumance of its flocks on the *meseta*, and this activity was to support a dramatic expansion of Castilian authority and control.

After the successful southward expansion of León, Castile and Aragón in the thirteenth century, transhumance became more ambitious and began to involve trans-peninsular movement on a grand scale. This was soon dominated by Castile, where from an earlier scattering of local shepherds' co-operatives, a new and powerful association of sheepowners was organized by 1273 known as the Honourable Assembly of the Mesta of the Shepherds of Castile.[3] Taking full advantage of the extensive winter grazing lands recaptured from the Moors, the *Mesta* laid out a system of special sheep walks known as *cañadas* across the Spanish peninsula for hundreds of miles from north to south. (Fig. 2) It represented sheep ranching and long-distance transhumance on a scale unique in medieval Europe. Indeed, by the early fourteenth century, Castile had become the continent's greatest wool producing and exporting region.

The core of Old and New Castile was thus the focus of a spectacular overland movement, the great central gathering-ground and passageway linking Iberia's 'Humid Crescent'—northern Portugal, Galicia, the Cantabrian Mountains, and the Pyrenees—to the dry, warm south. Flocks began to leave the northern mountains and plateaux in mid-September and had usually arrived in the south by the end of October, to lamb and over-winter on the pastures of Extremadura and Andalusia. Departure began in the following spring, usually in mid-April, with shearing carried out *en route*. By the end of May or early June, the flocks were back on their home pastures, grazing on the fresh summer feed. Many of the sheepmasters owned a few hundred head only; wealthy landowners, however, including the Church and the Military Orders, despatched flocks of up to 30,000-40,000 head. As a result, the *Mesta* became a huge integrated corporation moving millions of sheep back and forth across the Peninsula, with the *cañada* system the first coherent network of communication from north to south since Roman times. **A genuine institutional tie-beam had been inserted by Castile.**

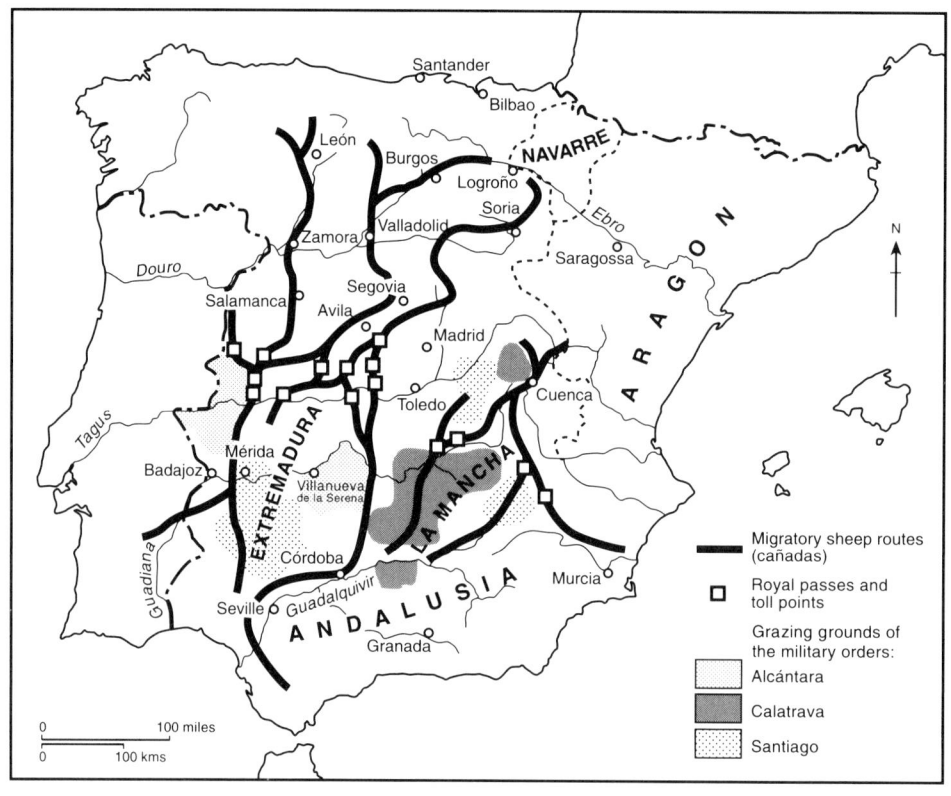

Figure 2 Major North-South tie-beams in Castile's compression structure. Migratory sheep routes controlled by the Crown and the *Mesta* in 15th–16th-century Spain.
(Based on J. Klein, *The Mesta*, Harvard University Press, 1920)

Shepherds were employed for the annual round trip, with sheep divided into flocks of about 1,000 for the seasonal migration. Criss-crossing the plateaux, however, were whole armies of people and animals on the move, for sheep and shepherds were accompanied by endless processions of mules laden with supplies, by horses, donkeys, sheepdogs, pigs, goats and cattle—all winding slowly across the skylines of Spain.

As well as providing a distinctive pattern of long-distance, north-south movement across the Peninsula, the *Mesta* was also notable for the high degree of control and formality it possessed as a Castilian institution. *Mesta* officials patrolled the great sheepways and drove roads, protecting them from encroachment by farmers, and from enclosure. The *cañadas*, more than eighty yards wide in places, were demarcated only where they ran through arable land, vineyards and orchards, but it was in these very areas that the local population faced the strongest temptation to ignore the markers and expand on to land that legally could never be ploughed or cultivated. To local farmers, each *cañada* formed a forbidden corridor used by local graziers, and twice a year by an alien flock. Conflicts over trespass, locally-owned pasture and unauthorized trading proliferated, so that the legal protection and representation in court provided by the *Mesta* for its members was one of the organization's principal attractions. Such protection served to underline the greater prestige, influence, and security of operation enjoyed by the Castilian pastoralist compared with the settled agriculturalist, an economic and social tradition which was to have far-reaching consequences.

Strengthening the tie-beam

The sanctioning of supply points, rest areas and refreshment posts, the maintenance of law and order, and the organization of markets and fairs were all part of the *Mesta's* responsibility. At least until the mid-sixteenth century, the *Mesta* was regarded by the Crown as a vital structural element, isolating and counteracting separatism, and unifying support over thousands of square miles through a peninsular network of special codes and privileges. Crown protection survived in fact until the late eighteenth century, when the entrenched power of the *Mesta's* pastoral interests was still reflected in the general stagnation and restricted development of Spanish agriculture.

Revenue payable to the Crown by the sheepowners was collected by *Mesta* agents at the official toll centres established along the way. Several of these royal toll points were located in or close to passes through the central *sierras*, since despite altitudes of over 8,000 feet rising dramatically above the general level of the plateau, these mountain ranges have never been a major barrier to movement. Many passes occur, mostly associated with the numerous geological faults. In the peak years, when more than three million sheep were being moved across the Peninsula, the *Mesta's* unique bureaucratic and fiscal role was indispensable. Crown and *Mesta* together had produced a strong bond of political and economic purpose, creating a large compression structure which was stamped throughout with the mark of Castile.

New Institutional Tie-beams

2. *Royal Charters and the Growth of Cattle Ranching*

The long-range movement of cattle across the Iberian peninsula during the medieval period played a smaller but nevertheless significant role in linking northern and southern Spain. Like the sheepowners, cattlemen had taken advantage of the extensive grazing lands on the *meseta* that became available with the Reconquest. From about the twelfth century, wealthy landowners, including the Church and the Military Orders, as well as small-scale farmers from the cooler, wetter fringes of the Peninsula, learned to adapt to the drier conditions and began to develop a genuine form of cattle ranching on the interior plateaux of León and Castile.[4] Indeed, in scale and emphasis, Spain's cattle-ranching activities were also to become unique in medieval Europe, and here the 1250s–1260s had been a particularly critical phase in the Reconquest.

After the fall of Seville, much of the territory newly recovered by Castile had undergone a major economic transformation in which many Muslim farmers, craftsmen, and merchants either fled, or were expelled from both the rural and urban areas for security reasons, and to provide supporters with wealth in the form of land. Although some of the most gifted artisans were retained as a protected minority, the loss of skilled agricultural workers, coupled with Castilian ignorance of sophisticated agricultural techniques, resulted in the conversion of some of the best cropland to cattle ranching, and an expansion of the great estates or *latifundios*. In addition to cattle ranching (including a dairying zone on the marshlands of the Lower Guadalquivir), there was now to be an almost total reliance on *unirrigated* agriculture—especially wheat, barley, olives, and vines—all of them the indigenous, drought-resistant Mediterranean crops which can normally survive on the seasonal rainfall (although irrigation increases yield), or which possess long root systems giving access to the local water-table. Only the huge size of the land-holding units that increasingly characterized the south and south-west would now mask the neglect and, with few exceptions, the extremely low productivity of Castilian agriculture. By contrast, the Crown of Aragón showed greater tolerance of the defeated Muslims, at least in terms of population expulsion, and as the Aragón-Catalan forces spread south beyond the Ebro valley into the rich irrigated lands (*huertas*) of Valencia and Alicante, Muslim farmers were encouraged to remain as skilled tenants or serfs of the new ruling class.

It was *Castilian* practice, however, which spread southward into Extremadura and Andalusia where, by the fourteenth century, *latifundistas* holding extensive tracts under new royal *repartimientos* had developed a lucrative, highly organized economy completely dominated in some areas by cattle ranching. No attempt was made, either by the ranchers or by the Crown, to establish a specialized association of cattlemen on the lines of the sheepowners' *Mesta*. Royal charters, however, allowed cattle to be moved for long distances along some of the *cañadas*, and until the fifteenth century, herds of 500–1,500 head were regularly trailed southward from León-Castile into Extremadura and thence to the plains of the Guadalquivir. As well as being distinguished by its sprawling agricultural estates, Andalusia increased its uniqueness by becoming the only major region in the Peninsula where cattle ranchers outnumbered sheepmen.

New Institutional Tie-Beams

3. *Trans-peninsular Trade and Transport*

> I have been thinking how little gain or profit there is in searching for adventures in these wastelands and crossways . . . Mark you, sir, along all these roads you meet no men of arms but only muleteers and carters.
>
> (Sancho Panza to Don Quixote)

Long-distance transport in medieval Spain was undertaken by pack animals, mainly mules. The rugged surface of the *meseta*, the

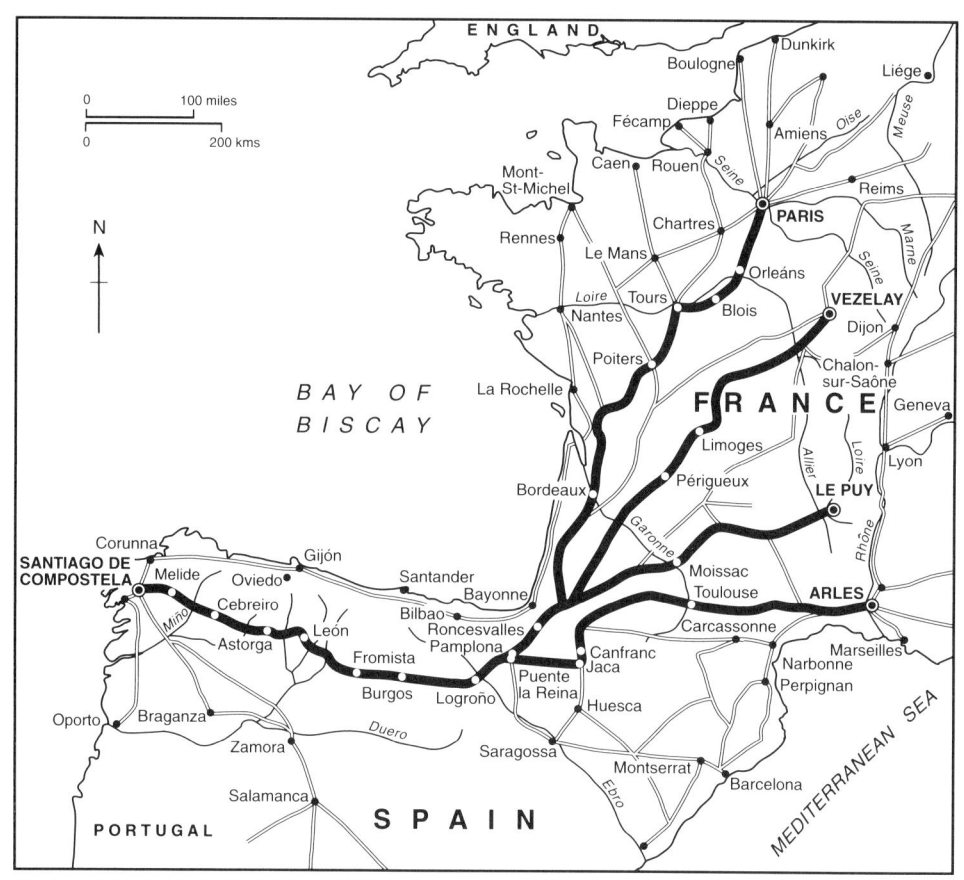

Figure 3 The first East–West tie-beam in Catholic Spain: the medieval pilgrimage route to Santiago de Compostela.

winding passes through the *sierras*, and the steep plateau escarpments overlooking river valleys and narrow coastal plains were negotiable only by mule train along a loose network of trails or dilapidated roads. The road system was still basically that of the Romans, although the medieval Pilgrim Road to Santiago de Compostela developed into an international highway after the site became the most famous place of pilgrimage in western Europe during the ninth century. Indeed, the location of the shrine in the far north-west corner of the Peninsula, coupled with the popular image of St. James as Christian Spain's own warrior-saint—'a holy Moor-slaying knight', forged an early and extremely effective east-west tie-beam between the Pyrenees and Finisterre. In the late eleventh century, the pilgrim route from Roncesvalles was shifted from north to south of the Cantabrian Mountains to pass through Burgos and León, after the northern Christian kingdoms had consolidated their territorial gains from the Moors. (Fig. 3)

The roads for the most part were badly maintained, and often impassable in rain, slush, or thick dust. The bridging points however, most of them established by the Romans, had remained key strategic sites for all trans-peninsular movement—Roman, Arab, and Christian *Reconquista*. In the early Middle Ages, wheeled traffic was mainly found only near towns. Late medieval Spain developed a simple two-wheeled oxcart, and by the fifteenth century, the Castilian freighting cart was frequently assembled into trains of twenty or thirty carts (usually the *carreta* with small solid wheels) for transporting major consignments of wool, ships' timbers, guns, rams or ammunition. Long-haul freighting by cart, however, was not developed more extensively until the seventeenth and eighteenth centuries, mainly with the growth of Madrid, and larger, four-wheeled wagons were not widespread in Spain until the nineteenth century.[5]

Even so, long-distance transport across the Peninsula by mule train was a significant feature of medieval Spain. Castile's highly profitable wool export to Flanders, France and England, via the Cantabrian ports, drew on supplies from as far south as Extremadura and La Mancha, and underlined the increasing Spanish reliance on the export of raw materials—Castilian wool, Basque iron ore, Catalan and Andalusian salt—rather than on development of the manufacturing sector pioneered centuries earlier by Arab craftsmen. Textile manufacture at this time remained a distinctive feature only of Catalonia. Since the nobility and other large land-owners were the direct beneficiaries of raw wool export, pastoralism imposed a peculiar character on Castilian society, "permitting the formation of a broad social class which did not cultivate the land but lived from it."[6] At the same time, pastoralism consolidated the *latifundia* system which always hindered the development of a class of well-to-do peasants. It was undoubtedly because of this pervasive seigneurial economy, argued Suárez Fernández, that Castile's interest in manufacturing was slight. In theory the Crown's aim was to encourage industry by protection, and a few traditional centres survived (e.g. for iron, textiles, leather, ceramics, and Toledo sword blades), but in practice there was no real stimulus to industrial production. "In the fifteenth century, Castile's economic evolution lagged behind that of the other European countries which, like England and France—not to speak of Flanders or Italy, which were exceptionally advanced—were then attempting, with relative success, the creation of powerful national industries." [7]

Fairs had given a major boost to long-distance trade and transport in the thirteenth and fourteenth centuries. Burgos became the main wool centre in the north, and mule trains laden with bales made their way down to Bilbao and the other northern ports handling Castile's wool and iron exports. During the fifteenth century, however, Medina del Campo surpassed all other fairs in the Peninsula, becoming the Crown of Castile's primary centre for collecting *Mesta* revenues and for overseas purchasing. Medina's fair lasted 100 days, divided into two periods between May and October. Merchants were drawn to it from all over Castile, as well as from Lisbon, Barcelona and Valencia. Genoese and Flemish merchants were also prominent, buying wool and hides, and selling manufactured and luxury goods. In fact, since the end of the thirteenth century, Italian merchants had been settling permanently in Seville, Córdoba, Cádiz and Cartagena, and had become an increasingly influential element in Castilian commerce.

FINAL TESTING AND STRENGTHENING OF THE CASTILIAN COMPRESSION STRUCTURE

As diverse cultural elements intermingled, Andalusia had become the testing-ground in which the Spanish state, essentially the Castilian state, was finally constructed, and from which the men and machinery of empire were carried into the New World.

The growing concentration of power in the two royal houses of Castile and Aragón, accompanied by new religious fervour, had revitalized the medieval concept of kingship and resulted in a greatly increased authority for the Crown, whose thrust was strengthened now by a more carefully controlled and more highly disciplined Church. Together, they had emerged as powerfully unifying factors in the life of the Peninsula, honed in the context of Spanish experience, instinct, and temperament. Intermittent, but seemingly interminable *guerrilla* fighting against Islam in the early years had become an inseparable part of the cultural tradition, particularly of the Castilian cultural tradition. Subsequently, crusading came to be regarded more as an attitude of mind, an epic narrative passed on from one generation to the next.

The Reconquest, however, was not complete. Following the marriage of Isabella and Ferdinand in 1469, Isabella's accession to the throne of Castile in 1474 and Ferdinand's to Aragón in 1479 led to a union in the conduct of foreign affairs.

Removal of the remaining major sources of tension

At the same time, with the introduction in Castile of the 'New Inquisition' in 1478 amid growing intolerance of the Muslim and Jewish communities in Spain, Queen Isabella's deep and uncompromising Christian conviction also led to a dramatic revival of military crusading. This became concentrated in the 1480s upon the last surviving Muslim enclave of Granada—well populated, prosperous, and enhanced by the strategic 300-mile section of the Mediterranean coast. (Fig. 1) The final surrender came on 2 January 1492, and the royal banners raised on the towers of the Alhambra at last proclaimed that the Peninsula was completely in the hands of Christian monarchs.

A few days later, the Catholic Sovereigns began to reconsider the project of a Genoese navigator, Christopher Columbus, who for nearly ten years had been presenting his proposals for a western approach to Asia to the courts of Europe.[8] The project had already been turned down by Portugal and Spain. Bartholomew Columbus, working on his brother's behalf, fared no better in England and France. Eventually, after what seemed like a lifetime of rejection, Christopher Columbus found Spain ready now to take a chance. Queen Isabella made the decision; Columbus, 'Admiral of the Ocean Sea', was granted permission in April 1492 to prepare for the voyage to the Orient, and test his conviction that a feasible, more direct route to the East could be secured by sailing fewer than 3,000 miles to the west. Overall, Columbus had underestimated the size of the world by about twenty-five per cent, but in addition he had also relied on estimates which exaggerated the longitudinal width of Asia. As a result of these combined errors, Columbus had calculated the distance between the Canaries and Cipangu (Japan) as only 2,400 nautical miles, less than a quarter of the true distance.

Spain's mood was soon to be one of triumphant vindication. A unique blend of ambition, self-confidence, religious zeal, and surplus energy was to inspire future Castilian policies. North Africa presented the obvious field for expansion, and Spain was to capture and garrison a few key sites, but in general, Muslim resistance there was too strongly entrenched to encourage a major offensive into the African continent. Portugal's claims to the Canary Islands had finally been abandoned in 1479 in the face of Castile's determination to strengthen its own position along the African coast. But the real significance to Spain of the Canary Islands, lying on the edge of the Trade Wind belt, was not to be their position in relation to Africa, but as the point of departure for the new transatlantic movement. With the astonishing coincidence of Columbus's discoveries, and his return only fourteen months after the fall of Granada, the direction of Spain's subsequent expansion was suddenly determined, just as its scale and dimensions were enlarged.

Viewed in retrospect, the preparation for empire had been harsh, prolonged, and eminently successful, with the final stages of construction greatly strengthened by the Catholic Monarchs' new administrative reforms. Without pause or interruption, Spain sailed out across the Ocean Sea to extend and organize its new possessions. Although the size and significance of the discoveries were yet to be recognized, the self-assurance displayed by the Crown concerning its fitness for the task of empire remains one of the most remarkable aspects of this whole remarkable venture. Indeed, Spain's immediate readiness to meet the challenge of the West never ceased to amaze, and to influence, all those who followed Spain into the dreams and destinations of the New World.

4
Laying out the First Site-Lines in the New World

GROUNDWORK AND FOUNDATIONS
Basic Principles

In large undertakings, first explore the ground, ascertaine its capabilitie, and relate your findings to the nature and scope of the edifice proposed.

(Builder's Manual, sixteenth century)

Regarding the Foundations, one indisputable fact is this: whatever the shape of a building or structure and whatever the nature and number of its supports, the whole weight of the building must come down to, and be supported by, the ground. It is therefore essential that, for any proposed structure, sufficient knowledge be obtained of the nature of the supporting soil and its load-bearing capacity.

(W. Morgan, *The Elements of Structure*)

INITIAL RECONNAISSANCE

SPAIN'S DISCOVERY OF THE WEST ATLANTIC AND THE CARIBBEAN, 1492–1519

What they dare to dream of, dare to do.

(J. R. Lowell, *Commemoration Ode*)

Among the many distinguishing features of the first great westward transmission of men and ideas into the Americas, none was more significant than the timing of events. It was an early migration, medieval still in its contact, heritage and ideals. Continuity was preserved between the late Middle Ages in Spain, and the early institutional and cultural life of the American colonies. Despite, or perhaps because of the huge Atlantic void between them, it is in the Spanish New World that we find one of the last vivid expressions of medieval Europe. As Luis Weckmann noted:

> Columbus, the first link between the Old World and the New, stands in a clearer light if we envisage him not so much as the first of the modern explorers but as the last of the great medieval travellers ... impelled by medieval quests and geographical puzzles towards the exploration of new routes of navigation.[9]

Since the first expedition had been specifically authorized by Queen Isabella of Castile, it became her project and Columbus her Admiral. No time was lost upon his return to Spain in March 1493 in seeking confirmation from the Spanish Pope Alexander VI of ownership by Castile and León of all the lands discovered (Papal Bull, 3 May 1493). The response was to be history's boldest and most uncomplicated delimitation of political spheres of interest on the global scale; the allocation of the land was made by a division of the ocean.

By the Papal Bull dated 4 May 1493, Spain's right to hold and exploit its new discoveries was confirmed by a line drawn from Pole to Pole passing 100 leagues west of any of the Azores and Cape Verde Islands (where Portugal had already been granted right of sovereignty by Papal Bulls issued between 1454 and 1481). The Crown of Castile and León was granted all the land lying west of this new dividing line, provided it was not already in the possession of a Christian ruler by Christmas 1492. This is not to say, as some do, that the 'New World' was knowingly allocated at this time, since its existence as such was not yet known. Portugal received a similar concession on lands to the east of the line, and by 1493 abandoned its earlier proposal for a latitudinal line passing through Cape Bojador (26°N), just south of the Canaries, which would have divided Spanish interests in the north from Portuguese interests in the south.

The immediate recourse to Rome for political decision-making on the grand scale emphasized the fact that the Catholic Church embodied Christendom's only international law. No matter that Protestant monarchs would shortly dispute such absolute authority in this, as in other affairs—that they would, in effect, like Francis I of France, demand to see the clause in Adam's will which excluded them from any part of the free world. The Pope could not give away what he did not own, and effective occupation would in time become the basis of political territorial claims, in the Americas and elsewhere. But the fact remained that for the two Iberian States at the close of the fifteenth century, a world apportioned by Papal injunction endorsed the claim that the resources, as well as the responsibilities, of the new empires were theirs by divine authority. It was an exceptionally powerful corroboration.

Portugal, however, was dissatisfied with the '100 league line', largely because it afforded insufficient clearance for Portuguese operations to continue unchallenged in the Gulf of Guinea and the south Atlantic, but also because if Columbus's discoveries were indeed part of Asia, Portugal needed to be near enough to maintain its claims in the region. Lisbon demanded a major adjustment which was incorporated in the Treaty of Tordesillas in 1494; Spain was forced to accept the shifting of the line to a point 370 leagues west of the Cape Verde islands. Despite the uncertainty over which island in the Cape Verde group was to be used for measuring the point of departure west, to say nothing of the fact that there was still no method of calculating longitude precisely, a Line (or Zone) of Demarcation was generally agreed. Further exploration revealed that it passed through the mouths of the Amazon and the island of Santa Catarina. The zone between 48°W and 50°W was acknowledged to be a realistic approximation, and Spanish activity was thus removed to a safe distance from existing Portuguese interests in the Atlantic. (Fig. 5)

In effect, the Tordesillas Line yielded the world's land hemisphere to Portuguese enterprise and the ocean hemisphere to Spain. The ocean hemisphere would soon be found to contain an immense land-mass of its own, a New World, but in the race to the Far

East, and with growing rivalry between Portugal and Spain for the India and China trade, it was more important to confirm the position of the Tordesillas Line in the Orient than in the Americas. No one at this stage could be certain of the relationship between the Orient and the Americas, even supposing they were two, and not one and the same. Whatever the relationship was between Asia's Indies and the Indies of Columbus, the Spice Islands remained the prize. Once it became clear that the Tordesillas Line's Atlantic demarcation could go full circle and "divide the world like an orange",[10] who got what could only be settled by encompassing the world, and staking a claim. Global political allocation by hemisphere was not only simple, it was also conducive to transoceanic perspective, to long-range expansion, and to a new concept of imperialism.

All things considered, the late fifteenth-century discovery of the Americas had initially done no more than interrupt the voyage to the Orient. How great an obstacle lay between Spain and the Spice Islands of the East remained to be seen. Columbus was still busy sketching the broad outlines of the Caribbean. His first voyage had located the Bahama group, Cuba and Hispaniola; the second (1493–96), Dominica, Guadeloupe, the Leeward and Virgin Islands, Puerto Rico and Jamaica. South America was discovered on the third voyage (1498–1500), which revealed part of the Venezuelan coast, Trinidad, and the great delta of the Orinoco, Columbus's first indication of the presence and scale of the land mass lying to the south. (Fig. 4)

With his fourth and final voyage in 1502–04, Columbus completed the framework of the Caribbean by following the Isthmian shore, and identifying it as a part of the Malay peninsula. Until his death in 1506, Columbus appears to have believed that he had reached his original destination, the coasts of China, Japan, and the Spice Islands. Indeed, for some years, no one could be absolutely certain of what Columbus had discovered; if it was not another island archipelago in the Atlantic, the legendary islands of Antilla, and the Seven Cities, perhaps after all the Admiral had been right, it was Asia, but an unknown corner, remote from the commercial centres he had sought.

Vexed and impatient, Spain began to search desperately for a strait through which to continue the westward voyage. With each successive survey, however, the continent appeared to become more extensive and more impenetrable. The combined efforts of the explorers and the map-makers were meant to close the gaps in the

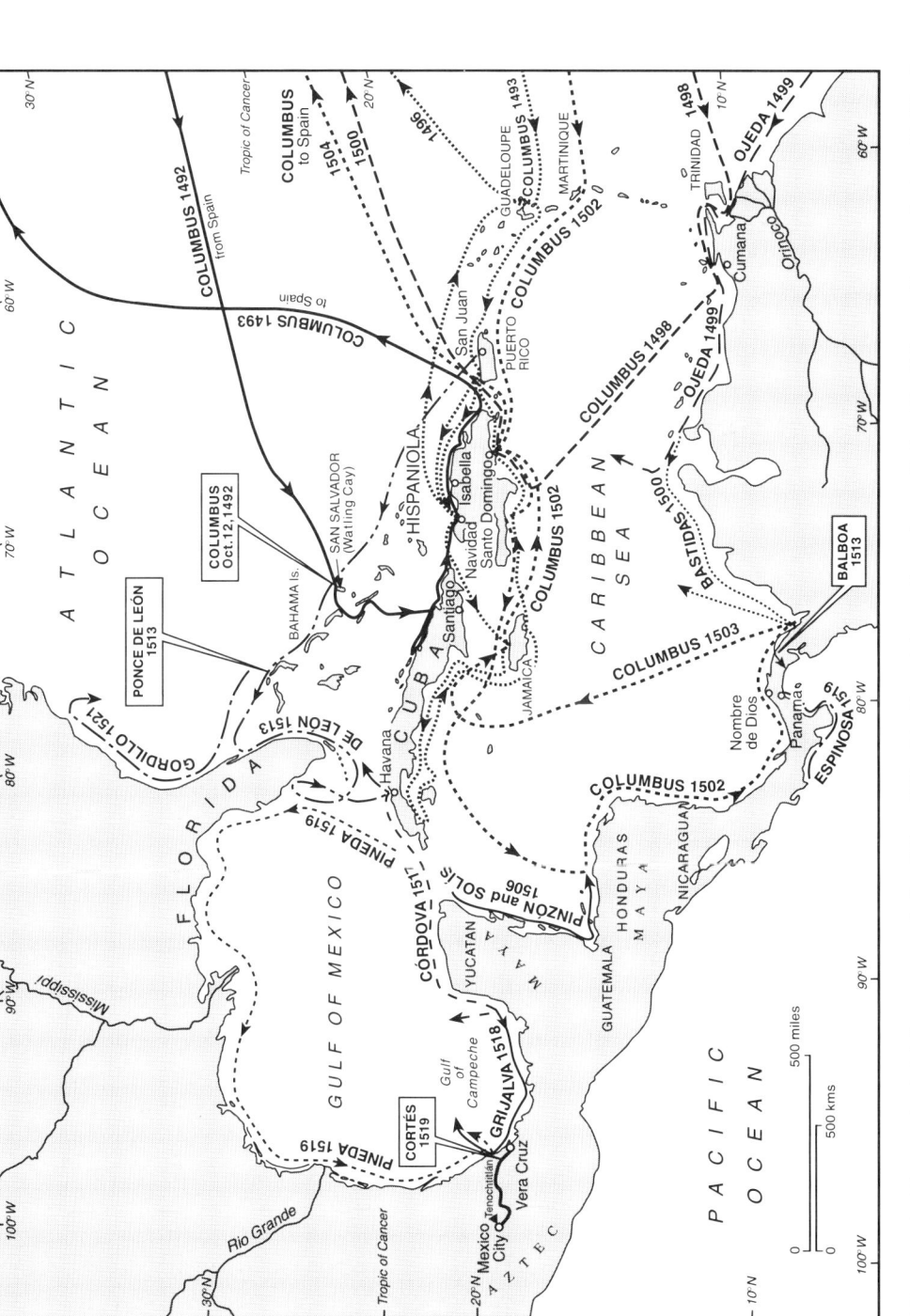

Figure 4 Europe's initial survey of the New World: Spanish exploration of the Caribbean Sea and the Gulf of Mexico, 1492–1519.

coastline, but not too literally. More systematic reconnaissance was urgently needed to supplement Columbus's discoveries, and in a burst of activity between 1499 and 1506, new voyages were authorized to explore different sections of the coast. The leaders of these expeditions sailed under special licence from the Crown but at their own expense, or through privately negotiated sponsorship. More often than not, ships' captains caught the tide with whatever they and their crews could beg, borrow or steal.

These secondary expeditions were usually under the command of men who had already sailed with Columbus on his early pioneering voyages. Between them, in caravels normally of only 50–60 tons, a handful of mariners added thousands of miles of new coastline to the charts as they worked their way around the abundance of islands and peninsulas forming the Americas' Atlantic rim. In 1499–1500, Alonso de Ojeda became the first to extend exploration along the whole of the Venezuelan coast, west of Trinidad. Niño and Guerra wisely concentrated on the island of Margarita and the 'Pearl Coast', while Yañez Pinzón and Diego de Lepe completed a survey of the South American coast east of Trinidad as far as the great shoulder of Brazil.

Meanwhile, Amerigo Vespucci, the Florentine navigator, had joined in the search. Sailing on behalf of Spain in 1499 (his second voyage), Vespucci concentrated for a time on the region around the mouths of the Amazon. His party separated from the main group and alternately sailed and rowed for many miles along low, indistinguishable shorelines completely curtained with rain forest. Eventually, all attempts to land were abandoned and the decision taken to sail north-west and rejoin Ojeda. Undeterred, Vespucci returned to South America in 1501–2, this time in the service of Portugal, and extended his exploration southward along the coast of Brazil. He sailed as far south as the Río de la Plata, and into the wide bays of Patagonia (to approximately 50°S), before returning to Lisbon with the latest report on the extraordinary size of this strange and perplexing land mass. Prophetically, Vespucci's letter to Lorenzo Pietro di Medici in 1503, describing his third voyage, was entitled *Mundus Novus*. In 1507, the German cartographer Waldseemüller named the land-mass *America* in honour of Vespucci—a New World, so far as it was known or conjectured, separated from the Old.

With no sign of a sea passage westward, Spain renewed its efforts along the isthmian coast. In 1500–05, Rodrigo de Bastidas and Juan de la Cosa (Columbus's old pilot) had explored the Gulf of

Urabá and Darien, convinced that it must form part of the elusive western strait. In 1506, Yañez Pinzón and Juan de Solís had followed the line of the Yucatán coast around the Honduras embayment with the same conviction and the same negative result. Farther north, by 1519 the Florida foreland and the curving line of the Gulf of Mexico had been traced, and similarly written off in exasperation as a possible way out of this new Spanish sea.

Locating the initial structure

In the Caribbean and the Gulf of Mexico, Spain had discovered the Mediterranean of the Americas, a two-bayed marine enclosure open to the Atlantic but otherwise encircled for 6,000 miles by the coastal sweep from Florida to the Orinoco. Unlike the Mediterranean of the Old World, so intimately linked to its *terrestrial* surroundings and to a complex set of small, distinctive circulations, the Mediterranean of the Americas at once formed part of Spain's *maritime* world. Where a section of the great American cordillera splits and curves to form the arc of the Indies, the ocean has drowned the intervening plains to create the Middle Seas. But the concept of the Middle Seas was not indigenous to the Americas; it was post- not pre-Columbian in origin, a Spanish concept developed at Spain's new transatlantic terminal in the centre of the New World. At first, however, the Caribbean and the Gulf of Mexico were simply the end of the Atlantic, exceptionally spacious but nevertheless a cul-de-sac. Spain was trapped against the Americas, and forced to discover the truth of the early geographers' definition of a continent: 'A great land not separated by the sea.'

To make matters worse, Spain was faced with the fact that in the first two decades of the sixteenth century this great land had provided neither the economic resources nor the political prizes to justify all the effort and trouble involved. Portugal had obviously pursued the wisest course by following the outline of the Old World, and pushing its ships around Africa to reach India and the Spice Islands by more traditional means.

In 1520, Magellan's discovery of an all-water route into the Pacific provided the longed-for practical demonstration that, in Mackinder's phrase, "the ocean was one ocean all the time." But in one respect, Magellan had confirmed Spain's worst fears about America: that the remote southern tip of the continent would prove to be the only uninterrupted western exit from the Atlantic Ocean.

Spain's final attempt at this stage to find a substitute was made by Esteban Gómez, who in 1524–5 sought a north-west passage along the coasts of Maine and Nova Scotia, but all in vain. The northern strait continued to elude Europeans. Without knowing the details, the site-surveyors had now discovered the essentials of a unique geographical phenomenon: the Americas formed a north-south barrier of land and ice which blocked the sea-lanes across 140 of the 180 degrees of latitude between the Poles.

The search for a continuous sea passage westward had remained the main objective of Spain's great coastal reconnaissance in the late fifteenth and early sixteenth centuries, but there were limits to how far Spain would go to avoid overland transfers. Magellan's strait was too isolated, too slow and too risky to be considered as a practical proposition at this stage. Seven years before Magellan sailed into the Pacific, Nuñez de Balboa had sighted this new ocean from the Isthmus of Panamá. Balboa had accompanied Bastidas and Juan de la Cosa in 1501–2 on their preliminary exploration of the Urabá-Darien gulf, and then decided to stay on in the region. In 1513 he led a small group across the Isthmus to the shores of the Pacific, and claimed the ocean and its surrounding lands for Spain, unaware that the Portuguese had captured Malacca two years earlier, and that in 1513 Portugal's Antonio de Abreu had also sighted the Pacific, looking eastward from the Spice Islands of the Moluccas.

At this stage, no one knew the enormous size of the Pacific, but it was Balboa's action that proved to be decisive in shaping the geographical patterns of Spain's future empire. The discovery of the existence of the Pacific must rank as one of the most amazing revelations in the history of exploration; knowledge of its extent, only eight years later, became another. The discovery of the Isthmus of Panamá had led the way, and Spain was to give this narrow neck of land a name befitting its value to the Crown— Castilla del Oro, Golden Castle. It was one of the most important finds ever made in the Americas.

In the event, Magellan's discovery of the sea-lane into the Pacific in 1520 had coincided with Spain's first great discovery of wealth thousands of miles farther north, in Mexico. In both the Old World and the New, wherever the costs of sea travel become excessive because of vast distance, or because of delays and dangers from storms, or calms, or pirates, or naval attack, alternatives were always sought. Transhipment of men and supplies overland for *short* distances was not regarded as a major hindrance in the sixteenth century. Many of the cargoes were of high value in relation to their bulk, ships were small and crew labour usually adequate if all else failed.

The riches of the Aztec empire set between the Atlantic and Pacific, and Balboa's crossing at Panamá, together established the key structural role that Mexico and Isthmus would play in tying Spain's two great ocean circulations. The American continent's immense length would serve a useful purpose after all; it would keep European intruders out of the Pacific.

SCALE, PROPORTION AND SAFETY

The designer seeks some kind of objective assurance about the strength and stability of whatever he is proposing to make. If one is unable to make the right sort of modern calculations then the obvious thing to do is either to make a model or else to SCALE UP from some previous smaller version of the structure which has proved to be successful.

What medieval craftsmen did was to make something very much like what had been made before . . . And there are some special reasons why it is sometimes safe and practicable to SCALE UP . . . relying simply on experience and traditional proportions.

(J. E. Gordon, *Structures*)

5
Design Enlargement

As soon as Spain was confronted with the need for new construction, it followed traditional medieval building practice and **scaled up** the design for an overseas empire from its own existing Peninsular model. **This was already remarkably sophisticated for the period since by the late fifteenth century, the Spanish state had created a uniquely-styled compression structure with Castile as the strongest component—its political and economic working space linking Biscay to Andalusia, its tie-beams in place, and its thrust lines increasingly centred and stabilized by the Crown and the Church.**

Spain's initial assessment of its discoveries

In economic terms, the Caribbean islands were a major disappointment to Spain. Matched against expectations, the returns were meagre, the prestige trifling. The limited supplies of gold in Hispaniola, Cuba, Puerto Rico, and the Isthmus declined after 1520 and were soon exhausted. Exploration of the Caribbean rim had been swift and thorough, but Jamaica, the lesser Antilles, and the mainland fringe yielded next to nothing to justify systematic colonization. An empire could not be built on cargoes of dyewood, pearls and parrots.

The Indian population had been decimated by European diseases, abuse, overwork, and despair. The indigenous labour supply, therefore, always limited, got rapidly worse, and land without labour remained unattractive to the Spanish settler. Land grants by the Crown would often include an allotment of Indians under *repartimiento*, the system of land distribution and colonization operated by Castile during the Reconquest, and introduced into the Indies via the Canary Islands by Columbus. The older term, *encomienda* (which stressed responsibility for, rather than simply the allocation of, the Indians), was more generally adopted after 1509. *Encomienda* involved the commending by royal grant of a specified district or region to the care of an individual (the *encomendero*), who was thereby entitled to demand tribute (and initially labour also) from the Indians settled within it. In return, contractually at least, *encomienda* carried the obligation to care for the Indians, to instruct them in the faith, and to provide military protection if required.

The continuity with Spanish medieval tradition was clear, although as a legal institution in the New World, *encomienda* did not include rights to the ownership of Indian lands. Even so, there was never sufficient manpower to shoulder the mundane tasks so disagreeable to the Spaniards—the laying out and building of new settlements, bringing in food, portaging supplies, clearing forest and planting crops, and, if gold was discovered, the sheer monotony of washing and panning. The remaining Indians grew increasingly hostile. The *repartimiento* system spread with the expansion of ranching and later of the sugar estates, where the import of African slaves was intensified in the 1520s. Additional crops and livestock from the Peninsula and the Canaries were introduced, but by this time, standards of living among many of the colonists had declined to little more than subsistence level. Despite the stringent penalties if they were caught, many restless, dissatisfied elements abandoned the islands to swell the stream of new immigrants from Spain and become the vanguard of the second great phase of empire. For in 1520 Spain stood poised upon the threshold of one of the greatest continental expansions the world has ever known.

Early site-lines strung in 1492–1519 revealed the western margin of the Atlantic Ocean, the nature of the Caribbean, and the existence of the Panama Isthmus and another Ocean. An immediate start was made on transferring elements of the Peninsular model to the Indies, but the open Atlantic beyond the Canaries had already introduced the first severe tensile strain into the structure and this influenced the next stage of operation.

Tests for stability confirmed that none of the responsibility for future design and construction would be given to the surveyors. Familiarity with local conditions, and adjustment to them, were neither required nor recommended qualifications for building the compression structure Spain had in mind. This was a key design decision of fundamental significance.

Primary building requirements: the need for increased compression

Columbus was relieved of his administrative authority at a very early stage in the proceedings. On the first voyage, Hispaniola had been selected as the site of Spain's first permanent settlement in the Indies. Columbus had sailed as 'Admiral of the Ocean Sea, Viceroy, Captain-General and Perpetual Governor' of the islands and mainlands he discovered, and from which one-tenth of the profits of his discoveries were to be his. The emphasis at this stage, despite the full implications of these new titles, had been on rapid ocean reconnaissance, at which Columbus excelled, rather than consolidation and administration of what was taken in the process.

The Indies presented a major administrative problem by any standards, a tropical archipelago of great physical variety, widely scattered across more than a million square miles of the Caribbean. Some islands consisted simply of low, coral platforms, barely visible above the horizon; others were steep and rugged, spiked with volcanic peaks of over 5,000 feet. "All are most beautiful," wrote Columbus, "of a thousand shapes." But Hispaniola's great bulk was unmistakable, its central mountains soaring to more than 10,000 feet. "Española is a marvel," the Admiral recorded, "so lovely and so rich . . . a land to be desired and, when seen, never to be left."[11]

Columbus's second expedition to the Indies had been a much more ambitious undertaking than the first. A royal fleet of seventeen ships and more than 1,200 men had sailed with great ceremony from Cádiz in September 1493, a mere six months after the completion of the initial voyage. And for the first time, priests, farmers, artisans, and strangely assorted cargoes of cattle, pigs, horses, mules, seeds, plants, tools and equipment, were all included in the transatlantic crossing to form Spain's, and Europe's, first colonizing expedition to the New World.

The implications of 'Scaling-Up': new compressive force

In 1499, however, during Columbus's third voyage to the Indies, investigation was begun on behalf of the Crown into complaints made against his and his brother Diego's mismanagement of the colony on Hispaniola. Before long, another Governor was appointed, Frey Nicolás de Ovando who, as Knight Commander of Alcántara, was a high-ranking officer in one of the three Military Orders founded originally to garrison Christian frontier outposts in Spain against Islam. Ovando's arrival in 1502 at Santo Domingo marked the rebellious colonists' first real contact in the Americas with the absolute authority of Spain. At the same time it heralded the style of Spain's own solution to the problems of remote control.

The Caribbean adventure had demonstrated the self-interest and lawlessness of an aggressive, late medieval Castilian frontier society suddenly separated by more than 3,000 miles from the metropolitan centres of power. It had revealed the problems rather than the prizes of empire, and provided a foretaste of the difficulties which lay ahead, particularly those of government and administration.

Nevertheless, valuable experience had been gained at virtually no expense to the Crown. Whether *America* or *Columbia*, *Antilla* or *Cíbola*, the legendary name of *Atlantis* came closer to recording Spain's first, and in many ways greatest discovery—the transatlantic. The Caribbean formed part of this maritime world so new to Spain, a Spanish pond at the western edge of the Atlantic Ocean. As a hastily-constructed field laboratory for testing the severe tensional stresses and strains introduced by distance, the Caribbean phase had served its purpose. So far as the Crown was concerned, the New World already called for meticulous, centralized administration. **Designs for empire would simply 'scale-up' Spain's Peninsular model, rely on tradition and experience, and insert whatever heavier, stronger elements were necessary to keep tensile forces to a minimum**. It was clear that the roles of the discoverer and the administrator—surveyor and builder—must be separated, and remain so.

As a result, much of Spain's basic imperial organization, enduring as it did for centuries, was established in the span of a single decade. Indeed, the structural components of empire were shipped out from Seville to form one of Spain's first exports to the New World. "No date can be set for the end of medieval Spain," observed one historian, "for medieval Spain invaded the Americas and left there a permanent projection of the Spanish Middle Ages in space and time."

6

Extending the Ground-Plan of Empire 1519–1543

> Exploration of the Americas and discovery of the extent of the Pacific Ocean by the second wave of site-surveyors confirmed the need to resist the huge increase in tensional stress and strain. The vast perimeter ground-plan was delineated by the 1540s, but Mexico and Peru were identified as the central work space, where the main load-bearing walls in the New World would be erected and the 'live load' concentrated.
>
> Nevertheless, Spain was building a Spanish, not an American empire. Spain was to remain the centre of the compression structure, however eccentrically it was sited.

CONTINENTAL EXPANSION:
THE LAND AND THE RIVERS, 1519–1543

> Where we must give the world a proof
> Of deeds, not words.
>
> (Samuel Butler, *Hudibras*)

The mainland gamble put Spain squarely on to *Tierra Firme*, the name applied to the land-mass encircling the insular world of the Caribbean. The first deep penetration of the American continent was undertaken by men, who, if they found Indian labour and precious metals in sufficient quantity, were called *conquistadores*. Otherwise they regarded themselves as failures.

The initial phase of exploration had taught one basic fact of location: there were no raw materials of empire lying conveniently close to any of the thousands of miles of new coast discovered by Spain. Expansion became a spectacular and explosive assault upon the American continent—a land rather than a marine reconnaissance, whose speed, range and accomplishment astonished Europe, and began a new era in the history of geographical exploration.

The invasion of Mexico in 1519 was mounted from Cuba and commanded by Hernán Cortés, the first of the new wave of conquerors. After exploring the coasts of Yucatán and Campeche, and founding the municipality of Vera Cruz, Cortés burned his boats (literally) and began the great march inland. During the next few months, 600 Spaniards and about three times as many Indian porters and auxiliaries climbed from the fever-ridden coast up to the central plateau to discover and, by 1521, to conquer the cities of the Aztecs. The scale and dream-like quality of the temples and palaces, lakes and causeways, dazzled the Spaniards, just as the hoard of golden treasure delighted them. An Aztec (Mexica) 'empire' consisting of several subject Indian communities (many of them fiercely resistant to Aztec domination) straddled part of Middle America from coast to coast, its total population perhaps as many as 15–20 millions.[12] Population density on this scale accelerated exploration of the intermontane region, and both the Atlantic and Pacific shores.

While a secondary expedition pressed southward into the jungles of Guatemala, Cortés supervised the building of Mexico City on the ruins of Tenochtitlán, and ordered the construction of a small fleet on the Pacific coast to continue the search for the western strait. This was still a matter of urgency. Apart from local timber, all the material for building the ships had been brought across the Atlantic from Spain and then been discharged at Vera Cruz, repacked, and carried by Indian porters under appalling conditions over some 600 miles of mountain and plateau to reach the Pacific. Shipbuilding began in 1522. Cortés regarded the eventual launching of the first ships in the Pacific fleet in 1526 as one of his greatest achievements, an act, he wrote, given his continued encouragement of shipbuilding on the Pacific coast of Mexico and Nicaragua, that would undoubtedly lead to Spain's mastery of the world.[13]

Southward extension

At this stage, however, most of the *conquistadores* turned their attention southward. Persistent rumour about new sources of wealth lying somewhere within the great land-mass of South America had already swept the Caribbean and the Isthmus. Explorers had worked their way down the west coast, southward from Panamá, and reported dramatic contrasts with the Atlantic side of the continent. The Pacific coast plunged steeply from an almost unbroken wall of mountains. Dense rain forest soon gave way to scrubland and then to desert only a few degrees south of the equator. But there was exciting evidence also of being somewhere on the fringes of a rich and well organized society. This was enough to send two illiterate but experienced adventurers from the Caribbean campaigns, Francisco Pizarro and Diego de Almagro, back and forth along the shores of the Pacific between Panamá and northern Peru for nearly eight years—searching, suffering, and gradually consolidating their positions at a few base camps along the coasts of Colombia and Ecuador. Finally, 1,000 miles from Panamá and more than 5,000 miles from Spain, the march inland began.

In 1532–33, from a point on the coast near Tumbes, Pizarro climbed into the Andes with fewer than 200 fellow-adventurers, about sixty horses and a few small cannon. As Cortés had discovered, horse and cannon were unknown to the American Indians. Amid all the noise and confusion, in a lofty and strangely theatrical setting, and with a mixture of courage, deception and cruelty, Pizarro captured the heart of the Inca empire. Its wealth was prodigious, its influence far-reaching, for gold and then silver were to flow from Spanish America into the economies and polities of Europe and the Orient—"oceans of monies" down the years, swirling through a system of linked circulations across the Old World and the New.

The marvellous discoveries in Mexico and Peru had proved at last the value of Spain's great *Ultramar*. To a Court fed on hopes and promises, the cargoes now filling the quays, the warehouses, and the royal mint at Seville were a triumph of fact over fantasy—and not before time, the King reflected, since in 1529 Spain had finally acknowledged Portugal's rightful claim to the Spice Islands of the Moluccas. The *conquistadores*' role as a task force commissioned to open up the Americas with all possible speed was now obvious, both to the Crown and to its willing agents in the New World. Deep penetration of the continent was necessary, deeds not words, and the 1530s and 1540s witnessed a dramatic new series of long-range overland expeditions which sketched the vast ground-plan of empire.

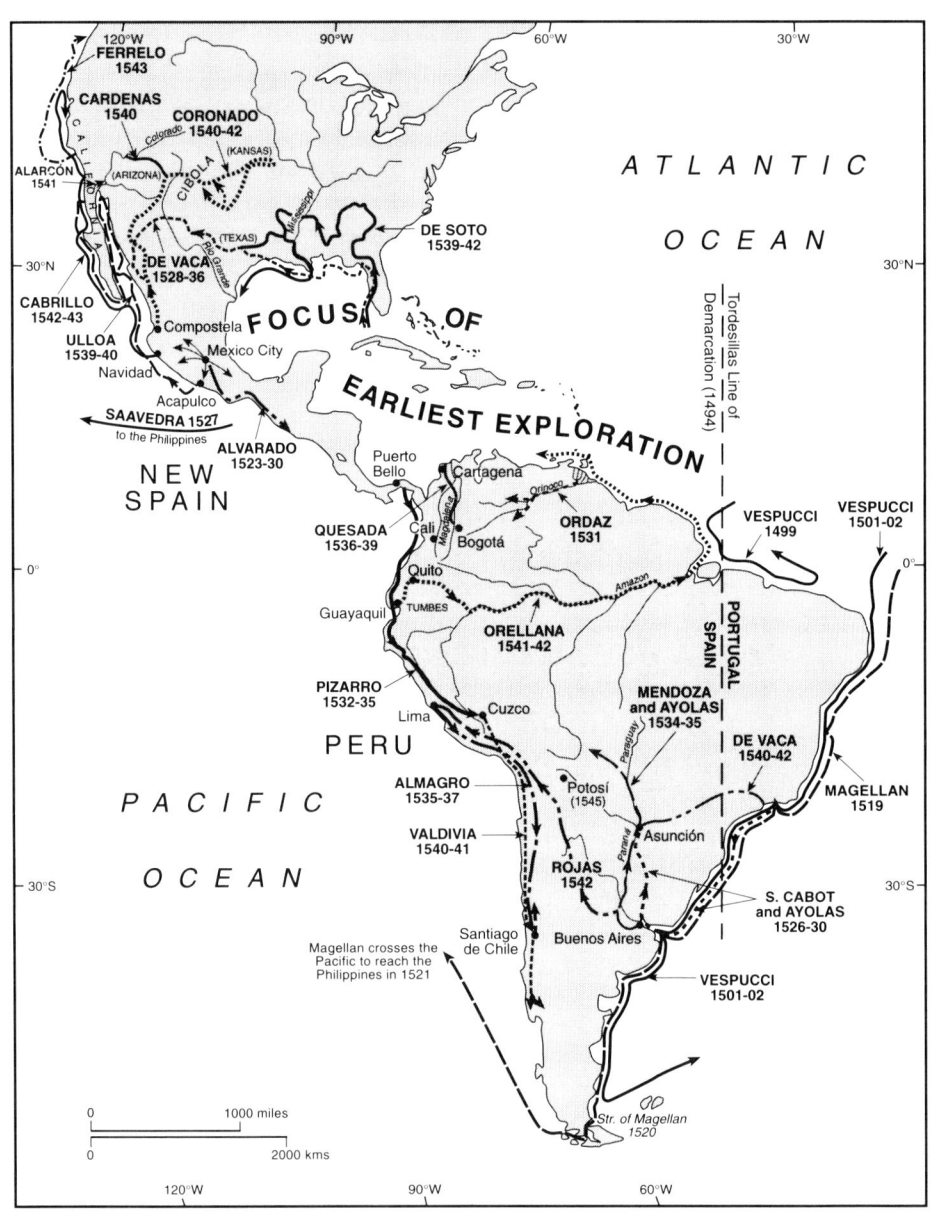

Figure 5 The ground-plan of empire: Spanish exploration of the American continent, 1519–1543.

Continental perimeters in the Andes

Gonzalo Quesada's discovery of the Chibcha (Muisca) Indians was made in 1536. This distinctive community formed a small but densely populated enclave set high in the Colombian Andes, an area rich in emeralds and noted for its inhabitants' exceptional skills in gold-working and agriculture. Although not on the scale of the Peruvian discoveries farther south, the Bogotá region was an important addition to empire. Apart from this gem, however, the efforts to emulate Cortés and Pizarro proved bitterly disappointing. The medieval knights of the Americas took on a continent, tilting at mountains, deserts, forests and swamps, and at distance itself. Desperation drove men to make protracted journeys into the interior, to ransack the New World from Kansas to Chile, and to pursue every lead and every myth to its wretched conclusion.

Physical hazards alone failed to deter the would-be *conquistador*, whatever his age. In 1535, Diego de Almagro began a new expedition out of Peru. His men marched southward from Cuzco along the Andean *altiplano*, two-and-a-half miles above sea level, and thence down into central Chile over some of the bleakest, most exposed country in the western hemisphere. Finally, in 1537, they marched northwards back into Peru, through the 800 miles of the Atacama desert. Despite the hardships, the worst suffering of all was being forced to endure the humiliation of returning empty-handed. Almagro was followed later by Pedro de Valdivia, who reached the Chilean heartland in 1541 and struggled to extend a military frontier against the hostile Araucanian Indians beyond the Bío-Bío. Like Almagro, however, Valdivia found no new treasure hoard, no more lost Empires of the Sun.

Problems in co-ordinating the ground-plan

1. *The Rivers of South America*

"This is a hard land that opens no passage to Spain."

Wherever men turned, one of the most striking features of the geography of expansion was Spain's inability to use the great rivers of the New World as the key to penetration and settlement. At first, the focus of this frustration was simply that the rivers were not straits, offering an uninterrupted seaway westward to the Orient. Surely, mariners had continued to ask themselves as they probed every wide bay and river mouth for thousands of miles along the

Atlantic and Pacific coasts, surely this new continent did not really stretch unbroken virtually from Pole to Pole? But as each apparent gap in the shoreline was tested, salt always gave way in the end to brackish or fresh water amid the confusion of deltas, islands and distributaries facing the little boats despatched to bring back details.

Entrances

The appearance of many of the river entrances was unlike anything seen in Europe. Huge volumes of fresh water, silt and mud poured far out into the Atlantic. In 1499, Vespucci had found that twenty-five miles out from the mouths of the Amazon the ocean was still fresh enough to fill the casks of drinking water; Yañez Pinzón had discovered the same marvel of this strange new land when forty miles offshore. In fact, the Amazon, *Mar Dulce* (the Freshwater Sea), makes the Atlantic drinkable for at least 200 miles offshore where this immense inland waterway system of some 15,000 tributaries carries one-fifth of the world's fresh water through the great rain forests and into the ocean.

Farther south, the entrance to the Río de Solís (later called the Río de la Plata) at first appeared more promising. Probably discovered by Vespucci and Coelho in the famous coastal reconnaissance of 1501, the river was entered again in 1516 by one of the veterans of the Caribbean, Juan Díaz de Solís. It proved to be the last of his many attempts to find the elusive western strait, for he was killed by Indians upon landing. The great embayment was found to be another dead end, narrowing eventually after 200 miles into the silt-choked throats of the Paraná and Uruguay rivers.

The force of the current racing away from the great river mouths helped to identify the navigable channels but often made the approach to them well-nigh impossible. It was the practical difficulties of entry, not the dimensions, that presented the real problem. Indeed, size alone was potentially attractive, since the Spaniards viewed the rivers of the New World as extensions of the ocean, and of ocean navigation. Spain had produced men of the mountains, plateaux and coasts, not of the rivers. In general, the rivers were always more useful for irrigation than for navigation (although, even then, much potentially irrigable land in Castile remained dry grazing). Streams cross the gentle gradients of the *meseta* in seasonal mood, often bringing devastating floods in late spring, but shrinking into braided shallows during the summer drought. At the steep resistant edge of the *meseta* or the Catalonian Mountains, rivers like the Duero, Tagus, Guadiana, and Ebro tumble through spectacular gorges on to the coastal plains, and ocean-going vessels are narrowly confined to the lower reaches, or to tidal lagoons.

The Arabs were able to develop extended river navigation only on the Guadalquivir, their 'Big River', and still the only major navigable waterway in Spain. Arab ships (like those of the Romans) were able to reach Córdoba, but the Moors preferred the more accessible site of Seville, over 100 miles downstream of Córdoba, and even then, still nearly sixty tortuous miles from the sea. Elsewhere around the coasts of the Peninsula, the long branching estuaries (*rías*) of the north-west, with their deep sheltered anchorages, had encouraged the great seafaring traditions of Galicia and the Atlantic borderlands. But small, localized fishing fleets had long been a feature of the Peninsular economy, and these also made a significant contribution to the diffusion of ideas and skills between the Mediterranean and Atlantic worlds.

Castile created its maritime tradition, however, by crossing the Atlantic, not from its Peninsular heritage. In this early, brilliantly innovative period, Spain learned to make do with small numbers of experienced mariners. Cargoes of landsmen were carried west, their lives in the hands of God, the ship's master, and the pilot.

For those who had spent weeks scanning an empty ocean, the great river entrances of the Americas were merely narrow seas— difficult to negotiate, often dangerous, but rarely daunting to transatlantic men. The volume of water and speed of outflow from the Orinoco was noted without undue concern by all who had accompanied, or followed, Columbus along the coast of Venezuela, although penetration was obviously not going to be easy. A similar problem was encountered to the north, on the Florida side. In 1528, as part of the Narváez expedition, Cabeza de Vaca reached the mouth of a huge river (it was the Mississippi) while coasting along the Gulf of Mexico beyond Florida. All efforts to breast the violent current resulted in his party being swept farther out to sea. After battling for more than two days against wind and river, they abandoned the effort and continued west. "Our destiny," De Vaca decided, "lay toward the sunset."

INLAND

The great rivers extended their ribbons of frustration far into the continental interior. The **PARANÁ-PARAGUAY** system was the first to be explored, since the failure of Solís's expedition in 1516 encouraged Sebastian Cabot, ten years later, to sail into the bay and see what the region still had to offer. At first, the signs were encouraging; silver and gold ornaments were being worn by Indians living around the Río de Solís, now dubbed by Cabot as the Río de la Plata. But the 'river of silver' proved to be nothing of the sort. Rumours of a distant ocean (the Pacific), and of a fabulously wealthy mountain kingdom lying somewhere in the northern interior kept the river party led by Juan de Ayolas winding slowly upstream between 1527 and 1529—sailing, rowing, punting, towing—around the huge meanders of the Paraguay. But the river dwindled into unnavigable shallows long before any sources of silver were reached.

The northern kingdom was of course the Inca empire, and the gold and silver ornaments worn by the plains Indians far to the south had been obtained from the Andes by long-distance barter. West of the Paraguay river, the trans-Chaco trail into the mountains soon proved to be long and hazardous, cursed alternately by drought and flood, and plagued by hunger, thirst, flies, and Indian attack. To cap it all, the *pampas* and *chaco* plains yielded nothing to make the suffering worthwhile. The small river port of Asunción, founded in 1537, was to remain one of Spain's most isolated outposts—a world of its own, drowsing in the sun.

The ORINOCO river had been the first of the great American rivers to be discovered (by Columbus in 1498), and in 1531 it became the second major waterway to be navigated inland by Spain for any appreciable distance. To those ranging over Mexico and the Caribbean, the rumoured kingdoms of gold lay not in the northern interior but somewhere to the south. Any number of different routes appeared possible given the physical variety of the Caribbean coasts. The prospect of finding a way but losing the race, of arriving just in time to witness the booty being divided by others, constantly drove men to action.

Some *conquistadores*, like Francisco Pizarro, had used the west coast and its great parallel cordilleras as the guideline south. Others remained in the Caribbean, where the curving edge of the Andean system frays into a complicated pattern of troughs and ranges which plunge seaward in massive promontories. Several corridors beckoned the explorers southward from the coasts of Colombia and Venezuela but none of them, with or without major river systems, offered an easy passage. Extremely broken country, drenching rains, dense jungle, extensive tracts of swamp forcing wide detours, limited vantage points from which to get one's bearings, all combined to turn weeks and months on the march into one long undivided struggle for survival. Under these circumstances, river navigation appeared to have advantages.

Diego de Ordaz had been with Cortés in Mexico, and was one of those determined to penetrate the southern continent with the help of the rivers. Fresh out from Spain, Ordaz and his men approached the equator. In a fruitless attempt to find the main channel into the Amazon, squalls and sandbanks took their toll of three caravels that had just completed the transatlantic crossing from Tenerife without difficulty. It was a sobering start. Ordaz sailed north-west along the coast in his one remaining ship, ordered the construction of special river boats, and then in 1531, with nearly 300 men, he struggled into the Orinoco. The high humidity, clouds of insects, sickness, shortage of food, and occasional Indian attack bedevilled the slow passage upstream. Rowing against the current was an endless nightmare. On every side, the *llanos* in the rainy season presented a dreary prospect: seas of floodwater, riparian forest, scrub woodland and grassy swamps.

After following the broad curve of the river around the Guiana Highlands for more than 800 miles, cataracts blocked further progress and the men finally turned back. Advice from an Indian guide to go west—toward the Andes in other words, rather than the Guianas—was ignored. The Meta river, it is true, rises only twenty miles north-east of Bogotá, but whether any of Ordaz's party could have forestalled Quesada's discovery of the Chibcha Indians in 1536 by this route remains doubtful. River boats would soon have had to be hauled, then abandoned, because of rapids and falling water levels, while the climb into the Andes would have faced some of the steepest and most deeply dissected mountain terrain in the Americas.

A few die-hards, led by Alonso de Herrera, returned to the Orinoco in 1533 and once more struggled up-river to explore the Meta route. Only death or disappointment awaited them. Quesada, in fact, was to use the more direct **MAGDALENA** corridor on his expedition southward into Colombia, and he began by navigating the river with a small part of his force. Before long, most of Quesada's men found it less difficult to hack their way overland, and to use the rivers only as a guideline to locate Indian villages, food supplies, and trade routes into the mountains.

After the discoveries in Peru and Colombia, any number of footloose, freebooting elements who had followed their leaders into the continent, watched the spoils vanish and their continued presence discouraged in no uncertain terms. Winners and losers went their separate ways. Hardened explorers, short of alternatives, disappeared into the wilds to search for 'lost cities' or 'lost kingdoms'.

Hopes of finding isolated hoards of treasure in the eastern Andes, along the fringes of the Inca empire, became tangled with stories about the gilded man, *El Dorado*, the epitome of concentrated riches.

Before long, *El Dorado* was to be associated with Lake Guatavita, and with local Indian ceremonies high in the Andes a few miles north-east of Bogotá. The gilding of the body of each new ruler (with gold dust over resin), and the dropping of golden ornaments from a raft into the centre of the lake had formed part of a dramatic ritual practised until shortly before the arrival of the Spaniards. As a legend, however, *El Dorado*, had a much vaguer geographical location; whether person or place, *El Dorado* shifted enticingly about the New World—from one mountain to the next, from the nearest valley to the farthest jungle, across the deserts and across the centuries too, always just beyond reach, in the land of dreams.

In the saga of the rivers, the AMAZON was to have a last word. During Gonzalo Pizarro's expedition to search for *El Dorado*, as well as for new sources of cinnamon and other spices in the eastern forested slopes of Ecuador, an extraordinary journey took place: Francisco de Orellana's equatorial crossing of the Americas, from the Pacific to the Atlantic Ocean. In 1541, Orellana had marched up from Guayaquil on the west coast with a small band of followers to join Pizarro somewhere beyond Quito. The combined force was to spend several months wandering hopelessly through the *montañas*, struggling in and out of the gorges which slash the eastern cordillera, and starving in the midst of apparent plenty.

While searching for food in a specially constructed launch, Orellana and others became separated from the main group; by the time they reached the Napo river, still short of food, most of the party decided that they had neither the will nor the energy to force their way back upstream. The river could carry them on, dead or alive. Eight months later, in August 1542, the astonishing 2,000-mile voyage was completed, and Orellana and most of his men floated out into the Atlantic. Survival had depended on good luck and abundant good management. Orellana's own resourcefulness and powers of leadership were outstanding, but in political and economic terms the enterprise was dismissed as worthless. The Indian communities scattered along the banks had provided no evidence of new treasure hoards hidden somewhere in the rain forest. As a line of communication, the mighty river simply flowed in the wrong direction; one journey was all Spain needed to prove that the Amazon would never provide a practical approach to Peru.

Orellana's great continental river-road was ignored and later abandoned to Portugal.

The increasing revenues from the Andes, particularly after the discovery in 1545 of the great 'silver mountain' of Potosí in Upper Peru (later Bolivia), confirmed Spain's earlier findings. The gold-working Indian cultures of the Americas were not riverine; they were all lodged in the high western Cordilleras. Unless the great rivers of South America revealed new local sources of wealth, their value as routeways would be assessed solely in terms of the access they afforded to the established Andean centres. In this, the rivers would have to compete with the Isthmus and the Pacific Ocean. None of the South American waterways made life easy. None matched size with usefulness to Spain.

Problems in co-ordinating the ground-plan

2. *The Rivers of North America*

Meanwhile, the *conquistadores* pursued fame and fortune by land and river for thousands of miles across North America. Hernando de Soto had taken part in the conquest of Peru. Determined to match Pizarro's now-legendary achievement, De Soto sailed in 1539 from Havana to Tampa Bay, Florida with about 700 men. To anyone who had actually gazed upon Inca gold, life in the forests and swamps of what became the south-eastern United States was nothing short of disaster. For three years, De Soto and his followers trudged through the wilderness of the Deep South, discovering the MISSISSIPPI river in 1541, but unhappily little else. The following year, still searching, De Soto died and was buried in the Mississippi, near the present site of Natchez. The remnants of his party eventually built some small craft, and travelled down the river and out into the Gulf of Mexico—the only time the Mississippi played any part in their continental exploration.

Other Spaniards tackled the west. Small groups marched or stumbled through the deserts, mountains, and high plains of what are now Texas, New Mexico and Arizona. Indeed, after abandoning his attempt to enter the Mississippi in 1528, Cabeza de Vaca had coasted west as far as Galveston Island, Texas and then continued overland to complete the first transcontinental journey across the Americas north of Mexico. With a party reduced from four hundred to four, De Vaca followed Indian trails, contacted different Indian communities, "passing from one strange tongue to another", endured captivity, and wandered through some of the hottest, driest sections of southern New Mexico and Arizona. The overland journey west, begun as a tailpiece to the Florida expedition, involved a sweep of well over 1,000 miles across mountains and desert basins, with shorter treks along the banks of the Pecos and the Río Grande. Finally, in the upper Gila valley, the men turned south towards the Pacific. In 1536, eight years after he had landed near Tampa Bay, Alvar Núñez Cabeza de Vaca emerged from the wilderness, a stranger returned from the dead, full of tales of adventure for his audience in Mexico City about Indians, and deserts—and cities farther north he had heard of but never seen.

Four years later, after fresh hopes had been raised by Friar Marcos de Niza's exploration in 1539, an elaborate expedition was organized under the leadership of Francisco de Coronado to explore this new north, an overland reconnaissance which carried the banner of Spain all the way from Mexico into present-day Oklahoma and Kansas. But Coronado was to discover that the fabled Seven Cities of Cíbola were no more than clusters of Zuñi Indian *pueblos* in Arizona and New Mexico. Across the continental divide and onto the Great Plains in 1541, Coronado entered the Mississippi drainage basin to wander over the level, seemingly endless grass-and-buffalo country of the Brazos, Red, and the Cimarron valleys. He reached as far as the great bend of the Arkansas, and the Smoky Hill River. At exactly the same time, 400 miles to the south-east, Hernando de Soto was toiling through the forests and flood plains of the lower Arkansas valley—two knights of Spain, unknown to each other, searching for new kingdoms of gold in the heart of a continent.

Meanwhile, López de Cárdenas had turned west from Coronado's main expedition and discovered the rim of the Grand Canyon on the COLORADO river. This great waterway once again presented enormous difficulties, both in its middle and lower sections. The barren, dissected canyon lands formed a major barrier to movement over the surface of the plateau, and nowhere was there evidence of gold and docile Indians to justify all the effort involved.

At the lower end of the Colorado valley, the Spaniards were faced with the all-too-familiar problem of entrance. As part of the great northern reconnaissance mounted from Mexico, Hernando de Alarcón had been commissioned to support the western flank by an approach from the Gulf of California. Unlike Francisco de Ulloa who in 1539 had simply reached the head of the Gulf, Alarcón also managed to get his ships over the sand bars and into the Colorado river. But he soon found the force of the current too strong to make any headway, and the decision was taken to haul smaller boats and tramp along beside the river for some 200 miles. At the mouth of the Gila tributary, however, they turned back. The Colorado valley could be seen running back into the mountains through a dramatic, brilliantly coloured desert landscape, but into nowhere that was of the slightest interest to Spain. There were no signs of the cities of Cíbola, and no useful contacts made with the expeditions of either Coronado or Cárdenas.

By 1542, hopes of penetrating North America via the Colorado river along either the middle or lower valley sections had been abandoned. Arid west and humid east, the lands of the Colorado and the Mississippi had contributed simultaneously to Spain's disappointment. Evidence of copper was not enough when one expected to find gold; turquoise was no substitute for emerald. There were in fact no Indian city-building cultures north of Mexico to compare with those of the Maya, Aztec and Inca. Widely dispersed over tundra, mountain, desert, woodland, and prairie, the North American Indians (apart from the concentrations in south central Mexico) probably numbered fewer than four million at the beginning of the sixteenth century. In the great continental excursions northward from Mexico City and the Caribbean, Spain had so far found nothing—no gold, no silver, no converts to speak of, no labour supply, no western strait; it was a northern borderland sans everything.

The confirmation of Castile's basic design principles: scale up, increase compression, reduce tension

The *conquistadores* had roamed the continent, scouting the New World to extend the site-lines of empire. Within a single generation they had established a basic network of towns and cities scattered over five million square miles which others would organize as the great urban centres of Hispanic America. Not only was the collective record impressive; personal achievements were often astounding. Countless adventures and adventurers remain unknown, but the immense distances covered by many of the *conquistadores* as a matter of routine, and the range of experience of different American locations and contrasted American environments that was concentrated into individual lifetimes was rarely equalled, let alone surpassed, in the Americas until the nineteenth and twentieth centuries.

Thousands of miles were logged across the continent by solitary explorers, small detachments, and by countless numbers of Indians forced to act as guides, bearers or labourers, never to return. Scouts and runners chased across the Americas, often back-tracking over great distances to contact ships waiting at anchor, to find passes through the mountains, firm paths through the swamps, or routes to the 'other ocean' and, with monotonous frequency, to check reports from far-away base camps of rebellion, or betrayal.

At the start, many a Spanish *conquistador* rode out looking every inch the medieval knight, plumed and helmeted, with a coat of mail, quilted tunic and leather trappings. Heat and humidity soon took their toll. Most Spaniards were familiar with the landscape of drought—the hot, choking dust of the *meseta*, and the brown unirrigated tracts of Extremadura, La Mancha, and much of Andalusia. But the humid tropics had no counterpart in southern Europe. Spanish explorers detested the closed vistas and damp, enervating heat of the tropical forest; moreover, they consistently overestimated its productivity. The luxuriant vegetation wrapped the ambitious and the inexperienced in a dark green world in which many of them starved. For many, the search for gold became instead an even more desperate search for food. Supplies seized from Indian villages on which the *conquistadores* normally depended after initial stocks ran low, were usually inadequate. The men were lost, soaked to the skin, and tormented by insects, as well as by fever, sores, and disillusion; and in the forest, as so often elsewhere, the *conquistadores* were perpetually hungry.

The great period of primary continental reconnaissance closed effectively in 1543, little more than twenty years after the conquest of Mexico. Whether in North, Central or South America, the day of the *conquistador* was soon over. It represented the initial, highly spontaneous aspect of empire, a contract with the Sovereign to undertake the risks of a personal crusade into the New World. Despite the astonishing epic quality of their performance, most of the *conquistadores* died without lasting reward. The future development of Spanish America was not to be entrusted to these first agents (*adelantados*) of the Crown. Significantly, *adelantado de frontera* was a term which had its origins in the Reconquest of medieval Castile from the hands of the Infidel; in the New World, these agents were once again to be the founders but not the builders of empire.

Their passing marked the end of Spain's tolerance of the power challenge of the individual—the autarchic feudal lord whom the

Crown had already struggled to subdue at home. The *conquistadores* had served their turn and were discarded. Although those who survived gained the gratitude of the Sovereign, the rights to administer their discoveries were rarely included among the honours bestowed. Hernán Cortés, for example, graced with a dazzling array of lands and titles, was not rewarded with the post of Viceroy of Mexico. Private enterprise was replaced, firmly and deliberately, by a centralized bureaucracy controlled from the other side of the Atlantic, a fully-structured Civil Service whose authority derived solely from the Crown.

The *conquistadores*, however, had restated Spain's role as a continental power. Whereas the seaborne empires of the Portuguese and the Dutch, the French and the English, would for the most part develop coastal bases linked by sea power, the Spanish seaborne empire was perceived from the outset as a land empire tied by sea-lanes. It was an important structural distinction.

7

Spain crosses the Pacific: Delimiting the Western Perimeter of Empire

> The Atlantic is a stormy moat; and the Mediterranean
> The blue pool in the old garden, . . .
> But here the Pacific—
>
> (Robinson Jeffers, *The Eye*)

The world had turned out to be so much larger than expected. Spain was the first to discover this fact and the two Iberian states the first to exploit it. The increased global dimension was not, however, simply the result of expanding the overall size of known geographical features. Indeed, in the early sixteenth century, estimates of Asia's breadth, though clearly still enormous, had to be substantially reduced. Marco Polo's detailed accounts of his long overland journey to Cathay, and the extensive missions he had undertaken there for the Great Khan led him, and others, over the years to exaggerate the continent's east-west span and lend support to the idea that Cipango (Japan) lay a mere 2,400 nautical miles west of the Canaries. The discovery of the Atlantic and the Pacific jointly dispelled the error. Increased global dimension, therefore, had largely come about by the addition not of land, but of ocean.

But where did all this lead? What did it signify that a major step had been taken towards the knowledge that more than seventy per cent of the world's surface is covered by the sea? Awareness of the existence, and then of the extent of the Pacific did little to change the habits of the Old World. European and Middle Eastern trade with the Orient continued to make its way around the margins of the 'World Island' (Europe, Africa and Asia). Moreover, given the short overland linkage between the Nile and Suez, traders soon revived the more convenient Mediterranean-Red Sea routeway

The first crossing of the Pacific Ocean

Ferdinand Magellan, a Portuguese navigator sailing in the service of Spain, had sailed from Seville in 1519, his small fleet westward-bound, like Columbus, to find a route to the Moluccas—the Spice Islands of the Orient. Three years later, the one remaining ship, the *Victoria*, slowly wound its way up the Guadalquivir with just eighteen exhausted survivors. Magellan had entered the Pacific on 28th November, 1520 and then without finding any more supplies of fresh food, had taken three months and twenty days to cross the ocean and reach the Marianas (Ladrones). Apart from two small uninhibited islands, the starving and scurvy-ridden crews had seen no land at all before sighting Guam on their transoceanic passage of more than 12,000 miles. Death from hunger was one of the great unsuspected dangers of the Pacific, as the famous eye-witness recorder of the expedition, Antonio Pigafetta, makes clear in his journal. The size and emptiness of the new ocean were staggering—"that exceeding vast sea," Pigafetta reported . . . "I do not think such a voyage will ever be made again."[14]

Magellan was killed in the Philippine Islands in April 1521, but the experienced Basque navigator who finally assumed command, Sebastian del Cano, went on to reach the Moluccas and bring the *Victoria*, laden with spices, safely home around the Cape of Good Hope. The sale of this single cargo paid the costs of the entire expedition, with profit to spare. A delighted monarch granted Del Cano a coat of arms which represented the double achievement: a terrestrial globe encircled with the words *Primus circumdedisti me*, to which were added the symbols of twelve cloves, three nutmegs and two bars of cinnamon.

The purpose of Magellan's exploration, however, had been to open an all-Spanish passage to and from the Spice Islands. Circumnavigation of the world had not been planned in advance. It had meant sailing well beyond the Tordesillas antimeridian (assumed to pass very close to the Moluccas), and then deliberately invading Portugal's hemisphere and Portugal's routeways. But this was a calculated risk, less daunting than the prospect of trying to find a way back across the deserts of the Pacific, whether to the Isthmus, to Magellan's strait, or to some unknown point on the unknown west coast of the Americas. With the return of the *Victoria* in 1522, three points became clear: the fringes of the Orient lay close to the farthest limits of Spain's world, the Pacific Ocean would have to be crossed to reach them, and Magellan's route outward-bound via his newly discovered strait (however he had planned to return) was a long and pointless diversion. There was no hesitation. After one more unsuccessful attempt to develop Magellan's route, new orders were given. Hernán Cortés, already working tirelessly to organize Mexico, expand the frontiers of New Spain, and explore both the Atlantic and the California coasts, was commanded to despatch the first American-based transpacific expedition to the Moluccas without delay.

Extending the site-lines

Three ships under Álvaro de Saavedra sailed from Mexico in 1527; they survived the crossing, but none managed to find the way back. Despite the formidable distances involved, this was an unexpected failure and a serious setback to the state that had demonstrated the art of transatlantic navigation so convincingly to a startled and envious Europe. The failure would prove to be only temporary. For the moment, however, Spain was forced to break its stride across the western hemisphere and come to terms with the size and emptiness of the Pacific on the one hand, and with the pressing need to organize the sprawling wealth of the Americas on the other.

Nevertheless, the global perspective remained strong. The Pacific was undoubtedly "a vast and mighty sea", but it was a Spanish sea, and Spain would control it.

Successful two-way communication across the Pacific was achieved for the first time in 1564–65. After that, the **'double ocean' ground-plan** became an essential part of Spain's imperial design, and Mexico increased its structural importance within the hugely extended dual system of maritime exchange.

Five separate expeditions had reached the Philippines and the Spice Islands from the Americas before a single ship had managed to return across the great 'South Sea'. Once again, the discovery of the wind systems held the key. The complications introduced both by monsoon and typhoon made the passage around the island of Luzon one of the most dangerous ever encountered by Spanish sailors. Ships sailed west from Mexico in the North-East Trade Wind belt and on return had originally attempted to pick up the Westerlies somewhere between 32°N and 37°N. Gradually, vessels began to run farther north, although such wandering was officially discouraged lest it develop into spontaneous exploration of the Pacific. By the mid-sixteenth century, such initiative was already a thing of the past so far as Spain was concerned.

In 1559, with a new sense of urgency, the Crown authorized preparations for an expedition under Miguel López de Legazpi to cross the Pacific and colonize the Philippines. Legazpi's principal pilot on the outward voyage (which left Navidad, Mexico in 1564) was the seaman-friar Andrés de Urdaneta who rightly deduced that the key to the successful return trip to the Americas lay in high latitudes, much farther north than anyone had searched systematically before. Bearing in mind the Atlantic wind circulation used so effectively by Columbus, Urdaneta hunted for a home wind in the 40°N-42°N zone and in 1565 discovered the main belt of Westerlies on which the regular return passage from the Philippines to Acapulco was to depend.

With the practical problem solved, Spain's fundamental principle could be restated: the Pacific was legally Spain's ocean, routine transoceanic connection with Asia must be introduced, and that in doing so, extremely long, unbroken voyages would have to be faced.

The new trans-Pacific tie-beam: the Manila Galleon

Spain demanded the same basic approach to transpacific communication as had been established in the Atlantic. Regular sailings to the Philippines had begun in 1565, following the discovery of 'Urdaneta's Passage'; the last galleon sailed from Manila to Acapulco in 1811, and returned in 1815.[15] The annual voyage across the Pacific, there and back, was thus maintained for two-and-a-half centuries, with some inevitable delays but relatively few interruptions. In terms of distance and durability, the Manila Galleon was by far the longest, and in some respects the most impressive of all Spain's structural tie-beams. Not until the eighteenth century did Spain withdraw its claim to be the legal and sole owner of the Pacific—the Spanish Ocean. A few more exploratory voyages were made after the mid-sixteenth century, but nothing of any economic value was discovered. The emphasis, therefore, remained on the *entirety* of the Pacific crossing—coast to coast, continent to continent. In some respects, the Pacific assumed the same relationship to the Americas as the Atlantic did to Spain; both were regarded as western seas linking their respective Spanish worlds. "There are three oceans," wrote one traveller at the beginning of the eighteenth century, "the Atlantic, the Indian, and the American."

One or two galleons were scheduled to leave the great harbour of Acapulco in March, carrying silver and other merchandise, as well as official passengers and despatches:

> All the merchants of Mexico bring their Spanish commodities down to Acapulco to ship them for China [wrote Sebastian Biscaino from Mexico City in 1590]. It is one of the best harbours in all Nueva Espanna, and where the ships may ride most safely without all kind of danger . . .
>
> Of China, it is the goodliest, and richest, and most plentifull countrey in all the world . . . But here we have an order from the King of Spaine that a Spaniard may not dwell in China above three years, and afterwards must return again into Nueva Espanna.

The transpacific galleons ranged from 500 to 2,000 tons, and were among the largest and strongest in the Spanish fleet, and in the world.[16] Most of them were purpose-built in the Philippines to strict specification, using local teak and other hardwoods. In June or early July, the galleons sailed from Manila back to Acapulco, laden with Chinese silks and East Indian spices.

In time, Indian cottons, Persian carpets, gemstones, ivory, jade, porcelain, and tea were added to the Manila galleons' cargoes of silks and spices which, in return for American silver, often made their way almost completely round the world before being unloaded in Spain. The fortunes of the Spanish colony in the Philippines literally sailed with the ships, and Manila emerged as one of the great entrepôts of the Far East. The appalling length of time and the hardship involved on the homeward run—normally from five to six months, sometimes nine months, at sea compared with ten to twelve weeks on the outward voyage—led to repeated pleas by Spanish officials in Manila for a permanent port of call to be established on the Upper California coast. But merchants in Mexico rejected the idea of adding yet more delay to the arrival of their cargoes, and the Crown refused to sanction the extra protection which would be required at some remote site in California against pirates, smugglers, or other foreign predators. **On balance, a regular new port of call would mean more expense, more risk, the introduction of a new, unmanageably oblique thrust line, and more tension.** For the most part, therefore, the galleons kept going without interruption, following the California coast southward from Cape Mendocino and sailing on until they reached Acapulco. (Fig. 7) As the galleons were sighted, the port roused itself from months of lethargy, *tiempo muerto*; merchants, officials and carriers hastened to town in a flurry of activity, and mule trains were assembled close to the quay, ready to wind their way along the 'China Road' up to Mexico City.

Few interlopers ventured into Spain's huge *mare clausum*. Drake's daring entry into the Pacific via Magellan's Strait in 1578, and his looting of Spanish treasure and supplies all the way from Valparaíso to the Isthmus of Panamá, sent shock-waves down the west coast of Spain's New World. Drake's booty was fabulous, perhaps as much as £20–40 million worth of silver by modern standards, and a dazzling reminder to north-west Europe of the wealth of Spain's empire. Queen Elizabeth was able to discharge the whole of her foreign debt out of the proceeds, and invest part of the remainder in the Levant Company, whose profits later laid the foundation of the East India Company, and some of England's most successful overseas trading connections in the seventeenth and eighteenth centuries.[17]

New buttressing constructed to support increased compressive load at key points

Stunned by Drake's unexpected and devastating appearance in the 'Spanish Ocean', Spain installed defences at major centres along the Pacific coast for the first time, and ordered Magellan's Strait to be colonized and fortified. But Drake's adventure, and the occasional raids which followed (most notably the capture of the eastbound Manila Galleon by Cavendish off Lower California in 1587, with further captures in 1709 and 1762, and the westbound, silver-laden Galleon by Anson off the Philippines in 1743), were isolated incidents punctuating centuries of seclusion. Although daring attacks along the coast were mounted from time to time by Dutch, English and French buccaneers, particularly during the seventeenth century, the size and inaccessibility of the Pacific remained its best defence.

No regular armed convoy system was ever introduced on the Manila run since the hazards of the Pacific were almost entirely physical. "The broad South Sea before us, and no land," wrote one mariner at the start of his voyage, identifying the greatest hazard of all. Fierce storms, and extremes of heat and cold had to be endured. Mutinies were common on the long, uninterrupted voyages. Conditions aboard were bad even by the standards of the time; the galleons were overcrowded, overladen, and swarming with rats, while crews and passengers were ravaged by scurvy and starvation. The mortality rates on some of the worst voyages between

Manila and Acapulco were among the highest on peacetime record, as 'ghost ships' coasted home with exhausted skeleton crews. One passenger, who sailed from the Philippines to Mexico in 1697, recalled the voyage as

> the longest, and most dreadful of any in the world; as well because of the vast ocean to be crossed, being almost one half of the terraqueous globe, with the wind always ahead; as for the terrible tempests that happen there, one upon the back of another, and for desperate diseases that seize people, in seven or eight months lying at sea, sometimes near the line, sometimes cold, sometimes temperate, and sometimes hot, which is enough to destroy a man of steel, much more flesh and blood.[18]

Spain apparently never discovered the Hawaiian Islands which could have provided the mid-ocean port of call and victualling point so desperately needed. The Hawaiian Islands lay outside the sea-lanes selected by the galleons, *between* rather than within the seasonally shifting tracks of Trades and Westerlies, and Spain's astonishing Pacific circulation passed them by. If any castaways ever drifted and found refuge on the Hawaiian Islands no records survived, and no use was made of the islands by Spain. The Philippines, particularly the magnificent port-site of Manila, remained Spain's outpost of empire by agreement with the Portuguese, to be formally administered by Mexico City as part, however remote, of the Viceroyalty of New Spain.

8

Oceans Apart: Spain's Search for Certainty in the New World

THE MAJOR CONSTRUCTION PHASE

Once the general layout and design were confirmed in the early sixteenth century, the compression structure was *massively* built. Risk reduction—the avoidance or minimizing of tensile forces—now dominated administration, Church, immigration, towns, trade and transport.

The immense size and weight of Spanish legislation and bureaucracy, reinforced by interminable delay (itself a powerful compressive factor) carried the thrust lines safely down from the Crown and the Peninsular Councils, through the colonial hierarchies, to the foundations of empire. Horizontal delegation, the overlapping of responsibility, and the endless cross-checking, did not minimize the downward pressure of centralized authority. They simply acted as balancing, bracing, or mortaring agents in a compression structure. The function of mortar is not to 'glue' the bricks or blocks together but merely to transmit the compressive load more evenly.

Weight was essential at all levels. Gothic cathedrals soared heavenward as an act of symbolism, but their medieval builders raised walls to great heights in order to maintain compression and keep the thrust lines well centred, i.e. well inside the edges of the walls and the supporting pillars. Even when large windows and delicate tracery were introduced, Gothic cathedrals were always more solid than they looked, a brilliantly designed system of arches, piers and buttresses carrying the thrust lines down to the ground. It was no coincidence that Seville possessed the largest Gothic cathedral in Spain, indeed, one of the largest and most breathtakingly beautiful cathedrals in Europe.

SPAIN'S 'REDUCED RISK' CONSTRUCTION POLICIES

I. THE ADMINISTRATION OF EMPIRE

Vaster than empires, and more slow.

(Andrew Marvell, c. 1670)

Every aspect of Spain's imperial administration revealed reaction to 'the tyranny of distance'. Isolation encouraged the erosion of authority, identity, and purpose, and Spain responded to this challenge by increasing the rules and administrative complexities of empire and placing them within an elaborately constructed framework of state and church bureaucracy, much of it based on existing Peninsular practice.

Responsibility for the political organization of the Spanish American empire lay with the Royal Council of the Indies (*Real y Supremo Consejo de las Indias*).[19] Although founded officially in 1524, the Council had been initiated by Queen Isabella as early as 1493 with the appointment of an Adviser to the Crown on all matters relating to the newly discovered lands. This Adviser was Juan Rodríguez de Fonseca, archdeacon of Seville, whose mastery of detail and organizational skills were well displayed in his first assignment—that of swiftly assembling the large fleet of men and materials that sailed with Columbus on his second voyage in 1493.

For centuries, Spain declined officially to adopt the name 'America', and continued to use '*Indias*' as a collective term for both its mainland and island possessions in the New World. With supreme control under the Habsburgs of all legislative, administrative, judicial, financial, and religious matters, the Royal Council of the Indies remained subject only to the Monarch, and for much of the time consisted almost entirely of lawyers, notaries, accountants, and clergy, few of whom until the late eighteenth century had ever served in the New World in the 300 years of the Council's existence. Nevertheless, they were tireless structural engineers. The growing mass and complexity of Spain's legislation concerning the colonies resulted in more than 400,000 edicts (*cédulas*) being officially in force by the 1630s. Passed on from one generation to the next, **the Council's task was an everlasting process of cutting, shaping, and then carefully mortaring the blocks, so that the compressive forces were transmitted over the whole area of the joint and not just at a few high spots.**

> **All structures have weight, and their own weight is one of the loads that they have to carry.**
>
> (A. J. Francis, *Introducing Structures*)

An immense increase in **dead load** and **compressive force** had been added to Spain's imperial structure in the sixteenth and seventeenth centuries. The Crown's involvement expanded rapidly under Philip II (1556–98), whose passion for detailed documentation was matched by an unwillingness to delegate decision-making. The King's sense of personal responsibility for organizing Spain's far-flung empire, while continuing to defend Catholicism in Europe and the Mediterranean against the inroads of Protestant, Jew, Arab, and Turk, reinforced absolute monarchy, and built a huge, complex State bureaucracy that slowed inexorably under its own weight—and in doing so, greatly increased its compressive force. In 1681, after nearly a century of effort, revised legislation was collected into the *Recopilación de Leyes de los Reynos de las Indias*, astonishingly detailed volumes which still contained some 6,400 laws regulating Spain's territories and responsibilities overseas. The ceaseless flow of new legislation continued. Indeed, a painstakingly prepared new edition of the *Recopilación de Leyes* awaited publication at the beginning of the nineteenth century.

Thus, the legitimate exercise of power in the Americas remained strictly controlled by the Crown and its Council and Committees in Spain. Spain's concern with matters of major policy was to be expected; its close watch on detail, however, and its continued involvement with the minutiae of everyday colonial affairs were the real evidence of the fundamental principles governing imperial design—**enormous structural weight, strong, well-centred thrust lines, and a multiplicity of architectural features to distribute the compressive load throughout the structure and down to the ground.**

As one contemporary master-builder noted on the subject of stability and thrust:

> There must be an exquisite care to place the *Columnes* precisely, one over another, that so, the *solid* may answer to the *solid*, and the *vacuities* to the *vacuities*, as well for *beautie*, as *strength* of the *Fabric*.

> **THE ELEMENTS OF ARCHITECTURE**
> **Basic Principles**
>
> In *Architecture*, the *end* must direct the *Operation*. The *end* is to build well. Well building hath three Conditions: *Commoditie, Firmenes,* and *Delight*.
>
> Concerning the Parts . . . they be these:
>
> The *Foundation*.
>
> The *Walles*.
>
> The *Apertions or Overtures*.
>
> The *Compartition*.
>
> And the *Cover*.
>
> (Henry Wotton, *The Elements of Architecture*, 1624)

The Cover

MONARCHY, and its role in Spanish society, both produced and centred strong thrust lines within empire. The relationship between the Castilian Crown and the Indies was always proprietorial; what the Crown owned, only the Crown could bestow—in land, title, and authority. While others could recommend, royal licence remained a separate and distinct royal act. The **roof** and **vault** of monarchy covered the main structure, but like all vaulting it also added greatly to the *weight* and to the *cost of maintenance* that had to be borne by, and distributed through, the structure as a whole.

Walls and Compartments

VICEROYALTIES. Within the political hierarchy, the viceroyalty became the primary administrative division in the New World as in the Old. Its legal boundaries were major load-bearing walls that delimited the perimeter of empire and divided the interior space. The post of viceroy remained the highest office the Crown could bestow, normally upon Spanish aristocrats, senior statesmen, archbishops, and high-ranking military or naval officers. Added to Castile's existing seven viceroyalties in the Peninsula and the Mediterranean, Spain's entire transatlantic and transpacific possessions were grouped originally, and *for the next two centuries*, into two immense viceroyalties, New Spain and Peru.[20]

THE VICEROYALTY OF NEW SPAIN (TO c. 1750)

Spain's earliest possessions in and around the Caribbean, and in North America, were administratively regrouped in 1535 to form the Viceroyalty of New Spain, with its capital in Mexico City. Even the Philippine Islands were later included in this widely scattered territory.

Within the Viceroyalty, the *audiencia* was the oldest compartment of empire. Hispaniola had remained the centre of regional government in the early years, and it was here that the first *audiencia* (high-court and court of appeal) in the New World was established at Santo Domingo in 1511, consisting of three resident judges (*oidores*) sent out from Spain.

Audiencias, already operating in Castile by the fourteenth century, were to provide the strong internal framework for distributing Spain's legal and administrative compressive load throughout the Americas, where they acquired a much wider range of political and administrative responsibility than their original purely judicial function. Subdivisions of authority at local level—the *alcalde* (municipal magistrate), the *cabildo* (town council), and the *regidor* (councillor)—were similarly transferred from Spain into the New World. Spanish municipalities overseas, however, soon lost much of their autonomy due to increasing intervention by the *corregidor* (provincial governor), or by the viceroy himself in key areas.

The policy of 'scaling up' the Peninsular model for New World construction purposes was well demonstrated by the introduction of *corregidores*, royal officials combining judicial and administrative roles who had been appointed to all the principal Castilian towns for the first time in 1480, in order to establish the primary authority of the Crown and weaken the role both of the regional aristocracy, and of independent town privileges originating in the Reconquest. Increased Crown intervention was also evident at lower levels. After 1528, for example, Mexico City's *cabildo* comprised nominees by the Crown, an important extension of royal patronage, and a curb on the extension of local privilege. The Crown also moved towards life appointment for *regidores*, setting aside annual election, and despatching some of them straight from Spain. As a result, **thrust lines were centred, compressive forces strengthened, and localized sources of tension reduced or eliminated**.

One of the clearest demonstrations of Castile's intention *not* to 'scale up' the Peninsular model in the New World where high risk was involved was the Crown's refusal to introduce the *cortes* component there. Not only was Mexico City's petition for a vote in the Cortes of Castile firmly rejected at an early stage, all subsequent requests from the colonial cities for representation in the Castilian Cortes were also refused.[21] The decision not to introduce the *cortes* into the Indies was logical, since such regional assemblies of representatives from the major towns were regarded as potentially dangerous sources of challenge to Castilian authority, and to the well-centred thrust of state control.

A second *audiencia* had been established at Mexico City in 1527, in the wake of the conquest by Cortés, and well before the formal creation of the viceroyalty. The *oidores* there, however, soon found themselves seriously overworked, and with far too large a territory to supervise effectively. To the south, the mountainous provinces of Central America (Guatemala, Honduras, Nicaragua and Costa Rica), which had been penetrated from both Mexico and Panamá, remained extremely difficult to contact and administer from either Santo Domingo or Mexico City. In fact, Spain found this rugged, densely forested terrain some of the most impenetrable country it ever encountered, despite the narrowness and apparent accessibility of the Isthmus. Sustained attention was focused only on the Panamá crossing, administered not from Mexico City but from Lima or Bogotá. Concerned about the isolation of the Central American provinces, the Crown established the viceroyalty's third *audiencia* there in 1542 (based permanently at Guatemala City after 1570), although communications in Central America remained slow and often ineffective, with the result that the provinces maintained considerable *de facto* autonomy.

The fourth *audiencia* in the Viceroyalty of New Spain was created in 1548, to administer the north-western province of New Galicia following the rich Zacatecas silver strike in 1546. The court was originally sited in the village of Compostela, but in 1560 it was moved to the larger centre of Guadalajara, where it remained.

The far western perimeter of empire was firmly drawn with the creation of a fifth *audiencia* in the Viceroyalty of New Spain at Manila, initially in 1583 and permanently after 1598.

Reinforced structural units

CAPTAINCIES-GENERAL had been a key element on the frontier during the Reconquest of the Peninsula. They combined military and political control, and in Spain's New World, were characteristic of the more remote frontier regions where fighting Indians was still commonplace. Elsewhere, they were often found alongside other authorities where a routeway or a region of major strategic importance required additional military support. Later in the sixteenth century, certain captains-general began to increase their political responsibilities, particularly in the most isolated areas, becoming governors independent of the viceroy, and subject directly to the Crown and the Council of the Indies in Spain.

Beyond the 'inner frontier' of New Galicia, remote as it was from Mexico City, the outposts of New Spain presented a continuing problem. Much of this far northern territory remained a wild, unprofitable area, lacking the *bonanza* silver strikes of such centres as Zacatecas, Guanajuato, Durango, and San Luís Potosí. In the desert and sage country, hostile Indians, particularly the Chichimecas, held off any steady northward Spanish advance over a wide front, just as the Aztec advance had been repulsed by the Chichimecas at an earlier period. Even after their defeat in the Mixtón War of 1541–2, the Chichimecas continued to attack Spanish supply wagons bound for the silver mines of New Galicia, and to interrupt mining operations.[22] Neither military operations by Spain, nor pacification policies based on large, regular gifts of livestock, food and clothing, brought a permanent solution to the problem. Moreover, Philip II was dismayed to learn that both approaches were equally expensive to the Royal Treasury. It was in the 1580s and 1590s, however, during the long struggle with the Chichimecas, that Spain first organized the mission system as an integral part of imperial control among nomadic tribes. This was extended by the late 1590s to include the practice of moving large groups of Indians into new 'congregations' where they could be Christianized more easily and also supply a fixed labour force. By the end of the sixteenth century, both Franciscans and Jesuits had pioneered the distinctive techniques of the 'mission frontier' on the northern borders of New Spain.

As a distant outpost of empire, New Mexico was first colonized by the Spaniards in 1598 under Juan de Oñate, who financed virtually the entire expedition himself by drawing on the fortune made by his family in the silver mines of Zacatecas. Ten Franciscans accompanied the party. San Juan/San Gabriel in the upper valley of the Río Grande became the first European settlement, and Santa Fe, founded in 1610, the official regional capital, although the whole area was lost during the Pueblo Indian rebellion of 1680, to be reconquered and recolonized in 1693–6 under Diego de Vargas. In general, however, Spain saw nothing to justify the enormous extra effort and expense involved in elaborating the administrative frontier in the far north. *Presidios* (military garrisons), mines, and missions were scattered thinly across the region, but for centuries the vast northern fringe of New Spain was left largely to its own devices.

THE VICEROYALTY OF PERU (TO *c.* 1750)

Until the Bourbon administrative reforms in the eighteenth century, the Viceroyalty of Peru comprised the whole of Spanish South America except the coast of Venezuela. Established in 1544 with its capital at Lima, Peru's fabulous wealth first in gold and then in silver established Pizarro's new 'City of the Kings' as the heart of the American empire, and appointment as viceroy to Lima frequently represented the final promotion for the viceroy in Mexico City.

Within the Viceroyalty of Peru, *audiencias* were created throughout the colonial period as the Crown responded to local strategic and economic requirements: Panamá in 1538, Lima in 1543, Bogotá in 1548, Charcas in 1559 (following the prodigiously rich silver strike at Potosí in the central Andes in 1545), Quito in 1563, and Santiago de Chile in 1563–73, refounded in 1606.

Bogotá (Santa Fe de Bogotá) gradually assumed greater administrative responsibilities for that part of South America lying closer to the Caribbean and the Isthmus. This region, known as New Granada, became a captaincy-general in 1563, while in 1739 its status was substantially improved by the creation of a new viceroyalty, a rank it had temporarily attained in 1717. Access to the inland city of Bogotá was never easy, but the decision to establish the Viceroyalty of New Granada finally acknowledged the even greater difficulty of trying to administer the northern sector of South America adequately from Lima. This had proved to be impossible. New Granada was an important area, responsible for the maintenance of security in the Panamá-Cartagena passage, as well as for the supervision of gold and emerald production, and for control of the increasingly prosperous Spanish agricultural settlements in the Antioquia and upper Cauca valleys. Venezuela, a province within the Viceroyalty of New Granada, enjoyed virtually complete independence from

Bogotá after 1742. Quito continued to regard itself as far removed from its new viceregal capital of Bogotá as it had been from Lima.

Elsewhere, attempts were made to resolve the problems of control and administration on the distant southern frontiers of the Viceroyalty of Peru. Mobile, warring Indians (mainly Toba, Mataco, and Chiriguano) repeatedly destroyed Spanish military and colonizing expeditions in the Chaco and along the south-east Andean foothills, expeditions which had been mounted both from Lima and from Asunción.[23] Much of this continental interior was to remain hostile, untamed country. Colonization of southern Chile was checked by the Araucanian Indians. Indeed, Chile remained one of the most isolated outposts of empire, but it had more strategic and economic importance than the Chaco, and remained a military frontier—a role confirmed by the creation of the Captaincy-general of Chile in 1778.

* * *

SPANISH INITIATIVES IN PRESTRESSED CONSTRUCTION

> **THE IMPORTANCE OF *PRESTRESSED* COMPONENTS:**
>
> In PRESTRESSING, an initial permanent state of stress is introduced which makes the load-bearing object work more efficiently . . .
>
> Materials which are strong in compression but weak in tension require a COMPRESSIVE PRESTRESS to make them more effective.
>
> (A. J. Francis, *Introducing Structures*)
>
> In the case of the *prestressed beam*, forces are applied to the beam *prior to its positioning in the building* to place it in compression . . . With competent design the compression initially imparted to the beam is of such an amount that, even when the beam is fully loaded, no tensile stresses are produced at any point, or at the worst there are only very small tensile stresses, which can be sustained safely without cracking.
>
> The deflections of *prestressed beams* are usually small, and there is a high resistance to fatigue.
>
> (W. Morgan, *The Elements of Structure*)

Spain proceeded with caution and deliberation, making full and effective use of **prestressed components** within the imperial structure—a design innovation of lasting significance. As a result, most of the senior administrative officials—viceroys, captains-general, governors, presidents—remained Spaniards born in Spain, not in America, i.e. *peninsulares* not creoles. Although the appointment of *peninsulares* inevitably characterized the early period of empire, tradition and conviction combined to maintain the practice, so that the selection of creoles for posts of major responsibility became the exception rather than the rule. Indeed, where slackening of the *peninsular* principle was uncovered, particularly during the late-eighteenth-century reforms, the policy was restated and reinforced. **The scale of Spain's deployment of prestressed components throughout its empire for more than three centuries has never been matched in the history of imperial construction, either before or since, with the exception of the 70-year Soviet system.** Control of the State machinery was in the hands of King's men, men whose background, contacts and loyalties lay with Spain. Thus, with few exceptions, each new senior appointment represented a fresh, transatlantic injection of Spanish authority and Spanish influence into the Americas—the assignment of known and dependable civil servants on whom the Crown could rely.

The system undoubtedly favoured those who would act predictably and according to the rules. Spain required conscientious officials who, in cases of doubt, would refer back for instructions rather than seek to gain a reputation for initiative and flair, qualities which could so readily introduce tension and oblique thrust lines within the vast compression structure. In any event, alongside the prestressed components, the whole administrative framework depended upon a complex and time-consuming code of cross-checking and balancing at all levels between the Crown and the various officers and their departments in order to maintain the *status quo*. **It represented, in accordance with Spain's normal imperial building practices, the regular analysis of internal stress and strain patterns within the structure, and the maintenance throughout of adequate compressive force to meet safety requirements.**

As noted earlier, until the final years of the eighteenth century, neither the Monarch nor the majority of the members of the Royal Council of the Indies had ever resided in the Americas. The king never did so. Nevertheless, from first to last, Spain was aware of the unwieldiness of empire. While waves of royal *cédulas* surged across the Atlantic, the time and distance separating Spain from the viceroy, and then again separating the viceregal capital from the regional centres, established their own power hierarchy in practical terms. Reports trickled back and forth through the system. Paperwork accumulated along the passages of state. In the end, isolation and painfully slow transport across the mountains, jungles, deserts and swamps could render the prescribed procedures null and void. *Obedezco pero no cumplo*—I obey but I do not fulfil—was in some cases the final viceregal reconciliation of duty and reality.

One great structural advantage emerged, however. Much of the *risk* inherent in Spain's overstretched lines of communication was mitigated by such exhaustive procedure and red-tape. Delay increased compressive force. Despite the many abuses of the system, there was little tolerance of incompetence or stupidity, at least among the senior ranks. Many of the appointments were filled by professional lawyers from Spanish universities or by other experienced administrators, able and dedicated men who wholeheartedly supported the Crown in principle, and as far as possible in practice. They shared the Crown's determination to maintain colonial America's close ties with Spain. In general they served the empire well.

SPAIN'S 'REDUCED RISK' CONSTRUCTION POLICIES

2. THE ROLE OF THE CHURCH

THE CHURCH operated in two ways:

First, it added enormous **WEIGHT AND COMPRESSIVE FORCE** to the imperial structure as a whole, and kept the thrust lines well centred both in the outer walls and buttresses and in the internal arches, pillars and shafted columns. Literally and figuratively, the Church also added much of the additional compressive weight to the top of the structure. Medieval builders added statues, pinnacles, copings, and heavy decorative balustrades to increase the compressive force on the walls, and to control oblique thrust lines. But these additions to the great cathedrals also embellished the architecture, and helped to make the structure both highly expressive and instantly recognizable.

Second, the Church formed a series of **TIE-BEAMS**, resisting tensile forces both within the main structure, and beyond it where extreme isolation left parts of Spain's empire outside the thrust lines of the main walls. In the latter case, Church and State together soon began to make more use of the **CANTILEVER BEAM**, fashioning this component with remarkable skill and economy. Missions formed these long cantilever beams to claim and hold outlying provinces in the sixteenth and seventeenth centuries (in northern Mexico, Florida and Paraguay), and again in the eighteenth century (in Texas and Upper California), beams which were often reinforced with small military garrisons. The cantilevers were constructed by the great religious orders, which were better organized and frequently better disciplined than the secular clergy.

Building Church and State

> We have a strong city;
> God makes salvation its walls and bulwarks.
>
> (Isaiah xxvi)

> So if we ask: 'Who made it?' the answer is:
> 'It was God.'
> If we ask: 'By what means?' the answer is:
> 'God said, "Let it be"; and it was.'
> If we ask: 'Why?' the answer is:
> 'Because it is good.'
>
> (St. Augustine, *City of God*)

Church and State combined to establish Spanish culture and Spanish authority overseas. Doctrine and internal discipline aside, the Church was in practice an agency of the State, a major compressive force in government and empire, and an established point of political control over colonists and Indians. It focused loyalty, discipline and orthodoxy; a revolt against the Church was effectively a revolt against the State, and implied a political misdemeanour. The Church in Spain's empire was controlled less by Rome than by the Royal Council of the Indies. Indeed, the immense power of patronage held by the Crown made the Church, in a very real sense, another branch of royal government. The Papal Bulls of 1493 and 1501 culminated in that of 1508 when the Spanish Crown received the coveted *Patronato Real* over the Church in the New World. Before long, with further concessions, the Monarchy had acquired a unique power over the Church in its American colonies, and much greater control than it possessed in its European territories.[24] This was the essence of Castile's cultural imperialism, developed during the Reconquest, and brought to a fine art by Isabella and Ferdinand.

The succession of Papal Bulls confirmed that lands and titles awarded in the Americas were a trust received in return for winning Indians to Christ, the continuing theme of duality in political and religious responsibility. The two were not of course always compatible, and the Church added tension to the compression structure with its complaints to the Crown about the ill-treatment of Indians.[25] Nevertheless, with the passage of time and the expansion of the empire, the Crown assumed the greater degree of executive power. Spain was always to be torn between theory and practice, between what it should enforce and what the colonists would tolerate. Brutal exploitation of the Indians elicited many complaints from the Church, as well as many anguished deliberations and well-intentioned royal ordinances to stop such abuses. But the greed of the local population, the needs of the Royal Treasury, and the inability of local officials to implement the ordinances led for the most part to no lasting change of approach. In fact, any comprehensive policy designed to balance Spain's manifold economic, political, social, and religious interests in the New World was totally unworkable in practice.

Conflicts of wealth, ideals and attitudes, where these existed, could therefore polarize the concerns of Church and State. Yet, taking even this into account, few other agencies of empire represented so completely the centralized authority of Spain in the Americas, **and no other set of structural components contributed more to the 'dead load's' ability to withstand and absorb the 'live load's' daily wear and tear on the imperial fabric.** The Church remained one of the greatest of all regulative mechanisms for the control of the *Ultramar*.

The empire's ecclesiastic hierarchy paralleled the State bureaucracy in many ways, **increasing, and at the same time distributing, the compressive load through walls, pillars, multiple arches, and new ground-buttress and flying-buttress support. Through procedure, style, and substance, the Church also mixed its own unique mortar to transmit the compressive load more evenly throughout the structure. While some historians have focused on the fragmented nature of Church and State authority in the Spanish empire, the structural engineer recognizes the skill with which the blocks and 'fragments' of authority were positioned and mortared in ways which successfully distributed very high levels of compressive stress over a huge area.**

Many of the familiar frictions and rivalries between *peninsular* and creole for positions of power and trust in the Church were soon apparent, and again **prestressed components** were favoured. Franciscans, Dominicans, Augustinians, Mercedarians, and Jesuits were recruited in Spain and sent out by the Crown to be allocated by viceroy or bishop. As far as possible, all friars, like other responsible churchmen in Spanish America, were officially required to be loyal Spaniards. Thomas Gage, for example, a young English Dominican friar in Spain, anxious to see America, was engaged without official clearance in 1625, to go to Mexico and on to the Philippines. Just before his departure, however, the Governor of Cádiz received orders to search for Gage and prevent his departure, as it was "the King of Spain's will and pleasure that no English should pass to the Indies, having a country of their own to convert." Nevertheless, Gage was rowed out in secret to his ship, where he hid in an empty biscuit barrel while the vessel was searched. Eventually, undetected, the 'English-American' as he was called, sailed out of harbour to begin his great adventure in the New World.[26]

The day-to-day maintenance of the Church, like that of the secular colonists in many regions, depended on Indian labour. The system of forced labour (*mita*) was not confined to the mines; the clergy also attempted to justify their reliance on it, and on *encomienda*, for the building and upkeep of cathedrals, churches, monasteries, and convents, for working the church estates, and for domestic service. Forced labour and the payment of tribute had not of course been introduced into the New World by the Spaniards; pre-Columbian America was not the gentle paradise that is sometimes depicted by the biased or the romantic. Both the Aztec (Mexica) and Inca empires depended on forced labour and tribute well before the arrival of the *conquistadores*. The scale and severity of the practice after the Conquest, however, were devastatingly new. Even the so-called free labour (hired and paid) was not free in the sense that the labourers were free to accept or refuse the work and still remain legally in the area. There were scattered exceptions; some of the most remote frontier regions such as the Mexican silver-mining centres in the far north, and the cattle and mule-raising *pampas* in the far south, retained considerable initiative as areas of free, paid labour, whether *mestizo*, *mulatto*, poor creole, or migrant Indian.[27] But although conditions could vary with the location, and with the personalities involved, the basic principle of forced labour operated virtually everywhere—in the mines, workshops, farms, church missions, and in building and public works. The use of Indians as slaves was expressly forbidden by the Crown. But as Thomas Gage observed while travelling through Central America in the 1630s:

> Certain it is, these Indians suffer great oppression from the Spaniards, . . . are under hard bondage, and serve with great rigour . . . Though the Kings of Spain have never yielded to what some would have—that the Indians should be slaves—yet their lives are as full of bitterness as is the life of a slave.

As one of the major property-holders in the New World, with land held in perpetuity, the Church derived huge additional wealth (and compressive force) from a complex system of tax exemptions and tithe collection. In Mexico particularly, the wealth of the Church gave it considerable political power. C. H. Haring called the monasteries the banks of Spanish colonial America, but it was capital largely tied to the maintenance of property and personnel, rather than mobile funds made available for local development purposes.[28] The prodigal establishment of monasteries in many parts of Mexico and Peru resulted in a formidable disproportion of clerics among the colonists; by the end of the sixteenth century, for example, an estimated ten per cent of Lima's population consisted of priests, canons, friars or nuns.

The weight and compressive force exercised by the Church at all levels of empire increased inexorably during the seventeenth century, well illustrated by the immensely heavy, extravagantly decorated additions to the structure that distinguished the Spanish Baroque. Such passion for display and lavish ornament in its most complex and ostentatious form became known as the Churrigueresque style, and, as Pevsner noted, "It was in fact in Mexico that the Spanish architects celebrated the wildest of all orgies of over-decoration."[29]

Cantilever beams

> A 'cantilever' is a beam one end of which can be considered as being 'built in' to some rigid support, such as a wall or the ground. The other end of the cantilever sticks out and supports the load.
>
> (J. E. Gordon, *Structures*)

It was on the frontiers of empire that the political role of the Church was most obvious, for the mission became Spain's most widespread pioneering device in and after the 1590s. As H. E. Bolton emphasized, "the amount of government aid, and the ease with which it was secured, depended largely upon the extent to which political ends could be combined with religious purposes."[30]

The Crown's chosen agents for the mission frontier were the great religious orders, institutional components that were already tightly structured and highly dedicated. The mission frontier in time extended from the deserts and wooded swamplands of the north to the rain forests, savannas and pampas of the south—from Florida, New Mexico, Texas and California to eastern Bolivia, Paraguay and Argentina. Along this huge periphery, the Spanish mission and the Spanish presence lay far beyond the mining frontier, which remained driven firmly into the high cordilleras.

Jesuit construction

One striking example of cantilever construction was provided by the Jesuits in Paraguay. In many parts of the American empire, the Jesuits introduced and operated some of the most efficient *haciendas*, *estancias*, factories, colleges and universities to be found anywhere on the continent. They arrived in Paraguay in 1605, and by 1607–9 had begun a systematic program of mission expansion among the Guaraní Indians that involved the congregation of thousands of scattered, semi-nomadic Guaranís into compact, permanent settlements. The 'congregation' policy had been introduced into New Spain in 1598; in the seventeenth and early eighteenth centuries, it spread through eastern Paraguay and the Misiones province of Argentina until by c.1750 more than 100,000 Indians were concentrated into thirty Jesuit missions (or 'reductions' as they were known), some ten to thirty miles apart, raising crops, ranching cattle, and practising crafts.[31]

The mission *pueblos* were laid out in Spain's traditional urban style. Grouped around the plaza were the church and mission buildings, the priests' house, the school, the workshop, and the long rows of Indians' dwellings. As the wealth of the mission accumulated, church fabric and interior decoration became noticeably more elaborate—dressed and carved stone replaced timber and adobe. To the Portuguese, against whose flank the missions were set, the Jesuit 'reductions' represented wealth in the form of an abundant, amenable labour supply, and they remained a constant target for the slave-raiding Paulista *bandeiras*. Nevertheless, despite the damage done by the Portuguese, the increasing power of the Jesuits' Paraguay missions reflected a strong political as well as spiritual presence in the remote south-east. When, under the terms of the Treaty of Madrid in 1750, Spain and Portugal finally abandoned the old Tordesillas Line of Demarcation in favour of a more realistic acknowledgement of Portuguese possession, Spain offered to relinquish seven Jesuit missions in the Ibicuhy region in exchange for the eastern bank of the River Plate. So great was the protest by the Jesuits, and by influential public opinion in Spain, that the Spanish Crown submitted to pressure, and in 1761 the entire treaty was annulled.

By this period, the missions had become virtually autonomous, insulated from external contacts (except certain trade contacts) not only by their remote location, but by their own rules which discouraged anything more than transient outside control and influence. Official visitors were rare, for the whole region still lay in the political wilderness of the Viceroyalty of Peru; Lima was over 2,000 miles away, and no *audiencia* had yet been established any nearer than Charcas (present-day Sucre in Bolivia), in the silver-mining region of Upper Peru. Thus the missions of eastern Paraguay, like those among the Mojo and Chiquito Indians in eastern Bolivia, and later, those in south central Chile and the lower Orinoco, operated at the very limits of Spanish authority.

Removing sources of oblique thrust

The Jesuits, however, had in practice created powerful theocracies within their Mission Provinces, and introduced new tensile stress and strain into the imperial structure. Of all the major religious orders, the Jesuits had remained the most independent of the royal bureaucracy, and the most devoted to the Papacy. Characteristics viewed earlier as advantageous to imperial Spain were eventually seen as obstacles to state power, and as a direct challenge to the Crown. **The Jesuit thrust-line became increasingly centred outside the imperial structure—the condition for collapse. No longer serving as a cantilever beam nor suitable for reconstruction as a flying buttress, the Jesuit component was eventually removed.** Following similar action by France and Portugal, and as a prelude to the king's late-eighteenth-century reforms, the Jesuit Order was expelled from Spanish America in 1767.

Despite the size and politico-religious cohesion of the Jesuit Mission Province in Paraguay, its failure to lay the foundation for sustained social and economic development was soon revealed. Much of the apparent progress had remained extremely superficial under the Jesuits' heavy paternalism. Without the padres' own compressive thrust, regional organization collapsed, and most of the 'reductions' were quickly deserted. In the Treaty of San Ildefonso, however, drawn up by Spain and Portugal in 1777 to confirm their respective claims to South America, the debris of empire remained on site. The influence of the Jesuits lingered on, and the eventual boundary delimitation in the middle Paraguay-Paraná and upper Uruguay valleys endorsed the political effectiveness of the Spanish mission frontier in the continental interior. (Fig. 8)

New cantilever beams in the north

Meanwhile, the expansion of the mission frontier on the fringes of New Spain had continued. In Florida, it was the seventeenth century that marked the spread of Franciscan missions across the peninsula in response to increasing French and English activity in the interior. Farther west, missions were reestablished in New Mexico after the end of the Pueblo Indian rebellion of 1680–93, and Franciscan missions of stout, fortress-type construction were extended across the Nueces River into Texas after 1715, in response to the growing threat of French encroachment from Louisiana.

French expansion represented a dangerous assault on Spain's imperial structure. France had built Fort Natchitoches in the Red River valley in 1714, while La Salle's grand design in the 1680s for strategic French control of the Mississippi Valley and the Gulf of Mexico had led to the founding of several key points along the waterway, including New Orleans in 1718.

North-westward, Franciscans and Jesuits had begun building their first cantilever beams in the 1580s–90s. After the expulsion of the Jesuits, the work was undertaken by Franciscans and Dominicans in a final dramatic revival of frontier expansion into Upper California after 1769, in response to the threat of Russian encroachment.

These long cantilever beams, extended beyond the main load-bearing walls of empire, were never effectively cross-braced however. Although Spain made some attempts to establish lateral connection, in practice the cantilevers remained discrete salients of Spanish authority—an imperial presence of Church and State thrust both into Indian lands and threatened peripheries.

SPAIN'S 'REDUCED RISK' CONSTRUCTION POLICIES

3. THE ROLE OF THE TOWN

> An account of the ports, harbors, forts and cities which have bene surveied, edified, finished, made and mended, with those which have bene builded in a certaine survey by the king of Spaine, his direction and commandment.
>
> (from a report by Baptista Antonio, Surveyor for the King, 1587)

Scaling-up the medieval Peninsular model

The emphasis on urban settlement was a primary feature of Spanish colonization. The medieval Reconquest of Spain from the Moors had demanded the capture of key cities. It had also involved the re-colonization of the Peninsula with a network of new garrison towns, rather than encouraging the spread of essentially rural, isolated, unprotected farming units. The organized urban community represented one of the most direct examples of transfer from southern Europe into Hispanic America; Spanish *conquistadores* and colonists, the majority of them from the towns and cities, or the adjacent rural areas, were well accustomed to the urban traditions of the Mediterranean world.

If anything, the transatlantic passage strengthened the emphasis placed on the role of the town in the New World. Towns were not identified as such by the size of their populations or the impressiveness of their architecture; many a municipality was cut out of the wilderness with great formality by a handful of adventurers who had hastily erected no more than a collection of thatched huts. Towns were distinguished instead by their founding, however rudimentary the layout, and by their institutions, appointed officials and jurisdictions. The perception of the role of the town was what mattered; embellishment could come later.

Towns focused the authority and administration of empire and so had a vital structural as well as social function to perform. The rapid creation of some eighty widely-distributed urban centres in a matter of three or four decades injected a Spanish presence around and within the American continent. By the 1570s, there were nearly 200 Spanish municipalities in the New World, and by 1600, the Americas were dotted with about 300 Spanish towns and cities.[32] It was one of the most spectacular town-planning movements in history, breathtaking in its concept, effort, and achievement.

Towns transmit compressive load, centering thrust lines at local level

The urban hierarchy was dominated by the two viceregal capitals. By 1625, Mexico City had a population of at least 90,000, and Lima 60,000. The extraordinary silver boom-city of Potosí, perched at more than 13,000 feet in one of the harshest, most remote locations in the entire Andes, had already attracted a population of 14,000 by 1547, and over 100,000 by 1600—by far the largest city in the western hemisphere in the late sixteenth century and for much of the seventeenth century also.[33] Many towns in Spanish America, however, consisted of no more than 50–100 families. By the end of the sixteenth century, Spain's territorial empire in the New World was more than thirty times the size of Spain itself, but the total number of Spaniards who had emigrated to any part of the Americas by that time probably amounted to no more than 200,000–250,000, and in the early years many had returned to Spain.[34] Thus, while distance and difficult terrain often opened huge voids between the urban centres, each town was officially positioned in relation to its own frontier—its labour supply, tribute revenue, mineral or agricultural resources, communication lines, and political control. A fundamental reason why towns enabled small numbers to retain and project a Spanish identity was the town's legal role in local government. "From the standpoint of the law," as J. H. Elliott pointed out, "even those Spanish settlers in the Indies who lived in the countryside existed only in relation to their urban community. They were *vecinos* (citizens) of the nearest urban settlement, and it was the town which defined their relationship to the state."[35]

Harmonizing the design. The use of standardized units

The Crown's authority was definitive in the sanctioning of new urban centres, as well as in the maintenance of stylized form and layout. When Nicolás de Ovando replaced Columbus as Governor on Hispaniola in 1502, he was instructed to investigate without delay possible sites for new towns, and to establish these wherever appropriate. In the event, Ovando's first task was the restoration of Santo Domingo, destroyed by a hurricane soon after his arrival, and quickly resited and rebuilt on the gridiron plan—Spain's first use of this plan in the New World.

> **ON THE SITING AND BUILDING OF TOWNES**
>
> Be circumspect . . . lest the *Towne* be *finely built, but foolishly planted.*
>
> In seeking *Firmenes*, proceed *Logically*, that in Judging of the *Worke* itself, we be not distracted with too many things at once . . .
>
> (Henry Wotton, *The Elements of Architecture*, 1624)

The first Spaniard to arrive in America with precise specifications regarding the setting out of cities was Pedrarias Dávila in 1513.[36] His instructions were apparently first applied to Panama City in 1519 (Spain's first city on the Pacific), and read in part:

> A settlement should from the outset follow a definite plan . . . let the city lots be regular from the start, so that once they are marked out, the town will appear well ordered as to the place which is left for a plaza, the site for the church, and the plan of the streets; for in new towns proper order can be established at the start, and thus they remain ordered with no extra labour or cost. If towns are not begun with a formal layout they will never attain it, and order will never be introduced.

The consistency demanded in urban form reflected the Crown's determination not only that order and control be established, but that they should be clearly seen to have been established. Indeed, Spain's deployment of **the town as a standardized unit** throughout the imperial structure was highly effective, both visually and functionally.

The central plaza boldly focused civil and religious authority by its public buildings and distinctive architectural form. In 1573, a new set of Royal Ordinances relating to the laying out of towns in the New World was issued by Philip II.[37] His characteristically detailed directions included the choice of sites and the basic plan of streets and open spaces. A short extract ran thus:

> On arriving at the place where the town is to be laid out, the plan shall be determined, and the plazas, streets, and building lots laid out exactly, beginning with the main plaza. From thence, the streets, gates, and principal roads shall be surveyed, always leaving a certain proportion of open space, so that although the town should continue to grow, it may always grow in the same manner.

If the town is situated on the sea coast, the main plaza should be made at the landing place of the port. If the town lies inland, the main plaza should be in the middle of the town. The plaza shall be of an oblong form, which shall have at the least a length equal to one and a half times the width, inasmuch as this size is the best for fiestas in which horses are used, and for any other fiestas that shall be held . . .

From the plaza shall run four main streets, one from the middle of each side of the plaza; and two streets at each corner of the plaza. The four corners of the plaza shall face the principal winds, so that the street running from the plaza will not be exposed to the winds that cause much inconvenience. The whole plaza round about, and the four streets running from the four sides shall have arcades, for these are of considerable convenience to the merchants who generally gather there . . .

The buildings of the whole town generally shall be so arranged that they shall serve as a defence against those who may try to disturb or invade the town. So far as possible, the buildings should all be of one form for the sake of the beauty of the town . . .

To the Spaniard in a New World, the grid of streets, squares, main buildings, and house plots, represented a familiar urban style, well rooted in the Mediterranean region. It had been anticipated to some extent in the Americas in the larger ceremonial city lay-outs of the politico-religious organizations of Aztec and Inca, although the urban centres of Spain's *Ultramar* were extended well beyond these indigenous limits by the great city-building drive that distinguished Spain's assault upon the continent in the age of the *conquistadores*. Whilst the scale of their town planning and development varied according to individual temperament, opportunity, and resources, nearly all the achievements of these pioneers, however limited, displayed that same air of confidence and of monumental purpose which characterized Spain's urban expression in the New World.

Key centres whose sites proved unfavourable, whether from health hazard, earthquakes, flood, poor soil, or repeated Indian attacks were moved, not once but several times when occasion demanded, in order to fulfil their functions more efficiently. The original choice of site, often rushed and without adequate local knowledge, did not always stand the test of time. Santo Domingo, Vera Cruz, Panama City, Guatemala City, Havana, Guayaquil, Trujillo, Arequipa, Valdivia, Concepción, Salta, Jujuy and Buenos Aires, for example, were all shifted or refounded as conditions required, and without undue concern or more than temporary

Figure 6 Key structural components: cities, towns, and principal overland routeways in the Spanish American empire.

disruption of administration. Indeed, 'temporary' disruption could last for centuries without any fading of Spain's sense of permanence and continuity. Osorno, founded in southern Chile in 1558, at the very edge of empire, was destroyed by Araucanian Indians in 1600. Two hundred years later, it was rebuilt (in 1796) following the original town plan kept in Seville. Towns formed the municipal supports of imperial power driven hard into the American wilderness. They established stable features in the landscape, even in cases where the permanent urban population remained small. Military service, or obligations on *hacienda* or *estancia*, could mean long absence from town; periodic market activity could result in only periodic occupation. Once founded on behalf the Crown, however, legally incorporated towns were not to be lightly abandoned by the footloose, swept forward on the latest wave of restless opportunism.

Above all, towns and cities were established how and where they would best serve Spain's imperial design. They were strategically located in the first instance in order to fix the transoceanic tie-beams linking Spain to the New World, and the New World to the Philippines. Deep, sheltered harbours with fresh water supplies, where careening and caulking could be properly carried out, and large numbers of vessels be safely assembled, were highly valued as port sites in the transatlantic and transpacific worlds. The relationship between the ports and their immediate hinterlands was often of secondary importance.

It was not the ports, however, but the mountains and plateaux that located the vital workplace of empire. In the interior, towns formed the control points of local mining districts, and the local centres of bureaucratic and ecclesiastical power, all carefully set within a compressive hierarchical framework. For over three centuries, the imperial economy pivoted first upon the stored gold and, after the 1540s, upon the more important mined silver within the cordilleras. Judicial and fiscal authority, drawn into closer contact with the mining areas and the concentrations of Indian labour, enhanced the status of such towns as Potosí, Charcas (Chuquisaca), Bogotá and Guadalajara, while the prestige of bishopric and archbishopric as well as of university, increased the importance of several administrative centres.

In form and function, towns were also units of compressive prestress

Whatever its size and position in the urban hierarchy, each town was designed from the outset to be a steadying point, built to withstand local tensile forces and to remain conscious of its special relationship with Spain. As such, the town was the most widespread unit of compressive prestress ever constructed on site in Hispanic America. Structurally, Spain's colonization of the New World was as much about implanting the concept of urbanism as it was about the process of urbanization.

It was a fundamental design policy that remained virtually unchanged throughout the reforms of the late eighteenth century. Spain was still creating new towns in Argentina in the 1790s, and new missions in California until the 1820s. In the empire's coastal and mountain core areas, as well as on the periphery, the Spanish urban ideal found a durable and unmistakable expression, for the isolated mission, *presidio*, or *hacienda*, just as surely as the town or city, represented nodes of centralized organization and control—multiple images of Spanish power and influence reflected in the New World.

SPAIN'S 'REDUCED RISK' CONSTRUCTION POLICIES

4. IMMIGRATION CONTROL

> Spain's emphasis on 'dead load'—on the importance of maintaining weight and controlling thrust lines throughout the compression structure—did not divert its attention from the damage that could be caused by the people moving about inside the building.
>
> Strict IMMIGRATION CONTROL revealed Spain's intention to permit as little tensile stress and strain as possible to be produced by the 'live load'. This was where the *Spanishness* of the 'live load' played its structural role.
>
> Controls on immigration were part of a comprehensive policy designed to eliminate, or at least to reduce, major sources of internal tension which could become the hinge points of collapse.

I have marvelled sometimes at Spaine, how they claspe and containe so large Dominions with so few Naturall Spaniards; But sure, the whole Compasse of Spaine is a very Great Body of a Tree.

(Francis Bacon, *Of the true Greatnesse of Kingdomes and Estates*, 1625)

Spain's desire to retain exclusive control over the style and direction of imperial colonization was in the medieval Peninsular tradition of the Reconquest. So too was determination to exclude the potentially dangerous elements likely to give trouble to both State and Church authority overseas. Control to this extent involved, or at least conceived, State monopoly on a massive and far-reaching scale.

Scaling-up the medieval Peninsular model

Queen Isabella's early legislation in 1501 confining emigration to the Indies to subjects of Castile was a significant pointer to future Crown policy, since except for a short interval (1525–38) under Emperor Charles V, the right to emigrate to the New World was reserved (apart from slaves) to those classified as peninsular Spaniards. Such restriction could never be totally enforced, although within the rules, Spanish naturalization was possible, and certain non-Spaniards with necessary skills were allowed to enter the Indies under special licence. Even so, throughout the sixteenth century, only about 1,000 foreigners are thought to have been granted legal entry.

There was of course clandestine immigration, notably Portuguese and Italian. Forged passports were readily available in Seville, at a price. Some foreigners slipped through the official restrictions, while others simply passed themselves off as Spaniards. Nevertheless, it remained true to say that the overwhelming majority of emigrants to Hispanic America were Spanish citizens. In the sixteenth century, about a third came from Andalusia, nearly thirty per cent from Extremadura and New Castile, twenty-five per cent from Old Castile and León, and others from Galicia, the Basque lands, and the Canaries—a continuation of the great medieval southward movement through the central Peninsula, channelled and dominated by Castile.

Continuance of the policy to remove all remaining major sources of tension produced by the 'live load'

Controls on immigration were religious as well as secular. Absolutist practices, 'one king, one law, one faith', were developing rapidly in Spain. The fall of the last Moorish stronghold in Granada in 1492 had been followed by Columbus's first voyage to the west; but in a mood of increasing religious intolerance, the expulsion of all Jews from Castile and Aragón had also been decreed in that same momentous year, despite the dire economic consequences to Spain of such a loss. Estimates vary, but perhaps as many as 200,000 Jews crowded the ports in 1492, bound for North Africa and other destinations in and around the Mediterranean. Others accepted the alternative of conversion, nominal or genuine. In 1502, Moslems in Castile were given the same choice: expulsion or conversion, an ultimatum also faced by Moslems in Aragón and Valencia in 1525. Spain, in theory, at the start of the sixteenth century had become a totally Catholic bastion of the Christian faith, under the 'Catholic Monarchs'. Spain beyond the oceans would be no less clearly identified.

As a general rule, no Moslem, Jew or Protestant was permitted to emigrate. Neither was any 'New Christian'; no known recent convert to Roman Catholicism, nor any redeemed heretic was to be granted the privilege of carrying Spain into the New World.

Such 'New Christians' included the Jewish converts (*conversos*), and in time the Muslim converts also (*moriscos*), many of whom had remained in Spain after the 1502 and 1525 edicts as successful farmers, craftsmen and artisans. The basic problem of the *moriscos*, however, was one of integration; they remained a class apart, with their own language and religion and a way of life directed by Islamic law. In Valencia and Aragón particularly, where there had been rapid population growth among the descendants of those who had submitted to forced conversion, the *moriscos* formed a genuine enclave of Islam within Spain.[38] After increasing hostility on both sides in the sixteenth century, most of the *moriscos* were finally expelled as a religious and a political risk in 1609–14. At Castile's insistence, special evacuation fleets were assembled and an estimated 300,000 *moriscos* deported from Valencia, Aragón, Murcia, Andalusia and southern Castile—a mere four per cent of the country's total population, but a crippling blow to Spain's national prosperity and economic growth, especially in Valencia and Aragón where more than sixty per cent of the *moriscos* had been concentrated. Nevertheless, for the more immediate purposes of the Church and Monarchy, the Peninsular compression structure was greatly strengthened as a result.

As in Spain, so in empire. Foreigners and heretics who appeared in the New World by chance or by design, and without authorization, were summarily given notice to quit. Although evasion of these stringent controls could and did take place, overall, the non-Spaniard and the non-Catholic tended to provide the exceptions which proved the rule of Spanish loading in a Spanish world. The formal introduction of the Inquisition into Spanish America and the Philippines in 1570–1 (though inquisitorial powers had been extended to bishops in the Indies as early as 1517) revealed the necessity to maintain vigilance, and the determination to protect Spaniard and Indian from the influence of Jews, Moslems, and Protestants.

The Crown's control extended also to the prohibition of unmarried women as emigrants to the colonies, unless they were the relatives or servants of legal immigrants. Although by law married men were supposed to be accompanied by their wives (or to travel with their consent) the rule was often waived on the understanding that wives would join their husbands within an interval of two years, and thus maintain the Spanishness of the 'live load'. This requirement was frequently ignored or evaded by both husbands and wives. In addition to those women listed as official emigrants, some of course entered illegally as stowaways, or by roundabout routes from Brazil and other non-Spanish territories. In the first phase to *c*.1520, women probably comprised somewhere between five and seventeen per cent of the emigrants to the New World. In 1560–1580, some estimates suggest that as many as twenty-eight per cent of the emigrants were women.[39] But as male emigrants were much more highly dispersed throughout the two viceroyalties, and, proportionately, many more men than women escaped official documentation of any kind both in Spain and the New World, the apparently more sophisticated estimates for sixteenth-century female emigration to Spanish America may be greatly exaggerated. In the widely scattered empire as a whole in this period, as many as ninety per cent of the immigrants were probably men, and over the centuries young single men continued to form the mainstream of emigrants to Spain's New World.[40]

From the beginning, the Crown had encouraged the emigration of Spanish families to the Indies, but Spain was never able to populate the colonies adequately with its own family units, whether *peninsular* born in Spain, or creole born in the Americas. As Lavrin noted: "Studies of migration patterns after 1600 are scarce, but indicators such as parochial and municipal censuses, marriage and death records, suggest a sharp decline in the number of peninsular women migrating to Spanish America in the seventeenth century."[41] Nevertheless, major expansion of the mixed *mestizo* population occurred even in those regions where, with the passage of time, Spanish women (creoles in particular) became well represented, since miscegenation did not occur because of a lack of Spanish women. While significant differences in role and social status were apparent in different parts of the empire, especially in the more isolated, thinly populated regions, the broad picture created by Spanish migration to the New World is of a mixed *mestizo* society (many of whom were described and accepted as Spanish creoles), overlain by the small, elitist *peninsular* and wealthy creole classes—the *peninsulares* in particular representing their own distinctive and unequivocally Spanish presence in the front ranks of American imperial organization.

Some estimates suggest that as many as 243,000 migrants may have left Spain for the Indies during the sixteenth century, and a further 195,000 in the first half of the seventeenth century.[42] But with Spain's own population totalling about nine million at the end of the sixteenth century, even these estimates would indicate that the losses through colonization overseas were relatively small, despite the fact that Spain's population had plunged to six million by the end of the seventeenth century after a toll of domestic disasters. Spanish emigrants to the New World however included many of the most energetic and enterprising elements in the population. Indeed, while never among the prime causes of Spain's (especially Castile's) domestic problems during the seventeenth century, emigration to the Indies is often regarded as a contributory factor in Spain's severe economic recession and population decline in the 1590s–1680s period, during which the 'Spanish' population on the Americas (i.e. the *peninsulares*, creoles, and *mestizos* classed as white) grew steadily, both by emigration and natural increase. During the eighteenth century, only about 53,000 Spaniards are estimated to have emigrated to the Indies, a vigorous influx nonetheless, mainly from northern Spain—Galicians, Asturians, Cantabrians, Basques, and Catalans.[43]

Throughout the centuries however, it was the overwhelming and persistent *Spanishness* of the 'live load' that astounded outside observers. As John Campbell reported in 1714:

> Though there have been formerly some instances of Foreigners passing through the Spanish Settlements, and even residing in them, yet they are so rare, and attended with such extraordinary circumstances, that instead of admiring that such things have happened, we ought rather to wonder that they have not happened more frequently, considering the strong passion that Strangers have always had for penetrating unknown countries.[44]

The official controls upon emigration, the expense of the sea passage, and the lack of large-scale, organized systems of indenture (although some went to the Indies as indentured servants), all combined to regulate the flow of Spanish colonists across the Atlantic. Hispanic America was never intended to be the 'land of opportunity' for the heterogeneous elements of the Old World.

SPAIN'S 'REDUCED RISK' CONSTRUCTION POLICIES

5. TRADE CONTROLS

> **TRADE was the greatest source of risk to Spain's imperial compression structure. It produced the most numerous and the most dangerous points of tensile stress and strain, and made the task of keeping the structure under compression at all times more difficult because of the many oblique thrust lines it introduced.**

I might enlarge here upon the mighty Advantages to *Old Spain* by this restraint upon *Trade*, and how it has kept the Possession of *New Spain* so entire to themselves, undisturb'd and undisputed by the rest of Europe, that it is a kind of *Terra Incognita* to this Day, to all the rest of the World.

(*A Review of the State of the British Nation*, 1711)

Trade was regarded as a vital part of the great monopoly that tied a global overseas empire to metropolitan Spain. Economic dependence was designed to reinforce political dependence within the compression structure and this being so, stringent trade controls exhibited some of the Crown's most ambitious efforts to ward off foreign competition and foreign infiltration into its American preserves.

> **Strengthen the angles of the walls, that part which must strengthen all the rest.**
> (Henry Wotton, *The Elements of Architecture*, 1624)

Seville: the Castilian cornerstone

The *Casa de la Contratación de las Indias*, or Board of Trade, had been established at Seville in January 1503 in order to regulate and develop trade between Spain, specifically Castile, and its transatlantic colonies in the Caribbean. From that time, Seville with its outport of Cádiz (to which the *Casa* was eventually transferred in 1717) controlled the commerce of an ever-extending American empire, and became one of the wealthiest and most powerful cities in sixteenth- and seventeenth-century Europe. Gold and silver destined for Spain crossed the Atlantic and floated up the Guadalquivir, since all the major cargoes from the Indies entered Spain legally only through Seville and Cádiz. Although between 1529 and 1573, nine other Spanish ports were allowed to freight ships outward-bound for the Indies as a special concession, and small ships working out of the Canary Islands avoided the principal controls, the dominance of Seville over the in-coming trade was real and effective. Not until the reforms of 1765, when the trade of the Americas was permitted to return to seven other Spanish ports besides Seville and Cádiz, was this extraordinary 260-year monopoly officially broken.

Designated ports provided a dramatic punctuation at each end of the transatlantic line. One of the earliest and most explicit forecasts of the economic opportunities created for the Castilian ports by the discovery of America appeared in a memorandum addressed to the city fathers of Córdoba by Hernán Pérez de Oliva in 1524, in which Córdoba's council was rebuked for its neglect of the river Guadalquivir. It was, argued Pérez de Oliva, more important than ever to improve navigation along the waterway, "*because formerly we were at the end of the world, and now we are in the middle of it, with an unprecedented change in our fortunes.*"[45] Instead of Córdoba's ancient rival, Seville, being allowed to reap all the profits, the Guadalquivir could transport some of them farther upstream. "Take advantage of the great fortune that is now coming to Spain," Pérez urged the council. "Make your river navigable, and you will have opened for yourselves a road by which you can participate in this fortune, and bring to your families, and to your city, great prosperity . . . From the Indies will come so many ships laden with wealth, and so many will sail to them, that I believe they will leave a permanent imprint on the waters of the sea."

In the event, Pérez de Oliva was right to identify the Guadalquivir as the richly tapered end of Spain's great transatlantic routeway, but Seville could never have been seriously challenged by any of the ports upstream. Córdoba became increasingly isolated in the face of Seville's overwhelming geographical advantages as the terminus of the Atlantic run. Seville itself had to fight the disadvantages of being an inland port, safe from pirates, and well placed to serve a rich Andalusian hinterland but not the needs of a rapidly expanding transatlantic empire. Delays and congestion in the Guadalquivir river led to increased specialization of function, and gradually extended Seville's port facilities farther downstream to San Lúcar and Cádiz, thus creating one of the first great European port complexes of modern times. The large ships eased their passage along the Guadalquivir river, towering above the myriad small ferries and support craft darting around them. The transatlantic vessels had to be light-loaded over the San Lúcar sand bar some sixty miles downstream from Seville, and towed around the river's tightest bends. Seville itself, however, long remained unrivalled as the city of a thousand opportunities. Silver and gold poured in from the New World. Men and capital poured in from Spain, and from the western Mediterranean. For those who settled, or for those who left it to take their chances in the Americas, Seville—"the Lovely Light of Europe, and Blessed Queen of the Great Ocean"— had become the first capital of the transatlantic world, its population well over 100,000 by the end of the sixteenth century.

Facing the growing problem of oblique thrust lines

The origins of the cargoes carried down the Guadalquivir bound for the New World were to change. Ships laden with Andalusian wines, olive oil, cereals and flour had helped to sustain the tastes of a Mediterranean world newly arrived in the Americas. But distance worked selectively against the various attempts to duplicate Spain on the far side of the Atlantic. As food production in the Indies became better organized, and colonists grew familiar with the great range of indigenous American crops, including the staples of the 'maize and potato civilizations' of the highland Indians, the New World became more self-sufficient in food, wines and beverages. By the 1580s, at least for the majority, bulk imports of foodstuffs from Spain had ceased to be a significant part of the trade with the metropolitan area, but Spain was already finding it increasingly difficult to meet the growing demands of its American colonists for manufactured goods. Although home-produced manufactures still formed part of the outgoing cargoes in the sixteenth century, there was no widespread promotion of manufacturing industry in Spain, and the country's relative decline in this sector accelerated in the seventeenth century. "As to *Manufactures*," Defoe wrote tersely in 1711, "we all know *Spain* has none."[46]

Seville and Cádiz became the ports through which the manufacturers of France, Flanders, Holland, England, Germany and Italy shipped their products, legally or otherwise, and assumed the role Spain could not fill. This was particularly true in the late seventeenth and early eighteenth centuries, when more than ninety per cent of the manufactured goods imported into Spanish America were foreign in origin.[47] Many exports specifically identified as 'Spanish' were simply foreign goods re-labelled and re-exported by Spain. Even much of the carrying trade by that time was in foreign-built vessels, paid for with Spanish silver, although Spain's own Peninsular and Indies shipbuilding industry was to revive slowly in the eighteenth century.

The *Casa de la Contratación* regulated Spain's transatlantic traffic, faithfully implementing the political policies laid down by the Royal Council of the Indies. Every detail of the departure and arrival of ships, their bills of lading, seaworthiness, royal treasury revenues, customs duties, convoy taxes (*avería*), passenger lists, pilotage, navigation, and all other movement was recorded and supervised by this extraordinarily powerful agent of government control. Its compressive weight was reinforced by Seville's influential guild of merchants trading with the Americas, the *consulado* formed in 1543. As Seville's port functions became more complex, the business of empire became increasingly cumbersome and slow—"Let my death come from Spain," ran the proverb, "for then it will be sure to be long in coming." Delay, however, was itself a powerful compressive force. The *Casa's* survival for nearly three centuries maintained a heavy superstructure of regulation whose complexities, it was recognized, provided opportunity for corruption and for contraband trade. But until its gradual decline in the eighteenth century, and eventual abolition in 1790, the *Casa de la Contratación* remained second only to the Royal Council of the Indies in the authority it wielded over Spain's affairs in the New World.

MAJOR STRUCTURAL RESPONSES TO THE RISKS INTRODUCED BY TRADE

Weaknesses and irregularities occur in every structure—holes, cracks, sharp corners can raise *local stress* very dramatically. Yet, normally, structures are full of minor cracks, holes and notches without endangering the structure or interfering with its use. The weight of the structure in compression must cope with what occurs. Spain resisted many of the tensions in the structure by increasing the weight of regulation, by adding new pillars, struts and buttresses of trade bureaucracy to support the weight, and by inserting lattices of foreign suppliers, agents and middlemen into the Spanish structure—the trusses of the structural engineer.

JOINTS AND JOINTING

The growth of trade thus increased the number and variety of the structural components and the complexity of the jointing between them. JOINTS between the different materials forming the structure can be weak or strong; whether they are 'efficient' or 'inefficient' depends entirely on what they are being asked to do.

THE JOINT'S FUNCTION IS TO TRANSMIT THE LOAD (i.e. THE COMPRESSIVE OR TENSIONAL STRESS) FROM ONE STRUCTURAL COMPONENT TO THE NEXT. Careful mortaring was a method of spreading the compressive load more evenly. Allowing for a little 'GIVE' IN THE JOINTS was also common practice where both compression and tension were involved, since it permitted small amounts of movement to redistribute the load and so reduce stress concentrations, the bane of all joints.

Spain eased the compressive forces at certain points in the imperial structure by allowing, or by coming to terms with, a certain amount of 'give' at the joints—an easing or adjustment of the rules—e.g. by the issuing of special licences, by granting naturalization, by the sale of office, by bribery, by dependence on foreign manufactures, by tolerance within limits of contraband trade, by occasional compromise with colonial opposition, and by provision for conflicting or locally unenforceable legislation through the response: 'I obey but I do not comply'.

Spain's reaction to trade competition, therefore, as to any other challenge to its authority, was to maintain its *legal* claims—to the Americas, to the sea lanes and sea ports which surrounded them, and to Spain's monopoly of imperial trade. Rights could be yielded but not usurped; only rarely did the Crown and its most senior advisers officially acknowledge the difficulty of enforcing what was legally required. But when faced with an *uncontrollable* flouting of the rules, Spain's tendency in the end was to recognize the scale of the problem, and, wherever possible, to incorporate the violation into the jointing system—that is, to institutionalize it in some form, and tax it.

On the other hand, certain joints were greatly strengthened. Overseas trade, for example, was restricted officially to a very small number of ports for more than 200 years, and this was reflected in the exceptionally strong protective fastenings constructed at designated points.

Major ports as primary joints

The strict control of the transatlantic traffic in Spain was supported by similar sets of controls, at selected ports, in the Caribbean and the Gulf of Mexico. Together they provided one of the most striking examples ever seen of co-ordinated, long-distance transport.

Spain threw all its effort into identifying and safeguarding the basic essentials of transatlantic communication. The growing problems of piracy, privateering, and a vigorous contraband trade, especially by the English, French, Dutch and Portuguese, strengthened Spain's determination to restrict virtually the whole of the transatlantic traffic to a few selected ports in Middle America. Throughout the greater part of the colonial period there were no 'open entry' ports on either the Atlantic or the Pacific coasts of Spanish America, officially no holes, unauthorized and unchecked, through which foreign goods and influences could penetrate and the wealth of the Americas seep away. Bullion and other merchandise destined for Spain, such as alpaca and vicuña wools, quinine, sugar, cacao, coffee, cochineal, indigo, tobacco and hides, as well as the valuable cargoes shipped from Manila, had to be moved across Hispanic America by laborious systems of transfers. Goods were shifted slowly along the overland 'corridors', along the trails and through the subsidiary ports towards the Isthmus, the Middle Seas and their designated Atlantic gateway terminals.

At first, Santo Domingo controlled the entire Caribbean circulation; later the four key American ports became Havana, Cartagena, Vera Cruz-San Juan de Ulúa, and Puerto Bello (which replaced Nombre de Dios in 1598 as part of the great new program of port defence and security undertaken in the 1590s). Because of their strategic location in relation to the Atlantic and the Isthmus, and their role as the assembly points for the wealth of Mexico and Peru, the ports of Havana and Cartagena developed into key military and naval bases, crucial joints in the structure, heavily fortified and garrisoned against attack by buccaneers. These two fine harbours, "sufficient to receive a great store of ships", were protected by defences of such scale and massiveness that, even now, no more impressive evidence can be found anywhere in the Americas of Spain's concept of transatlantic maritime power. The old walls and fortifications of Havana and Cartagena are relics of empire, bold expressions of an earlier authority, and a once-significant location in the first Americo-Atlantic world.

THE DEVELOPMENT OF THE TRANSATLANTIC CONVOY

> It is manifest that the Indies, being as the stomach to Spain (for from it nearly all the revenue is drawn), must be joined to the Spanish head by a sea force.
>
> (Hollander, 1648)

Scaling-up the medieval Peninsular model

As with so many other elements of Spain's imperial organization, the transatlantic convoy was an extension of a system that had already operated in medieval Spain. By the mid-fourteenth century, Castile had introduced convoy protection for its seaborne trade with Flanders, and by the early fifteenth century, forty Castilian ships based in the northern Cantabrian ports were patrolling the Bay of Biscay and the English Channel.

New tie-beams

Global dimensions and transoceanic spans resulted in sea-lanes becoming important tie-beams in the imperial structure, their innovative use by Spain stimulating new, stronger design features. In 1526, Spain had forbidden its merchant ships to sail alone to and from the Indies. Instead, immobilised by government restriction, they were forced to await official grouping under armed escort—the world's first transatlantic convoys. The system was reorganized and refined in the 1530s and 1540s until in 1564, the *Carrera de Indias* began despatching two fleets annually to the New World, one sailing in May for Vera Cruz in New Spain, the other (the Tierra Firme fleet) leaving in August for Nombre de Dios and the overland crossing of the Isthmus to Panamá, which controlled the movement of cargoes along the Pacific coast to and from Peru.

Severe additional 'live loading' of the structure caused by environmental hazards

After wintering in the Gulf of Mexico or the Caribbean (at Cartagena), both fleets converged on Havana in March to prepare for their combined return to Spain. The annual departure from

Havana was supposed to take place not later than June, with the great treasure fleet entering the strong current of the Gulf Stream (discovered by Ponce de León in 1513), and following it through the Florida Strait into the Atlantic. Delay in leaving Havana was not unusual but it could be disastrous since ships were then liable to be caught in the hurricane season. This occurred between late July and mid-September, and vessels could be trapped anywhere between the Florida keys and the Hatteras shallows—the convoy scattered, ships sunk or disabled, and isolated vessels left to provide easy targets for pirates.

The frequency of the sailings varied with circumstances, but in the early 1550s, as the silver wealth from Potosí, consigned via Panamá, began to cross the Atlantic in greatly increased amounts—in volume and value the greatest transoceanic trade the world had ever seen—much stronger defence of the ships carrying bullion was needed. This resulted in heavier protection for the Tierra Firme fleet, which became known as the *galeones*, while that to Mexico, with fewer armed warships in attendance, was termed the *flota*. After Spain's spectacular loss of treasure during Drake's raid along the Pacific coast in 1578–9, a convoy system was also introduced between Arica (the main port for shipping the silver of Potosí) and Panamá—the *Armada de la Mar del Sur*. Other regional defence squadrons were deployed in the seventeenth century at vulnerable points on the transatlantic run; the *Armada de Barlovento* patrolled the Caribbean (although the area was too extensive for effective cover without a much larger force), while the *Armada del Mar Océano* guarded the eastern end of the route where the returning fleets approached home waters.[48]

DANGER POINTS

I come to *Apertions* . . ., in short, all *Inlets* or *Outlets*. To which belong these generall *cautions*. First, that they be as few in number, and as moderate in dimension, as may possibly consist with other due respects: for in a word, all *Openings* are *Weaknings*.

(Henry Wotton, *The Elements of Architecture*, 1624)

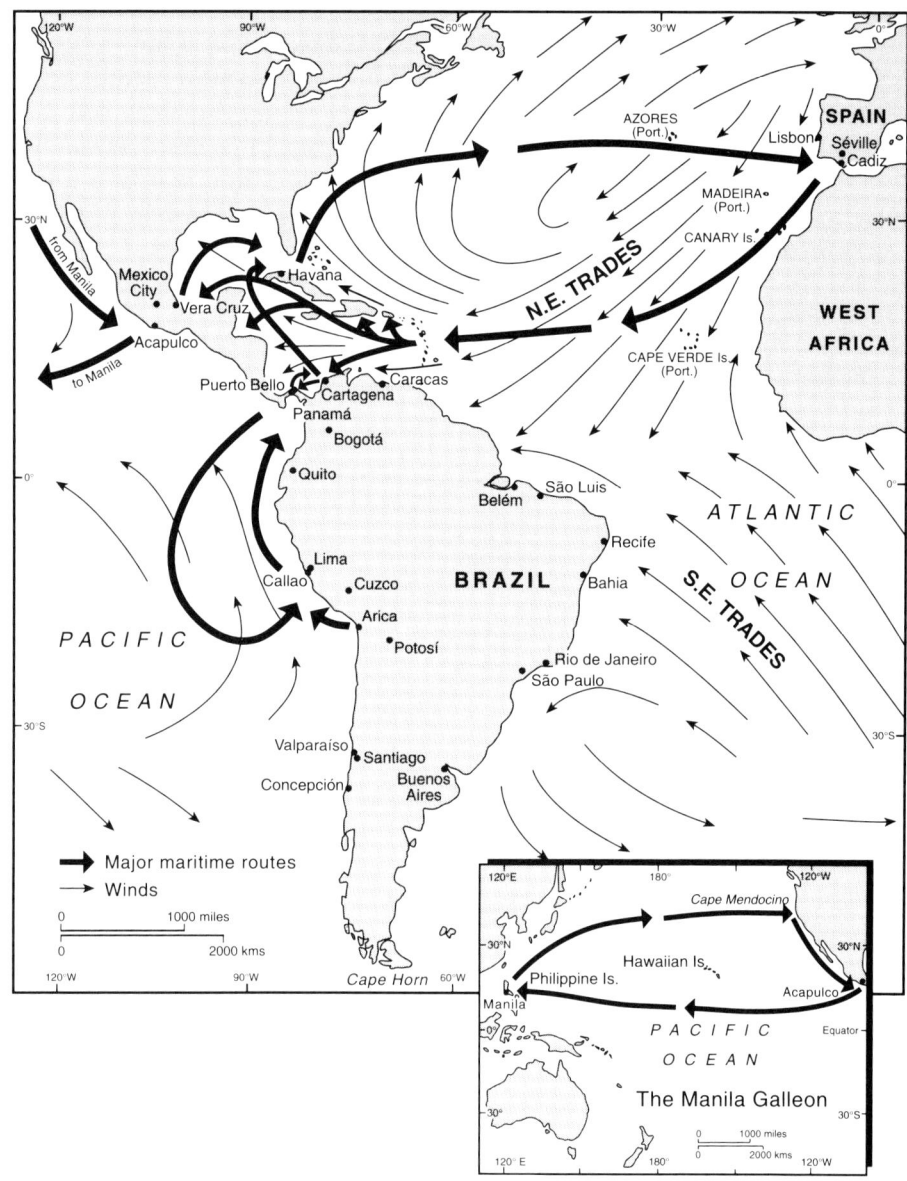

Figure 7 Spain's oceanic tie-beams: the early trans-Atlantic and trans-Pacific imperial routeways.
(Main map based on M. J. MacLeod, in *The Cambridge History of Latin America*, Cambridge University Press, I, 1984)

Despite the evasions and loopholes in the system, Spain struggled for more than 200 years to concentrate the bulk of its transatlantic trade on only *six* key ports: two in Spain (Seville and Cádiz), and four in the New World (initially Santo Domingo and Nombre de Dios, but soon the major sites of Vera Cruz, Puerto Bello, Cartagena, and Havana). The mainstream of trade, the *Carrera de Indias*, swirled strongly and unmistakably across the Atlantic, along the familiar routes, and in and out of the prescribed ports.

Reinforcing the great transatlantic tie-beam

The need for greater protection of the treasure and supply fleets led to the prohibition not only of unaccompanied vessels, and then of small fleets of less than ten vessels, but also to restrictions on ships of less than 80 tons crossing the Atlantic. This minimum was raised to 100 tons by the decree of 1544, and to 300 tons by that of 1587. Small ships like the invaluable caravels were never completely eliminated, but the size and armament of Spain's merchant fleet increased dramatically in the second half of the sixteenth century. Impressively stout vessels of 300–600 tons, initially square-rigged *naos* built in northern Spain, became a feature of the 200 or so crossings of the Atlantic made annually as the traffic increased. The trend towards larger ships also made good use of the limited numbers of skilled navigators available. Whatever the dangers from piracy and foreign warships, the physical hazards caused by storms, reefs, overloading, and navigational error, for example, took a heavy toll. The Atlantic crossing was always hazardous; then as now, only the inexperienced ever underestimated it.

No better expression of the style and purpose of Spain's seaborne imperialism could be found than the galleon fleets, ships of state in every sense. The Spanish galleon was developed in the 1550s, a three- or four-masted warship of 500 tons or more, with heavy broadside armament, good cargo space, and elegant lines. The *Armada de la Carrera*—armed convoy across the Atlantic—was expensive, highly organized, and extraordinarily successful. Only three of the transatlantic treasure fleets ever fell into enemy hands: in 1628 when the Dutch Admiral Piet Heyn captured the fleet in Matanzas Bay, Cuba, and when the English Admiral Robert Blake destroyed the fleet in 1656 (off Cádiz), and again in 1657 (at Tenerife).

The galleons were a visible and menacing sign of Spain's naval power, a formidable deterrent under normal circumstances to any small force or direct attack. The galleons protected the merchantmen and also served as floating bank vaults, carrying the royal silver. The annual rhythm of the armed convoys to the New World, *galeones* and *flota*, became a regular feature after 1564, and around the Atlantic and Pacific basins countless other rhythms were adapted to it. The system continued, though with some modification, for virtually 200 years. The transatlantic trade suffered general depression in the first half of the seventeenth century, particularly in the crisis years of 1629–31 and 1639–41, and during a decline in the volume and value of the trade with New Spain. Recovery was slow and uneven, although between 1650 and 1700, there was a *flota* to New Spain on average every two years, and a *galeones* to Tierra Firme every three (an average which reflected increased traffic in the 1690s). Moreover, larger galleons of 700–1000 tons were now not uncommon, and as many as ninety merchant ships at a time were convoyed across the Atlantic.

The ports of the New World sprang into life whenever the royal *armada* arrived to convoy the treasure fleets back to Spain, or when the fleets from Seville and Cádiz arrived with colonists and supplies. As Antonio de Ulloa noted in 1735:[49]

> The bay of Cartagena is the first place in America at which the galleons are allowed to touch, and thus it enjoys the first fruits of commerce by the public sales made there . . . the fair is a time of universal profit, shops are opened and filled with all kinds of merchandise . . . This commercial tumult lasts while the galleons continue in the bay; for they are no sooner gone, than silence and tranquility resume their former place. This the inhabitants of Cartagena call *tiempo muerto*, the dead time.

Puerto Bello (Portobello), on the Isthmus, was the site of an even larger fair since, with Nombre de Dios before it, for over a century it handled more than half, by value, of the rich South American trade. The port was heavily fortified, and was distinguished by a fine natural harbour (discovered by Columbus in 1502), two large plazas, and a substantial stone custom house close to the quayside.

> The town, so thinly inhabited . . . becomes at the time of the galleons, one of the most populous places in all South America. Its situation on the Isthmus betwixt the South and North Sea, the goodness of its harbour, and its small distance from Panamá, have given it the preference for the rendezvous of the joint commerce of Spain and Peru, at its fair.

While seamen set about using the ships' sails as makeshift tents, and merchants opened bales and arranged their goods, Ulloa watched...

> The land become covered with droves of mules from Panamá, each drove consisting of above a hundred, loaded with chests of gold and silver from Peru . . .
>
> He who has seen this place during the *tiempo muerto*, or dead time, solitary, poor, and a perpetual silence reigning everywhere, the harbour quite empty, and every place wearing a melancholy aspect, must be filled with astonishment at the sudden change, to see the bustling multitudes, every house crowded, the square and streets encumbered with bales and chests of gold and silver of all kinds; the harbour full of ships and vessels . . . and thus a spot, such a sickly place, at all other times detested for its deleterious qualities, becomes the staple of the riches of the Old and New World, and the scene of one of the most considerable branches of commerce in the whole earth.

From the end of the sixteenth to the early years of the eighteenth century, Puerto Bello was thus the periodic meeting point of two huge commercial circulations, the joint between two essential tie-beams. Seville merchants, or their representatives, were officially authorized to trade as far as Puerto Bello; Peruvian merchants took over at that point and together with the Crown's officials, normally stationed at Panamá, handled virtually the whole of the South American trade to and from the Pacific ports. Until the reforms in the eighteenth century, even Buenos Aires was *legally* required to receive its goods transhipped by this astonishingly long 'back-door' route via the Isthmus, the Pacific, and the Andean trails across Peru.

Puerto Bello was indeed "a sickly place", less so than the fever-ridden Nombre de Dios where the annual fair was held from 1575 to 1597, but still "an open grave" as Thomas Gage described it in 1637, "not *Porto bello*, but *Porto malo*". After the fair, which by the eighteenth century was permitted by the Crown to last up to forty days, men and merchandise departed from the Isthmus either towards Spain or towards Peru—two long journeys in opposite directions, two long ocean voyages separated only by this narrow continental parting of the ways.

In 1740, however, Spain authorized certain ships to sail from Spain and trade directly with the Pacific ports of South America via Cape Horn or the Magellan Strait, thus abandoning the official Caribbean–Isthmian monopoly of the West Coast trade. The *galeones* system was now in terminal decline in the Caribbean despite the prolonged attempts to maintain it as the only legal trade route to South America. Puerto Bello had become increasingly vulnerable to buccaneers, and to the even more damaging *contrabandistas*. No fair was held there between 1708 and 1722. Puerto Bello's capture by Admiral Vernon in 1739 at the start of the war with England (The War of Jenkins' Ear), followed by Vernon's systematic destruction of the port's massive fortifications in 1740, marked the final end; the fair of 1731 proved to be the last. It also marked the end of the Tierra Firme fleet. Indeed, Vernon's destruction of Puerto Bello, and the subsequent (though much less effective) attacks on Cartagena and Cuba, had concentrated on the major *joints* of empire in the Caribbean, and reflected his intention to weaken Spain's oceanic tie-beam by destroying its land connections.

Henceforth, all legal trade with the greater part of the Caribbean and with South America was by *registros*, individual ships sailing under licence from Cádiz. The exception was the *asiento*, the monopoly acquired by Britain in 1713 under the Treaty of Utrecht to supply Spanish America with African slaves—a monopoly transferred at this point to Britain from France, which had itself acquired it from Spain in 1701. In 1713 Britain had also gained an exclusive privilege to send one merchantman annually to Vera Cruz or Cartagena/Puerto Bello; the rights were granted to the South Sea Company until they were retrieved by Spain through purchase in 1750. Both the *asiento* and the Annual Ship had been dangerous new sources of oblique thrust, since they offered major opportunities for increased contraband trade.

The transatlantic *flota* to Mexico, though small and sporadic, was less affected by the turmoil further south in the Caribbean. In all, it persisted for some 240 years, continuing intermittently until 1789, when it was finally abandoned.

> **RESILIENCE**
>
> The quality of being able to store strain energy and deflect elastically under a load without causing permanent damage is called 'resilience', and it is a very valuable characteristic in a structure.
>
> (J.E. Gordon, *Structures*)

Much of the RESILIENCE of Spain's empire came from the structure's ability to store STRAIN ENERGY and to deflect under a heavy load without suffering permanent damage. New cracks could occur under these conditions, but these were 'SAFE' CRACKS well within the margins of tolerance. Where pieces of the structure did break off locally under tension it was never catastrophic since Spain allowed the most dangerous strain energy to convert to FRACTURE ENERGY along paths delimiting only non-essential areas. Some of the islands, ports and sea-routes in the Caribbean, together with the whole of the Atlantic seaboard north of Florida, even the vast South American interior—all these Spain could afford to lose, or at least, was prepared to lose. But fracture energy never separated Spain permanently from those parts of the imperial structure it was determined to keep. In this, Spain simply applied one of the basic rules of structural 'efficiency', *viz.* to avoid building, or remove if already built, 'idle' sections which distribute little or no stress, or which are actually weakening the structure by weight, or cost, or nuisance.

SEA TRADE WITHIN THE EMPIRE: THE PROBLEM OF THE PACIFIC RIM

The dangers of oblique thrust caused by direct trade between Mexico, Peru and the Philippines

As the geographical framework of empire became fixed in the sixteenth century, basic principles were confirmed. With few exceptions, trade between the two viceroyalties was either prohibited or discouraged, particularly where competition with Spain's own products or conflict with Spain's political interests was involved. In commerce, as in everything else, the purposes of empire were felt to be best served by centralized control—long tie-beams of regulated transoceanic movement secured firmly to Spain, rather than the innumerable oblique thrusts, and 'unsafe' cracks of inter-regional trade.

The distribution of goods by sea among the various Spanish colonies in the New World had of course operated since the early days. Supplies brought out from Spain and the Canaries had to be distributed from the primary ports, return cargoes moved back. The greatest potential for sea trade, however, envisaged by some of the earliest arrivals, was that between the two key centres of New Spain and Peru. It was New World-based, and focused on the Pacific, not the Atlantic. Cortés, the most entrepreneurial of the *conquistadores*, had dreamed of opening a vigorous trade between Mexico and Peru, beginning in 1536 with supplies of foodstuffs, arms and horses for Pizarro's newly discovered empire. Cortés foresaw a major southward expansion of trade, with Peru as the natural market for the agricultural produce of his west Mexican estates. Indeed, Cortés' promotion of the shipbuilding industry had as much to do with extending exploration and promoting trade along the west coast of the Americas as it had with establishing transpacific exchange.

Cortés died in 1547, his many initiatives and independent spirit having long aroused deep suspicion in Spain. Apart from the Crown's willingness to sanction trade between Mexico and Peru in emergencies, the prospects for steady, long-term growth and diversification declined in the sixteenth century.[50] The round-trip trade represented about four to six ships annually, ten at best, carrying local products or Spanish goods, but never regarded as more than a minor supplement to Peru's main line of supply and communication with Spain via Panamá. The tie-beam to Seville was stoutly constructed by the Crown, by the *Casa de la Contratación de las Indias* and by Seville's powerful guild of merchants, the *Consulado*; the firm distinction between the *flota* to New Spain and the *galeones* to the Panamá Isthmus and Peru was not to degenerate into a trade free-for-all on the west coast of the Americas.

Manila, however, founded in 1571, quickly became the great entrepôt for the wealth of the Orient, and it was the success of the Manila trade that caused so many problems. Spain had never intended to develop a major trade flow across the Pacific, merely to import controlled quantities of goods (silks, spices, porcelain and other wares) that Spain's own markets in Europe and the New World could absorb. A royal *cédula* of 1579 had permitted two ships to sail from Manila directly to Peru, but as soon as Philip II heard of plans to establish a Philippines–Peru trade on a regular basis, he immediately issued instructions (in 1582 and 1587) forbidding such navigation in the future, and forbidding all sale and purchase of goods from the Philippines in Peru. Peru simply ignored the prohibition. Such was the demand for luxury items, and so great was Peru's purchasing power in silver, that its merchants took matters into their own hands and carried on their trade illegally with the merchants in Acapulco. Wind patterns made the return southward sailing from Mexico slow and hazardous, indeed, seamen considered the transpacific voyage from Acapulco to Manila easier than the much shorter one from Acapulco to Peru, but this did not deter business. As a rule, the Philippine trade always offered Peru an excellent choice of goods at prices far below the cost of the imports from Spain, even on occasion below the cost of 'cheap' Mexican manufactured wares, including textiles, clothing and furniture.

In desperation, in 1631, Spain had forbidden all trade and navigation between the Viceroyalties of New Spain and Peru, but this merely promoted more contraband traffic. The true extent of the smuggling and the bribery of officials remained unknown and uncontrollable. No amount of Crown legislation could reduce Peru's hunger for luxuries, and the silver at its disposal to pay for them. Both Mexican and Peruvian silver drained into the Orient, perhaps as much as one-third of the total silver production of the New World. Chinese goods occasionally glutted the markets of Mexico City and Lima, but the persistent demand for silver in the East, and for silk in both Europe and the Americas, sustained the trade.

Not until the early years of the eighteenth century was the prohibition of trade between the two viceroyalties partially lifted, and only in 1774 were Mexico and Peru legally allowed to trade with each other. Even then, it was in local products only, not in Asian or European goods. Though often ignored, the official embargo on trade between Mexico and Peru over such a long period had at least discouraged a regional exchange that had greater potential for expansion and diversification (i.e. for *risk* from the Crown's point of view) than any other in Spain's New World. Mexico had imported cacao from Venezuela since the 1620s. Peru, however, had had the greater potential for coastwise internal trade, stimulated by the demands of Potosí, the shipbuilding capacity of Guayaquil, and its much greater isolation from Spain.

SPAIN'S 'REDUCED RISK' CONSTRUCTION POLICIES

6. THE PROBLEMS OF OVERLAND TRANSPORT

> Those who have describ'd these parts before
> Of trades, winds, hurricanes do tell,
> Of headlands, harbours, trendings of the shore,
> Of rocks and isles, wherein they might as well
> Talk of a nut, and only show the shell;
> The kernel neither tasted, touched nor seen.
>
> (Thomas Chaloner, London, 1648, on the lack of knowledge concerning the interior of Spain's New World)

Europe knew next to nothing about the great continental interior of Hispanic America. As time passed, more was learned by the seafaring world at large about the configuration and resources of the coast, the harbours, the reefs, and the navigable channels. But it was hard to find any reliable information about what lay inland. The drama of the early conquests, the continent's prodigious wealth first in gold and then in silver, the style of Spain's imperialism, and the prohibitions placed on foreign trade and immigration, all combined to shroud Spanish America in wonder and secrecy. Spain's possessions in South America were the most mysterious of all.

"Travail by land". The severe tension introduced by terrain and distance

The mystery was compounded by the fact that overland travel was dauntingly difficult. Since the huge river networks draining into the Atlantic had failed to provide a practicable means of reaching the continent's major mineral and labour resources, journeys into the interior from the major seaports became steep, nerve-racking ascents from the coastal swamps, forests, deserts, or scrublands into rugged mountainous terrain. Important trails leading back from the ports on the Gulf of Mexico, the Caribbean, and the Pacific coast had to penetrate high and difficult country almost immediately in order to reach centres lying for the most part between 6,000 and 12,000 feet among the intermontane basins and plateaux. Potosí, one of the highest cities in the world, was sited at 13,500 feet.

Reports to the Spanish Crown from viceroys, judges, intendants, churchmen, and others, often revealed the laborious efforts necessary to carry out official duties in the remote, virtually inaccessible corners of the American interior, cut off by time and distance from all but the most determined and robust representatives of Spain. Personal journals by foreign technicians and advisers travelling with special authority through Spanish America also provided rare glimpses of the hardships involved—the rough terrain, the continual danger to life and limb, the physical stamina required to keep going, and not least, the overwhelming sense of isolation felt by travellers once the trails were out of sight of the sea.

The great advantage of the passage across the Isthmus was its brevity—"this little journey", as Antonio de Ulloa aptly described it. Even the 45-mile land bridge between the Atlantic and Pacific Oceans included raft transport on the Chagres river, thirty-five miles south-west of Puerto Bello. From Cruces, at the head of navigation on the Chagres, a day's journey was usually sufficient to bring travellers into Panamá, but Spain continued to explore the possibilities of cutting a canal to link the oceans.

The South American mainland, however, presented the most formidable problems of accessibility. The Orinoco was virtually unused for trade. As a means of transport, the Magdalena–Cauca remained the only waterway of any value, in so far as it provided a link between the port of Cartagena on the Caribbean and a narrow section of the continental interior below Santa Fe de Bogotá. Fleets of covered canoes carrying passengers and merchandise took about two months of strenuous rowing, poling and hauling to make the journey upstream. The journey downstream could be managed in three or four weeks, but it was still extremely tiring and hazardous because of the torrential rains, storm surges, and the many alligators following the boats. Gold, emeralds, and silver from the mines of New Granada, however, generally reached the galleons waiting at Cartagena via the Magdalena.

Merchants in particular made every effort to reduce the distance goods had to be carried to and from the seaports. Apart from the crippling freight rates, long overland journeys, reported one observer, where mountains, ravines, floodwaters and soft muds had to be crossed and recrossed as a matter of routine, "expose the merchandise to a thousand accidents and make the undertaking totally impracticable." Swollen torrents brought traffic to a halt. "The rivers", Ulloa noted graphically "are too wide for the bridges of this country." The two Spaniards, Juan and Ulloa, experienced many of these problems in rapid succession as they made their way up to Quito from the Pacific port of Guayaquil in 1736, a route that Francisco de Orellana had pioneered 200 years earlier. The journey made the same dramatic geographical traverse from sea level to 9,000 feet, but recorded no improvement in land transport in the two centuries since the initial European penetration by the *conquistadores*:

> The bridges are equally dangerous, for these structures, all of wood and very long, shake in passing them; besides their breadth is not above three feet, and without any rail, so that one false step precipitates the mule into the torrent, where it is inevitably lost.
>
> The road from Tarigagua is very toilsome and dangerous, extremely steep and slippery . . . The trouble of having people going before to mend the road, the pains arising from the many falls and bruises, and the disagreeableness of seeing one's self entirely covered with dirt, and wet to the skin, might be the more cheerfully supported were they not augmented by the sight of such frightful precipices, and deep abysses, as must fill the traveller's mind with terror. For, without the least exaggeration, it may be said that in travelling this road, the most resolute tremble.[51]

Ulloa complained repeatedly about the *lack of maintenance* of the trail:

> The natural difficulty of all the roads among the mountains is increased by the neglect of them . . . If a tree, for instance, happens to fall down across the road and stop up the passage, no person will be at pains to remove it; and though all passing that way are put to no small difficulty by such an obstacle, it is suffered to continue, neither the government nor those who frequent the road taking any care to have it drawn away. Some of these trees are indeed so large that their diameter is not less than a yard and a half, and consequently fill up the whole passage; in which case, the Indians hew away part of the trunk, and assist the mules to leap over what remains. But, in order to do this, they must be unloaded; after prodigious labour, they at last surmount the difficulty, though not without great loss of time, and damage to the goods. Pleased with having got over the obstacle themselves, the Indians leave the tree in the condition they found it. Thus the road, *to the great detriment of trade*, remains encumbered till time has destroyed the tree. Nor is it only the roads over the mountains between Guayaquil and the Cordillera that are thus neglected; the case is general all over this country.[52]

The slowness of overland travel was constantly alluded to—the delays, interruptions and sheer unpredictability of making connections and reaching destinations on time compared with the relative ease and reliability of sea travel. **Delay could be a valuable**

additional compressive load within the legal and administrative imperial structure, but delay in the movement of supplies, and particularly in the movement of silver to the coastal ports, weakened the structure at its very foundations. The need to find the shortest overland trail to ocean navigation underlined one of Spain's basic principles of imperial organization—that of reducing wherever possible the length of the 'controlled corridors' of movement overland and, within reason, extending those at sea.

Nor was the extreme slowness of overland travel confined to the Andes. Wheeled traffic, save for local town use and religious ceremonial, remained extremely rare throughout the empire, but the gentle gradients across the *pampas* between Buenos Aires and Salta had encouraged the eighteenth-century introduction of ox- and horse-drawn wagons for transporting merchandise, passengers and baggage, as well as special passenger coaches known as *galeras*, 'the galleys of the plains'. The standard two-wheeled ox-carts (*carretas*) were roughly constructed of wood and rawhide in the distinctive medieval style of Castile, although on the *pampas*, the wheels were usually six to seven feet in diameter. Bigger carts, resembling the Mexican *carro* in appearance, also became a feature on the plains.[53] The slowness of the ox-drawn transport, however, and the sheer distances involved, resulted in journeys taking a month to reach Córdoba, and at least three months to reach the Andean foothill stations from Buenos Aires.[54] At Salta or Jujuy, freight and passengers were transferred to the mule trains, to endure another three hundred miles or so along the trail into the high Andes.

The trans-*pampas* routeway was one of the very few major wagon roads introduced into the Spanish American empire, but the irregularity and often low standard of its repair resulted in long delays and high freight rates. Even the ox-cart journey west to Mendoza took forty to sixty days, the track deeply rutted and highly destructive both to wagons and freight. Many travellers reported the frequency with which sections of road anywhere on the plains disappeared altogether. Nevertheless, *El Camino Real*, whether wagon road, sand-blown trail, mountain ledge, or narrow jungle track, represented the perception of royal authority, a line of movement pegging out a centuries-old tradition of toll and tax collection—in global terms, part of the Crown's imperial route system to and from Spain.

> Structurally, the official overland trails were thus the landward extension of the great oceanic tie-beams, a function in line with Spain's earliest perception of the Americas—that of a land empire tied by sea-lanes.
>
> Exactly where the major overland tie-beams were laid in South America soon came to depend to a large extent on the location of Potosí.

POTOSÍ'S INFLUENCE ON SPAIN'S STRUCTURAL DESIGN

The difficulties encountered in maintaining compression at key points, and in strengthening the new tie-beams

Of all the mining centres within the Andes, Potosí's extreme isolation coupled with its extraordinary wealth in silver emphasized the problems of overland transport faced by the Spanish authorities. The Cerro Rico, a conical mountain rising to almost 15,800 feet, was mined intensively after 1545 when old Indian workings were discovered close to the summit. Undeterred by the high altitude and the distance from the coast, treasure seekers rushed to one of the bleakest, least accessible points in the Andes, swiftly pursued by the men and machinery of State. Before long, Potosí had become one of the greatest boom towns of that, or any other, age—"the Imperial City, mainstay of empire", as the Spanish Crown thankfully dubbed it.

The immediate region was scoured for Indian labour and virtually depopulated as a result. The *mita* system of forced labour, inherited from the Incas, was thereupon greatly expanded as part of the large-scale organization Spain found necessary to operate the mines. By the 1570s, the designated area for supplying Indian workers was enormous, extending some 800 miles from Cuzco in the north to Tarija in the south, and up to 250 miles across the width of the Andes—an annual labour force of about 13,500 men, 4,500 of them working four months at a time on a seven-year rota—the largest *mita* in the New World.[55] Reorganization between 1692 and 1735 reduced the size of the Potosí *mita*, but still demanded an annual draft of some 3,000 to 4,000 men.

The overland extension of the Pacific tie-beam

In addition, over 1,000 Indians, as well as army units, guarded the mule trains and the silver routes to the ports, a vast human convoy system of overland transfer. On the 'Royal Road' to Spain, trails crossed the high sierras, the *altiplano*, and the Peruvian and Atacama deserts to reach Lima-Callao or Arica, which in 1574 was designated as the official port for Potosí.

> **OPENINGS**
>
> **Since all *Openings* are *Weaknings* . . . There is no part of a *Structure* either more expencefull, than WINDOWES; or more ruinous.**
>
> **Not only for that vulgar reason, as being exposed to all violence of weather; but because consisting of so different and unsociable pieces, . . . they are easily shaken.**
>
> (Henry Wotton, *The Elements of Architecture*, 1624)

Potosí's rich and unruly society, remote from the coast, presented acute problems to the officials of the Crown.[56] There were the persistent and ingenious attempts to evade payments of the 'royal fifth' tax (the *quinto*, reduced to the 'royal tenth' in 1735), the uncontrollable smuggling of silver especially to Buenos Aires and Brazil, the disturbingly high proportion of foreigners in Potosí, with or without authorization, and the *potosiños*' insatiable demands for luxury items which attracted merchants from all quarters of the trading world.

In addition to this lucrative but illegal circulation, legitimate long-range movements across Spanish America also developed as a consequence of Potosí's interior location.[57] Indeed, the economic stimulus given to agricultural and livestock production stretched from the Pacific coast to the Paraguay-Paraná-Río de la Plata plains. The needs of the mining centres supported the huge mule-breeding and cattle-ranching activities on the *pampas* of the Paraná-Plata region, particularly those on the gathering ground between Córdoba and Tucumán where the richest fattening pastures were located. From here, along with a flourishing trade in hides, more than 60,000 mules were sent north annually for sale at the great Salta fair, before being transferred by stages up to the harsh environments of the high Andes, to service the mining and urban communities.[58] This long-range trailing of stock across the *pampas* and into the Andes negotiated distances and changes in elevation that had no counterpart in the Iberian peninsula, but the movement itself, like stock ranching, had its roots in medieval Spain. **In 'scaling-up' the Peninsular model, Spanish patterns, greatly magnified, had crossed the Atlantic**. Endless processions of mules wound their way slowly across Hispanic America—from the plains into the cordilleras, between the mines and the camps, through the towns and the cities, and between the mountains and the sea. Agricultural products from the foothill zone, *yerba mate* from eastern Paraguay, and special hardwood constructional timbers from the *quebracho* forests of the *chaco* were also transported slowly to the markets of Upper and Lower Peru.

Inserting the overland section of a new Atlantic tie-beam

In 1776, the long 1,600-mile overland connection between Potosí and Buenos Aires was legally acknowledged by the creation of the new Viceroyalty of the Río de la Plata. Upper Peru was detached from the jurisdiction of Lima and transferred to Buenos Aires. This major structural adjustment strengthened Spain's official exchanges between two of its key structural components—the Andes and the Atlantic. Potosí silver production had declined in the second half of the seventeenth century and fluctuated during the eighteenth, but other centres in Upper Peru such as Oruro became important producers, and Potosí still had great potential, since its registered annual output had increased to 3 million pesos by the 1790s.

while maintaining the overland section of the Pacific tie-beam

One-third of the imports into the central Andes continued to come via the Pacific. The Pacific ports retained a substantial share of Upper Peru's trade despite the transfer of the region to the Viceroyalty of the Río de la Plata. Small quantities of minted gold and silver from Upper Peru continued to be exported via the Pacific ports of Arica and Cobija, and the in-coming trade remained broadly based: mercury from Huancavelica, and foodstuffs, especially sugar, wines and brandies from the irrigated coastal valleys, were despatched into Upper Peru. So, too, were dried fish, guano fertiliser, tobacco and cotton fibres, as well as woollen cloth from Quito, cacao from Guayaquil, coca and woollen goods from Cuzco, wheat, copper, hides and tallow from Chile, and a range of imported manufactured goods.[59]

Potosí was indeed "the axis of an immense world", as Bolívar later described it. Between the Pacific ports, Upper Peru, and Buenos Aires, the empire's overland tie-beams spanned Hispanic America for distances of up to 4,000 miles. Without the discovery of the Cerro Rico, Spain would never have sustained such deep penetration of the South American interior, never have dragged its administrative machinery so far into the central Andes. Yet despite Potosí's fame and importance, and its far-reaching economic and political influence on Spain's overseas strategy, in many ways the city remained a legend—unseen, unreal. Long journeys to and from Potosí, and the time and energy needed to make them, emphasized its isolation. Officials even at the height of Potosí's prosperity complained that correspondence from Spain sometimes took as long as two years to reach them. From the beginning to the end of empire, Potosí's elevation, harsh environment, and extreme remoteness within the widest section of the Andes made it unattractive both as a posting, and as a stable, permanent centre of commercial operation. Rootlessness, or alternatively, hostility to outside interference, continued to characterize much of the population, whether Indian, creole or European. Potosí had become in some respects a necessary evil of empire.

The 'Port' of Potosí

Spain's own perception of the location of Upper Peru was revealing. **Essentially, it had a structural, not a geographical, location. It was the true end-fixture of the oceanic tie-beam.** Whether as part of the Viceroyalty of Peru or the Viceroyalty of the Río de la Plata, Potosí was invariably seen as the *end* of a very long tortuous line of maritime communication reaching out for thousands of miles from Spain. Potosí was a port, a great inland port, a 'port of the mountains' in true medieval Castilian style. For the trans-Peninsular routeways through the high, landlocked central *sierras* of Spain converged not on the passes, nor on the gateways, but on the 'ports' of the mountains—not *paso*, nor *puerta*, but *puerto*.

In South America, the primary line of communication pierced the continent officially first through Lima and later through Buenos Aires. In both cases, the responsibility for Potosí's revenues was seen as the means of boosting the prestige, patronage and authority of the coastal cities. The viceroys in turn spent much of their time worrying about Potosí—its control, supply, productivity, and transport problems. But from whichever direction they were officially administered, Potosí and its surrounding settlements felt equally remote from both their Pacific and Atlantic viceregal masters—closer, indeed, to the spirit and traditions of Spain. Despite the long-range regional exchange sponsored by the needs of the mining zone, so far as Spain was concerned, if Upper Peru had any use to America it was to assist in underwriting the viceregal capitals, one at a time. While its resources were used to strengthen the political structures of the coastal zones, Upper Peru itself kept its distance, landlocked and with a regional identity which owed nothing to a sense of continental linkage.

Spain's perception of long-distance overland transport in the Americas: Interoceánico *not transcontinental*

Given the emphasis on its structural rather than its geographical location, Potosí did little to stimulate a genuinely *transcontinental* awareness in this huge area, *i.e. an awareness of the potential of the routeway itself as an agent of change and development in the regions through which it passed.*

This is not to say that the overland routeways between Potosí and the Pacific, and Potosí and the Atlantic, had no impact on the areas through which they passed. A number of centres were established during the sixteenth century in the sprawling Viceroyalty of Peru for tax collection, administration, and livestock sales—indeed, when mapped, such centres trace an impressive line of towns right across South America. (Fig. 6) Much of the activity at these centres, however, was periodic and localized. What cartographically looks like a purposeful set of linked urban growth points through the mountains and across the plains remained, for most of the time, a series of self-contained settlements servicing local needs and local jurisdictions—in effect, isolated ports-of-call separated by intervening seas.

There was no policy of systematic regional development and no *structural* imperative at any stage to link, much less to bind, the two edge cities of Lima and Buenos Aires overland—an essential feature of transcontinental construction. The many internal customs duties, taxes and permits discouraged long-distance trade, while Spanish policy fostered the division of influence and the division of role between Lima and Buenos Aires with regard to the Potosí routeway and the wealth of Upper Peru.

Spain's enduring perception of overland linkage in the Americas as *interoceanic*, not transcontinental, reflected the reality of seaborne empire. Even the physical problems of overland transport were not of paramount importance in highlighting the crucial role of oceanic connection. The technology of land transport had of course lagged behind advances in the maritime sphere. The great fifteenth-century flowering of ideas and experiment in navigation, and in hull, superstructure and rig design had created fresh opportunities for empire. The development of three-masted and four-masted fully-rigged vessels dominated ocean navigation for nearly 400 years until the coming of the steamship. The Atlantic and the Caribbean could be crossed in less time than it took to reach Bogotá from Cartagena. The Pacific Ocean could be crossed from Acapulco to Manila in less time than it took to struggle overland to Potosí from either the Pacific port of Arica or from Buenos Aires. The improvements to marine transport were unmatched by anything on land until the coming of the railway. Spain founded and maintained its empire with two long-distance vehicles—the full-rigged sailing ship and the mule.

The unity and continuity of ocean connection could not be duplicated on land in the early days without the help of long navigable rivers or canals. Without such assistance, the distances and extremely difficult geographical conditions over much of the North and South American interior were daunting—heat, cold, desert, forest, mountain, and swamp. Nevertheless, such dangers and hardships should not obscure the fact that these were rarely *primary* factors in reducing the number of Spain's overland imperial cross-ties. This was structural policy, not geographical determinism.

The physical unity of the Pacific coast and the western cordillera encouraged the trails up into the mountains to be regarded in the global view as no more than short projections from the seaports, however slow and hazardous these 'short' projections were in practice. Spain's New World was undoubtedly a land empire, but overland connection remained entirely ancillary to interoceanic structural design, never a purposeful means of interior development. Based on mastery of the Oceans, Spain constructed one of the most extensive and distinctive *inter*continental empires the world has ever known, but a *trans*continental empire in the Americas was neither perceived nor desired.

The lasting effects of the earliest encounter

Columbus never saw North America. The Admiral discovered Central and South America for Spain, and it was in Middle and South America for the most part that Spain consolidated its position and concentrated its efforts for the next 300 years. Columbus had drawn Castile south-westwards across the Atlantic into the great Caribbean embayment and in doing so had immediately carried Spain to the *western* margin of the continent. The Middle Seas of the Americas extended the mid-Atlantic passage by a thousand miles *and allowed Spain in effect to sail past South America*. Portuguese interests along the eastern seaboard were left far behind by Spain's networks; so too were the small Dutch, British and French Guianan wedges subsequently pushed by the European challengers into the frontier zone between the two Iberian powers.

The fact that the continent's Middle Seas—Caribbean and Mexican Gulf—formed a unique extension of the transatlantic run was to have a lasting influence on Spain's attitudes to overland communication. The Panamá Isthmus provided a land bridge a mere forty-five miles wide at the lowest section of the great continental divide. A climb of less than 300 feet separated the Caribbean from the Pacific Ocean, and thus the Isthmus remained part of the seaman's, not the landsman's, world. Indeed, *the Isthmus reduced the break in the sea-lanes to Peru to such an extraordinary minimum that from the outset Spain was relieved of any real need to find a better alternative*. This was the lasting significance of Balboa's march from the Atlantic to the Pacific Ocean, twenty years before Pizarro's discovery of the treasure of the Incas. After that, when Incan gold and silver had promptly earned western South America its pride of place in the Spanish American empire, the Panamá solution to continental circulation was irresistible. Spain placed its signposts to Lima and Potosí, as well as to Mexico and Manila, in the Middle Seas. Spain sailed west, and for centuries the mining centres in the interior of Peru were officially approached by trails running *eastward* into the Andes from the Pacific ports. The west coast of South America had become the true rim of Spain's Atlantic world. (Fig. 14)

Spain's first overland crossing of the American continent via the Isthmus, coast to coast, had been little more than a short walk. So short in fact that the image of interoceanic linkage never left the mind. Even when the overland crossings involved much greater continental distances, the concept of *interoceánico* was to remain remarkably durable in Spain's perception of overland movement. Indeed, **the perception of the major overland tie-beams as extensions of the great oceanic tie-beams was part of the great strength of Spain's imperial structure. It would only become a weakness in the age of independence.**

Since the Pacific-Potosí and the Atlantic-Potosí tie-beams were not inserted in order to stimulate regional growth in the intervening areas, they formed 'controlled corridors' of overland movement which, like the medieval *cañadas*, often had very little productive contact with the regions through which they passed. This was not based on distance, but on structural purpose. The tie-beams' imprint on the land remained linear rather than spreading.

Only in parts of Mexico, noted Morse, could scattered examples of a complex, internally integrated regional economy be found.[60] Even then, the great imperial routeway between Mexico City and Spain remained dominant. As P. W. Rees observed, with reference to the Mexican colonial road:

> For the Spaniards, the Mexico City-Veracruz highway was merely the first link in what was to become a political and economic axis on a grand scale between colony and homeland. In its direct path, minimizing both distance and elevation, it was a typical colonial route . . .
>
> The economic effect of the transport link on the intervening land between the terminals was incidental, since the primary purpose was to facilitate external rather than internal trade.[61]

J. Lockhart picked up the same point:

> The centre is perhaps more a line than an area—a trunk-line leading from silver mine to great capital to major port. Elaboration and Hispanicization will concentrate all along this line and be less intense in areas to the side of it, even though they be located in Mexico or Peru. Parts of southern Mexico and the central Peruvian highlands which had dense sedentary Indian populations but were off the silver line still had a sixteenth century aspect at the end of the colonial period.[62]

The fundamental difference between *interoceánico* and *transcontinental* in the perception of long-distance overland connection in the Americas was crucial, for perception was to influence practice, and both were to have lasting significance in the contrasted structural designs developed in the New World.

9

The Survival of Empire

> Of course it is a bad thing for walls to crack, and it should not be allowed to happen in well-regulated buildings, but it does not necessarily follow that the wall is going to fall down immediately.
>
> (J. E. Gordon, *Structures*)

Preoccupation with the problems of Spain's overseas empire can cause us to lose sight of the extraordinary success with which Spain held its empire intact. The evasion of regulations, the fluctuations of trade, the attacks of pirate and privateer, the scale of the empire and the sheer cost of its upkeep—all these and more challenged Spain's authority and control. Given the huge initial claims to the American continent, some 'rights' were yielded over time, but no territory was permanently lost that Spain was determined to retain.[63] In the search for security and reduced risk, certain routes were avoided, and several Caribbean islands ignored or abandoned, but in the struggle to hold an empire that had stretched from Italy and the Low Countries to the Philippines, it was the structures in the Americas that were most strikingly preserved. Spain used the geography of empire to assist in its defence—the size and emptiness of the Pacific Ocean, the length of the Americas, the narrowness of the Isthmus at Panamá, the height and complexity of the Andes, and the isolation of the west coast. The Atlantic, not the Pacific, seaboard was the battleground. It was the Portuguese, not the Spanish, colonies that bore the brunt of North-west Europe's efforts to dislodge Iberia from the New World.

Spain craved stability in the *Ultramar* and achieved it, by and large. The creation and maintenance of empire on such a scale demanded a degree of conviction and self-assurance, coupled with a mastery of bureaucratic procedures which were unique at this period, and too often underestimated. The weaknesses of the system cannot hide the durability of the structure. In an age before the steamship and the railway, Spain selected its key sites and key routeways overseas, and concentrated effort where it was most needed: on naval power, armed convoys, military garrisons, fortified cities, and mine labour supply. Overall, many of the problems remained no more than superficial cracks in the compression structure. An empire which reached its zenith between 1580 and 1630 nevertheless survived as a formidable going concern for almost another 200 years.

Spain's fundamental principle of a Peninsula-based power structure did not change, for it was based on the firm belief in Spanish, essentially Castilian, authority, and on the need to control the *encomenderos* in the New World and prevent the emergence of a unilateral feudal aristocracy in Spain's American colonies. There was strong support for the integrity of the Spanish empire, and the role of the monarchy. If Spain's colonial system did not greatly differ in certain essentials from other colonizing nations of that age, its uniqueness in some respects was remarkable. No other European power had ever ruled so vast an empire with such intensity, and none could compare with Spain in the reach and exercise of royal authority. More than one European state was to underestimate Spain's fundamental antipathy to division; 'Spain entire' was no minority conceit, whatever the regional loyalties. As one eighteenth-century English political commentator observed: "What do you mean, when you talk of *Spain*, or of a *king of Spain* in general, but a *king of all the Spanish Dominions*." Too narrow a focus on the 'cracks' in the imperial structure can magnify the internal tensile stresses and strains, which, after all, had been successfully accommodated from Spain's point of view for more than 300 years. It is perhaps easy, therefore, to mistake the purpose and exaggerate the scale of the Bourbon reforms.

> **THE BOURBON REFORMS** introduced no fundamental change to the basic design principle of the Spanish empire. Reform was neither swift nor radical since compressive forces remained as indispensable as ever. The Habsburg empire was not a flexible structure in practice, as some have suggested—resilient certainly, but not flexible.
>
> The Bourbons began their detailed survey of the existing structure only in the 1760s. Localized damage to the structure, together with the build-up of strain and stress concentrations, were then carefully examined. The purpose of the survey, however, was to restore the greatness of Spain—*to strengthen the structure, not to redesign it*. Insofar as reform was applied to the American empire, it was simply to further that goal.

A few preliminary adjustments to improve efficiency had been made in the first half of the eighteenth century. In 1717, the *Casa de la Contratación*, the merchants' *Consulado*, and the entire administrative machinery of the *Carrera de Indias*, were moved from Seville to Cádiz. There was confirmation of the new Viceroyalty of New Granada based in Bogotá in 1739, and permission granted in 1740 to trade around Cape Horn with the relaxation of the Tierra Firme-Panamá monopoly. Earlier commercial concessions to France and England, following the War of the Spanish Succession and the Treaty of Utrecht (1713), had forced some easing of Spain's official trade controls. But new Spanish monopoly trading companies were also established (notably for Cuban tobacco and Venezuelan cacao), with instructions to increase business, eradicate contraband traffic, and boost profits for the Crown.

The major period of Bourbon reform was delayed until the 1760s, and even then, change was not triggered internally but mainly as a result of Spain's humiliating defeat by Britain in the Seven Years' War (1756–63). After its late entry into the war on the side of France in 1761, Spain's mortifying, if temporary, loss of the strongholds of Havana and Manila in 1762, together with a huge haul of treasure and stores, forced Charles III to introduce a series of political and commercial reforms. But the purpose of the reforms was Peninsula-based—to tighten control, to strengthen the American contribution to Spain's sagging economy, and to restore Spain's international reputation as an imperial power.

Surveying the damage

In 1765, Spain began by sending an intendant to Cuba, and inaugurating a fast monthly royal mail packet service between Corunna and Havana. It was the first of a series of general inspections (*visitas*) to investigate and report on conditions in the Indies.[64] In all, thirty-six such commissions were sent to virtually the whole of Spanish America by the end of Charles' reign in 1788, their work accelerated by the successful war of independence waged by Britain's North American colonies between 1775 and 1783. Although Spain's traditional alliance with France and hostility to England had led Charles in 1779 to support the American colonists in their fight for independence, he was well aware that by doing so he was playing a dangerous, and basically, a most alien role. In the Spanish world, the king was still a maker, not a breaker, of empire.

Figure 8 The major load-bearing compartments: Spanish viceroyalties in the New World in the late 18th century. New internal walls, piers, beams, and buttresses, and more prestressed components, were also added by the Crown in this period to strengthen the imperial structure.

Reporting the damage and instituting repair work
The specification included:

> (i) The addition of a new and exceptionally strong BUTTRESS to a weak section of the outer perimeter wall. This involved the creation of the Viceroyalty of the Río de la Plata, and the upgrading to viceregal capital of Buenos Aires. Bracing included new TIE-BEAMS overland: the Potosí-Buenos Aires and Buenos Aires-Santiago de Chile routeways.
>
> (ii) The insertion of NEW INTERNAL COMPARTMENTS, with new pillars, struts, and trussed beams to support or reroute an increase in the compressive load—additional *audiencias*, captaincies-general, internal provinces, and a few additional legalized ports.
>
> (iii) The construction of a new CANTILEVER BEAM in the far north-west. Franciscan mission, *presidio*, and *pueblo* colonization was extended into Upper California to deter foreign encroachment on the remote outer margins of New Spain.
>
> (iv) The introduction of more PRESTRESSED ELEMENTS into the compression structure—more *peninsulares* and even fewer creoles in positions carrying real responsibility. This included the insertion of new, highly efficient prestressed components in the form of Intendants: professional administrators appointed in Madrid who were distributed virtually throughout the empire by the end of the 1780s.

The new outer buttress

In 1776, a major division of the sprawling Viceroyalty of Peru created the Viceroyalty of the Río de la Plata, its capital at Buenos Aires and its revenues secured by the inclusion of Potosí and the whole of the rich mining region of Upper Peru within its boundaries. New overland tie-beams linked Buenos Aires both to Potosí and to Santiago de Chile, although Lima retained its responsibilities for Chilean settlements west of the Andes, and the 'Kingdom of Chile' remained part of the Viceroyalty of Peru. Structurally, Santiago was now doubly braced—to Lima and to Buenos Aires.

New internal compartments and a new cantilever beam

Reform at viceregal level was accompanied by systematic strengthening within, as new internal divisions and new supports were built to carry greatly increased compressive loads at vulnerable points.

New *audiencias* were created in Buenos Aires (1785), in Caracas (1786), in Cuzco (1787), and in Puerto Principe, Cuba (1797) following transfer from Santo Domingo. New Captaincies-general were established in Cuba (1764), in Caracas (1777), in Chile (1778), and in Florida (1783) after Spain re-acquired it from Britain under the Treaty of Paris. The remote northern frontier of New Spain, including Lower California, New Mexico, Texas, Sonora, New Vizcaya, Coahuila, New León, New Santander, and New Galicia, was reorganized in 1776 and 1786 as the Internal Provinces under a Commandant-General. It was a new viceroyalty in all but name, largely independent of Mexico City, with its capital first at Arizpe in the Sonora desert, and later at Chihuahua.

New *presidios* and new mission sites were also built in New Mexico and Texas, while a remarkably long, reinforced cantilever beam consisting of 21 missions, 4 *presidios*, and 3 *pueblos* was constructed north-westward through Upper California between 1769 and 1823.

Re-routeing part of the compressive load

The 'free trade' legislation introduced by Charles III in October 1778 meant no more than permission for a freer trade between certain parts of the Spanish empire. **It was designed to release strain energy, and to insert a few more joints into the structure where controlled 'give' would allow safe redistribution of load and a reduction of local stress concentration.** This *Reglamento para el Comercio Libre* was the single most significant structural modification introduced between 1765 and 1789, but as with the other adjustments introduced in this period, its prime purpose was to benefit Spain, not Spanish America.

In 1774 the Viceroyalties of New Spain and Peru had been authorized to trade their own products among themselves, but not goods from Europe or Manila. That still represented too dangerous a degree of oblique thrust in the imperial structure. Colonial industry, and intercolonial trade, were never to be officially allowed to compete with the metropolis, or with metropolitan interests, in any part of the world.

In 1777, Buenos Aires' trade with other Spanish colonial centres was sanctioned at certain specially registered ports. A few years earlier, in 1765, Spain's Caribbean islands had been permitted to trade direct with seven ports in peninsular Spain in addition to Cádiz and Seville, and by 1778 a total of thirteen Spanish ports could legally trade direct with Spanish America.[65] In 1789, 'free trade' finally replaced the *flota* to New Spain which had survived for another fifty years after the *galeones* monopoly was ended, but completely free trade between all parts of the Spanish empire was still banned, as was trade (other than slave trade) between Spanish America and non-Spanish territories without special licence from the Crown. In practice of course, Spanish America's 'free trade' had existed for centuries as contraband trade, which represented the colonies' direct trade with the world market that the Crown struggled to curtail. In 1789, therefore, trade with the Indies had been opened to all the major ports of Spain, but it was a reminder even then of the continued 'Spanishness' of the official thrust lines in the imperial compression structure. Not until the following year did that powerful Castilian institution, the *Casa de la Contratación*, finally close after nearly 300 years of operation.

New prestressed components

> **New components under *compressive prestress* were inserted into the imperial structure. *Already primed to bear additional loads and to resist tension*, they were capable of increasing the strength and stability of a structure designed to be kept under permanent compression.**

The most significant single element in the drive for structural 'efficiency' was the introduction of Intendancies (a French system already operating in Spain), and with it, the insertion of **new, highly prestressed components in the form of Intendants**. These professional administrators, mostly *peninsulares* appointed in Madrid, were placed in the Viceroyalties of the Río de la Plata in 1782, Peru in 1784, and New Spain in 1786. By 1790, intendancies were the primary internal administrative division throughout Spanish America except where military governors controlled the most distant frontier provinces.

The new intendancies created smaller compartments, i.e. more internal walls and pillars through which the compressive load could be distributed more evenly and the thrust lines kept more carefully centred. Within the Viceroyalty of the Río de la Plata, for example, Upper Peru's single, sprawling *audiencia* was subdivided into eight new intendancies in 1782, each intendant responsible directly to the Viceroy. While this new concentration of authority and control often produced local tension between the intendant and existing officials, here and elsewhere, this was where the need for new prestressed components was frequently most urgent so far as Spain was concerned. But in fact, reform at local level often proved impracticable, sometimes impossible if new and independently-minded officials who were required to assist the intendant could not be found. By contrast, as Brading noted:

> It was in the provincial capitals that the reform made it greatest impact. For here the intendants were at their most active, paving streets, building bridges and prisons, and suppressing popular disorders. Assisted by a legal advisor and treasury officials, the intendant was living proof of the new executive vigour of the monarchy.[66]

The Crown, always reluctant to encourage a creole elite, continued to emphasize the role of peninsular Spaniards as the agents of reform. The chief architect of reform, José de Gálvez, who began his work as Visitor General to New Spain in 1765–71, went on to supervise the structural repair—including the expulsion of the Jesuits in 1767, Spanish settlement of Upper California in 1769, viceregal status for Buenos Aires, and the creation of the new viceroyalty in 1776. He cut costs and improved efficiency wherever he went, becoming permanent secretary of the Indies in 1776–87, and making no secret of his preference for peninsular Spaniards to the exclusion of creole candidates wherever possible in all branches and levels of colonial government. Gálvez had been heavily critical of the extent to which by the 1760s American-born Spaniards were filling government, church, and military posts in the New World, and he became the driving force behind the replacement of many creole office-holders by men born in Spain.

New, well trained civil servants, coupled with a vigorous new wave of Spanish immigrants at the end of the eighteenth century, increased the thrust of the *peninsulares* and the alienation of the creoles, a fresh reminder to Spaniards born in America of one of Spain's oldest, most fundamental principles of empire. The most senior positions had always been dominated by *peninsulares*. During the entire colonial period, of the 166 viceroys and 558 captains-general, governors, and presidents who held office in Spain's American kingdoms—in all 724—only 18 were creoles.[67] At lower levels, certainly until the late eighteenth century, there were numerous rank-and-file creole judges, magistrates, and other local officials, but **the dominance of peninsular Spaniards in the more responsible positions, i.e. in the critical structural positions, was permanent and extreme.** And although the situation was not quite so marked in the Church and the army— in New Spain about fifteen per cent of all archbishops and bishops appointed by the Crown were American-born, and creoles were well represented as middle-ranking army officers—key posts with few exceptions were held by peninsular Spaniards.

The Royal Council of the Indies was also greatly strengthened by the late-eighteenth-century reforms which, in 1776, required the appointment to the Council of men with colonial experience. These were soon to represent the majority of the membership. It was a significant modification of centuries-old policy, but it was not a break with the past. The members were *peninsulares* still, but now *peninsulares* who had already distinguished themselves in colonial service, and who, assembled together in Madrid, could provide expertise from every major geographical division of Spain's American empire. As Burkholder observed: "Staffing the Council with colonial veterans coincided with the Crown's most vigorous efforts to reassert control over the Indies."[68]

* * *

The need for greater administrative efficiency in order to increase the empire's contribution to the Spanish economy was based, as always, on the Crown's perpetual need for money. Much of the immense wealth acquired from the Americas was squandered on wars in Europe and the Mediterranean in defence of empire and Catholicism, on foreign loans at high interest rates, on grain imports for a still agriculturally backward Spain, on palatial building and imported luxury goods.

An inflationary movement had spread through Spain to Europe at large during the sixteenth century; by 1550 commodity prices had more than doubled in thirty years based on supplies of gold from the New World, and by the end of the century they had doubled again, based on the prodigious silver imports from Potosí and Mexico. By 1600, prices were thus four times higher than those of *c.*1500. The Spanish Crown was officially bankrupt in 1557,

1575, 1596, and again at intervals throughout the seventeenth century. Mounting foreign debt meant that consignments of gold and especially silver were often transhipped immediately from the quays at Seville to the German and Genoese banking houses, as well as to manufacturers in France, Flanders, Holland and England. Indeed, at the nadir of Castile's economic collapse in the early 1680s, two-thirds of the New World's silver went directly to foreign creditors without entering Spain.[69] Despite widespread belief to the contrary, the wealth of the Americas never provided more than twenty to twenty-five per cent of the Crown's total annual revenues, and for part of the time it was as little as five to ten per cent, but its great advantage was that it was a cash asset, with its arrival from the New World generally predictable.

To the terrible burden of wars in Europe were added the costs of the defence of empire and the need to protect the routeways, ports, forts, and bullion stores, **all of it part of the routine building and maintenance costs of the imperial structure's 'dead load'**. As responsibility for defence was assigned to the viceroys, Lima found that by the mid-seventeenth century, at least twenty per cent of Peru's silver was being spent on fortification of the Pacific coast, from Panamá to Valdivia, before any of the remainder began the journey to Spain. Overall, the expense of maintaining the American empire is estimated to have swallowed as much as fifty per cent of Spain's revenues from the New World at the end of the sixteenth century, and a staggering eighty per cent or more at the end of the seventeenth century after a period of heavy military expenditure.[70] In addition, the scale of the financial losses from fraud and contraband cannot be calculated with any degree of accuracy. "We have witnessed," wrote a contemporary observer, "Spain's mismanagement of the greatest fund of wealth in the world."

Yet Spain showed considerable powers of survival and recovery. Silver remained of fundamental importance to Spain's imperial economy; production in both Mexico and Lower Peru increased dramatically in the late-eighteenth century, and in 1796–1820, silver still represented seventy-five per cent by value of New Spain's exports, and eighty per cent of the Río de la Plata's (i.e. Upper Peru's) exports to Spain.[71] If the basic equation of Spain's imperial trade foundered—bullion one way, Spanish manufactures the other—it was Spain's manufacturing base that failed to respond. Here, the lingering effects of Spain's medieval tradition had exacerbated the problem. Although foreign policy had been consolidated with the union of Castile and Aragón in 1479 under Isabella and Ferdinand, the internal customs barriers had not been removed. Even in the seventeenth century, customs posts still remained between Castile, the Basque provinces, Navarre, the Aragonese provinces, and Andalusia, impeding the free movement of goods and materials. With the added burden of numerous municipal and seigneurial tolls, it was frequently cheaper to import foreign manufactures by sea than to place orders within Spain.[72]

Spain's own share of manufactured goods exported to the New World (a trifling percentage in 1700) had grown to about thirty-eight per cent by value in 1778, and to a peak of fifty-two per cent between 1782 and 1796, although the true extent of the relabelling of foreign manufactures as 'Spanish' goods remains unknown. Despite the fact that agricultural producers in Spain were somewhat more responsive than the industrialists to the late-eighteenth-century 'free trade' opportunities, Bourbon commercial reform failed to promote a significant alteration in the structure of the Peninsular economy, one of its primary aims.

Events in Europe, however, again took a decisive turn. After Spain's unsuccessful opposition against Revolutionary France in 1793–5, the country, now allied with France, entered the war against Britain in 1796. This triggered a British blockade of Spain's trade with the New World that forced Madrid to allow neutral commerce into Spanish America in 1797–9, 1801–2, and 1805–8. The concept of imperial trade being continued by 'neutral carriers' was an act of desperation, and marked the end of the Bourbons' Spanish 'free trade' system, since Spain's own trade was paralyzed by war and blockade in 1796–1802 and again in 1804–8, and legalized neutral commerce undermined the principle that foreigners were excluded from trading freely with the Spanish American colonies. It was an opportunity that the Anglo-American colonists in particular seized, and never relinquished. **As always, trade's oblique thrust lines were the greatest source of risk in the compression structure.**

In bold outline, Spain's imperial policy was based on Spanish men, of orthodox faith, and of unimpeachable loyalty to the Spanish Crown, sailing forth in Spanish ships, under Spanish convoy, laden with Spanish supplies to fulfil Spain's spiritual and temporal obligations in the New World. In return, the wealth that accrued from such enterprise was to be reserved for the furtherance of Spanish power at home and overseas. Such policy built a huge imperial structure suffused with Spanish sentiment, ceremony, and custom. Although the gap between theory and practice inevitably widened, the structure was stabilized for more than 300 years by an astonishing range and manipulation of compressive forces. It was braced by the Spaniards' respect and affection for the Crown as an institution, and, despite creole frustration, by a generally willing acceptance of the centralized State and the Catholic Church as the formal framework of empire. Once in place, the architectural design resisted drastic modification and survived minor adjustment. Spanish America was indeed no idle boast.

> The Bourbon reforms, though uneven and in places unfinished, have sometimes been identified as an unmanaged disturbance, and, in the new Age of Enlightenment, the main cumulative cause of Spain's imperial collapse in the New World. But *the imperial structure did not collapse from Bourbon repair work, from additional compression, from resonance, or from structural fatigue.*
>
> It did not collapse from external assault on its massive foundations, nor from any sudden failure of its internal load-bearing components. Collapse *began* with the removal by Napoleon in 1808 of what was still the main compressive force—the image and authority of the Spanish Crown. After that, tension hinges opened, in some cases along very old cracks and joint planes, and the walls started to fall.[73]
>
> Even then, much of the structure remained standing, and this was to have far-reaching consequences. As well as shaping the compartmented ground-plans of the newly independent states, the slow, only partial collapse of the great structure also maintained a continuity of structural style, keeping in place the age-old reliance on weight and mass; on costly, complex superstructure and compressive thrust; and on the familiar dependence on 'give' at the joints—minor adjustment, in form rather than substance, to ease local points of stress and strain inside the institutional framework, instead of the need to face the difficulties and the risks of producing a fundamentally new design.

Part II

The United States' Tension Structure

A siren sang, and Europe turned away
From the high castle and the shepherd's crook.
Three caravels went sailing to Cathay
On the strange ocean, and the captains shook
Their banners out across the Mexique Bay.

And in our early days we did the same.
We crossed the sea . . .
And saw, enormous to the little deck,
A shore in silence waiting for a name.

(Louis Simpson, *To the Western World*,
Middletown, Connecticut)

THE UNITED STATES' TENSION STRUCTURE

While Spain maintained its huge compression structure, the United States had begun to build a **TENSION STRUCTURE** whose major design challenge from the outset was the diversity and energy of the 'live load'.

Medieval builders had used the structural necessities of their buildings as the basis of their design. The United States did the same, *but now the structure showed less ecclesiastical, more secular, influence*, and *more engineering than architectural awareness*. There would be experiment; less certainty, more risk.

10
The English Initiative

> Those truths are fled and left behind
> A real world and doubting mind.
>
> (John Clare, *The Shepherd's Calendar*)

Europe's seventeenth-century settlement of North America's eastern seaboard had its origins in dissent and self-help. Whereas Spain had carried medieval certainties to the New World, the Reformation shattered medieval unity in northern Europe, opening the way for Protestantism, the Enlightenment, and the Industrial Revolution. The transatlantic passage from seventeenth-century Europe to the rim of a huge, unfamiliar land also demanded a passage of the mind, from the political and religious upheavals of the Old World to the political and geographical uncertainties of the New.

The style of England's imperial structure in the New World

Before the 1680s, English immigrants formed over ninety per cent of the total population scattered along the Tidewater between the rocky coasts of Maine and the sandy shores of Carolina. American Indian communities were widely distributed, and African slaves had already arrived in Virginia—the first in 1619, a year before the Pilgrims landed on Cape Cod.

Diversity increased with accelerating immigration, but up to the end of the seventeenth century additional waves of German, French, Swiss, Dutch, Swedish, Finn, Scots and Irish settlers were sufficiently well absorbed (or surrounded) by English settlers and the English colonial administration to form a varied but indisputably Anglo-America. English remained the dominant language, 'broken' English to be sure, often spoken gutturally, hesitatingly and infrequently, but nevertheless the language that every second generation would have to learn.

> **FLEXIBILITY**
>
> **Strength is not the same thing as stiffness . . . *Flexibility* is the ability to bend easily without breaking.**
>
> (J. E. Gordon, *Structures*)
>
> (A. J. Francis, *Introducing Structures*)

English political institutions were to offer sufficient flexibility to accommodate the rapidly changing socio-economic conditions and population growth of the American colonies. The many formal and informal political declarations in this period (whether identified as Compacts, Contracts, Fundamental Orders, Orations, Sermons, Agreements or Debates), reveal the wide range of contemporary organization and polemic among local communities, a uniquely Anglo-American structural characteristic in the wider world of empire. For unlike the Spanish and French imperial initiatives, the English colonies had originated not in Acts of State but in the venture of joint-stock companies or of individual proprietors. As the colonies were gradually brought under the control of the Crown, the habit of self-government was continually adjusted, not without friction, to the authority of the Royal Governor. In practice, however, despite the Governor, the English colonies remained virtually self-governing in their own internal affairs, and much less compliant with metropolitan decision-making than the colonies of Spain, Portugal, France or even Holland.

LAYING OUT THE FIRST SITE-LINES
AND STARTING CONSTRUCTION

Internal mechanisms for distributing stress and strain

The first permanent English colony, mainly farmers and tobacco growers, was established at Jamestown, Virginia in 1607. Agrarian rather than urban, large-scale landholding and increasing social stratification characterized its development. By contrast, after 1620, New England settlement was to demonstrate how well Puritan conviction could turn its hand to the building of small, self-reliant communities. The Congregational church was a linked group of going concerns, not a monolithic or hierarchical structure. In church, meeting-house, schoolroom, and workplace, the practical application of Calvinism to New World society was part of everyday life—action rather than dogma.

Strict orthodoxy had marked the early settlements. Only Church members (the bulk of the population) had full political rights; there was no pretence at religious toleration. In 1637, eight years after the chartering of the Massachusetts Bay Company, its General Court in Boston ruled that no one should be permitted to settle within the colony without having had his orthodoxy approved by the magistrates, a principle Spain would have found no difficulty in recognizing. Disagreement, however, led to dispersal. What would have led to expulsion in the Spanish empire, or to the creation of a new Puritan sect in England, simply produced another colony in New England. Whether in other parts of Massachusetts, in Rhode Island, or in Connecticut, **dissent encouraged geographical displacement, a physical adjustment within the structure to reduce local concentrations of stress and strain, rather than the application of increased compression** and a confined intellectual debate.

Rapid growth and diversification of the 'live load'

During the second half of the seventeenth century, economic and population growth injected fresh energy and fresh challenges into established systems in both religious and social fields. Many scattered settlements consolidated or were annexed, while new colonies were organized, or reorganized, after the Restoration of the Monarchy in 1660. After the beginning of the eighteenth century, only Georgia was chartered as a new area for settlement and border defence (1732), but thousands poured into the older colonies. Immigration and natural increase combined to double the total population approximately every generation, i.e. from $c.250,000$ in 1700 to more than two millions in 1770.

This dynamic population growth from increasingly varied sources became the key factor in eighteenth-century American political development, just as the overwhelmingly English origins of the settlers dominated that of the seventeenth century. Even so, in the mid-1770s at least sixty-six per cent of the total white population were still of English stock, and the proportion remained at sixty per cent in 1790. Leaving aside the issue of slavery, however, greater diversity was accompanied by the reaffirmation of traditional attitudes to the rights and responsibilities of the individual, and, particularly in the northern and middle colonies, to locally-designed political approaches to coherence and order. Society was regulated but not static; with the exception of Virginia, a high degree of social mobility, both vertical and horizontal, produced for its period an extraordinarily varied and open class structure. Although the colonies' mercantilist role remained fundamental to Britain's imperial design, the weight and vitality of so much of the 'live load' made it the greatest source of risk in the imperial structure.

During the eighteenth century, the various lower Houses of Assembly within the colonies grew more powerful and became increasingly regarded by their members as the colonial equivalents of the English House of Commons.[1] Election in all the colonies was on the basis of a comparatively wide franchise; approximately sixty to seventy-five per cent of the adult, male, white population were entitled to vote (a far higher percentage than in England), and it was a franchise stoutly defended if not always exercised. Although the property qualification was fundamental, there was a growing tendency in the eighteenth century to broaden suffrage by admitting personal property on an equality with land. Assemblies focused the challenge to the powers of the colonial governors and hammered out the rights or demands to make constitutional changes, *each colony* a varied compartment of political and environmental response to the imperial system.

The diversity of the 'live load' took many forms. There were great contrasts, for example, in the initial purposes and perceptions of the colonists, in the extent of their knowledge (or interest) beyond the immediate locality, and in their experience of continuous hardship or relative ease. There was marked variation in the range and frequency of combined effort, in the need for co-operation, and in the interaction of rural and urban life. Many groups had little in common with each other, and no inclination to mix. There were important differences in the economic and social exchanges with England, and in the degree of political sympathy, or conflict, with the Crown. Much of the north and the south and the Piedmont remained in the pioneer state, although isolated settlers often had group support within hollering distance. In regional circulation, Tidewater merchants drew on their agents and suppliers in both the near and more remote back-country, while in the towns the growth of commerce, crafts and professional

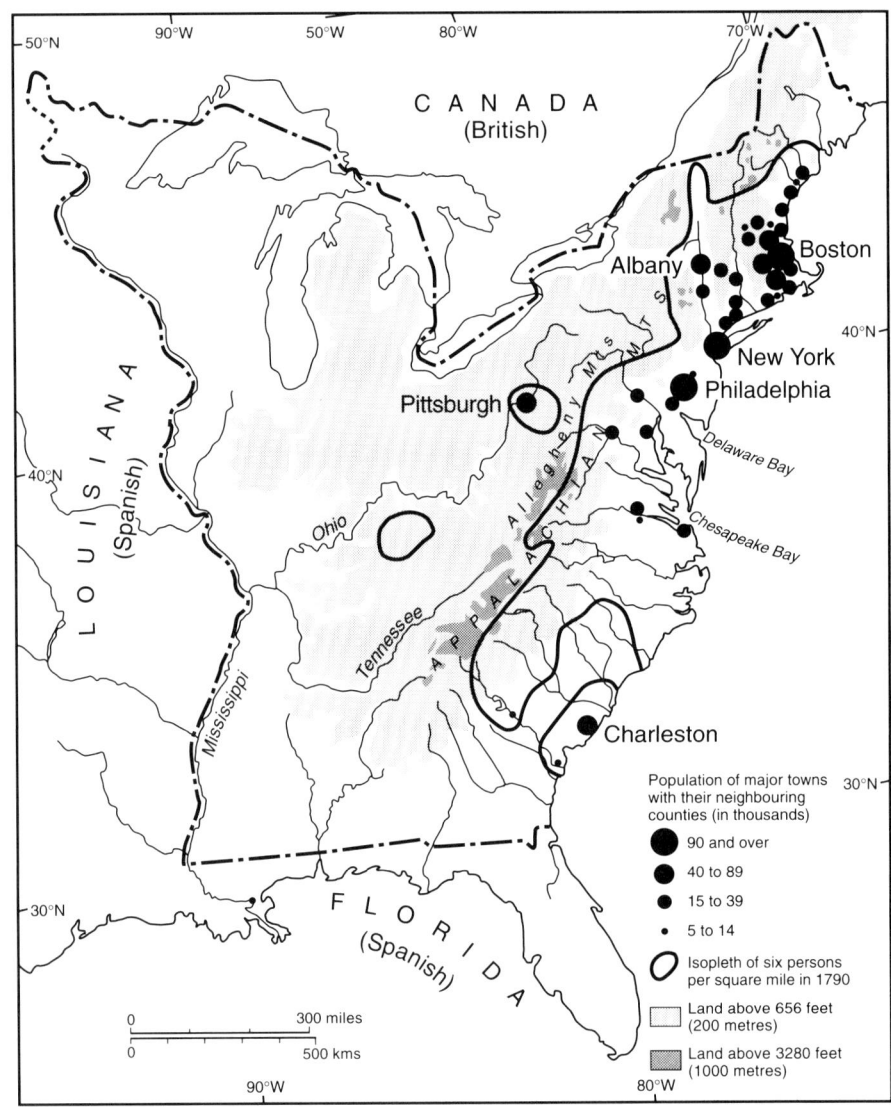

Figure 9 The distribution of towns and neighbouring county populations in the United States in 1790. The boundary along the Mississippi followed the river's median line.
(Based on J. R. Borchert, 'American Metropolitan Evolution', *Geographical Review*, 57 (1967); C. L. and E. H. Lord, *Historical Atlas of the United States*, New York, 1953; and *A Compendium of the Ninth Census*, Washington, D. C., 1872)

skills sponsored libraries, colleges, lecture tours, trade associations and countless societies. Newspapers were particularly effective as regional ties in the northern and middle colonies.[2] Yet towns were still small; even the largest cities in the colonies—Philadelphia, New York and Boston—were dwarfed by Mexico City and Havana, while there was nothing to match the other regional centres containing 20,000–50,000 inhabitants to be found in Spanish America in the late eighteenth century.

Over-emphasis by some writers on the relatively 'compact' location of the Anglo-American colonies along the Atlantic seaboard when compared with the much greater scale and more widely distributed population clusters of colonial Spanish America, tends to obscure the fact that immense areas of wilderness also characterized the whole of colonial Anglo-America. Once across the Delaware, and south beyond Chesapeake, huge desolate tracts expanded the wilderness still more; even small towns became scarcer, and the 'live load' as a whole much less mobile and less diversified. (Fig. 9) Nevertheless, despite contrasts in settlement pattern and socio-economic structure, the South was firmly included within the imperial structure in a number of ways. There was the broad unity provided by imperial organization, and the prestige of the South's role within it; Virginia, the most populous colony, was the oldest and strongest pillar in the empire, while only the Carolinas and Georgia showed a profitable imperial trade balance with England. The port of Charleston was the richest town in the colonies, 'the Pearl of the South'. Its wealth, influence and trade with the northern ports and the West Indies tied it into the American as well as into the transatlantic system, permitting many southern merchants, lawyers and landowners to form part of an efficient kinship, social and political tie-beam laid along the Tidewater. Yet at the same time, any practices amounting to a thinly-disguised feudalism on the part of the large estate owners and planters towards their white indentured workers were curbed by the availability of freer conditions elsewhere, and by a characteristically American physical and social mobility to move on and find them. Divergent opinions and lifestyles were accommodated but excesses (apart from slavery) tended to be checked. Virginian plantation owners, for example, did not favour the custom of absentee landlords like their counterparts in the British West Indies, where Spanish influence had been dominant. Indeed, whether by virtue or necessity, ruling Virginians also differed from some of their counterparts in the English landed gentry by neither despising trade nor admiring an idle aristocracy.

New tensile forces in the West

By the middle of the eighteenth century, new pressures were building. "The first drudgery of settling new colonies, which confines the attention of people to mere necessaries, is now pretty well over," wrote Benjamin Franklin in 1743. An increasingly important element in society had staked out a place in the imperial structure to become the voice and outlook of the West. The trend was eventually highlighted in the early 1770s by the new Provincial Congresses which marked the beginning of a political transformation and a westward shift of power. They drew on a larger representation, often doubling the numbers in the Assemblies and bringing in new faces—unknown men from small up-country farming communities, less transatlantic and more continental in their attitudes and experience. The Provincial Congresses, with their new Constitutions or Declarations of Rights, became strong centres of political innovation and oblique thrust within the imperial structure. They prepared the way for the Continental Congresses, proposed by Virginia in May 1774 and convened first in Philadelphia the following September. During the eighteenth century, therefore, Assemblies and Congresses became the colonies' principal political workshops, all of them actively absorbed in test and experiment, in the production of practical, not theoretical, models. As events were to prove, they were also preparing to design and build a major new political structure to replace the old.

The dismantling of the British imperial structure

To acknowledge that the Revolutionary War was part of an evolutionary process merely emphasizes the internal patterns of diversity, disagreement, co-operation and tolerance which had long characterized Britain's American colonies. **Along the Atlantic seaboard, the empire's architectural variety and structural flexibility had produced levels of managed stress and strain unmatched elsewhere in the British, or any other empire up to this time.** Predictably therefore there was no unanimity of purpose—commitment, hostility and even more apathy to the idea of rebellion were found everywhere, whether within districts, towns or individual families. Many issues were not clear-cut, nor the solutions to grievance all that obvious. After the early months when trade was stimulated, costs mounted uncontrollably and serious inflation set in by 1777. Inability or unwillingness to pay taxes regularly, once the prospect of a long war had to be faced, led to increased profiteering and bankruptcies by 1779.

Nor is it possible to give an accurate assessment of the numbers loyal to the Crown since many of these varied in their allegiance over the years. Probably they averaged about thirty per cent, but they were well distributed and by no means confined to the dedicated Tory. Some, for a time, had emphasized the need for a link to the Crown, not in the likeness of Spain but as a protest against British Parliamentary rule. In his *Summary View of the Rights of British America* (1774), Thomas Jefferson rejected the right of Parliament to legislate for the thirteen colonies, claiming that their link to the mother country was solely by, and through, the Crown. John Adams took up the same point in 1775: "We owe allegiance to the person of His Majesty, King George III, whom God preserve." The principle of 'King of Great Britain and Ireland, King of Massachusetts, King of Rhode Island . . . ' was a possibility. Liberty was the priority, and liberty within the empire had certain advantages provided American liberty was not curtailed by Parliament in London.

Confrontation with Parliament increased however, and fresh local sources of tension were introduced. Pacifists were particularly numerous in Pennsylvania and New Jersey. Recent immigrants often had little understanding of, or sympathy with, political debate; many others remained doubtful of the rebels' competence to organize their promised land even if, in the unlikely event, they managed to win the war. Still more were reluctant to commit themselves either way, wanting simply to be left alone to make their own way in the New World, free from political pressures of virtually any kind. Physical isolation left some relatively untouched.

On balance, however, the Revolutionary War did much to unify the political, economic and social life of the thirteen colonies, particularly by the intensive period of problem-solving it presented. Rural New England supplied half the soldiers for the Continental Army, but Charleston had to supply much of the money. There was the everlasting fund-raising, the widely dispersed military and naval engagements, and the consultation networks developed to harmonize campaign strategy, tactics and logistics. There was the need for skilful management of French assistance, for desperate patching of the economy, for rallying, in Thomas Paine's words, "the summer soldier and the sunshine patriot".

The timing, well constructed argument, and carefully edited prose of the Declaration of Independence typified the reasoning man's approach to political rebellion in the Age of Enlightenment. Though still premature, it was a declaration of intent, a political testament, printed and displayed in town square and private home to mark the essential point of political reference and departure. For this reason it is neither the first shots at Lexington and Concord in 1775 nor the final Treaty of Independence in 1783 but the year of the Declaration, 1776, which is rightly celebrated by the USA as the first great emotional, intellectual and ideological date-line in the political development of the state.

Even so, the lack of strongly centralized control proved a major problem in the War of Independence, and was one reason for the protracted, indecisive campaigning into which the Revolution degenerated. The colonists' ultimate success immediately transferred the search for compatibility away from the military or quasi-military sphere back into politics. One way or another, extreme Loyalists to the Crown were given notice to quit; others, prepared to take new loyalty oaths, were absorbed. The grace with which this was done varied with the location and value of their property and with the personalities and numbers involved, but it was the strength and widespread distribution of the neutrals that discouraged a sustained witch-hunt.[3] Despite many harsh measures, the post-war attitude towards the Empire Loyalists was pragmatic rather than punitive, an indication that these and other sources of tensile stress and strain would be an integral part of the post-war structure.

11

The Failure of the First Tension Structure

> Since great internal variety and a relatively pliable imperial framework had characterized the British colonial structure in North America, these were given even greater prominence after the Revolution. Thus the newly independent United States designed for maximum flexibility. *It quickly discovered that it may be as bad for a structure to be too flexible as it is to be too weak.* The collapse of the Confederation after only six years (1781–87) was probably the most profitable failure that the country has ever experienced. The Articles of Confederation emphasized State sovereignty and limited government. The thirteen 'Free, Sovereign, and Independent States' were structurally no more than an open row of small individual dwellings in their own garden plots.

Under the Articles of Confederation, drawn up by the Continental Congress during the War in 1777 and ratified in 1781, the powers accorded to Congress were so slight as to reduce it to little more than an advisory body. It could not enforce taxes nor directly govern the citizens of the States unless they were in the army, in the western territories, or on the high seas. It could not regulate commerce effectively nor impose import duties. It had no power to support commercial expansion or to retaliate against foreign discrimination. At the same time, no State working independently could finance the improvement and expansion of the inland waterway and road networks, or upgrade the postal service. None could cope in isolation with a present (or future) 'Indian problem'. No State was safe from invasion by a foreign power, and a common defence, though desirable, might now be impossible to organize effectively. The demand to keep government close to the people, coupled with deep suspicion of out-of-State interference (now perhaps only 30 or 300, rather than 3,000 miles away), thus required time, disillusion, and a renewed threat to survival before work could begin on the design of a new structure.

By 1787 all but the State of Rhode Island had acknowledged the need to seek some 'more perfect union', either by a simple revision of the Articles of Confederation or by more radical engineering work. Time was short; the extremists were now to be left out of the serious business of practical politics, at least for the time being. There was a clearer continental perspective, and a growing awareness of the friction of distance upon political loyalties and political control. In the colonial assemblies, the Tidewater had already become tuned to a western note, sounded then from the Piedmont and the Appalachian corridors. Tensile stress and strain in the West was becoming stronger and fraught with risk.

12

A Newly Designed Tension Structure: The Invention of Federalism

> Many little supports held together in a bundle are capable of bearing a greater load than if they are separated from each other . . . the increase of carrying capacity is entirely dependent upon the firmness of the binding; if loosely connected the total load becomes merely the sum of the loads each can carry separately.
>
> (Leonardo da Vinci, *Manuscript collection*)
>
> It is very rarely possible to avoid compression. Even in a predominantly tensile structure like a suspension bridge, the tensile forces in the cables must be balanced by the compressive forces in the towers.
>
> (A. J. Francis, *Introducing Structures*)
>
> The modern form of suspension bridge was invented by James Finley of Pennsylvania about 1796. He introduced the first stiffened, level roadway, suspended from cables and supported by high towers—"a most ingenious invention," wrote Thomas Pope in the influential *Treatise on Bridge Architecture*, New York, 1811.
>
> (*A History of Bridge Design*)

Federalism allowed two governments to operate on the same people simultaneously, both governments sovereign in the areas of responsibility assigned to them. This functional, two-tiered structure had added a new deck of more centralized 'national' authority to the popular colonial/State governments—"a device which now seems so normal and simple," wrote one twentieth-century political scientist, "that it is hard to understand how original it was."[4]

The design comprised a newly stiffened structure, a linked, two-tiered span of state and State polities suspended from, and supported by, the main cables and towers of the Constitution.

> **The cables of a suspension bridge take up the best shape automatically, because a flexible rope has no choice but to comply with the resultant of all the loads which are pulling on it . . . It may be regarded as defining a 'thrust line' in tension.**
>
> (J. E. Gordon, *Structures*)
>
> **A rope can only take tension. A suspension cable exerts a pull, and this must be resisted by adequate anchorages.**
>
> (W. Morgan, *The Elements of Structure*)
>
> **In the design of tension structures, the stress system in the end-fitting is a great deal more complicated than simple tension. There is plenty of scope for theory in the design of tension end-fittings, but there is also a very great deal of experience, . . . and experience will often dictate the design.**
>
> (H. L. Cox, *The Design of Structures of Least Weight*)

The invention of Federalism was the product of nearly 200 years of open experiment in the Tidewater-Piedmont country, and nearly four months of analysis and synthesis behind closed doors in Philadelphia. The new bi-cameral Congress acknowledged through the representation in the Lower House (based on free population numbers) where the financial burdens would fall; the equality of representation in the Senate, however, increased the appeal of Federalism to the small States, as well as to new areas admitted later to the Union on equal terms. The opportunity for admission to full Statehood backed by legal guarantees, the separation of Church and State, the rejection of monarchy and titles of nobility, and the enlightened approach to public domain and small-scale private ownership of land were to prove immensely attractive to the flood of new immigrants surging west with that uniquely American brand of social opportunity and political collateral.

The word 'national' was carefully avoided in the wording of the Constitution, as it had been in the Declaration of Independence. As John Adams observed: "the colonies had grown up under constitutions of government so different, there was so great a variety of religions, they were composed of so many different nations . . . that to unite them . . . was certainly a very difficult enterprise."[5] The States' delegations meeting in 1787 to design the new tension structure comprised a Continental, not a National, Convention. The United States of America were in the process of building a serviceable *state* structure in the legal sense, not a national one. Indeed, the gradual evolution of the United States would be that of 'state into nation', not 'nation into state'. 'National identity' was never a structural component of the new Federalism; 'American' identity, though more clearly delineated by the Revolutionary process, was still neither deep nor evenly distributed. The United States was a state before it was a nation.

> **THE IMPORTANCE OF ECONOMY IN CONSTRUCTION**
>
> Economy denotes the proper management of materials and of site, as well as a thrifty balancing of cost and common sense in the construction of works. This will be observed if, in the first place, the Architect does not demand things which cannot be found or made ready without great expense.
>
> (Vitruvius, *De Architectura*)

The Federal structure had to be both plain and economical. It also had to be a structure that would allow an increasingly hopeful and demanding 'live load' new mobility and opportunity. The chance to amend the Constitution under Article V was crucial. As Washington himself commented in October 1787:

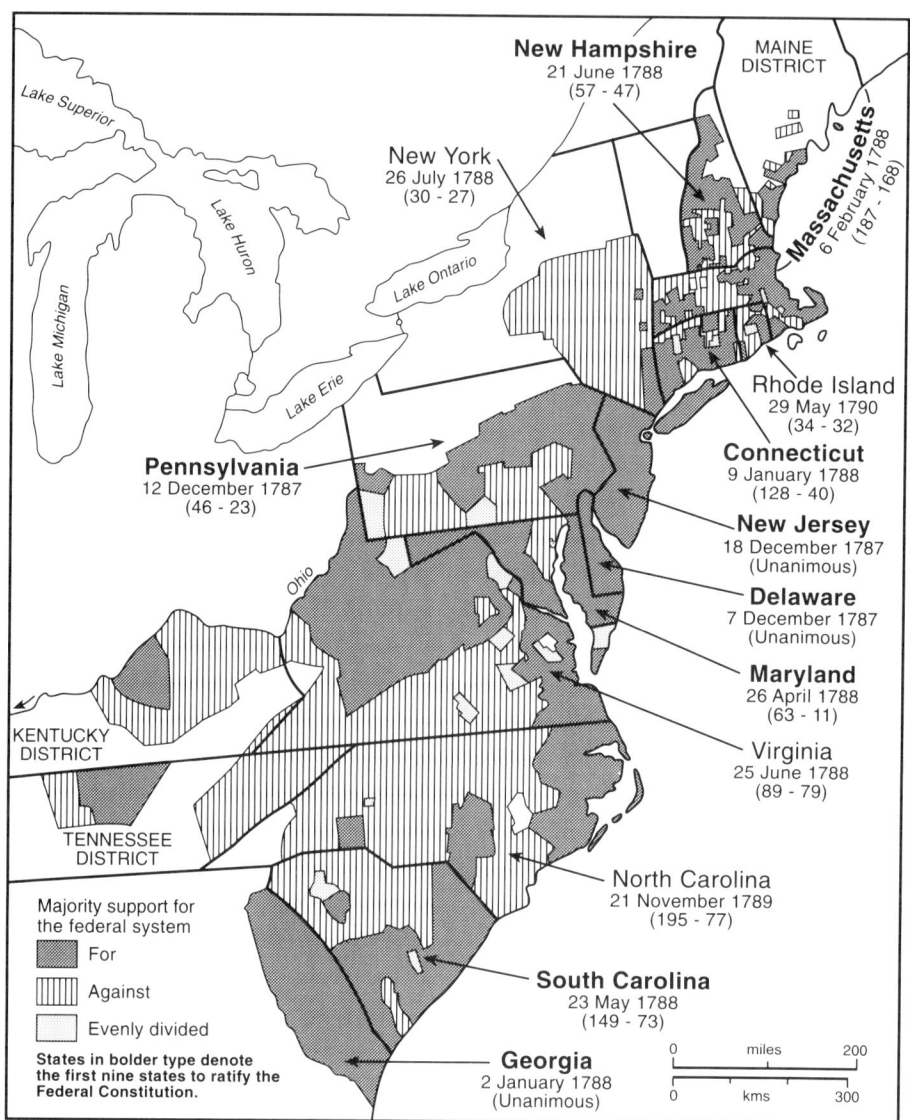

Figure 10 Conflicting attitudes in the United States to the proposed new Federal structure, 1787–90. The internal distribution of support and dissent, including the dates of ratification of the Federal Constitution, and the votes for and against it in the thirteen states.
(Based on M. Gilbert, *American History Atlas*, Weidenfeld & Nicolson, 1968, and on other sources)

> The Constitution that is submitted is not free from imperfections, but there are as few radical defects in it as could well be expected, considering the heterogeneous mass of which the Convention was composed and the diversity of interests that are to be attended to. As a Constitutional door is opened for future amendments and alterations, I think it would be wise in the People to accept what is offered to them.[6]

Risk: the new structure's severe internal tensions

By June 1788, the necessary nine States had ratified the Constitution, enabling it to be put into operation. Ratification by Virginia and New York was soon to follow. But confederal sentiments had been strong since the mid-1770s, and those favouring Confederation in some amended form, while still insisting on relatively weak central government, became known as Antifederalists.[7] Antifederal opinion now formed a major source of tension *within* the structure, both in its strength and geographical distribution, and because of the energy and discussion it generated among convinced Federalists by way of response. The eighty-five essays written by Hamilton, Madison and Jay for the people of New York State in 1787–88, for example, known as *The Federalist Papers*, include outstanding examples of political insight and judgement. Indeed, the great body of argument upon the nature of Federalism contained in the various addresses spoken or published in the States, for and against adoption of the Constitution, comprises one of the finest collections of political discourse ever produced—innovative, painstaking construction work in the Age of Reason.[8]

Federal, a new word to describe the new Constitutional structure, had thus entered the language in the mid-1780s. As Jefferson confirmed in 1786: "We can no longer be called Anglo-Americans. That appellation now describes only the inhabitants of Nova Scotia, Canada, etc . . . I had applied that of Federo-Americans to our citizens."[9]

The geographical patterns of support and dissent

Internal tensional stress and strain permeated the entire structure. The distribution of support for the new compressive forces introduced by Federalism revealed extremely complex socio-economic and environmental influences operating within the core area. The

Antifederalists based much of their politics on the opinion that the core area itself and what lay beyond were already too diverse to be organized and regulated by one body. Federal sympathies were strongest in the Tidewater settlements *and in those regions and routeways most readily accessible to them*; the valleys of the Connecticut, Lower Hudson, Delaware, Potomac, Shenandoah and Savannah, for example, became important diffusion paths extending Federal sympathies into the interior. Indeed, *within* Appalachia, the differing patterns of accessibility to the eastern seaboard had already produced marked internal contrasts in Appalachia's own economic development, and these were now to be strongly reflected in the differing political attitudes to Federalism.

Throughout the core area, from Maine to Georgia, Federalism had overwhelming support in the urban centres, not only on the Tidewater, but also at such outposts as northern New England, Albany, Pittsburgh, and the southern Piedmont.(Fig.10) Significant exceptions occurred only in the small, self-contained towns of the New England interior, and of Rhode Island. The Constitution's political and fiscal reforms were widely favoured by merchants and commercial interests, by the wealthier property-owners, and by many professional men.[10] The well-organized press network was more skilfully used by the Federalists. Antifederal sentiment was often associated with the more remote western or up-state rural areas, with small farmers and tenants. Even so, many of the isolated western frontier regions of Virginia and Georgia, for example, provided interesting exceptions by their decisive support for Federalism, for the protection it could offer them against the Indians, and for Federal guarantees to open free land.

Massachusetts' and Maryland's decisions to ratify proved critical; without the latter Virginia would have been lost and New York with it. In fact, Maryland had played a leading role in persuading Virginia and New York, with others, to relinquish claims to territory west of the Ohio River, thus freeing land from which new States would be formed. It was a crucial feature in the structural design. Virginia, wealthy and prestigious, the home of such influential figures as Washington, Jefferson and Madison, could claim (like certain others) that its early charter had extended the colony all the way across the continent to the Pacific, the 'South Sea'. While the future development of particular Tidewater States would be tied to the western interior, the ties would become economic and commercial, not those of territorial ownership. The future would show that Virginia, unlike New York, was already yielding at the start of independence the key position it had held in the imperial Tidewater structure.

One important new structural component included in the Federal Constitution was yet to be put in place. The decision to create a purpose-built Federal capital on land ceded by the States of Maryland and Virginia was recorded in the Act of 1790—a 'ten-mile square' which in 1791 was named the District of Columbia.[11] After the Declaration of Independence, the Continental Congress had assembled in various centres; New York became the headquarters after 1784, and it was in Wall Street in April 1789 that George Washington took the oath of office as the first President of the United States. Philadelphia was subsequently chosen as the capital during the transitional period from 1790 to 1800, when Washington, D.C. ('Federal City') became the permanent seat of Federal government. The District of Columbia was legally regarded as belonging to *all* the States, and therefore as rightfully (i.e. structurally) to be administered by *all* of them through Congress. Westward expansion was already marked by the westward shift of a number of State capitals. But in creating Washington, D.C., and thus rejecting the rival claims of existing towns and cities—some of them particularly well favoured for federal capital status by location and political experience—Congress had established a strong argument against all similar claims from future cities still unborn. **Inserted into the south-centre of the Tidewater's structural core, Washington, D.C., both in site and function, was to become an increasingly strong 'end-fitting' in the Federal structure as a whole.**

The supreme achievement of the new Federal design was to be the political guarantees it offered to those going west. In debating and reconciling many of the antagonisms thrown up by the core area itself, based on differences of size, tradition, resources, economy, and western access, for example, the new Federal Constitution (1787; ratified 1787–90) and the Bill of Rights (1791), had produced a strong but astonishingly flexible structure. The *Constitution* was now to be the new imperial framework for balancing and distributing compressive and tensional forces, for as Daniel Webster was later to note: "No monarchical throne presses these States together." **While Spain's huge baroque imperial compression structure still straddled the Americas to the south and west, the United States' tension structure had adopted plain, unadorned functionalism.** The success, or otherwise, of such innovative design remained to be seen.

There was urgent need for effective practical steps to support the structure through Federal action. In 1792 Congress began subsidizing the Post Office which was soon handling mail on the frontier, and promoting newspaper circulation by the introduction of low mailing rates. At the same time Congress began to debate "the imperious necessity in this extensive territory of tying together the whole community by the strongest ligatures . . . roads and canals."

There was another vital element among the components gathering and transmitting the compressive load, as well as those strengthening the suspension cables and hangers: it was the acceptance of only one *de facto* official language—English. English was the language of the Constitution, of Congress, the Courts, and the Administration. Periodic petitions to Congress to print Federal documents in other languages (e.g. the proposal in 1795 to print all Federal laws in German as well as English) were rejected, mainly on principle, but also on practical grounds of economy. The encouragement, or even tolerance, of official bilingualism (or multilingualism) was rightly seen as a potential fundamental structural weakness in the United States' tension structure. It was an early recognition of what, if adopted, would have been revealed at every future stage of construction as a basic and permanent design flaw in the system. The 'live load' would (and will) always have to learn, sooner or later, that English is the only 'structural' language of America—American English of course, since John Witherspoon, in his discussion on the language, had already invented the word *Americanism* in 1781.

Diversity and tension had thus been regarded as basic and permanent characteristics of the design, not simply as initial risks that time would remove. The opportunity to amend the Constitution reassured many of the waverers, but these, along with the convinced Antifederalists, represented that substantial majority of Americans who would ultimately respond only to the successful practice of Federal politics. This strong challenge to the theory of Federal union was thus included within the ideological structure of the core area from the outset. Antifederalism had been brilliantly countered in Ridge and Valley, Piedmont and Tidewater; Federalists had successfully argued that **all tension structures must contain some compressive force.** Yet the very existence of doubt and dissent proved invaluable since it would continually question, and normally renew, the state's confidence in its ability to accommodate diversity, and control it.

Utility
Economy
Expansion
Maintenance

> The United States had begun building a purely utilitarian structure, in which much of the construction work would continue at great distance by unspecialized labour. The designers had nevertheless followed one of the basic rules of construction—they had attempted to predict and in some cases to calculate, how the various parts of the engineering structure would share the load between them, a task here made more dangerous and unpredictable by the need to increase the weight and energy of the 'live load'. *In contrast to Spain's emphasis on increasing the 'dead load' of its imperial structure*, the dominant role that the 'live load' would play in the United States' tension structure, and the additional strains and stresses it would put on the framework's engineering as the structure was enlarged, presented a permanent challenge both to building and maintenance. For the true cost of a structure is not just the cost of designing and building it, but of maintaining it afterwards in good condition.

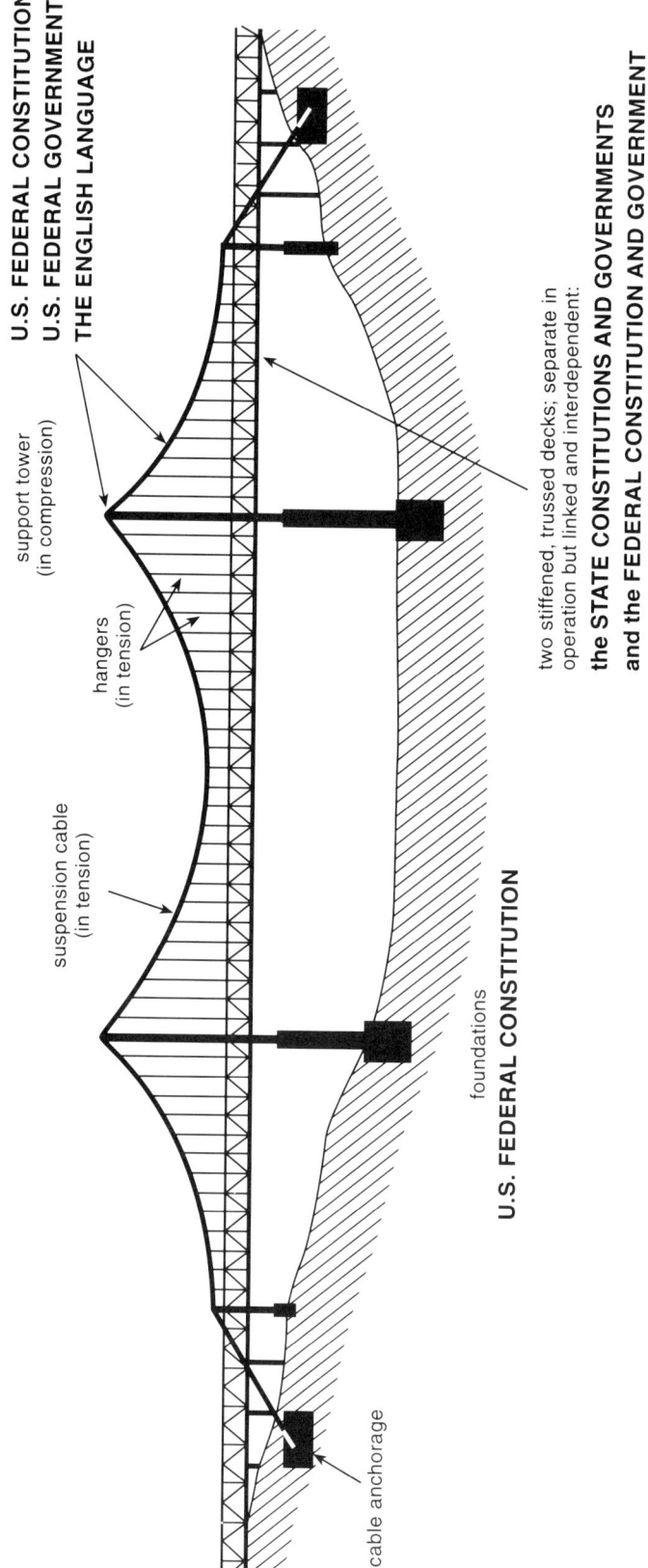

Figure B. A diagram of the United States' Federal tension structure

13

Spain's Influence on the Early U.S. Perimeter Ground-Plan: I

The Mississippi 'Coast'

> Though remote from the main centres of population, the Mississippi River formed the United States' first 'west coast' and immediately became the most politically sensitive of all the new boundaries, given the demands by the trans-Alleghany's 'live load' for free navigation on the river from source to mouth. *Potential fracture energy* was subsequently reduced in the western lands by the 1790s–1803 diplomacy, but the Mississippi problem focused American attention at a very early stage on the *perimeter* of empire, and at the same time provided evidence that the new tension structure was capable of managing *risk* on an enormously expanded scale.

"Let this person speak in Castilian, since we are in Castile, and he will be heard."

(Tomás Portell, Spanish commandant of New Madrid, Louisiana, on the Mississippi River, 2 July 1794, following a petition made to him in English by an American colonist)[12]

With the inherited western boundary of the United States at independence already on the Mississippi River, the original tension structure spanning the thirteen Tidewater States at once represented only about one-quarter of the total state territory.

Under the terms of the peace treaty with Britain in 1783, the western boundary of the United States was a median line along the Mississippi demarcating Spanish Louisiana as far south as 31°N. (Fig. 9) The United States had no south coast at all, since Florida and the Gulf of Mexico still belonged entirely to Spain. An extensive, if landlocked, north coast was provided by the Great Lakes shoreline, but the main perspective lay westward and, despite other external threats, the most politically sensitive boundary ran with the waters of the Mississippi. This was based on the fact that although south of 31°N the Mississippi ran entirely through Spanish territory, the peace treaty with Britain stipulated that the navigation of the Mississippi, *from its source to the ocean*, should forever remain free and open to British subjects and United States citizens.

Ironically, the Americans' most recent reminder of the importance to them of the entire Mississippi routeway had been provided by Spain. After Spain entered the War of Independence on the side of the colonists in 1779 (though without recognizing their declaration of independence), Havana had remained the control centre but New Orleans had become Spain's operational base. As early as 1776, Spanish silver, munitions and supplies were being moved both by sea to Philadelphia and by the 'back road' river route from New Orleans to Fort Pitt. George Rogers Clark's successful campaigns at Kaskaskia, Cahokia and Vincennes had used Spanish *matériel*, and French and Spanish support had been important in protecting the north-western interior from British attack.

Spanish support for an independent United States soon faded, and freedom of navigation on the Mississippi became an immediate issue after Spain reacted to the 1783 British-U.S. treaty by closing the river to United States navigation in June 1784. Madrid complained that it had not been party to the treaty (a separate treaty having been signed by Britain and Spain in 1783 which omitted all reference to Mississippi navigation), and that it was therefore not bound by Britain's guarantees to the United States on freedom of navigation through Spanish territory. Moreover, Spain was angered by a boundary line placed at 31°N rather than 32°30′N, where the old boundary of West Florida, the port of Natchez (31°35′N), and the Yazoo River confluence at Nogales (32°21′N) were all claimed. (Fig. 6)

The population of the trans-Alleghany West had been increasing even during the Revolution, particularly in Kentucky and Tennessee Districts which by the end of the War contained about 30,000 new American settlers. The flow accelerated as the rich farm lands along the Ohio and in the fertile Blue Grass country received the first hard thrust of post-war migration into the interior; wheat, corn, flour, salt beef, pork, bacon, lard, hemp, whisky, livestock, and tobacco all moved down the great Ohio-Mississippi river-road to New Orleans and the markets beyond:

> The Americans [wrote John Jay], almost to a man, believed that God Almighty had made that river a highway for the people of the upper country to go to the sea by ... The inhabitants would not readily be convinced of the justice of being obliged either to live without foreign commodities, and lose the surplus of their productions, or be obliged to transport both over rugged mountains and through an immense wilderness, to and from the sea, when they daily saw a fine river flowing before their doors, and offering to save them all that trouble and expense, and that without injury to Spain.[13]

George Washington had toured the trans-Alleghany West in 1784 and emphasized its crucial role in the future economic prosperity of the United States:

> The flanks and rear of the United States are possessed by other powers, and formidable ones too ... The western states stand as it were upon a pivot. The touch of a feather would turn them any way ... Smooth the road [down the Mississippi], and make easy the way for them, and then see what an influx of articles will be poured upon us, and how amazingly our exports will be increased by them, and how amply we shall be compensated for any trouble and expense we may encounter to effect it.[14]

But Jay was later to be involved in a compromise offer to Spain over its closure of the Mississippi in 1784, an offer which above all revealed the internal weakness and limited international bargaining power of the Confederal structure in place at the time. The northern Tidewater States were willing to accept the closure of the Mississippi for a twenty- to thirty-year period in return for trade privileges with Spain. Closure of the Mississippi, New England reasoned, would have the added advantage of discouraging westward migration, regarded by some as a threat to the Northeast's prosperity, perhaps even to the Northeast's survival. The northern attitude outraged the trans-Alleghanians, and, although negotiations with Spain broke down in 1786 after the five southern States vetoed Jay's proposals, and Spain reopened the Mississippi to U.S. navigation in 1788 (though duty of between six per cent and fifteen per cent had still to be paid at New Orleans), the West continued to regard the whole issue as crucial to the survival of the Union.

Spain's attempts to strengthen the edge of its imperial compression structure in the Mississippi Valley

While the United States began to work on the design of a new tension structure in the late 1780s, Spain attempted to strengthen its own outer perimeter defences in the Mississippi Valley. Efforts to protect Louisiana (Luisiana) and thus New Spain, by encouraging large numbers of new Catholic settlers, mainly Spanish and French, into the region, met with little success. Spain turned instead to the encouragement of American frontiersmen, inviting colonists to become Spanish subjects in one form or another, whether west or east of the Mississippi.[15] Spain's most immediate concern was control of the trans-Alleghany country and here the degree of independence and lack of stiffening in the United States' confederal structure prepared the ground. In the mid-1780s, Spain envisaged the erection of separate States under a loose U.S. Confederation which were nevertheless free to place themselves under Spanish protection and to gain exemption from Mississippi river and port taxes.

By 1787, Spanish immigration officials had been appointed in Kentucky and elsewhere, and for the first time (under new orders from Spain in 1788) there was tacit agreement that Protestant settlers would be acceptable, provided there was no overt Protestant worship, no local self-government, and no free-ranging land speculation. Although much of the United States Tidewater saw Spain as the instigator of Western unrest, demands for action and for greater autonomy in the trans-Alleghany country were the Westerners own. Whether Indian tribes or American settlers, Spain's preference was for Spanish protection, i.e. *accommodation within the Spanish imperial structure*, not for separatism. Yet semi-automonous groups established or projected on the western frontier, notably the self-styled Vandalia, Westsylvania, Transylvania (Kentucky District), Watauga, and Franklin, had been a growing feature since before the Revolution, and by the late 1780s, the pace of new settlement in Kentucky and Tennessee, now containing two-thirds of the United States' Western population, had increased tensile forces to dangerous levels. As Jefferson observed in 1787:

> I will venture to say that the act which abandons the navigation of the Mississippi is an act of separation between the Eastern and Western country [i.e. between the Tidewater States and the trans-Alleghany West] . . . If they declare themselves a separate people, we are incapable of a single effort to retain them . . . They are able already to rescue the navigation of the Mississippi out of the hands of Spain, and to add New Orleans to their own territory.[16]

The Kentuckians made the same point: "The free use of the Mississippi *by Constitutional means, if shortly;* if not, *by any means.*"

Spain perceives the Mississippi River as a tie-beam of empire

The Mississippi was thus on the perimeter of both the Spanish and the United States empires, and both were working on the fringes of their respective authorities. Even here, operational contrasts between the compression and the tension structures were stark. Spain had increasingly come to regard the river (since its acquisition from France) as an *imperial* river, delimiting and tying part of the imperial structure. The King of Spain's *Royal Mississippi River Squadron*, based at Natchez and comprising up to five armed galleys and galiots, patrolled the lower river for defence and the supervision of other river craft. Occasional patrols also worked the upper Mississippi between St. Louis and Prairie du Chien.

The concept of the Mississippi armada was daring; American frontiersmen had seen nothing like it before. One has only to study the detailed specifications and hand-coloured maps of new emplacements and projected forts for the defence of the Mississippi prepared in New Orleans in the late 1780s and lodged with the Council of the Indies in Seville, to appreciate the scale and consistency of the design policy of Spain's imperial compression structure.[17] As it was, the *Royal Mississippi River Squadron* never engaged in combat so far as is known, but its presence helped to dissuade Americans from attacking Natchez, Nogales and New Madrid.

Spanish officialdom nevertheless marked out the boundary of empire. To Americans, alternately bewildered and exasperated, it was a strange world of permits, passports, stop-and-search, delay, and endless formality—the long shadow of Spain's towering imperial compression structure cast across the Mississippi Valley.

The growing influence of the United States' 'live load' at the edge of the tension structure

The overwhelmingly Antifederal vote recorded in the Kentucky and Tennessee Districts during the 1787–90 general vote on the new Federal Constitution reflected their conviction that free navigation of the Mississippi would be traded away by the Federalists under the commerce clause. At the time, Westerners still represented less than six per cent of the total population, but most of them remained angry and determined. Their tensile force was now pulling within the Federal, rather than the Confederal, structure but both stresses and strains were becoming stronger, as the vital importance of the Mississippi routeway dominated the patterns of internal communication and the needs of the export market. Alexander Hamilton was well aware that the promised benefits to be derived from the new Federal tension structure, along with the advantages of its new Constitutional compressive force, were going to be tested immediately, and on site:

> Let it be supposed that Spain . . . persists in the policy she has hitherto pursued, without the slightest symptom of relaxation, of barring the Mississippi against us; where must this end, and at a period not very distant? Infallibly in a war with Spain, or separation of the western country, [which] must have an outlet for its commodities. This is essential to its prosperity, and if not procured to it by the United States, must be had at the expense of the connection with them . . . Free navigation of the Mississippi to the sea is of the first moment to our territories to the westward; without it, they will be lost to us.[18]

They were not lost. Kentucky was admitted as a State of the Union in 1792, the first west of the Alleghanies; Tennessee would follow in 1796. In this context, A. P. Whitaker's observation on the style of their admission serves, coincidentally, to reinforce the structural theme of empire presented here, since the first building extensions of the two-tiered Federal span relied on the already familiar, serviceable components:

> It is remarkable [wrote Whitaker] how little the law and constitutions of Kentucky and Tennessee differ from those of Virginia and North Carolina, how few changes the frontiersmen had to make. It is still more remarkable how little they desired to change . . . their purpose was not creative but reproductive. They were indeed State-builders, but they found their plans and specifications ready made.[19]

The United States now increased its pressure on Spain over the Mississippi and the right of free deposit New Orleans, backed by a surge of American migration into Spanish Illinois, West Florida and Lower Louisiana.

The Spanish-American Treaty of San Lorenzo el Real (the Pinckney Treaty) which followed in 1795 had far-reaching effects because the new legislation for the Mississippi River was to mark the first major step towards a wider interpretation (in Europe in 1815) of the principle of international rivers. Under Art. IV, Spanish subjects and U.S. citizens were granted the right to navigate the Mississippi 'from its source to the ocean', i.e. along the shared portion of the boundary as far south as 31°N, and south again, through Spanish territory, to the sea. Natchez was formally ceded to the United States, its population already largely American. Under Art. XXII, U.S. citizens were also granted the right to deposit their merchandise at New Orleans, and export it again duty-free (in the first place for three years), but the port was often either closed, or access and handling delayed:

"We have a vast number of boats in our harbour from the American Settlements," the U.S. Consul at New Orleans informed the State Department during the Treaty period, "boats laden with flour, tobacco, bacon, salt pork, beef, cordage, hemp, and cotton of Natchez and Tennessee." But the port restrictions imposed by Spain were intolerable—American vessels were "forever stopping, starting, meeting new officials, and facing new ceremonies of inquiry."[20] The trans-Alleghany West remained frustrated and impatient.

The Pinckney Treaty, however, was regarded as conciliatory by Spain, and by the United States as a major success for the stronger Federal structure. Spain had feared that the trans-Alleghany westerners (and increasing numbers of trans-Mississippi westerners also by this time) would simply take New Orleans by force. The Spanish Crown was already regretting the relaxation of its rules in its attempts to secure the Mississippi Valley as an outer defence for New Spain, a relaxation later withdrawn by Madrid after the damage had been done. Spain had compromised cherished traditions in seeking new settlers, particularly in its toleration of Protestant colonists. The Spanishness of the 'live load' had been reduced, the compressive force weakened, the joints rather than simply being permitted to 'give' within tolerable limits had gaped open, and the oblique thrust lines were totally unmanageable. The sheer size and turbulence of the new 'live load' were beyond control; by the end of the decade, the population in the West had reached half-a-million.

Once across the Alleghany/Appalachian watershed, the American settlers had at last found rivers that were flowing in the direction they wanted to go. Like the American Indians and the French before them, but now in much greater force, **the Americans drew river transport into the design of the ground-plan of empire, and into the routeing of its 'live load' in ways that Spain had never been able to do anywhere in the New World.**

Louisiana itself, where numerous Americans had become Spanish subjects for convenience sake, was an expensive wilderness Spain discovered, and quite useless as an imperial buffer zone. Moreover, new settlers had ignored all Spain's earlier commercial restrictions, while subsequently deriving huge benefits from trade with the West

Indies and with Europe during the 'neutral commerce' period. The American colonists were never content; whatever was yielded, they wanted more. As George Washington had already remarked: Westerners showed "a predisposition to be dissatisfied."[21]

The question of the ownership of New Orleans itself now took priority, and here the problem was overtaken by events in Europe. Once Napoleon had reclaimed Louisiana from Spain in 1800, there was not only the matter of New Orleans but also the need to renegotiate navigation rights on the Mississippi. As Alexander Hamilton wrote in 1802:

> You know my general theory as to our Western affairs. I have always held that the *unity of our Empire*, and the best interests of our nation, require that we shall annex to the United States all the territory east of the Mississippi, New Orleans included.[22]

And whatever their other disagreements, Hamilton's emphasis on the structural importance of the Mississippi and of New Orleans was also underlined by Thomas Jefferson: "France placing itself in that door assumes to us the attitude of defiance. Spain might have retained it quietly for years. . . . I would not give one inch of the waters of the Mississippi to any nation, because I see in a light very important to our peace the exclusive right to its navigation, and the admission of no nation into it, . . . but with our consent and under our police."[23]

The famous bargain was struck with France in April 1803. Jefferson's request to purchase New Orleans and the Florida bank of the Mississippi at the same time as the navigation rights were being negotiated was answered instead with New Orleans and the west bank of the river, in the atmosphere of uncertainty and opportunism which surrounded the Louisiana Purchase.

* * *

ENLARGING THE STRUCTURE
The Federal tension structure builds new support towers along the Continental Divide, lengthens its span, and confirms the advantages of suspension bridge design

> When designing and constructing a **LONG-SPAN BRIDGE**, the great weight of the structure, the dynamic effects of moving loads . . . give rise to problems which call for the greatest knowledge and ingenuity in their solution . . . The construction of a long-span bridge is a great achievement.
>
> When spans are large, **SUSPENSION BRIDGES** are the most economical.
>
> (W. Morgan, *The Elements of Structure*)

The Louisiana Purchase more than doubled the size of the United States at a stroke, and extended the boundaries of the state beyond its original limits for the first time. Debate concentrated on the wisdom of such a huge acquisition of territory a mere twenty years after independence, and fears voiced earlier were raised again concerning the increasing isolation of the eastern seaboard and the inevitable loss of population westward, both of which would weaken, and later possibly challenge the survival of the Union. Significantly, doubters questioned how the trans-Mississippi West could be *controlled*, not how it could be peopled; the trans-Alleghany movement had answered that. The advantage of owning *both sides* of the Mississippi River now appeared overwhelming to those who had settled within the Mississippi Valley. As Senator Breckenridge of Kentucky reminded Congress, there was no standard extent for a republic:

> Why not then acquire territory on the west, as well as on the east side of the Mississippi? Is the Goddess of Liberty restrained by water courses? Is she governed by geographical limits? . . .
>
> I believe that the more extensive the Republic's dominion, the more safe and more durable it will be.[24]

Extending the Federal tension structure west of the Mississippi

"There are *high destinies* in the West to which the United States is hereafter to be called," wrote the French representative Louis Beaujour while travelling through the country after the Louisiana Purchase; . . . "Back settlers, American buccaneers, restless, adventuring, and always pushing westward as if in search of their own El Dorado."[25]

Experience had given fresh confidence to the builders of the tension structure whose new support towers had now been erected in the Rocky Mountains. While primary reconnaissance would be undertaken by such official government explorers as Lewis, Clark, Pike and Long, it would be a highly varied and mobile 'live load'—mountain men, prospectors, soldiers, engineers, freighters, traders, farmers, ranchers—who would become the main site-surveyors and early builders of the Federal span soon to be constructed from the Mississippi River to its western watershed.

As Jefferson observed in his Second Inaugural Address in March 1805, emphasizing a point already made by Madison in the 1780s:

> I know that the acquisition of Louisiana has been disapproved by some, from a candid apprehension that the enlargement of our territory would endanger its union. *But who can limit the extent to which the federative principle may operate effectively?* The larger our association, the less will it be shaken by local passions.

Momentous as the huge Louisiana land purchase was in scale and technical challenge, the design policy had been shaped by the Mississippi river, America's first west coast. The Mississippi in turn became the base-line from which to survey and map new far-western construction to the Pacific. Despite Jefferson's earlier reservations about the wisdom of a major trans-Mississippi expansion by the United States, there had been no more avid reader of Alexander Mackenzie's journal recording the 1789-93 exploration across Canada to the Pacific Ocean than Jefferson himself.[26] In a projection of the internal waterways policy, Jefferson's instructions to the Lewis and Clark expedition in 1803 had emphasized the importance of finding a river route to the Pacific in order to produce a balanced continental Mississippi network, sea to sea. In fact, the concept of the integrity of the Mississippi basin had been extended west into the semi-arid and mountainous regions where the rivers themselves became unnavigable, and the United States was to face its first challenging adjustment to the dry lands.

Within a few years, the continued determination to make the Mississippi-Missouri an all-American waterway was decisive in the new Great Britain-United States Canadian boundary convention negotiations of 1818–19. The final agreement ran the line from the Lake of the Woods to the Stony (i.e. the Rocky) Mountains along the 49th parallel, and thus kept the boundary north of the Missouri, and well to the north of the source of the Mississippi, wherever its exact location might be. In the same period, the Floridas East and West were finally acquired from Spain and for the first time, a western boundary line was extended along the 42nd parallel beyond the source of the Arkansas river all the way to the Pacific.[27]

Steamboat transport had begun on the Mississippi in 1811, revolutionizing the network's efficiency and greatly enlarging its continental influence as a structural tie. Under Art. III of the 1819 U.S.-Spanish Treaty, Spain's right to navigate the Mississippi was quietly dropped, as Britain's had been in 1814. "The whole of the Mississippi, and our option open in the West"; despite the fact that the United States had surrendered its claim to Texas, Secretary of State John Quincy Adams was well satisfied.

* * *

> Bidding the eagles of the west fly on . . .
> In a miracle of health and speed, . . .
> They leaped the Mississippi, blue border of the West.
>
> (Vachel Lindsay, *Bryan*)

The Mississippi had demanded American adjustment to American space. It focused 'Western Waters' diplomacy, settlement and trade. Instead of remaining a remote, virtually unknown boundary to the majority, the river had immediately been drawn into the political calculations of Americans on both sides of the Appalachians. The Mississippi had raised political issues and design risks involving the state structure as a whole; dissent and sectionalism, core area and frontier were all represented. Whether the horizons were physical or mental, the Mississippi had provided the Tidewater with a truer westward scale measurement than the Alleghanies/Appalachians had ever done. Now the great river had become a *mid*-continental component in the American design.

By 1810, the population west of the Appalachians was over 1 million; a decade later it was approaching 2,250,000. In 1820, western settlers in five of the ten new States of the Union had already taken themselves and their two-tiered Federal structure right to the Mississippi 'coast'; some had even completed the first sections of the next span on the other side. The transcontinental preparation, about to start, was in some ways already over.

14

Spain's Influence on the Early U.S. Perimeter Ground-Plan: II

The Development of Transoceanic Empire

> In addition to the early role played by the Mississippi River, the rapid design enlargement of the United States was also strongly influenced by Spain's 'double ocean' ground-plan—the *continental* and the *global* dimensions of New World empire. Moreover, it was at the *outer edges* of Spain's huge compression structure that the north-eastern United States saw their own greatest immediate opportunities for growth.
>
> The silver supply and the commercial backwardness of the Spanish empire combined to present the perfect target to those bent on the expansion and management of *risk*—an intrinsic design feature of the United States' tension structure. Thus, while the Spanish seaborne empire became weakened and more distracted by events in Europe, the emergence of the *New England seaborne empire* was one of the most remarkable features of this early period. As carriers and suppliers, New England pursued Spain around the entire edge of its empire—to Spain and the Mediterranean, Cuba, New Orleans, Mexico, the River Plate, Chile, Peru, and California. By 1787–90, the commercial site-lines had been extended to the Orient.
>
> New Englanders had always been the most versatile component in the American colonies, the most dynamic element in the 'live load', and by far the greatest single source of tension in Britain's imperial structure. Now, while New York traders opened the Cape of Good Hope route to China, Boston traders followed the Spanish westward across the Pacific. Before long, the ports of Boston and Salem on Massachusetts Bay had drawn their own 'Tordesillas Line' in the Pacific—Salem vessels bound for China using the Good Hope route, Boston the Cape Horn route. The merchants of Boston and Salem divided their spheres of interest in the great Ocean, and in a crucial early period became 'the Spain and Portugal of the Pacific'.

The Revival of long-range seaborne empire in the New World
New England: Stability and Risk

Northward, till everlasting ice besets thee
And South as far as the grim Spaniard lets thee.

(W. C. Bryant, *Rhode Island Meditation*)

United States independence in 1783 brought both political and economic separation from the British Empire, denying Americans access to many markets and sources of supply that had previously sustained a highly profitable colonial commerce. This was particularly true of New England whose lack of a staple crop with which to fit neatly into the imperial mercantilist system had encouraged an early development of the fishing, shipbuilding and carrying trade.

After 1660, shipbuilding had become a leading industry in Massachusetts as the great Puritan emigration was renewed, bringing many shipwrights and master-builders. Supplies of good oak timber and pine spars were so plentiful that building ships to order or on speculation for the English market was soon a thriving industry. London capital in its turn helped to build New England's own merchant and fishing fleets.

The English Navigation Act of 1651, restricting colonial commerce to English and English colonial vessels, had already given an extra boost to New England's shipbuilding, since before then the Dutch yards at New Amsterdam had been serious competitors. The capture of New Amsterdam in 1664 (and finally in 1674) removed this focus of Dutch maritime activity from the Tidewater, and brought New York and New England into a closer working relationship. Before long, vessels built and owned in New England were doing the bulk of the carrying trade between the northern and middle colonies, England, Spain, and the rest of Southern Europe. Boston in addition, since the 1640s had become "the mart town of the West Indies", its business community frequently supplanting the London merchants and ignoring English laws regulating trade.[28] Many smaller ports also worked the West Indies; in 1650 the first Connecticut ship, appropriately named the *Tryall*, had left to seek markets in the Caribbean with a cargo of barrel staves.

Essentially, New England was a coastline of *harbours*, not navigable rivers. Capital built by shipping, commerce and manufacturing by an increasingly diversified social and religious merchant class in the late seventeenth and early eighteenth centuries was kept mobile, versatile and wide-ranging—venture capital in every sense.[29] Post-Revolutionary War depression in New England was initially severe, its shipbuilding orders and main carrying trade lost, its adjustment slower than that of Virginia. Yet the terms of the peace treaty with Britain in 1783 were not harsh, and owed much to the shrewdness and skill of Benjamin Franklin, the United States' chief negotiator. Americans retained full fishing rights on the Grand Banks and all other banks around Newfoundland and in the Gulf of the St Lawrence, as well as drying and curing facilities along any unsettled portions of the Nova Scotia, Magdalen Islands, and Labrador coastlines. It was the route to recovery.

Shipbuilding was reviving strongly by the mid-1780s, and despite the fact that in 1783 Spain had attempted to end the 'neutral commerce' clause, New England remained determined to increase its carrying trade with the Spanish empire. Havana was pivotal. In terms of its capacity and location, "the port is not only the best in the West Indies but perhaps one of the finest in the Universe," wrote an eighteenth-century observer.[30] American colonists had assisted Britain in the capture of Havana in 1762 during the Seven Years' War, and had contributed to the spectacular growth in the port's economy during the occupation. Spanish silver was as vital to Yankee recovery in the 1780s as it had been to the rebels during the Revolutionary War. Although Spain had never meant to make 'neutral' trade (in specified items) a permanent feature, Cuban merchants had welcomed it as an unfettered opportunity. After 1783, Yankee traders continued to bring a wide range of supplies from the Tidewater and the Mississippi Valley into Cuba, either as hidden contraband or as 'in distress' emergency landing (another example of Spain's permitted 'give' in the joints) until the Spanish clampdown in 1784–5.

As Spain tightened its control of Havana, Boston in particular grew more desperate for Spanish specie, more impatient with Spain's restrictive practices, and more determined than ever that Americans operating in the Gulf of Mexico and the Caribbean should provide the nearest warehouse for supplying the Spanish trade. There was a huge increase in contraband traffic, along with the growing risk of confiscation and arrest. But as the United States moved towards adoption of its stronger Federal structure, and Europe again became disrupted by war, the Yankees were fast becoming the main carrier and *de facto* supplier of Spanish America.

Meanwhile, increasing restrictions imposed by the Governor, Captain-general, and Intendant in Havana encouraged New England, New York, Philadelphia and Baltimore to develop stronger trade links with the east coast of South America. American carriers appeared in growing numbers on the River Plate, most notably after 1795 in the permitted periods of 'neutral commerce' that accompanied war and blockade among the European powers. Boston vessels dominated the U.S. merchantmen in both Buenos Aires and Montevideo, bringing in flour, lumber, tobacco and manufactured goods, and loading silver, hides, tallow, wools, sheepskins, Peruvian bark, and Brazilian sugar and coffee.[31] Yankee captains ran four separate naval blockades of Buenos Aires by Spain, Brazil, France and Britain between 1810 and 1848, and until mid-century, South America remained an important market for New England timber, fish, and ice (and for New England's own manufactured goods also where these were competitive with the British).

In general, during these critical early years of independence, United States trade flourished when the Great Powers were embroiled in war and slumped when peace was restored in Europe. Soon after Havana had been given responsibility for Spain's defence of the Caribbean in 1793 (in return for the port's demand for virtual free trade with the United States), nearly 1,000 American ships arrived in Cuba, by far the greatest single contingent, and almost twice as many as Spain's own vessels. But early in 1802 the U.S. Consul in Havana reported tersely: "Times have been harder since peace." He complained to the Spanish Governor that many U.S. vessels had arrived at, or very shortly after, the latest embargo, and were now riding at anchor, loaded with provisions but forbidden to land. The response was brusque:

> As the trade with the United States has never been *open*, but only *suffered*; and as the Americans knew the tenure upon which the intercourse was held, they could not, or should not, have extended any concerns beyond the reach of a very short period to adjust.[32]

In 1805, 'neutral commerce' was again permitted, and within a few weeks of opening Havana, the U.S. Consul recorded that "upwards of 600 American vessels have entered it, whose average tonnage is 130 tons, and not thirty vessels of every other nation . . . The wants of the Island (about 400,000 souls) are great, . . . and almost wholly supplied through the commerce of the United States."[33] Havana dominated the trade, supplemented mainly by Santiago de Cuba, Matanzas and Trinidad.[34] By the early nineteenth century, at least thirty New England ports were trading with Cuba, in addition to the ports of New York, Philadelphia, Baltimore, Charleston, Key West, Tampa, Pensacola, Mobile, and the Mississippi Valley via New Orleans. "The Americans have enriched themselves by the wars which have desolated Europe," wrote a visiting French official. "They have taken the place of the Dutch in the carrying trade, and of France and Spain in the trade with their own colonies . . . The Americans have been like a bridge connecting Europe with the other parts of the world, an entrepôt for the trade of all nations."[35]

Increased structural tension in New England

Legal trading was again interrupted in 1806–7 after Napoleon's decrees forbidding both France's allies *and neutrals* to trade with Britain or the British colonies. Britain retaliated in 1807–12 by subjecting the whole of Napoleonic Europe to British blockade; the Yankees, the great neutral carrier, now found themselves barred from European trade and much else besides. Thomas Jefferson responded with an Embargo Act (22 December 1807–15 March 1809), which forbade American vessels to sail to foreign ports, and placed American coasting and fishing vessels under heavy bond not to land their cargoes outside the United States. In addition, the import of many British goods was prohibited. New England suffered most from the Embargo Act and was the main source of opposition to it. In practice, many of the restrictions were circumvented by a huge increase in the smuggling trade across the Canadian and Florida borders.

Before long, Massachusetts, Connecticut and Rhode Island were also to become increasingly hostile to pressures in Congress for war with Britain—pressures produced by a combination of frontier and maritime grievances advanced by 'war hawks' from the West and South. The War of 1812 was opposed by New England, particularly in 1814 when the British naval blockade was extended to include New England's ports for the first time. Indeed, in 1814–15, New England was talking openly of secession from the Union. But the war reached stalemate, peace terms were soon agreed and the tension eased. Besides, New England had one foot in sea, and one on shore; however peripheral the region's location, it was already obvious that New England's opportunities for growth, risk and reward were much greater by remaining within the continental Federal structure than by detachment from it.

Furthermore, the setbacks caused by Jefferson's Embargo Act and the War of 1812 had stimulated the development of New England's own manufacturing industry. This was characterized by an extraordinarily wide range of factory products, reflecting human skills, the virtual lack of domestic raw materials, the broad distribution of good water-power sites, the long experience in the shipbuilding and carrying trade, the available venture capital, and the remarkable versatility of the merchant class. By the 1840s, southern New England was predominantly a manufacturing region, and Boston's population was over 100,000.

New England enters the Pacific

Boundless risk must pay for boundless gain.

(William Morris, *The Wanderers*)

The 360-ton *Empress of China*, out of New York, had reached Canton via the Cape of Good Hope in 1784 and opened the United States' lucrative trade with the Far East. Aboard was a young Revolutionary War hero, Samuel Shaw of Boston, who went out as Commercial Agent; the following year he made his next voyage as the first U.S. Consul in China.

Boston itself was to pioneer America's *westward* route into the Pacific. After Magellan, a few Dutch, English and French seamen had penetrated 'Spain's Ocean' over the centuries, but it was the three wide-ranging explorations of the Pacific by the English Captain James Cook, culminating in his discovery of the Hawaiian (Sandwich) Islands and the charting of the British Columbian and Alaskan coasts between 1776 and 1780, that were of the greatest significance to the United States. After the official accounts of the voyages were published in 1784, the commercial possibilities of transpacific trade were the talk of Boston, where the pursuit of Spain and Britain into the Pacific roused more excitement than Spain's closure of the Mississippi ever did.

As part of an expedition led by a fellow New Englander John Kendrick, Captain Robert Gray sailed from Boston in September 1787 with the *Lady Washington* and *Columbia*, rounded Cape Horn, and then proceeded north to load sea-otter skins obtained from the Indians in the Nootka Sound-Vancouver Island region until July 1789. Gray then crossed the Pacific (via Hawaii) to mark Boston's entry into the Far Eastern fur trade, where Canton was the world's greatest market at that time. Gray continued his voyage round the world in the *Columbia* (the first United States vessel to circumnavigate the globe), returning triumphantly to Boston in August 1790.[36] The world trade route Boston-Northwest Coast-Hawaii-Canton-Boston was soon established. In a zone already in dispute between Spain and Britain, the United States' entry into the 'Spanish Ocean' and the 'Spanish Coast' had particularly angered Madrid. Kendrick and Gray had narrowly avoided the capture of their vessels at Nootka in 1788, and in 1789, Spain's Mexican authorities instructed officials in Upper California to seize "a ship named *Columbia* which they say belongs to General Washington of the American States," should it arrive at San Francisco.

After only a month back in port, Captain Gray left Boston again in the *Columbia* in September 1790, loading furs and skins along the Pacific inlets in 1791–2, and in 1792 discovering and naming Gray's Harbor and the Columbia River, before returning to Boston via China in 1793. The Spanish had already seen and mapped the 'Columbia River' estuary in 1775, but Gray was the first (apart from the local Indian communities) to negotiate the difficult entrance and sail up the river for about twenty miles.[37] Soon, the Pacific Northwest—'The Coast' as it became known in Boston—became the primary source of sea-otter, seal, and beaver skins in the Chinese market, together with sandalwood loaded in Hawaii.

It was not surprising to find English, French, Spanish and Russian ships surveying and patrolling the Pacific coast of North America in the 1780s and 1790s. What was surprising was to find New England there also, as the small, successful revolutionary city of Boston shouldered itself in among the great European powers.

Meanwhile, back on Massachusetts Bay and less than twenty miles from their powerful Boston rivals, Salem merchants developed the Old World route to the Orient. Elias Derby of Salem had despatched the first United States merchantman to St. Petersburg in 1784 and was soon active from the Baltic to the Far East. But Salem left the trade of the Pacific Northwest and the adjacent zones to Boston, concentrating instead on East and West Africa, Arabia, the Indian Ocean, the East Indies and Manila. Boston had in fact followed Magellan, while Salem followed Vasco da Gama. As S. E. Morison observed: "Boston was the Spain, Salem was the Portugal, in the race for Oriental opulence."[38]

Boston's regional shipbuilding industry was now booming—on the North and the Mystic Rivers, at Salem, and on the

Merrimac—as New York and New England merchants ordered vessels to develop both the Horn and the Good Hope routes to China, India and the East Indies. The *Massachusetts*, 820 tons and co-owned by Samuel Shaw, was launched at Germantown, near Quincy in 1789. It was the largest merchant ship ever built in the USA up to that time and large vessels were favoured for the Good Hope route. But the demand was varied. Boston captains working the winding inlets of 'the Coast' to load furs and skins preferred small sturdy brigs of 100–250 tons. These also proved to be extremely successful in rounding the Horn; none apparently was ever lost, a fitting tribute to outstanding skills in shipbuilding and seamanship.

The remarkable revival and diversification of Boston's economy between 1790 and 1820 now co-ordinated a New England sea-borne empire which was active in both the Pacific and the Indian Oceans, as well as in the earlier trading realms of Europe and the Mediterranean, the West Indies, Brazil and the River Plate. Indeed, Captain Gray of *Columbia* fame, took the brig *Alert* into Montevideo and Buenos Aires in 1798, returning with hides and specie.

Back to New England and New York came teas, silks, cottons, porcelains, enamels, spices, coffee, pepper, carpets, hemp, jade, ivory, and indigo, much of it re-exported from the major entrepôts of Boston and Salem. But it was Boston that developed the trade so long resisted by Spain's imperial controls, that of bringing silks and other goods directly across the Pacific from the Orient into the warehouses of Lima, Valparaíso and Buenos Aires. And it was Boston that dominated the Manila trade, where Boston merchants long-resident in the Philippines, such as Henry P. Sturgis, Josiah Moore and Jonathan Russell, were frequently in charge of the U.S. Consulate, and where Boston ships took the lead in expanding the age-old maritime trade between Canton, Manila and Spain.[39]

New England and the Pacific whaling industry

> I thought I would sail about a little
> and see the watery part of the world.
>
> (Herman Melville, *Moby Dick*)

The first American sealers from Connecticut appeared off Chile as early as 1778, but the whaling industry expanded rapidly after 1791 when Nantucketers began to follow Boston traders round the Horn, hunting the sperm whale along the South American coast and soon all over the Pacific. On the New England mainland, New Bedford became the centre of the industry, its spacious harbour focusing the quays, refineries, cooperage and other manufacturing and ancillary services that spread from Buzzards Bay to New London.[40]

By 1820, Nantucket captains had located major new hunting grounds west of the Galapagos, off Japan, and before long off Kamchatka, Alaska and the Bering Strait. The first American whaleship entered Honolulu Harbor in 1820, and by 1823, up to sixty whaleships were calling at Hawaii's ports. John C. Jones of Boston had been appointed U.S. Commercial Agent in Honolulu in September 1820, and wrote in his report of 1827:

> Since the discovery of whale fishery on the coast of Japan, the Sandwich Islands have become indispensable to the American commerce employed for that purpose, for provisioning and refitting ships, and for manpower. There is no place in this ocean which can afford them equal advantages.[41]

Between 1820 and 1860, more than 100,000 New Englanders were involved in the Pacific whaling industry. It was rough, often dangerous work, and crews were treated harshly, often brutally as the industry expanded. Many were not seamen at all but New England farm boys, drifters or criminals. As U.S. Consul Turrill reminded the State Department in 1848:

> Men and boys were collected from our rail-roads and canals by agents sent for that purpose, many of them ruined both in morals and in constitution. These individuals, entirely ignorant of the business in which they were about to engage, were placed on board ... Many crew are on the sick list here, seeking discharge or deserting.[42]

The rapid expansion of Yankee whalers around the entire Pacific Rim during the 1820s had prompted President John Quincy Adams, himself from Massachusetts, to advocate systematic exploration of the Pacific. Within a few years, Congress authorized the U.S. Navy's Exploring Expedition in the Pacific (1838–42) under the command of Lieutenant Charles Wilkes, whose responsibilities in the Pacific and Antarctic Oceans included the charting of sea channels, harbours, and victualling ports for use by American whaling vessels. Indeed, New Bedford and Nantucket whalers made an immense and a unique contribution to knowledge of the Pacific, a practical demonstration of the *entirety* of the Ocean that Spain had claimed 300 years earlier in law.

The Pacific whaling industry remained a virtual United States monopoly, 'whitening the Ocean with its canvas', in Wilkes' own graphic phrase. By 1846, there were approximately 900 whaling vessels in the world, and 730 of these had American registry. Many whalers worked off Japan in the winter and the Arctic in the summer, stopping at Hawaii in the spring and fall to store or tranship their cargoes of whaleoil and baleen (whalebone). In June 1843, the U.S. Consul was able to report that "nearly 40,000 tons of American shipping, manned by nearly 3,000 seamen, have touched at these Islands in the past five months."[43] Whalers in particular derived great benefit from the eventual removal of all port charges by Hawaii's Legislative Council and Royal Sanction. Whaleships were also allowed to land and sell up to US$200-worth of merchandise duty free.

There was huge expansion in the whaling industry during the 1840s, growth which helped to finance New England's industrialization. In 1850–60, more then seventeen million gallons of whaleoil and fourteen million pounds of baleen were transhipped from the Hawaiian Islands to the United States. The 1850s represented the climax of the Nantucket-New Bedford whaling era in the Pacific. The whaling fleet was halved during the Civil War, and the use of kerosene and gas for lighting reduced the market for whaleoil. Nevertheless, steam whalers (many of them still owned and registered in New Bedford) were working in the Pacific by 1879, while San Francisco, at the terminus of the first transcontinental railroad, became a major whaling port and overland shipper of oil and baleen until the U.S. whaling industry effectively ended in 1900–1910.

New England missionaries

The first American missionaries arrived in Honolulu from Boston in 1820, the same year as the first American whaleship. Their frame houses, furniture and printing-press were shipped round the Horn, their Congregational church later built of coral blocks to replace the palm hut erected in April 1820. Amos Starr Cooke of Danbury, Connecticut and his wife founded the Royal School in Hawaii and taught the royal children, and others, for many years. Critical as the missionaries were about some of the Yankee whaling and trading practices, they set about adding their own strong cultural component to this New England outpost of empire.

Francis Warriner, ashore briefly from a U.S. naval frigate which was visiting Honolulu in 1831, made the point echoed by many:

> Could I have forgotten the circumstances of my visit, I should have fancied myself in New England . . . the dress, the framed house, the carpets, the furniture, the hymns, the tunes, the sermon, the Sabbath school, the Bible class.[44]

As advisers and teachers, as well as preachers, the missionaries' influence was greater than their actual numbers would suggest. The Hawaiian Constitution of 1840 was largely their work, and they supported the diplomatic mission to Washington, D.C. in 1844 to secure confirmation of U.S. recognition of Hawaiian independence.

The Hawaiians themselves favoured continued independence, if this was ever going to be possible amid the growing rival strategic interests of Britain, France, and the United States in the Pacific throughout the nineteenth century. Against the background of the dramatic American territorial expansion in Oregon and California in the 1840s, Hawaii's independence was confirmed for another fifty years, but during this period it became an increasingly vital component in New England's, and the United States', 'ocean empire'.

Boston traders

Boston traders had been developing 'the Coast and Canton' route via Hawaii since the 1790s. As early as 1812, the Winships of Boston had obtained a trading monopoly in sandalwood from King Kamehameha I in return for a percentage of the profits. By the 1820s–1830s, several New Englanders resident in the Islands had purchased vessels via Boston and, under the Hawaiian flag, were trading independently to China, Manila, and the Pacific ports of North and South America. As individual enterprise gave way to corporate effort, the major Boston merchant houses consolidated their position through firms such as Lamb, Perkins, and Bryant and William Sturgis. Given the rivalry between French, British and U.S. commercial and strategic interests in Hawaii, Boston merchants set out to make Honolulu a showcase for New England manufacturers. Indeed, 'the Hub' of Massachusetts became in a very real sense the United States' 'Hub of the Pacific'.

Boston firms were increasingly trading with the South Pacific islands by the 1830s–1840s, crossing the earlier demarcation line into Salem's trading sphere, and revealing a shifting of power between the two rivals that was also evident in Massachusetts Bay, where Salem lost ground to Boston. For Boston was exploiting its ties with the port of New York, both as a linked entrepôt for the European and worldwide import, re-export, and carrying trade, and as a shipbuilding, crewing, and insurance base for the New York business houses.

The tradition continued into the period of the clipper ship, which was built and rigged for speed. Introduced by New York *c.*1845 after pioneering work in Baltimore in the 1830s, clipper ships were perfected by Boston to meet the special demands of the California goldrush trade. Sailing time for the 15,000-mile course from New England-New York to San Francisco via the Horn had been reduced over the years from 8–9 months to an average of 160 days. But the first clipper ship arrived in San Francisco in 1850 after only 97 days, and in 1851 the *Flying Cloud*, built in Boston, entered the Golden Gate only 89 days after leaving New York. The clipper *Great Republic*, built in the same East Boston yard in 1853, was the largest ship in the world for many years.

The heyday of the clipper ships was brief, 1850–1855, when the lucrative California run paid for the high costs of building and maintenance, and the clippers' high freight rates had yet to feel the competition of the Panama Railroad, which was completed in 1855. But their effect was far-reaching. The speed of the clipper ships tightened the structural connection between the Eastern seaboard and the West Coast. They broke every record on every trade route around the world, remaining important throughout the 1850s on the Australia, China/Manila, and Cape Town runs. In an age of fast sailing ships, clippers helped to stimulate trade between California, Hawaii and Japan, which was first visited by Commodore Matthew Perry in 1853, and opened as a limited residence for U.S., English, French, Russian and Dutch merchants in 1859.

What is sometimes forgotten is that these sleek, powerful clippers also increased the isolation of the west coast of South America at this time. Bound direct for California from Cape Horn, they swung well out into the Pacific, harnessing the Trade Winds and crossing the Equator between 105°W and 125°W. "The Yankee clipper-ships dash by the ports," reported a U.S. Navy officer in Valparaíso in 1852; "it has already become as rare for ships to call, as it previously was for them to pass by."[45]

> Morison described the Yankee clipper-ship as being "stately as a cathedral, beautiful as a terraced cloud." Indeed it was, and a very New England-style of cathedral at that. Boston's 'cathedrals' were not the massive compression structures of medieval times, but towering complexities of compression and tension. Fully-rigged sailing ships, whatever the design, collected the compression loads into a small number of masts, and distributed the tensile forces through a complicated system of ropes and sails. The hull in turn had to be strong and rigid enough to withstand the pull of the rigging and the downward thrust of the mast.
>
> The structural technology behind all this was superb of its kind, noted one twentieth-century engineer . . . "the design of the rigging was ingenious, while the masts of the big sailing ships represented perhaps the most elaborate and certainly one of the most beautiful systems of trussed cantilever structure which has ever been developed."

Boston and the California hide trade

Boston's fur trade in the Northwest declined as 'Coasters' met increasing competition from the Hudson's Bay Company, Astor's American Fur Company, and the Russian-American Company, which had founded a settlement at Ross (short for Russia), some seventy miles north of San Francisco, in 1812. Boston began to switch its attention farther south, where the first Boston 'Coaster' had already appeared at Monterey, in Spain's Upper California, in 1795. This stretch of coastline from Catalina and the Channel Islands to Monterey Bay and the Farallones had become a smuggling base in the last phases of the Spanish empire, as well as a zone for poaching sea-otter and seal skins on this most remote and exposed fringe of New Spain. Trade expanded however after Mexico declared its independence in 1821 and opened the ports to foreign commerce in 1821–2.

The California market was now wide open to any merchants willing to service it. Mexico City could offer no funds to administer California, nor send in adequate supplies, since even the annual supply vessel from San Blas was unreliable. Californians continued to maintain a quasi-independent existence. "California holds hardly the relation of even a colony to Mexico," wrote Alexander Forbes from Tepic, the customs centre for San Blas, in 1835; "Mexico has more intercourse with China than with California."[46]

Within a few weeks of the legalizing of foreign trade, Boston's Bryant & Sturgis company had established their agent in Monterey, squeezing out initial competition from the English merchant house which had despatched a representative from Lima and contracted to buy cattle, hides and tallow from the California missions. This English initiative was short-lived. So too were the Russian initiatives, although Boston was keenly aware of the risk of competition. For in March 1822 José San Martín had reported to the Mexican authorities that:

> On July 23, last, the Russian frigate, *Centurion*, anchored in Monterey, proceeding from St. Petersburg with a cargo of goods . . . For this reason and because other Russian vessels have sold a quantity of goods in Monterey, the place is well supplied at prices with which those that our vessels bring from San Blas cannot compete . . .
>
> The Port of Bodega of the Russians is immediately north of the mission of San Francisco, and their garrison has always wished to extend more to the south; it is to be feared that under the present circumstances they may be more active about it.[47]

The speed and the force with which Boston's seaborne empire seized the California trade proved decisive. Although not the only Boston traders involved, Bryant & Sturgis alone were soon supplying two-thirds of California's imports, and were unbeatable in the range of New England manufactured goods—cloth, shoes, clothing, furniture, tools, cutlery, hardware, jewellery, luxury items, novelties, notions, as well as coffee, tea, sugar, and spirits—that were exchanged for hides, horn, and tallow. Not least among the assets of Bryant & Sturgis was their long-term resident agent in California, Alfred Robinson of Boston, whose ability and enterprise greatly enhanced the company's business reputation.[48]

Dana's classic account of his 1834–6 voyage from Boston to California and back in the *Pilgrim* revealed the brig as a typical Bryant & Sturgis floating department store: "assorted cargo, that is it consisted of everything under the sun."[49] Sales to the *pueblos*, the ranches, and the missions were organized by the company's resident agent, while in addition many parties of customers were rowed out to the ship. As Juan Bautista Alvarado (a native of Monterey and later Governor of California, 1836–42) observed, recalling the days "before Boston arrived":

> Although we had meat and wheat in California, we lacked chocolate, coffee, sugar, medicines, stockings, hats, dress shirts, porcelain, and a host of other articles which, through being of a daily use, are indispensable for rendering existence comfortable.[50]

Nowhere is Boston's role as the replacement supplier of merchandise to Spain's former empire better seen than in Spanish/Mexican California, which got most of its goods from Boston until mid-century.

Monterey remained the only legal initial port of entry for foreign vessels, which were fined if it was discovered that they had touched at any other port before entering Monterey and paying their duties. Direct initial entry into San Francisco remained forbidden by Mexico, although the Californian authorities were willing to sell special licences under certain conditions, and frequently ignored any Mexican law which conflicted with their own and other local interests. Whaling ships were also permitted to call and buy provisions, and allowed to sell small quantities of merchandise in order to do so. Whalers normally carried a few hundred dollars-worth of New England manufactured goods for the purpose. In general, port duties and other tariffs on foreign trade were left to finance virtually the whole of the costs of the Mexican government's outpost in California. They did so handsomely. Reporting in January 1846, U.S. Consul Thomas Larkin (from Massachusetts) noted that the *annual average* of duties received by the Californian authorities for the previous seven years amounted to US$85,985.[51]

Duties were payable at the Monterey Custom House before trading began, duties of one hundred per cent or even two hundred per cent which inevitably increased the smuggling activities elsewhere along the coast. Even so, it remained a highly profitable Yankee trade in the 1820s–1840s. Dana's vessel returned to Boston in 1836 with over 40,000 hides (which had been cured, dried and stacked in Bryant & Sturgis's own hide-houses on San Diego beach), together with 30,000 horns and several barrels of otter and beaver skins. Throughout the period, a cargo of 30,000–40,000 hides remained typical of a vessel's return voyage to Boston after two to three years' work up and down the coast. The California hide trade did not reduce hide imports from the River Plate and elsewhere since demand was soaring. California hides were cheap and plentiful however, and Boston merchants were determined to develop the seaborne California trade. Most of the tallow was shipped to Mexico and Lima after sale to local and U.S.-Hawaiian traders. In this, as in other commercial exchange, the Hawaiian Islands played a key role in New England's 'two-ocean' framework since they pegged the transpacific routes, and facilitated Boston's trading expansion around the whole of the Pacific Rim.

The word 'Boston' in fact had quickly become a synonym for the whole of the United States in Hawaii, as it did on the Northwest Coast and in California—a singular reminder of the huge range and strong identity of New England's seaborne empire, and of the wealth-creating contribution of the Boston region to the United States' tension structure as a whole.

* * *

Americans did not discover the Hawaiian islands, nor did they originate the fur trade, the China trade, the whaling industry, the hides and tallow trade, or missionary work in the Pacific. But New England enterprise expanded and developed all these activities. Before the start of the war with Mexico in 1846, and the Gold Rush to California after 1848, Boston's interests in the West Coast's resources and untapped potential had already rehearsed the advantages of acquiring it. For the West Coast was assessed in the first instance from the perspective of the Pacific Ocean, and thus stressed the importance of securing the *coast* and the *ports* in order to safeguard the United States' new maritime world.

So far as the 500-mile stretch from San Francisco to San Diego was concerned, it was the hide trade in particular that had led to Boston's economic annexation of California, and through its business and social contacts helped to prepare the way for political acquisition by the United States. For a well-defined movement for the annexation of California had been developing in the United States since the 1830s.[52] In response to the growing number of reports by seamen, trappers, travellers, and Americans residing in the province, enthusiasm for its climate and agricultural potential became more widespread, and organized *overland* immigration into California began in 1840–1. John Sutter, who had arrived in 1839 and settled on a huge Mexican land grant near the present site of Sacramento, became a focal point for newcomers to the Valley by developing an impressive range of farming, ranching, forestry, and fur-trading activities. Indeed in 1841, Sutter took over Fort Ross from the Russians. Additional new settlers arrived from Oregon, while others, having changed their minds *en route*, turned off the Oregon Trail and headed directly for California.

The overland movement was viewed "partly with alarm, partly with acquiesence" by the local government officials, but by 1844 the growth of an American population in California was for the moment being tolerated, even encouraged, by Mexico. Consul

Larkin reported from Monterey in 1844 that "while a few Americans come by sea, many now come by way of the Rocky Mountains." Three-quarters of all the foreigners in California were American, Larkin estimated in 1845, the other quarter dominantly British. "A person travelling from San Diego to San Francisco or Bodega can stop at a foreigner's farm house almost every few hours and travel without any knowledge of the Spanish language."[53]

By now, the United States had appointed an additional Vice-Consul at San Francisco. There was no local loyalty or sense of attachment to Mexico, Larkin informed the State Department. Nor could there be any question, he added, of California simply "being passed from one European power to another." The sale or transfer of California from Mexico to Britain, France or Russia would not be tolerated. The United States government needed no persuasion. Following the annexation of Texas in 1845, in 1846–8 the country acquired the Oregon region from Britain, and the California/Utah/New Mexico territories, and west Texas from Mexico—a huge territorial expansion greater even than the Louisiana Purchase in 1803. At the same time, the United States had gained an additional prize—the four key inlets of Juan de Fuca Strait/Puget Sound, the Columbia River, San Francisco Bay, and San Diego Bay that together pegged out the Pacific Coast strategy of President Polk's administration.

New England consolidates the United States' 'second' west coast

Nothing could demonstrate more clearly New England's adjustment to the United States' colossal westward expansion than the fact that the acquisition of California found its strongest popular support in the Northeast. And in California itself, as Robert Cleland noted, it was hard to find more than one or two resident Americans of any prominence in California at this time who were not of New England origin. From the period in the mid-1780s when fears of the growth of the trans-Alleghany West had raised doubts in New England about the survival of the United States' Federal structure, and certainly about New England's own future within it, the next few years had witnessed the region's firm grasp of the opportunities of continental scale and Pacific-based commerce.

Changing attitudes to scale and to risk had been pioneered by New England's own seaborne empire, stimulated by the need for silver, and by Spain's poor commercial performance. The Spanish empire had created cities, routeways, demand. New England could follow, overtake, enlarge. Moreover, it could do what Spain had never been able to achieve—New England could become the manufacturing workshop of its own empire.

The remarkable strength of New England was thus the *interlocking* of its interests, its quick response to new market opportunities, and the powerful support its merchant marine and whaling fleet received from New England's own shipbuilding and manufacturing base. Boston's sweep of the Pacific and the Pacific Rim had challenged earlier fears of isolation in an expanding Union, and shaped a new confident attitude to the trans-Mississippi West.

The diversification of New England's commerce and manufacturing had depended on the lengthening and strengthening of New England's maritime connections. These had stabilized and invigorated the region's internal economy in the first half of the nineteenth century. They had also given New England a vital role in strengthening the peripheral supporting towers, cables, end-fittings and anchorages of the Federal tension structure, which by 1850 stood on both the Atlantic and Pacific seaboards.

Senator Daniel Webster of Massachusetts, who had earlier declared that in terms of overland transport he would not "vote one cent to bring the Pacific nearer to Boston than it is now," was at mid-century welcoming the westward expansion of the United States as a glorious opportunity both for maritime and overland linkage. In March 1850 he exhorted the Senate:

> The United States has received a vast addition of territory. Large before, the country has now, by recent events, become vastly larger. This Republic now extends, with a vast breadth, across the whole continent. The two great seas of the world wash the one and the other shore.

United States enterprise could now be applied and realized "on a mighty scale ... Let our comprehension be as broad as the country for which we act, our aspirations as high as its certain destiny."[54]

15

The First Phase of Land Empire

> The early re-running of Spain's ocean site-lines by the northeastern United States fostered a global perception of commercial empire. But it was also a prelude to the building of strong overland tie-beams and well-braced spans to cope with growing tension and compression forces *within* the structure. Severe torsional stress and shear stress were added to the structure's existing tensile and compressive stresses and strains as loading and buffetting increased. During the first half of the nineteenth century, however, the 'live load' in the northeast and midwest interior was developing new building techniques and new trussing systems. As work progressed on the United States' tension structure, the North and West employed stronger cable suspension and more adaptable components that were of a markedly different design from those being developed in the less mobile, less urban, and less industrialized South.
>
> Despite the South's final demand in 1861 for separation from the Federal structure in order to build the looser, more flexible connections of a new Confederation of States, what the South had in fact produced were plans for a relatively small, multi-cellular *compression structure* since, for the time being, it lacked the skills, the components and the desire to build a genuine tension structure.

Spanning the Interior: The Problems of Diverging Styles of Construction, 1800–1860

> Listen! I will be honest with you,
> I do not offer the old smooth prizes, but offer rough new prizes,
> These are the days that must happen to you.
>
> (Walt Whitman, *Song of the Open Road*)

Building the great structural supporting towers at strategic points across the continent from the Atlantic to the Pacific had been a remarkably early phase of construction. Building work on the connecting spans, however—the intervening two-tiered decks of state and State—revealed that the people in the old, initially manageable Tidewater region were now constructing two highly contrasted western interiors.

Structural work in the North

The North's extraordinarily rapid economic growth after 1790 had produced an increasingly urbanized and industrialized economy based on manufacturing, trade, improved internal transport, and the dynamic growth of its own internal market. Although there were clear differences in the patterns of westward expansion through Appalachia between the northern and middle Tidewater States—particularly between those of New York State to the Great Lakes, and those of the Pennsylvania-Maryland-Ohio Valley routeways—both were combining to construct a distinctive *Northern* component linked to their merging trans-Appalachian Wests. As F.J. Turner observed in his influential study on the growth of nationalism and sectionalism in the United States in the 1820s:

> A flood of colonists was spreading along the waters of the west. In the Mississippi Valley the forests were falling before the blows of the pioneers, cities were developing where clearings had just let in the light of day, and new commonwealths were seeking outlets for their surplus and rising to industrial and political power. It is this vast development of the internal resources of the United States, the *Rise of the New West*, that gives the tone to the period . . .
> The nation was building an empire of its own, with sections which took the place of kingdoms.

After the highway initiatives taken by the turnpike companies in the 1790s–1820s, the need to insert a major overland tie within the tension structure culminated in the Federal government's National Road, the greatest road-building enterprise ever undertaken in the early years of the United States. Authorized by Congress in 1806 on a central axis, it was designed to link Baltimore and the Chesapeake–Potomac region to the West. The National Road (via Cumberland) reached Wheeling in 1818, Columbus, Ohio in 1833 and Vandalia, Illinois in 1850, although Congress (in 1834) had turned over its responsibility for the road's construction to the States.

Meanwhile, amid the insatiable demands for transport improvements in the North and West, numerous canal-building projects were undertaken to link, for example, Baltimore and Washington, D.C. to the Ohio Valley, Philadelphia to the Pennsylvanian anthracite fields, and the Hudson River to the Great Lakes. Other canals provided important cross-ties in the West between the Great Lakes and the Ohio River. "The whole design is destined to be the most extensive navigation system the hands of man have ever opened," reported Beaujour in 1814, assessing the vast continental lake-river-canal linkages already planned; "It means navigation into and through the very heart of the United States."[55] The spectacularly successful Erie Canal opened in 1825, while 500 miles farther west, the completion of Chicago's Illinois & Michigan Canal in 1848 marked the beginning of dramatic new growth in the Great Lakes–Mississippi River trade.

The great canal boom ended *c*.1850. In 1840, the United States had about 3,320 miles of canal and roughly the same length of railroad. But by 1860 the country had a railroad network of 30,600 miles, virtually all of it still east of the Mississippi. More significantly, well over two-thirds of the railroads were located in the North and West, where they now tied an extremely large and diversified mining and manufacturing region containing thousands of centres of highly specialized industrial and commercial activity. By mid-century, the manufacturing region straddled the Appalachian system from Southern New England and the Atlantic seaboard to the upper and middle Ohio Valley and the Great Lakes shores.

Integrated internal transport networks by road, river, canal, steamboat, and railroad had triggered the growth of service and handling centres, marketing and supply towns. Commercially isolated subsistence farmers, deprived of an urban outlet, were comparatively rare in the North and West. Subsistence was largely a temporary frontier condition, overcome as rapidly as transport to market could be improved. Transport projects dominated public works.

> **BASIC DESIGN CONSIDERATIONS**
>
> **Initial Form**
>
> **Maximum Use**
>
> **Minimum Weight**
>
> The problem with the concept of the "natural" flow of forces is that forces do not flow, other "naturally" or otherwise, until a solid object is interposed between the force and the foundation.
>
> When it is, the forces will certainly distribute themselves within it according to the law of minimum potential energy, *but this distribution will be entirely dependent on the initial form chosen for the member.*
>
> In addition, other criteria must be introduced:
>
> (i) *All material should be utilized close to its capacity.*
>
> (ii) *Minimum weight* should be achieved.
>
> (A. Holgate, *The Art in Structural Design*)

Structural problems in the South

A key structural feature at this time was the multiple linkage that the combined farming and manufacturing interests of the North had established with the South, i.e. that distinctive, though far from uniform, region lying roughly south of the Ohio–Potomac river line.

The South's 'live load'

In 1820, forty-six per cent of the total United States population of 9.6 millions lived in the South. By 1860, only thirty-five per cent of the U.S. total of 31.5 millions did so, and one-third of these were slaves. Indeed, in the Deep South slaves represented more than forty per cent (even up to eighty per cent in some districts) of the total population. Very little growth occurred through immigration. No other section of the United States' tension structure contained a 'live load' that, taken together, was so immobile, and so little invigorated, challenged or jolted by newcomers born outside the region.

Many colonial characteristics persisted, many had intensified, not least the South's lack of towns: "We have no townships," Jefferson had observed in discussing Virginia in the 1780s. "Our country being much intersected with navigable waters, and trade brought generally to our doors, instead of our being obliged to go in quest of it, has probably been one of the causes why we have no towns of any consequence." This overwhelmingly rural characteristic was aggravated by the fact that as plantations spread, many of them appropriated the typical 'small-town' services provided elsewhere by independent enterprise—the sawmill, brickyard, tannery, forge, chapel, schoolhouse, hotel, boarding-house, and regional store. The effect was to stunt, or even destroy, town growth.

Restricted circulation of the 'live load'

The South's extensive system of navigable waterways had maintained a heavy reliance on river transport. In 1860, as noted above, less than one-third of the United States' railroads were located in the South, where, as one study reported, the regional network was less developed than in any other area east of the Mississippi.[56] "Interconnections among the State-oriented railroad systems were so inadequate that most inter-State rail traffic had to move by indirect and roundabout routes." Railways were often regarded as individual port-city feeders only, and bedevilled by gauge variations, "in part reflecting a failure to appreciate the future of the railroad as a means for the long-distance transportation of freight and passengers . . . Not only were the southern railroads largely without internal integration," observed Taylor and Neu, "but they were also completely without direct rail connections with any other part of the nation. The lack of bridges over the Mississippi proved a barrier to the West as the unbridged Ohio River did to the North. Even in northern Virginia, where the gauges were the same as in Maryland, there was not a single direct connection with northern railroads, for at Alexandria and Aquia Creek the only means of transferring either goods or passengers was by steamboat."[57]

Apart from the lack of railroad bridges across the Ohio River (the first was at Steubenville in 1862–3), there was only *one* point along the entire length of the Ohio at which any significant length of Southern railroad touched the river bank opposite the Northern rail net. This was at Louisville, Kentucky (on 5ft gauge), which faced New Albany–Jeffersonville, Indiana (on standard gauge).

Although the Northern railroads were not all of uniform gauge, the early adoption of standard gauge by the major companies, including the Baltimore & Ohio, Pennsylvania, New York Central, and Illinois Central, had given an unrivalled speed and flexibility to *long-distance, through rail transport* in the North and Midwest—a structural tie of immense significance, since the railroad was eventually to triumph over all competing forms of transport. Turnpikes, canals, steamboats, and railroads had all been employed as man-made components on the United States' tension structure in order to stimulate and speed the overland movement of the 'live load'— people, goods, and services. None save the steamboat had made much impact in the South, and even that was on the region's periphery.

The popular image of stern-wheelers and side-wheelers busily plying the waterways of the South concealed the fact that many of South's rivers were useless for reliable, year-round, long-distance navigation. The 600-mile Tennessee River, for example, was characterized by rocky shoals, unpredictable currents and disastrous flooding which greatly reduced its value for transportation. Steamboats had been introduced on the Tennessee River in 1821, but they were designed for deep rivers like the Mississippi and at best could only be used effectively on short stretches of the Tennessee for a few weeks in the year. Although the Cumberland River was less hazardous, the South never contained any 'river-road' connection with the Mississippi to rival the Ohio.

While many of the transport initiatives in the North had been State-funded with Federal assistance, or privately sponsored by townsfolk, farmers or business enterprise, no part of the United States stood in greater need of *Federal* capital to provide internal improvements than the South. But little support for such projects came from this section.

The Economy of the South: conflicting objectives.
The 'live-load' becomes increasingly unskilled in building the tension structure

In the immediate post-War of Independence period, tobacco had quickly resumed its old dominance of the American export trade, providing about one-third of the exports by value. But between

1790–1814, the traditional mainstays of the colonial export trade, tobacco and rice, made little growth. Indeed, the plantation system itself had begun to decline before cotton gave it a new lease of life. Eli Whitney's invention of the cotton gin in 1793 revolutionized production. By 1800, the country's annual cotton crop had increased from 5 to 35 million lbs; by 1805 it had doubled to 70 million lbs, and in 1820–25 risen from 160 to 300 million lbs. The cultivation of cotton swept through the Southeast, ousting earlier sources of raw cotton in the English and French markets, and becoming by 1814 nearly half of the United States' export trade by value.

Cotton: the 'Spanish silver' of the Deep South

The South had now become committed to cotton, and the wealthiest elements of the 'live load' to heavy capital investment in slaves, land, and property. Cotton production boomed in the 1830s and with it came clearer evidence of the emergence of a major design problem in the United States' tension structure. For while raw cotton export had now become the country's most profitable single item of overseas trade, the wealth flowing back to the South from cotton exports (supplemented by rice, sugar and tobacco exports) flowed out again almost immediately to pay for imported domestic and foreign manufactured goods. Writing from Mobile in 1854, one Northerner reported: "A friend informed me that he found it cheaper to have all his furniture and clothing made for him, in New York, to order, when he needed any, and sent on by express, than to get it in Mobile." Textiles, tools, machinery, furnishings, and a wide range of luxury items were purchased from the Northeast, and as more land was put under cotton, increasing quantities of both the food and fodder needed by the South were bought from farmers in the Ohio Valley and the new Midwest.

Re-enacting Spain's Portobello trade fair: The South's merchants go North for supplies

Awareness of "a backward and tributary South" was not confined to Northern critics. H.R. Helper of North Carolina published a detailed analysis of the scale of the South's dependence in *The Impending Crisis of the South* in 1857:

> The North is the Mecca of our merchants, and to it they must, and do, make two pilgrimages per annum—one in the spring and one

in the fall. All our commercial, mechanical, manufactural, and literary supplies come from there. We want Bibles, brooms, buckets and books, and we go to the North; we want pens, ink, paper and envelopes, and we go to the North; we want furniture, crockery, glassware and pianos, and we go to the North; we want toys, primers, school books, fashionable apparel, machinery, medicines, tombstones, and a thousand other things, and we go to the North for them all.

Instead of keeping our money in circulation at home, by patronizing our own mechanics, manufacturers, and laborers, we send it all away to the North, and there it remains; it never falls into our hands again.[58]

Northern ships, particularly those registered in Massachusetts and New York were now the main carriers of the South's import and export trade. Charleston declined dramatically as a major port after 1830, its hinterland market too small to make it a gateway port for foreign ships. Since coastwise trading was effectively restricted to U.S. vessels, New York's superb natural harbour, together with its large fleet of intra-coastal freighters, attracted many transatlantic shippers. New York and Boston, with Philadelphia and Baltimore, dominated the re-export trade. In the South, only New Orleans expanded as a port after steam navigation had been introduced on the Mississippi River in 1811, allowing the Delta to become tied efficiently for the first time to the markets and producers upstream.

After 1840, however, New Orleans dropped steadily down the ranking of United States cities. New York, not New Orleans, became the great entrepôt of the South, while New York also became the financial centre for the cotton trade itself. Northern ships carried over ninety per cent of the South's merchandise, Northern companies insured it, Northern agents traded it, and Northern banks and venture capital financed the South's plantation expansion.

After 1815, therefore, the three regions of the Northeast, the West, and the South became increasingly distinct even if it was difficult to draw their boundaries precisely. The Northeast and the West were becoming more closely meshed with each other, while at the same time each could profitably service the South on different tracks. The borderland States of Maryland and Delaware were more closely associated with the North, those of western Virginia, Kentucky and Missouri more with the West. But inside this border zone, the Lower or Deep South fell further behind, neither marketing its own exports nor providing the consumer goods and services to supply its own needs. "Southern money just keeps draining North," observed *De Bow's Review*, "into Northern railroads and hotels, Northern merchants and shop-keepers, Northern shippers and insurers, and Northern theatres, newspapers and periodicals."

The South's cotton, like the silver of imperial Spain, was financing and twirling huge regional and transatlantic trade circulations without introducing genuine growth or change within the South itself. The United States economy as a whole would not have declined, or even stagnated, without the cotton *bonanza*, but the boost the economy received was undeniable. And certainly between 1820 and 1843, the cotton trade was the prime mover in quickening the pace of U.S. growth. Overseas demand for high quality raw cotton soared dramatically, and in the period between 1815 and 1860 cotton on average continued to represent half the value of the United States total exports. The figures fluctuated, varying between thirty-nine per cent by value in 1816–20, sixty-three per cent in 1836–40, and despite lower prices in the 1840s, over fifty per cent in 1840–60.

Under these conditions, cotton production and slaveholding moved steadily westward onto the Black Belt soils of Alabama, expanded along the Mississippi and the Yazoo Bottoms, and finally advanced into east Texas. The availability of new land to the West had widened what were really discrete zones of more concentrated cotton production, to create a generalized, and often misleadingly labelled region known as the "Cotton Belt". Within this region, cotton was the export staple but never the greatest acreage. Moreover, ever since the 1830s, high prices for cotton and the availability of new land had helped to mask the problems of low productivity, deforestation and soil erosion.

North and South: progress reports on building work and the shock of the U.S. Census statistics, 1850 and 1860

In the widely-read account of his travels through the South in the 1850s, F.L. Olmsted, farming in New York State, found "in the so-called cotton States much more evidence of waste land, forest, and poor corn smothered in weeds . . . The natural resources of the land were strangely unused, or were used with poor economy."[59] There was so much stillness, so little mobility, in the South:

> If all the wealth produced in a certain district is concentrated in the hands of a few men living remote from each other, it may possibly bring to the district comfortable houses, good servants, fine wines,

food and furniture, tutors and governesses, horses and carriages, for these few men, but it will not bring thither good roads and bridges, it will not bring thither such means of education and of civilized comfort as are to be drawn from libraries, churches, museums, gardens, theatres, and assembly rooms; it will not bring thither local newspapers, telegraphs, and so on . . . It will not bring well-constituted communities.[60]

In a period of mid-century stock-taking and reflection, the Seventh Census of the United States in 1850 presented the South with an unwelcome, and often shocking review of the structural state of the Union. The statistics jolted the analysts, in particular the detailed comparisons which revealed the outstanding agricultural productivity of the North and West. "Until we examined into the matter," wrote Helper, "we thought and hoped the South was really ahead of the North in *one* particular, that of agriculture." But the North's range of agricultural produce, together with the sheer productivity and value of the many small farms in the Free States, was overwhelming. "New York State alone produces more than *three times* the quantity of hay that is produced in all the slave States . . . With regard to agriculture, cotton has been shorn of its magic power, and is no longer King; *dried grass*, commonly called hay, is, it seems, the rightful heir to the throne."[61]

The part played in this "humiliating" report by the South's retention of slavery was of course fiercely debated. Despite their representative regional image for those outside the South, very large plantation owners and slaveholders were in a minority, though a very influential minority. In 1850, Virginia had the largest slave population of any State in the Union—472,528. With 894,800 white citizens, there were only 55,000 slaveholders (just six per cent of the white population), and of these more than half owned fewer than five slaves. Reporting this and other facts in his analysis of the 1850 Census, Daniel Goodloe of North Carolina, like Helper, identified slavery as the great obstacle to progress for both white and black: "For myself, though a Southern man, I am opposed to slavery. I have seen its effects in retarding the prosperity of my native State and of the whole South." The "real practical questions," he argued, were essentially structural. Slavery restricted the growth of cities and towns, held down land values, stifled commerce, manufacturing, and internal improvements, absorbed capital investment unproductively, and retarded general education.[62]

Paradoxically, the majority of white Southerners in the 'slave-owning South' owned no slaves at all. But in contrast with the

North, this reflected the fact that most of them lived *outside* the market economy in a perpetual 'frontier' condition. As the 1860 Census confirmed, while Virginia, South Carolina, Georgia, Alabama, Mississippi, North Carolina, and Louisiana (in that order) contained the largest slave populations in the 1850s, thousands of isolated subsistence farmers were scattered across the South—from Appalachia and Florida in the east, to the Ozark mountains of Missouri and Arkansas in the trans-Mississippi west.

Loosening the structural connections between North and South

The *dependence* of the Northeast and West (Northwest) on the South was already waning by the late 1840s. The rapid increase in immigration to the cities of the Northeast, the surge in the Northeast's mining and manufacturing, and the growth of fast trans-Appalachian rail communication, enabled Western farmers to send produce to the eastern seaboard markets, as well as to the Pennsylvania coal, iron and steel centres, to Chicago, and to other Great Lakes ports. Even on the Erie Canal, the late 1840s marked a significant point in the canal's history as *east-bound* cargoes of wheat, flour, cheese, meat, wool and lumber for the first time surpassed the total volume of west-bound traffic from New York State—mainly emigrants, furniture, tools, and general merchandise.

By 1860, New York and Brooklyn together contained well over 1 million, while Philadelphia had reached 566,000, having more than doubled since 1840. Baltimore's population was 212,000, Boston's 178,000. While these eastern seaboard port-cities remained trade-orientated, they had also developed a substantial manufacturing base. The Ohio River had earlier made Cincinnati the first metropolis in the West, and in 1860 (with a population of 161,000) it was still the largest city west of the Alleghenies and north of New Orleans (whose population was then 169,000). Chicago's explosive growth as a canal, railroad and lake port had already reached 110,000 by 1860. As cities, towns and manufacturing centres in the Northeast sucked in European immigrants and American migrants, the region became both a major domestic market for manufactured goods and a huge food-deficit area, particularly as much of the region's marginal agricultural land went out of production in the face of western competition.

Thus, while from 1815 to the mid-1840s, the South had been the *primary* market for farmers west of the Appalachians, a market supplemented by the export of foodstuffs through New Orleans to the West Indies, South America and the USA's eastern seaboard, in the late 1840s and 1850s the main direction of the North's interior trade began to shift dramatically to an east-west axis. In the Far West, California was becoming a major market for the Northeast's manufactured goods and services, including much New England–New York venture capital. The California trade, as noted earlier, also stimulated both shipbuilding and shipping companies on the northeastern seaboard, since trade to San Francisco was 'coastwise' trade, and therefore restricted to United States vessels.

The importance of economy and adaptability in structural design

> **TRUSSING**
>
> Of course the longest span bridges are suspension bridges, but the accompanying need for innumerable bridges of shorter span led to the widespread development of timber- and metal-truss bridges in America during the 19th century.
>
> In particular, there was a very active requirement in the United States for long—and cheap—wooden trusses, which could be made by ordinary joiners. Since the construction of these trusses was potentially profitable and since the Americans are an incurably inventive people, a very considerable number of nineteenth-century Americans seem to have spent their time in *inventing trusses*.
>
> A trussed girder is frequently used in bridge design *where the load is constantly moving*.
>
> Trusses can in fact be found in many possible configurations depending on the functional requirements of the building shape and bridge span . . .
>
> One important property is their *adaptability*—the opportunity to change the direction of the diagonals so that they can act either as tension members or as compression members, i.e. as ties or as struts.
>
> > (W. Morgan, *The Elements of Structure*)
> >
> > (J.E. Gordon, *Structures*)
> >
> > (W.T. Marshall and H.M. Nelson, *Structures*)
> >
> > (W.R. Spillers, *Introduction to Structures*)

TRUSSING

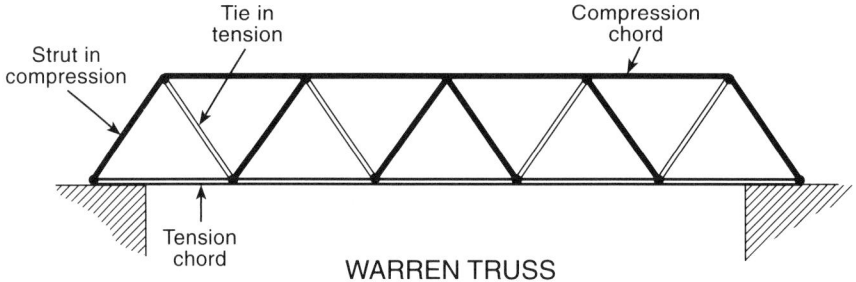

WARREN TRUSS

For bridging gaps, a solid beam could often be replaced by a lattice composed of shorter lengths jointed together in a correctly triangulated pattern. This is a TRUSS - an open web of rigid triangles, where components can be variously assembled to take compression or tension. Economy in weight and cost, basic strength and stability, and the adaptability of the components in construction, were vital advantages. The 1840s marked the beginning of a major expansion in the design and use of truss bridges in the United States.

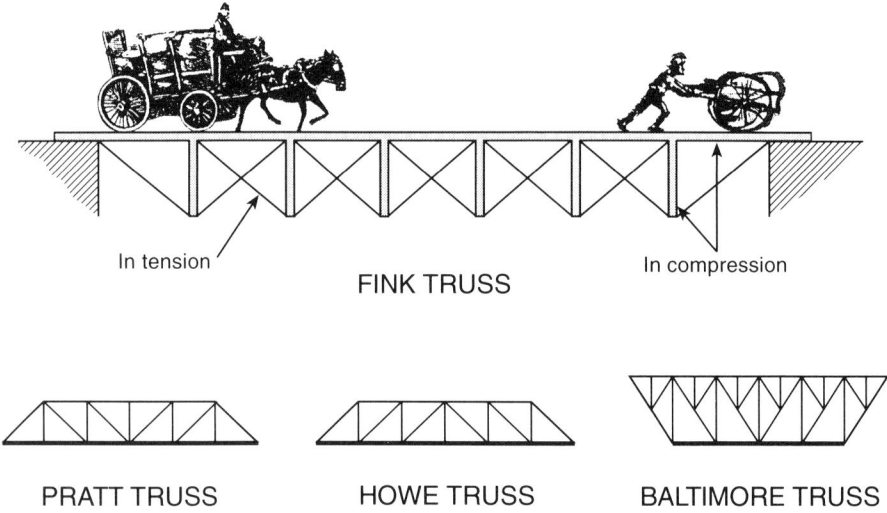

FINK TRUSS

PRATT TRUSS   HOWE TRUSS   BALTIMORE TRUSS

Innovation, speed of construction, the versatile use of components, and the ability to make local modifications on site, characterized both bridge building and strong regional economic development by the mid-19th century, most notably in the North and the West.

Figure C. Nineteenth-Century Truss Bridges in the United States

HUDSON RIVER BRIDGE
Albany N.Y., 1870-71

THE NEW UNION PACIFIC RAILROAD BRIDGE AND THE OLD WAGON ROAD BRIDGE,
Eagle Rock (Idaho Falls), Snake River, Idaho, 1878

ANIMAS RIVER CANYON,
near Silverton, Colorado, 1881

BROWN'S CANYON,
Arkansas River, near Leadville,
Colorado, 1880

**THE CENTRAL PACIFIC RAILROAD'S ARCH-
BRACED HOWE TRUSS BRIDGE,**
Truckee River, Nevada, 1868

**Figure C.   Examples of Nineteenth-Century
Truss Bridges in the United States**

> ## THE IMPORTANCE OF STRENGTHENING THE SUSPENSION SYSTEM
>
> ### IMPROVED TRUSSING TECHNIQUES MATCHED BY IMPROVEMENTS TO CABLES AND HANGERS
>
> During the first half of the nineteenth century, the North was showing greater flair (and greater need) than the South for improved trussing in a period of turbulent growth. In addition, through its diversification and development of manufacturing, agriculture, commerce, and transportation, the North was also making rapid advances in strengthening the major components of the suspension system, including the HANGERS which attached the bridge decks to the MAIN SUSPENSION CABLES.
>
> The mid-nineteenth century saw revolutionary developments in the engineering of steel cables, soon to be adopted in suspension bridge construction. *The early chains, their links made of flat iron bars, were now being replaced by thicker, tougher, multi-strand cables, spun on site*, and capable of resisting huge tensile force as the 'live load' crowded the decks and strained against the overhead suspension.

The Northeast, Northcentre (Northwest) and Far West were both integrating and diversifying their interests—decreasing their dependence on the South while increasing their interdependence on each other. Cotton still remained the United States' most important single export commodity, but whereas in the North cotton had helped to construct a variety of interchangeable components, increasingly versatile in their contribution to a well-braced, well-tied industrial economy, in the South cotton and slavery had helped to weaken the region's ability to maintain the Federal tension structure. Visitors from the North were often surprised by the rigid *classification* of workers in the South, not only among the slaves where it had originated, but as a widespread and extremely limiting characteristic of the white population also. There was little evidence of adaptability—apparently neither expectation nor will "to turn your hand to anything while bettering your circumstances."

Inside that outer tier of border States which was more closely jointed to the North and West, the South found itself gradually loosening and dismantling the connections to the Federal tension structure, partly from choice, partly from shortage of construction workers. There was increasing incompatibility of design. Despite the claim in 1861 that the Confederation of Southern States restored the more flexible design principles of the old Antifederalists with the rallying cry: "the Federal Government shall never interfere with the domestic institutions of the States," the South in reality had built a series of compression structures whose formidable 'dead load' was the great weight of the structure itself. Indeed, $c.3.9$ million slaves, well over one-third of the South's 'live load', were classed as property and structurally therefore formed part of the South's 'dead load'. More than any other part of the United States, the South exemplified the principle that all structures have weight, and their own weight is one of the loads that they have to carry.

Strain energy and Fracture energy

> **It is a fact of life that it is not possible to predict the strength of any material or structure with absolute accuracy until it has been tested to destruction.**
>
> (A.G. Smyrell, *Design of Structural Elements*)

As early as 1832, the South Carolinian Convention had voted to nullify the tariff which protected Northern manufactured goods. A Federal Constitutional power that permitted Congress to enact a protective tariff, it was argued amid a discussion of general principle, could also be used to free the slaves. But in 1832 no other Southern State supported South Carolina's action, and some outspokenly condemned it. South Carolina retreated on the issue in February 1833 and rescinded Nullification after a compromise reduction on the tariff had been agreed. **Strain energy had been converted to fracture energy, but this had been contained within the structure as a 'safe crack'.** South Carolina, for its part, had learned that although it had become a focus of anti-Unionism, the sentiment was not yet widespread through the South as a whole. The 'safe crack' had to be extended:

> **When a solid is broken in tension, at least one crack must be made to spread right across the material, so as to divide it into two parts.**
>
> (J.E. Gordon, *Structures*)

The growth of Sectionalism in the South, particularly during the 1850s, is well documented. The South complained that its views would always be dismissed as *sectional*, while the sectional interests of the North were described as *Unionist and national*. The fact that the South had become a permanent minority by mid-century reflected the contrasted demographic and economic history of the northern and southern United States after 1790. It also underlined the South's sense of urgency to expand into the West on to what remained of the territories acquired from Mexico in the 1840s, particularly after California had entered the Union as a Free State in 1850.

Although the issue of slavery was central in the move to secession, the principles involved were more complex. A deep sense of the need to preserve a 'regional' identity, strengthened by fear and envy of the North, was often decisive. Were the issues moral or economic? Were opportunities for the white working class severely curtailed by slavery? Was slavery itself a wasteful use of financial resources? Slaveholders in any case were in a minority, and even here, support for secession was far from unanimous—whether through a genuine belief in the principles of Federal Union or because of the certainty that the South could not win. **In 1860–61**, however, **the 'safe crack' widened to a length of nearly 2000 miles**. This time, the secession of South Carolina in December 1860 (after Lincoln's election in November) was followed by Mississippi, Florida, Alabama, Georgia, Louisiana and Texas in January-February 1861, and by Virginia, Tennessee, Arkansas, and North Carolina in April–May 1861, after Lincoln had made clear in his proclamation of 15 April that secession would be resisted by force.

Pseudo-flexibility and underlying compression—the basic design weakness in the South's Confederate structure

The Constitution of the Confederate States of America approved in Montgomery, Alabama, 11 March 1861, closely resembled the wording of the U.S. Constitution in many of its articles. The preamble however replaced the Federal purpose in 1787 "to form a more perfect Union" with the declaration that the Confederacy now comprised "each State acting in its sovereign and independent character." A crucial section stipulated that "the Confederate States may acquire new territory . . . In all such territory, the institution of negro slavery, as it now exists in the Confederate States, shall be recognized and protected by Congress and by the territorial government; and the inhabitants of the several Confederate States and Territories shall have the right to take to such territory any slaves lawfully held by them."

The Constitution authorized Congressional taxes "to pay debts, provide for the common defence, and carry on the Government of the Confederate States," but no duties or taxes were to be made on foreign imports in order "to promote or foster any branch of industry."

Neither was there to be any delegation of power to Congress "to appropriate money for any internal improvement intended to facilitate commerce," the only exception being funds to improve *river and coastal navigation*—a significant emphasis on the most important transport mode in the Confederate South.

In its key changes, the Constitution of the Confederate States was an extraordinarily dated document for mid-nineteenth-century America—naive and anachronistic, quite apart from its grim determination to maintain and extend the institution of slavery. Indeed, as a structural blueprint it was medieval in character, for alongside the setting up of an association of small independent sovereign states, there was a basic reassertion of the principles of compression, and the elimination of the oblique thrusts of change, all of which would have been recognizable to imperial Spain.

President Lincoln's first Inaugural Address on 4 March 1861 was to emphasize the structural as well as the legal and historical aspects of Union:

> Physically speaking, we cannot separate. We cannot remove our respective sections from each other, nor build an impassable wall between them.

"No State upon its own mere motion can lawfully get out of the Union," Lincoln reasoned, particularly as the running cracks, once started, could lead to further fracture: "a portion of a new confederacy may secede again."

This would almost certainly have occurred since the South no longer had any aptitude for managing strong tensile or torsional stress. The eleven State compression structures were linked together less effectively than any of them appeared to recognize, or at least was prepared to admit; with limited infrastructure, and low immigration and investment levels, the South could not have resisted the stresses and strains generated by further expansion into the trans-Mississippi West, to say nothing of the dangers of weakening still further the joints between the Upper and Lower South. Although the South claimed in effect to see the Confederated States as the ultimate tension structure, a successfully engineered tension structure must be *kept* under tension at all times. The economy and society of the South, however, promoted neither tension nor risk. The Confederacy was no more than an idealized tension structure, crafted unskilfully by Southerners who by now were more comfortable in practice with hierarchical, compressive design at State level.

Destruction and Reconstruction

The Confederate structure as such was short-lived. It was built under war-time conditions which ironically at once reduced States' rights and demanded more centralized organization. Given the nature of the *Federal* tension structure, the North was able to increase centralized compressive force; the South resisted it. The Union taxed its citizens more; the Confederacy had to rely heavily on borrowing and on the issue of paper money.

The Confederacy was tested to destruction in four years. Even so, neither side had anticipated how long and how costly the conflict would be. The majority of men in the Union forces (over two millions) had never seen the South before; the majority of Confederate soldiers (about one million) were moved around the South they were fighting for with totally unaccustomed mobility. All who survived experienced a new awareness of the sheer size of the eastern United States.

While the South formed the main battleground, the North continued to design and build the Federal tension structure during the Civil War. The Emancipation Proclamation of 1863 guaranteed an end to the institution of slavery after the War was won. Northern manufacturing industries (already four-fifths of the Union's total), were greatly stimulated by war, as was agriculture. Indeed, desperately-needed Northern foodstuffs, clothing and medical supplies, were bought by the South, and paid for with smuggled cotton.

The North retained the structural initiatives in the West. The Homestead Act (1862), with its opportunities of virtually free quarter-section (160-acre) land ownership for existing and future United States citizens, was restricted to those "who had never borne arms against the United States Government, or given aid and comfort to its enemies." The Pacific Railroad Act (1862), authorizing the construction of the Union Pacific-Central Pacific Railroad, heralded a vast new building program in the post-war period. And after Indian attacks on stage lines, supply posts and ranches increased in 1862 following the recall of army units from the Western forts, Congress again sent troops to enlarge key forts, and to protect vulnerable sections of the trails to Oregon, Montana, California and New Mexico, thereby encouraging Unionist emigrants to continue to move west. The Emigrant Overland Escort Service had been introduced by Congress in 1861, and annual appropriations of $25,000 to $50,000 continued throughout the Civil War, with allotments made for escorts along specific routes within the trans-Mississippi West.[63]

The continuing significance of the Mississippi tie

The vital structural importance to the Union of the Mississippi River revived sentiments reminiscent of the 1780s. Then, Spain had blocked the way by depriving the United States of free navigation on the waterway, and by its ownership of the whole of the Gulf coast. After 1861, the North was to be constantly reminded that the Mississippi had been the first margin of empire, and that again, the Lower Mississippi was in "foreign hands", this time Confederate hands. As the editor of *Harper's New Monthly Magazine* observed:

> A map of the Valley asserts to the eye what facts unfold to the reason, that this river system is the vital channel of the organic life of the region. To dismember it is death. Never while the world stands can the people of the Upper Valley consent to have the custody of the mouth of the river in foreign hands.

The need to preserve the political unity of the Mississippi basin was already one of the fundamental structural realities of the United States that Lincoln himself had stressed. In his Annual Message to Congress on 1 December 1862, he considered the dire geographical consequences for the Union's heartland if it was to be confined to the middle and upper Mississippi Valley:

> A glance at the map shows that, territorially speaking, it is the great body of the Republic . . . This great interior is naturally one of the most important in the world . . . yet this region has no sea-coast, touches no ocean anywhere . . .
>
> *Wherever* a dividing, or boundary line, may be fixed . . . still the truth remains, that none south of it can trade to any port or place north of it, and none north of it can trade to any port or place south

of it, except upon terms dictated by a government foreign to them ...
The people inhabiting, and to inhabit, this vast interior region ...
will not ask *where* a line of separation shall be, but will vow, rather,
that there shall be no such line.

In fact, the 'Message of the Mississippi' had never been silenced since independence. Every decade it had gained new force, new messengers, new conviction. By the 1840s, with the annexation of Texas and the huge expansion into the Far West, the role of the Mississippi was again as prominent in Congressional debates as it had been in the late eighteenth century. As John Hardin of Illinois emphasized in January 1845, voicing the "especial interest of the Northwest":

> We purchase our goods in the East, and find there a market for much of our produce; and we cannot, therefore, consent that the East should be separated from us. But the great natural outlet for our commerce is the Mississippi river; and let me tell southern gentlemen who have pictured in their imagination that El Dorado—a southern confederacy—that the free States situate on the Ohio and Mississippi will never permit the mouth of that river to belong to any other government than their own. And should an overruling God ever inflict the curse of the dissolution of this Union upon us, by means of this Texas or any other question, the southern confederacy will have to be formed wholly east of the Mississippi; for not all the united chivalry of the South would ever be able to hold it against the combined forces which would be concentrated to open that great outlet of our commerce.[64]

Even New England was now "ready to admit, and compelled to admit" the huge economic potential of the Mississippi Valley. "Can anybody suppose," asked Daniel Webster of Massachusetts, "that this population [north of the river Ohio] can be severed by a line that divides them from the territory of a foreign and an alien government, down somewhere, the Lord knows where, upon the lower banks of the Mississippi?"[65]

In 1862, Federal gunboats ascended the Mississippi and captured New Orleans. After Grant finally captured Vicksburg in July 1863, the Mississippi lay effectively in Northern hands and the South was cut in two.

The Civil War had highlighted the fact that, for the most part, the cities of the South, like the transportation system, were located on the perimeter of the region—a characteristic of the Spanish American empire also, whose major distributing and service centres lay round its edge. The

inertia of much of the interior was to remain one of the persistent structural weaknesses in the southeastern United States, associated as it was with an already weak transport infrastructure made worse by war, and with very low levels of manufacturing and immigration.

* * *

The North's Radical Reconstruction of the South began in 1867, and military intervention by the North in the South's political affairs lasted until 1877. For all the bitterness and humiliation that marked the decade of military and civil 'Reconstruction' in the South, the immediate post-Civil War period had much in common with the post-Revolutionary War reaction to Empire Loyalists in the 1780s. For the same basic reasons (page 148), *official* Northern attitudes to the losers were pragmatic rather than punitive. The need to get the Federal structure back in shape and full working order demanded new oaths of allegiance to the Constitution from the defeated States (including allegiance to the Fourteenth Amendment), but there was no widespread move to reduce their authority by territorial subdivision; even South Carolina escaped such retribution, which would in any case have disturbed the voting balance in Congress. In the event, only West Virginia, a consistently staunch area of Union support, acquired separate Statehood (in 1863), and between 1866 and 1870, the eleven States of the Southern Confederacy rejoined the Union.

But the problems of the Southeast in particular—the Deep South—were daunting. Racial segregation, racial discrimination, 'White Supremacy', and the subsequent disfranchisement of Black voters, became the means of increasing compressive, not tensile, force. For the next hundred years, a defeated White generation and its most politically active followers **clung to the medieval structural principles of 'risk reduction'**, wasting both its time and the energies of its potentially productive 'live load'—Black and White—in pursuit of the 'Lost Cause' of the Southern Confederacy. **In the United States' tension structure as a whole, the basic design principles were based on the productive management of increased risk and increased tension in society,** and for this, the more urgent post-war building program became focused on the trans-Mississippi West.

The Civil War has been called "the least avoidable of the great mass-conflicts of history up to that time." It certainly demanded a closer analysis and restatement of the building and maintenance principles underlying the Federal tension structure, and demonstrated by force key points in the construction of the Union which had been implicit rather than explicit in the Constitution until then. **It was now clear that so far as the territorial components and the citizens (though not necessarily all the occupants) of the tension structure were concerned, the request to become an integral part of the structure was voluntary, but that once built into the framework's span, the demand to leave it again was not. The tension structure's spatial design, and the continuous balancing of tensile and compressive forces, involved the structure as a whole, and as a whole, it would stand or collapse.** Now with the need to extend the bridging spans to the Pacific, where the great supporting towers were already in place, a major expansion in the numbers and energy of the United States' 'live load' was required. There would be new linkage between the North and the West, but a frequent by-passing of the Southeast in its long, tragic struggle to rebuild.

FROM FINLEY TO ROEBLING

After James Finley's invention in Pennsylvania of the first stiffened suspension bridge c.1796, the **STIFFENED ROADWAY** remained the indispensable feature of modern long-span suspension bridges.

The advantages of the design encouraged others to develop it. In the 1840s and 1850s, John A. Roebling began working in Pennsylvania and New York, adding **RADIATING CABLE-STAYS** from the towers to the decks to strengthen his bridges and to stabilize them against the wind. Stays and counterstays, as well as **STIFFENING GIRDERS**, would be part and parcel of all his bridges. Indeed, Roebling's innovative addition of cable-stays to his suspension bridges had a lasting influence on bridge design. His two-decked suspension bridge at Niagara, strongly trussed and stayed, was completed in 1855. His design for the Brooklyn Bridge (completed by his son and opened in 1883) included the world's first use of **STEEL CABLES** for suspension bridge construction.

The strengthening of the suspension bridge permitted longer spans and heavier loading. The importance of the **SUPPORTING TOWERS** and the **CABLE ANCHORAGES** remained crucial.

16

The Extension of Land Empire in the Trans-Mississippi West

1. New Structural Engineering in the Trans-Mississippi West
Strengthening the Foundations and the Supports
Stiffening the Spans, and Toughening the Surfaces

Post-Civil War construction (and reconstruction) was designed to strengthen the framework of the United States' tension structure, particularly since this construction phase coincided with a major expansion of the 'live load' into the trans-Mississippi West.

The Spanish periphery still exerted influence on the American ground-plan. Early site-lines in the form of trails to Texas, New Mexico, and California had linked the Mississippi to the fringes of the Spanish–Mexican empire during the early nineteenth century, but these connections were inadequate for heavier loads and heavier traffic. Stronger, reinforced beams were built across the West in the form of Federally constructed wagon roads, and these in turn were soon replaced or augmented by Federally assisted railroads which tied the Pacific coast to the Mississippi 'coast', and so to the Atlantic seaboard. In an intensively active period of new building and internal growth, the *foundations*, *supports*, and *suspension* of the United States' tension structure were all greatly strengthened by Federal government action as the huge two-tiered span of state and State was finally completed across the trans-Mississippi West.

Setting out the Ground-Plan

It has been supposed by some that all settlers who go beyond the Mississippi, will be forever lost to the United States. There is, I believe, little danger of this, provided they are not provoked to withdraw their friendship. The emigrants will be made up of citizens of the United States. They will carry along with them their manners and customs, their habits of government, religion and education . . . they will be Americans in fact, though nominally the subjects of Spain . . .

Besides, we cannot but anticipate the period as not far distant when the AMERICAN EMPIRE will comprehend millions of souls west of the Mississippi. Judging upon probable grounds, the Mississippi was never designed as the western boundary of the American empire.

(Jedidiah Morse, *The American Geography*,
1st publ. Elizabeth-Town, N.J. and Boston, 1789)

The first American site-line and overland tie to the Spanish Southwest

Before the overland trails to Oregon and California were established in the 1840s, the trail to Santa Fe, New Mexico had drawn American traders towards a market whose focus was located even farther south in the silver-mining centres of Chihuahua and Zacatecas. The silver resources and commercial challenge presented by the Spanish empire in the Southwest involved great risk—a long, arduous journey of some 800 miles from the central Mississippi Valley to the upper Río Grande—but the stimulus it provided, and the basic American response to new business opportunity, matched that of the sea-going traders. While New England's merchant seamen circled the maritime perimeter of the Spanish empire and its successor states, the Santa Fe Trail provided a slender overland tie—a land voyage to New Mexico and its 'port' in the mountains. Indeed, the regular designation of Santa Fe as a 'port' had carried the medieval Castilian tradition across the centuries.

Unlike the shorter sea- and river-based advance of American colonists into Texas, the Santa Fe Trail was a *land* route, a uniquely early overland approach to the Spanish empire that had already been traced by Indians and by eighteenth-century French explorers. Santa Fe itself attracted little attention in the United States until the report of Lieutenant Zebulon Pike's expedition to the region (1806–7) was published in 1810, but in 1821 two significant events

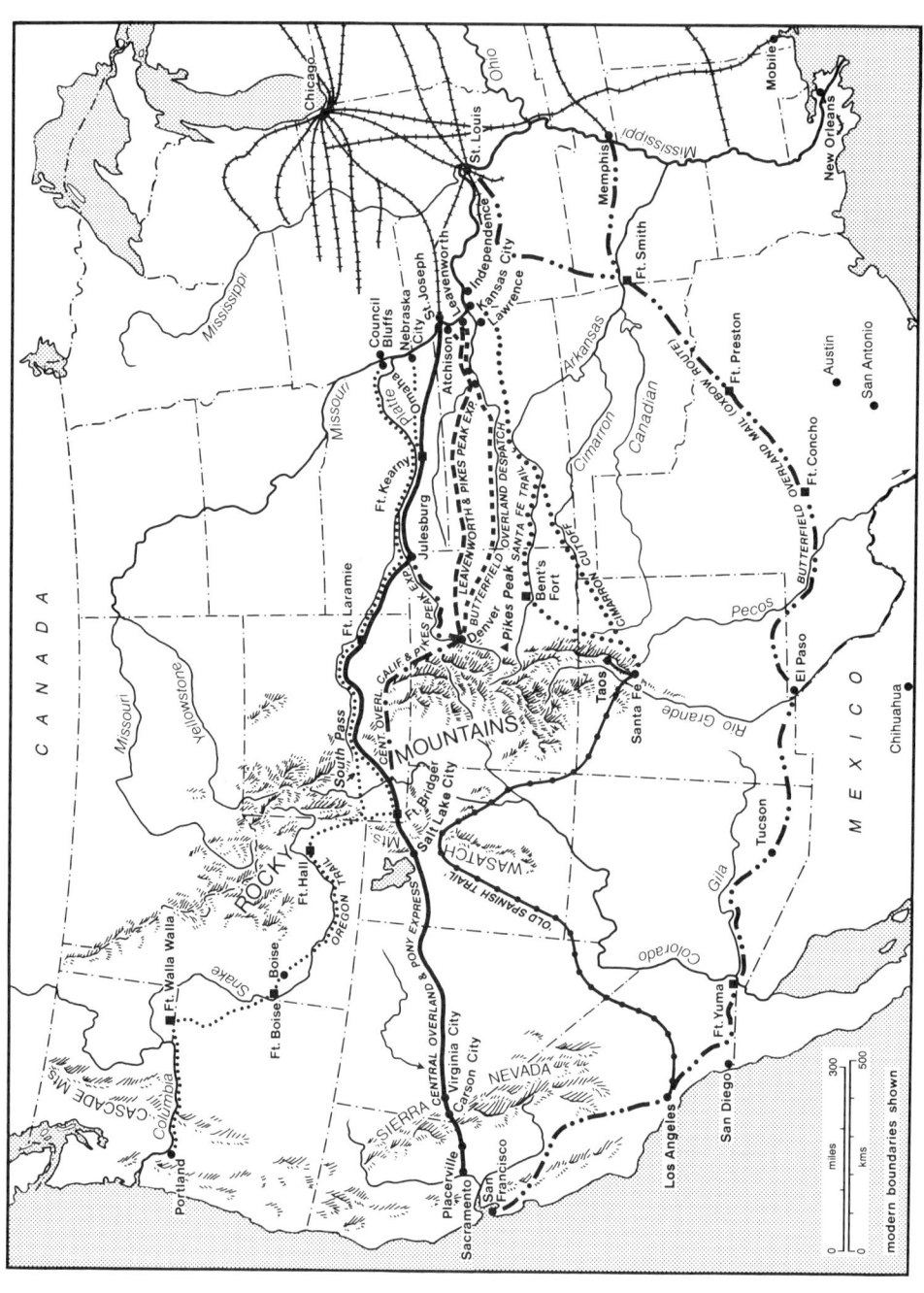

Figure 11 Early ties across the trans-Mississippi West, 1821–1861.

occurred: Missouri acquired Statehood, and Mexico declared its independence from Spain, opening its ports to foreign commerce. The same year, Missouri merchants blazed a trail to Santa Fe via the Arkansas Valley, and in 1822 added the Cimarron Cutoff—an arid route, vulnerable to Indian attack but one which shortened the total journey by ten days. (Fig. 11) The Santa Fe Trail offered new opportunities for springboard growth into the West, while at the same time Santa Fe could be used to challenge the Gulf port of Vera Cruz as the main supply base for Mexico's northern frontier. This was a crucial factor. Competition for Mexico's trade had once again increased among the foreign commercial houses in Vera Cruz, where the U.S. Consul in 1826 reported a fifty per cent decline in American trade in the face of vigorous English and French competition. "Perhaps," he added, wistfully recalling the boom years, "some fresh disturbance in Europe shall again throw the carrying trade into the hands of the Americans."[66]

Wagons were added to packmule traffic for the first time in 1824—"The caravan reached Santa Fe with much less difficulty than must have been anticipated from a first experiment with wheeled vehicles," wrote Josiah Gregg. "The route, indeed, appears to have presented fewer obstacles than any ordinary road of equal length in the United States."[67]

St Louis and Franklin had been the original departure points, but in 1827 Independence, Missouri became the eastern terminus of the trail—"the general 'port of embarkation' for every part of the great western and northern prairie ocean." Here the wagons and pack animals were loaded with what was known as "the Santa Fe assortment"—a wide range of silks, cottons, velvets, shirts, hats, dresses, ribbons, lace, trinkets, cutlery, hardware, and other dry goods. As with every other Spanish port roused into activity only once or twice a year, the arrival of the caravan at Santa Fe ended months of *tiempo muerto*. As Gregg observed, "Instead of the idleness and stagnation which its streets exhibited before, now one sees everywhere the bustle, noise and activity of a lively market town."[68]

The vital element in the return cargo was silver specie and gold dust, to which were added furs, wool, buffalo skins, blankets, and mules. The silver came from the mining centres of 'Old' Mexico. By the 1830s, merchants on the trail to Santa Fe (population 3,000) were extending their activities southward along Spain's old tie-beam, *El Camino Real*, to the larger settlements of Chihuahua, Durango, Aguascalientes, and Zacatecas. Here were some of the ancient supporting columns of imperial Spain—cities with populations of between 10,000 and 30,000. The size of these markets encouraged Missouri-based merchants to explore alternative, more direct routes across the plains. Gregg himself opened a route via Arkansas and the Canadian River in 1839, although all U.S. merchants trading overland from the Mississippi Valley into the Chihuahua–Zacatecas markets were in competition with European goods supplied through the Mexican seaports of Matamoros, Vera Cruz, Tampico, and Mazatlán.

Given the basic objective of opening trade at any likely point on the periphery of Spain's empire, merchants from the Ohio/Mississippi/Missouri country—the heart of America's river-trading region—found the lack of water transport to Santa Fe a new and unwelcome restriction on business in the 1820s and 1830s. It became an increasingly familiar problem in other parts of the trans-Mississippi West, but the Santa Fe Trail was the first extended Yankee trade route to have to adjust to the arid and semi-arid environments in the New World. Merchants were quick to recognize the scale of the problem:

> The chief natural disadvantage to which the Great Western Prairies are exposed, consists in the absence of navigable streams. Throughout the whole vast territory, there is not a single river, except the Missouri, which is navigable during the whole season. The remaining streams in their course through the plains are, and must continue to be, for all purposes of commerce, comparatively useless.[69]

So anxious were Americans to investigate the possibilities of extending navigation on the Río Grande, in 1846 the U.S. Army of Occupation in Mexico commissioned engineer Bryant Tilden to accompany an official exploration upriver to investigate the economic resources of the region, and to assess the prospects for navigation and commerce.[70] Tilden's survey of the "upper" Río Grande in the low-water season followed the river for some 700 miles upstream from the Gulf of Mexico as far as Laredo, where c.1,500 inhabitants were living on the Texas side, c.500 on the Mexican. With its location on the direct overland route from San Antonio to Monterrey, Laredo was regarded by Tilden as the logical future head of navigation for steamboats drawing four feet, "after a hundred thousand dollars shall have been expended in the proper improvement of the river above Mier." But following Tilden's report, Roma (near Mier), not Laredo, remained the head of steam navigation on the Río Grande for the rest of the nineteenth century, and indeed until 1907, when steamship service was discontinued.

Tilden saw little prospect for agricultural settlement along this portion of the valley, although there was scope for the rancher, the merchant, the trader, and the miner. "While there exists every natural inducement to draw speculators to these points, no man can honestly invite the American emigrant hither."[71]

The first step in strengthening the overland tie to Santa Fe

Federal involvement in the Santa Fe wagon trains began in 1829 with the introduction of a military escort as far as the U.S.-Mexican boundary on the Arkansas River in order to protect traders against Indian attack, as well as against raids on the silver and gold shipments in the 1830s and 1840s by bandits from Texas.

Charles Bent of St Louis had led this 1829 trading party to Santa Fe, and on the journey became the first freighter to borrow army oxen and use them successfully instead of horses and mules for long-distance wagon haulage across the plains. The following year, he settled in Taos (site of the original Mexican Custom House), where he co-founded what became the largest trading company in the Southwest—Bent & St. Vrain. With Santa Fe and Taos as his centres of operation, Charles Bent and his younger brothers, William and George, went on to establish large fortified trading posts on the Arkansas, South Platte, and Canadian Rivers.

Critics of the expense involved in maintaining the U.S. military escort were told that it was a necessary outlay, because, as the Governor of Missouri put it in 1830, "trade with the northern section of New Mexico had become an essential branch of the commerce of Missouri." U.S. Consuls had first been appointed in Santa Fe in 1825 although the consulate never appears to have been officially recognized by the Mexican government. Consular reports consistently complained of the high duties demanded by the Mexican customs officials, and the hazards of the overland route—attacks by *guerrillas* from the Republic of Texas, and Indian attacks at wells and river-crossings, on the warehouses at Taos, and on Bent's various outlying trading posts, where Bent was frequently forced to pay ransom to retrieve his goods.

At the Arkansas River crossing, the U.S. military escort was intended to be replaced by a Mexican troop for the rest of the journey to Santa Fe, but this rarely occurred, and U.S. Army escorts were soon discontinued by Congress on grounds of economy. Both the traders and the Consul, however, continued to demand U.S. protection and to emphasize the strategic and commercial importance of the route to "the Frontier Port of Santa Fe". As the U.S. Consul in Santa Fe informed the State Department:

> Despite the uninhabitable and immense prairies that intervene between the State of Missouri and Santa Fe, the distance from the seaports of Mexico, upon either maritime border, to Durango, Chihuahua, and other large cities on the tablelands is greater than from Independence, Missouri to Santa Fe. Our road across the plains is not only incomparably better than theirs, but the best upon the continent . . . With the rich State of Chihuahua, plus parts of Sonora and Durango, our trade over the Prairies is about *2 million dollars* annually, using 800–1,000 wagons.
>
> It is well known to those familiar with Mexican affairs that they are controlled by England, and English influence in the southern and most wealthy parts of the Mexican Republic extends to the States of Durango, Chihuahua and Sonora. Now give to us the commerce of them, which Nature ever intended to be our own . . . A thousand wagons with 1,500 men accompanying them, travelling twice a year through the prairies, would be more effective in commanding respect than any military force.[72]

Charles Bent, writing from Taos in 1843, emphasized the point that the U.S. Government must take a firmer hand:

> If steps are not taken by the authorities of our country to secure such rights as are guaranteed to American citizens by the treaty [of Amity, Commerce, and Navigation, 1831–2] between the two countries, we Americans shall be compelled to abandon the trade of this country to the English and French . . .
>
> The trade of this country is of some importance to the United States, and particularly to Missouri—there is annually taken to the United States in precious metals alone about half a million dollars, besides other property. Merchandise is brought by this route with less expense than through any other port, and would be greatly augmented if protected.[73]

Other American merchants opened for business in Santa Fe, however, even in the difficult early 1840s. James Webb, a young clerk in a Connecticut dry goods store, worked his way to New Mexico in 1844 and by 1849 had the largest store in Santa Fe, in partnership with two other New England merchants from Boston and Salem.[74] In 1846, Santa Fe had been taken virtually without opposition at the start of the U.S.–Mexican War by General Stephen Kearny's 'Army of the West', and a regular monthly stagecoach service, with army escort, began later that year between Fort Leavenworth, Kansas and Santa Fe. James Webb took the opportunity to expand his trade over much of the Southwest until 1861, organizing two shipments of goods annually from Westport Landing (Kansas City), Missouri, which had been favoured by Charles Bent, and which by the 1840s had replaced Independence as the eastern terminus of the Santa Fe Trail.

By 1855, annual trade into New Mexico Territory had reached about US$5 million, and almost US$10 million by 1860. The Santa Fe Trail's value was essentially commercial—a freight route, rather than a major path of westward migration.[75] Progressively shortened by the advancing railroad, it survived until the tracks reached Santa Fe itself, via Ratón Pass, in 1880.

Strengthening the Structural Connections between East and West

New building and maintenance work demanded fresh attention to problems caused by the enormous length of the span, and by the severe additional 'loading' on the tension structure caused by environmental hazards. These included:

(i) Distances of more than 2,000 miles between the Mississippi 'coast' and the Pacific.

(ii) the high proportion of mountainous terrain.

(iii) the widespread severity of the winters.

(iv) the fact that even after misconceptions had been set aside, desert and semi-desert conditions still characterized fifty per cent of the total surface area of the trans-Mississippi West.

(v) the *unreliability* of the seasonal precipitation over many areas west of 96°W. Irregular cycles of higher rainfall increased the risk by encouraging the introduction of small-scale arable and stock farms which failed in the drought years.

All presented serious obstacles to permanent settlement, and thus to the continued expansion of the 'live load' (which was now advancing not only into areas of greater natural hazard but also into Indian treaty lands).

The steps leading from Territory to Statehood, as safeguarded in the Federal Constitution, had been outlined earlier by Thomas Jefferson in his ordinances of 1784 and 1785, and were formally adopted in the Northwest Ordinance of 1787. Basic to the design principles of the United States' tension structure was the guarantee that States were to be *built on site*—not by Congress, but by the 'live load'. After the initial Presidential appointment of Territorial Governor, secretary, and three judges, the next stage was reached when the voting population of a Territory (or part of a Territory) had reached 5,000, thereby gaining an elected lower legislature and a non-voting delegate in Congress. When the total population had increased to 60,000 free white citizens, the Territory was eligible to apply for Statehood.

The long period of TERRITORIAL STATUS for much of the trans-Mississippi West meant that centralized control over the building and development of large parts of the region was retained by Congress for many years. There were advantages in this however. Since the Federal Government was largely carrying the cost of organizing the Territories, it was the primary supervisor and coordinator of the building program. But as well as being a regulator, the Federal Government was also the pioneer and facilitator of much construction work:

        in Exploration and Survey
- Administration
- Law and order
- Military campaigns and defence
- Indian affairs
- Postal services
- Roads
- Railroads
- Telegraph communication
- Daily Weather Reports and Forecasting
- Land Grants and Sales
- Homesteading
- Interstate Commerce

Providing for Increased Traffic into the West
The Great Federal Wagon Road Surveys of the 1840s and 1850s

"Good roads are both a tool of empire and a text for the basic principles of good construction"

> The average man would probably say that a ROAD is not a structure, but indeed it is a very complex one.
>
> Serviceability depends on good foundation. Maintenance, *to be economic*, requires only limited expenditure on surface-wear renewals, and this can be achieved only if the surface is laid on a sound foundation.
>
> Deterioration of the road surface is nearly always excused by the large volume of traffic, or by weather conditions, or by classifying the wearing surface as being composed of 'defective material'. But in most cases structural failure would not have occurred *if the base had not failed first*.
>
> It is the earth that eventually carries the load... Check and consolidate the foundation, for if the foundation becomes permanently disturbed, it is only a question of time before the road surface disrupts, no matter how tough or strong it is in itself.
>
> Be well prepared for the shocks and weight of traffic.
>
> (H.E. Brooke-Bradley, *The Structural Engineer*)

Roads had both practical and structural significance to the Federal Government. The need for road transport to the trans-Alleghany West had led to Congressional provision for "laying out, opening and making roads" as early as 1802; the start on the National Road in 1806, and particularly its extension westward beyond Wheeling after 1818, began a long-term commitment to Federal road survey and construction. By the 1830s, there were two separate bureaux within the War Department: the Corps of Engineers and the Corps of Topographical Engineers, the latter with responsibility for civil works including roads, bridges, and river and harbour improvement. While these were officially classified as *military* operations, their role in facilitating civilian stagelines, freight wagons and emigrant travel was immense.

In the 1840s and 1850s, the need to introduce or improve wagon transport between the Mississippi and the Pacific led to a series of army expeditions into the West which combined systematic exploration and mapping with the selection of routeways for both wagons and railroads. John Frémont led four wide-ranging expeditions through the trans-Mississippi West in the 1840s, and in New Mexico, after occupying Santa Fe in 1846, General Kearny instructed officers in the Topographical Engineers to survey new wagon routes to California. By January 1847, Captain Philip St. George Cooke and the Mormon Batallion had opened the first wagon road through the Southwest to California, via Santa Fe, Albuquerque, Rincón, Tucson, the Gila River, and San Diego.[76]

With this action the United States had joined the long search for a viable overland connection between the Gulf of Mexico/Río Grande Valley and the Pacific. Spain's early sweep of the imperial frontier had sent the Catholic Church on the heels of the *conquistadores*. In 1697, the Jesuit Father Juan Salvatierra established the first of a series of missions in Lower California at Loreto, the site of the future capital of the two Californias (Baja y Alta), while between 1687 and 1711, Father Eusebio Kino had travelled thousands of miles in the Sonora, Gila and Colorado River country, exploring, mapping, founding missions and ranches, and finally confirming (in 1701) that Lower California was a peninsula not an island.

The settlements founded by Salvatierra and Kino were not inter-linked however; the work of these remarkable Jesuit pioneers remained two discrete penetrations into the desert frontier. Structural improvement during the Bourbon reforms, on the other hand, was intended to create new lateral connections on the remote borders of New Spain. In 1769, Gaspar de Portolá made Spain's first sighting by land of San Francisco Bay. Juan Manuel de Ayala explored the Bay in 1775, while in 1775–6, Juan Bautista de Anza, with some 200 colonists, opened the overland route from Sonora to Monterey (which he had pioneered in 1774), and then pushed north again to establish the *presidio* and mission at San Francisco in the summer of 1776.

By the mid-1770s, Spain was also actively seeking to open another overland connection—a road between Santa Fe and the new *pueblos, presidios*, and mission settlements in Upper California that would insert a major cross-tie between New Mexico and the Pacific. To this end, following pioneer work by the Rivera expedition in 1765, a party of ten led by the Franciscan friars Domínguez and Escalante travelled for 2,000 miles in 1776-7 across New Mexico, Colorado, Utah and Arizona—though the wilderness of the San Juan Mountains, the Uncompahgre Plateau, and the Wasatch Mountains. But they were unable to cross the Sierra Nevada before snow filled the passes, and they returned to Santa Fe through deserts and dissected canyonlands that would continue to challenge United States army explorers and engineers a century later. Despite its designation as an important early routeway across the Southwest, the 'Old Spanish Trail' from Santa Fe to Los Angeles had been little used, and was never effective as an east–west tie-beam in Spain's imperial compression structure. In fact, Spain had only developed the first section of the trail (from Santa Fe to the Great Basin) in order to trade with the Ute Indians, although the term 'Old Spanish Trail' was later applied to the whole of the Santa Fe–Los Angeles routeway. (Fig. 11)

The section of the trail between the Great Basin and Los Angeles was not opened until the region had ceased to be Spanish territory. After gaining independence from Spain, it was the Mexican authorities who first opened a circuitous but regular trade route between Santa Fe and Los Angeles, via the 'Old Spanish Trail'.[77] Initiated by the Governor in Santa Fe, the trade operated on an annual basis from 1829 to 1848, exchanging New Mexican woollen blankets for Californian horses and mules, with sales normally held in the San Bernardino/San Gabriel/Los Angeles region. Although a few prospective settlers travelling overland to California in the mid-1840s also followed this trail, the majority chose the central, more direct route from Missouri across the plains and the Sierra Nevada to Sacramento. By the 1850s, apart from the section between Utah and Los Angeles (via Las Vegas, Nevada and San Bernardino) which was still followed by emigrants heading primarily for southern California, the great northern loop of the 'Old Spanish Trail' from Santa Fe had been largely superseded by Cooke's wagon road, with its southern loop across the desert to San Diego.

Texas had been persistent in its demands for Federal wagon roads following its admission to the Union in 1845 and the ending of the War with Mexico in 1848, which together with the Oregon territory acquired from Britain in 1846, were to add more than 1.2 million square miles to the United States—an increase of some sixty-six per cent to the total area, greater even than the Louisiana Purchase. In the 1850s, Texas was the most active military frontier in the entire West, with the greatest number of forts and army camps requiring the movement of troops, government stores and supply wagons.[78] At the same time, merchants in both San Antonio and Austin were anxious to acquire a wagon road to El Paso in order to tap the Chihuahua–Durango–Zacatecas trade route, and divert business from New Mexico into Texas. In fact, the diversion of trade from the Missouri–Santa Fe–Chihuahua–Zacatecas route at *any* point along the way had always been a Texan objective.

The Army on the other hand saw their work as part of the great structural development of the United States—helping the 'live load' of emigrants, prospectors, traders and soldiers to reach California.[79] The discovery of gold in California just three weeks after the drafting of the U.S.–Mexican Treaty at Guadalupe Hidalgo on 2 February 1848 provided a major boost for Texas, once the scale of California's new wealth became known. As Captain S.G. French of the Army Quartermaster's Corps reported in December 1849: "El Paso, from its geographical position, presents itself as a resting place on one of the great overland routes between the seaports of the Atlantic on one side and those of the Pacific on the other . . . a connexion that will strengthen the bonds of union by free and constant intercourse. The government has been the pioneer in the enterprise."[80]

The territorial acquisition of New Mexico and California by the United States in 1848 had indeed changed the strategic position of Texas, which became, as Lamar noted, "a middle passage" to the West rather than the farthest frontier.[81] But Texas did not become part of the primary span—the major structural cross-tie— to the Pacific. The *central* routes to California took priority. Kansas and Nebraska Territories were created in 1854, and government road-building policy remained clear: funds were to be spent first on making the route serviceable from end to end, and secondly on improvement of the most difficult sections. Reporting to the War Department after work in the Platte Valley and the Rocky Mountains, the chief engineer observed: "I have endeavored to carry into effect the instructions of the Secretary of War, namely, . . . to make all parts practicable before any part was elaborated."[82]

Building more bridges

> Bridges were landmarks in olden times; people traveling through the land would inquire from one bridge to another.
>
> (Anna Mary Robertson Moses ["Grandma Moses"], born 1860)

The Topographical Engineers continued the work of strengthening both the Federal foundations and the traffic surfaces across the trans-Mississippi West—building bridges, culverts and causeways, improving fords, embanking, draining and grading roads, cutting forest, clearing brush, grubbing out roots, shifting boulders, removing rock overhangs.

California had achieved Statehood by 1850 and immediately begun to insist that the U.S. Government use the initiatives it already possessed in the intervening Territories to construct a *continuous Federal wagon road* from the Mississippi–Missouri Valley to the Pacific. Emigrant families were needed to stabilize the population on the West Coast—farmers, artisans, construction workers. Although the term 'military road' was retained, by the 1850s the needs of the military were required less often to justify constitutionally the use of Federal funds for road construction. The organized protection and encouragement of emigrants, freighters, stagelines and mail services had long since defined the main military purposes of western defence. Indeed, the 600-mile 'military road' built in 1855–62 through extremely difficult terrain to link the upper Missouri to the Columbia River had little military value. It was mainly used by emigrants to the Pacific Northwest, and by miners in the goldrush to Idaho and Montana in the 1860s.

The Railroad Connection

During the 1840s and 1850s, there was an increasingly close relationship between wagon road surveys and the Pacific Railroad surveys in the trans-Mississippi West as new developments in transport technology were applied to the United States' basic structural design.

Three overlapping site advantages had now emerged to reinforce the structural significance of the State of Missouri in westward expansion:

(i) The regional importance of the central Mississippi basin in the overall development of the United States.

(ii) The magnitude of business energy generated by the State's location at the confluence of the Mississippi and the Missouri river traffic.

(iii) The State's location at the starting points of the Santa Fe, Oregon, and California Trails.

Passage to India?

One of the earliest and most persistent advocates for "inland communication across the continent" was Thomas Hart Benton, who had arrived in St Louis in 1815, established a successful law practice and quickly revived a long-standing interest in western politics. In 1819, following the new boundary agreements with Britain and Spain, he published his first essay on 'The North American Road to India'. Benton's original support for the Missouri–Columbia river linkage was soon to be reworked into a strong argument in favour of a Central National Highway, an all-American turnpike to San Francisco, and a new western route to the Orient, an idea which was strongly influenced by the growth of U.S. activity in the Pacific at this time, and the commercial opportunities in Asia. The proposal was pegged to a Mississippi crossing at St Louis and, predictably, Benton became one of Missouri's favourite adopted sons; he had been elected to the U.S. Senate and in 1821 took his seat for the new State of Missouri. A passionate speaker, Benton was soon emphasizing the advantages of Gallatin's 1808 Federal transport project, and calling for a "national fund to make roads and canals where the national interest requires them, without regard to population, direct taxes, or the size of States."

A new term, Pacific Overland, was in use by the mid-1830s along the early trails into Oregon. The idea of faster Pacific Overland connection *by rail* was promoted in the 1830s and 1840s largely through the efforts of individuals, several of them Midwest boosters, but some of the most effective in New York and New England.

The first to publish a plan for a Pacific Railroad from New York to Oregon appears to have been Judge S.W. Dexter in February 1832, in his weekly newspaper *Emigrant*, at Ann Arbor, Michigan. It caught the attention of several in the Northeast. Hartwell Carver and Samuel Barlow, for example, developed Dexter's ideas in articles published in New York and Massachusetts, and proposals for a railroad rather than a turnpike attracted fresh interest. In 1836, John Plumbe in Dubuque, Wisconsin Territory, began to lecture on the advantages of extending a railroad from Lake Michigan (Milwaukee) to the Mississippi (at Dubuque), and on through

Oregon to the Pacific. Plumbe had earlier worked as an engineer on the eastern railroads, and the rest of his life became a personal crusade for a Pacific Railroad to Oregon—through correspondence, speeches and petitions in the Midwest, California, and Washington, D.C.[83]

In the 1840s, the New York merchant Asa Whitney took matters a stage further. On his return from China (where the first official Sino-American trade agreement had been signed in 1844), Whitney prepared a plan which, in January 1845, was the first to be formally presented to Congress.[84] Whitney requested a grant of public land (sixty miles wide) on which to build a 2,160-mile railroad from Lake Michigan to the mouth of the Columbia River. The line would not only provide a direct westerly passage between Europe and China, but effective support for American interests in the forthcoming settlement of the Oregon question as well. As one Senator noted years later: "the importance of connecting the Mississippi to the Pacific Ocean by a railroad was first brought to our attention by Asa Whitney's memorial in 1845, and in some shape or form it has been before Congress ever since." Whitney's proposals attracted so much attention between 1845 and 1852 that many assumed he had originated the idea. The term 'Pacific Railroad' was now firmly established, both inside and outside Congress. Whatever the fears about the intervening wilderness, there was little serious or sustained opposition to the principle of extending a line to some point on the West Coast. "This is the time," argued Senator Seward. "To those on the Atlantic and Pacific coasts it can make very little difference; the location of this railroad concerns chiefly the *central inland States*, and is to them a matter of very great consequence."[85] It was a timely acknowledgement of the route as an internal development mechanism.

Whitney's plans, however, did not guarantee early completion. After the initial land grant from Congress "to himself, his heirs and assigns", Whitney was to be fully responsible for building and completing the railroad, i.e. for the sale of parcels of land to the settlers and, with the proceeds, the westward extension of the rails. Benton was bitterly opposed to this, insisting that the line be built and operated by the Federal government. In February 1849, he roused the Senate with demands that the Pacific Railroad to the Orient (via St Louis and San Francisco), must be "national in its design, national in its character, and national in its construction." Opposition to Whitney became widespread. "Memorials Against Mr. Asa Whitney's Railroad Scheme" accumulated in Congress as citizens from coast to coast petitioned for rejection. Significantly, opposition focused not on the principle of a railroad to the Pacific but on the method of achieving it, and did much to strengthen support for the role that central government would play. Congress eventually defeated Whitney's proposals in 1852.

Early in 1849, the "western route to China" had still sounded attractive. As an added incentive to domestic growth, much was made of the point that the Pacific Railroad would enable American merchants to send out their manufactured goods and haul back the wealth of the Orient. But Benton's Senate speech in February 1849 was to be one of the last occasions when the dual purpose, Pacific *and* Orient, would be stressed in this way. By 1850, debate in Congress on the Pacific Railroad focused on the military, financial, political and social necessity of "connecting California". In addition to the Federal wagon road, a new argument centred on California's "right" to have a railroad and magnetic telegraph link with the eastern networks on the basis of the equality of States.

The surge in the 'live load' and the varied origins of the crowds bound for California guaranteed traffic on even the most hazardous and circuitous routes into the region, whether overland (some sixty per cent of the total), via Panamá (where the Panama Railroad was built 1850–55), or round Cape Horn. And aside from consignments of gold dust, bullion, and specie, the enormous increase of mail alone between California and the East demanded quick government action to tie the structure securely.

The year 1852 marked an early peak in the California gold rush and in March 1853 Congress commissioned the official surveys for a Pacific Railroad by the Army's Topographical Engineers, some routes incorporating earlier surveys made for Federal wagon roads. Indeed, the realization that part of Captain Cooke's wagon road in the Tucson–Gila River area still lay in Mexican territory led to the Gadsden Purchase of the land in 1853 for $10 million; neither wagon road nor future railroad could be left outside the United States' boundary. By 1854, *five* possible rail routes had been found, and detailed maps submitted. (Fig. 12) Each railroad route slung its own political lobby across the trans-Mississippi West, but Congress was now deadlocked in this, as in other issues, by sectionalism and the likelihood of secession.

Meanwhile, the Government sanctioned temporary ties across the trans-Mississippi West. In 1858, the *Butterfield Overland Mail* began the first mail stage service authorized by Congress between the Mississippi (St Louis and Memphis) and California

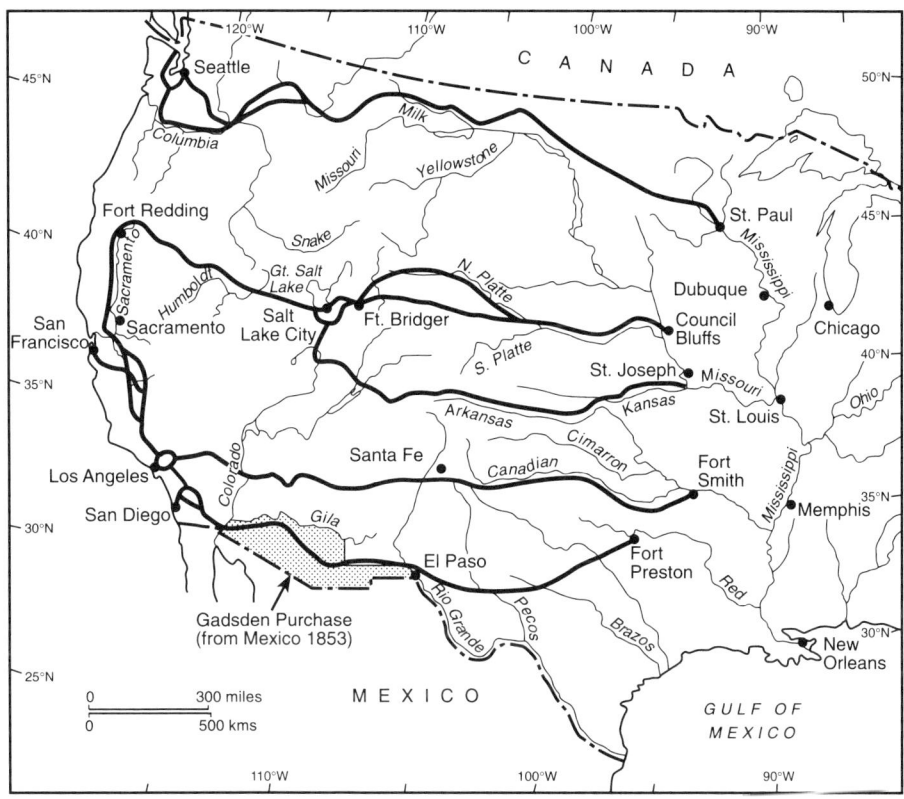

Figure 12 Strengthening the ties: the Pacific Railroad Surveys, 1853–54. The work was undertaken by the Army Corps of Topographical Engineers and, in a few sections, incorporated earlier Federal wagon road surveys made in the 1840s. (Based on Secretary of War Jefferson Davis's report and Lieut. G. K. Warren's original map, presented to Congress in 1855)

(Los Angeles and San Francisco). The journey took three weeks, and until it was re-routed at the start of the Civil War, made a great southern loop through Texas and New Mexico. (Fig. 11) The next year, the *Central Overland, California & Pike's Peak Express* started operating out of St Joseph, Missouri and from 1862 to 1866, Holladay's *Overland Mail & Express* dominated the central and northern routes out of Atchison, Omaha and Nebraska City. Many other operators fed these lines or duplicated parts of them. Distance measured in time was cut dramatically by the *Pony Express* which in April 1860 connected St Joseph, Missouri and Sacramento, via Salt Lake City, in only ten days. This mail and messenger service was never commercially viable, but it was a bravura performance, and of its type, the swiftest form of long-distance travel in the world. Eighteen months later, the telegraph link effectively ended it when in October 1861, the telegraph lines were joined in Main Street, Salt Lake City, marking "the completion of an enterprise which spans a continent, unites two oceans, and connects with nerve of iron the remote extremities of the body politic with the great government heart." The coast-to-coast wiring of the continent at the start of the Civil War had met the genuine political need for fast intra-Union information flow. **Many became convinced for the first time that if the technology was provided, no distance was now too great to prevent the Federal tension structure from working well.**

Lincoln signed the Pacific Railroad Bill in July 1862. The southern routes were now out of the question for a Union-sponsored enterprise. The *Pony Express* had confirmed the advantages of a central route to California, but one farther north than that out of St Louis; with much of the southern vote withdrawn into the Confederacy, there was no longer any need to balance the northern and southern lobbies, and a resurveyed central route was chosen. Lincoln stipulated that the railroad should operate as *one continuous line*, and that construction should go ahead without interruption, despite the war between the States. A line of States, the first north–south section of the two-tiered Federal structure west of the Mississippi, was already in place from Minnesota to Louisiana. The Pacific Railroad was to start at the gateway to the Territories, and Omaha in Nebraska Territory was selected. *The Territorial status of the entire route in 1862 as far as the California State line reinforced the key initiatives and controls that could be exercised by the Federal Government*. This was an important structural factor, since some in Congress had once again questioned the power of central government to build, or assist in building, a highway within State boundaries.

The Union Pacific Railroad Co. was organized, and the Central Pacific Railroad Co. in California recognized by Congress for the joint construction of the line. The accompanying incentives of Federal land grants, loans, concessions, bonuses, and completion clauses speeded the work on what was to become, at that time, the longest and highest railroad in the world.[86] The last spike linked the Union Pacific and Central Pacific tracks at Promontory Point, near Ogden, Utah on 10 May 1869, seven years ahead of schedule; within twenty-four hours, the first train from the east had passed over the link and was on its way to San Francisco Bay.

Widening the United States' tension structure and inserting new girders

> We tunneled the mountain, we bridged the river,
> we split the Rockies and they're split forever,
> we coasted down to Pacific foam,
> but now I'm dying and I want to go home.
>
> (Conrad Aiken, the railroad worker in *The Last Vision*)

The years between 1883 and 1893 marked the great climax of transcontinental railroad construction in the United States. In a single, spectacular decade, four new lines to the Pacific were completed: the Southern Pacific (1883), the Northern Pacific (1883), the Atchison, Topeka and Santa Fe (1885), and the Great Northern (1893). As a result of transcontinental railroad construction, the country's four standard time zones were established in 1883.

In 1855, Senator Butler from South Carolina had voiced widespread opinion with his statement to Congress that "if we are to have a railroad to the Pacific, *one road is enough*." Not even the most determined railroad boosters had envisaged five roads, a transcontinental rail and telegraph *system* in fact, well before the end of the century. (Fig. 13) Railroad construction on this scale was already beginning to tilt the global balance of sea and land power in favour of the latter, and nowhere was land power emerging so strongly as in the United States.

What of the Passage to India? Earlier forecasts concerning the role that the Pacific Railroad would play in drawing off much of the Asian trade soon faded—in part through the advantage Europe gained by the opening of the Suez Canal in November 1869, only

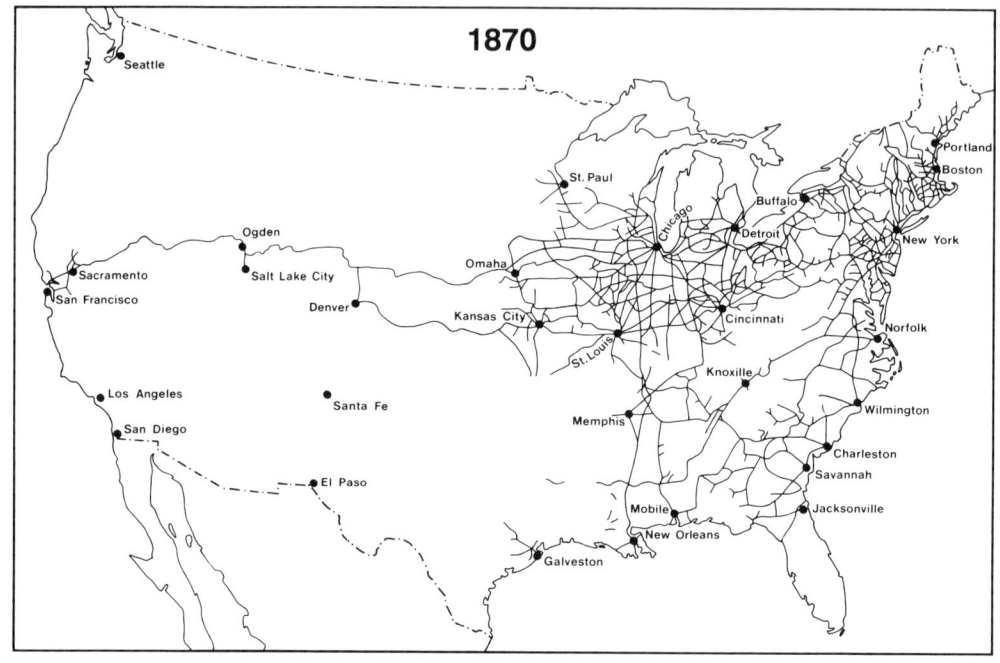
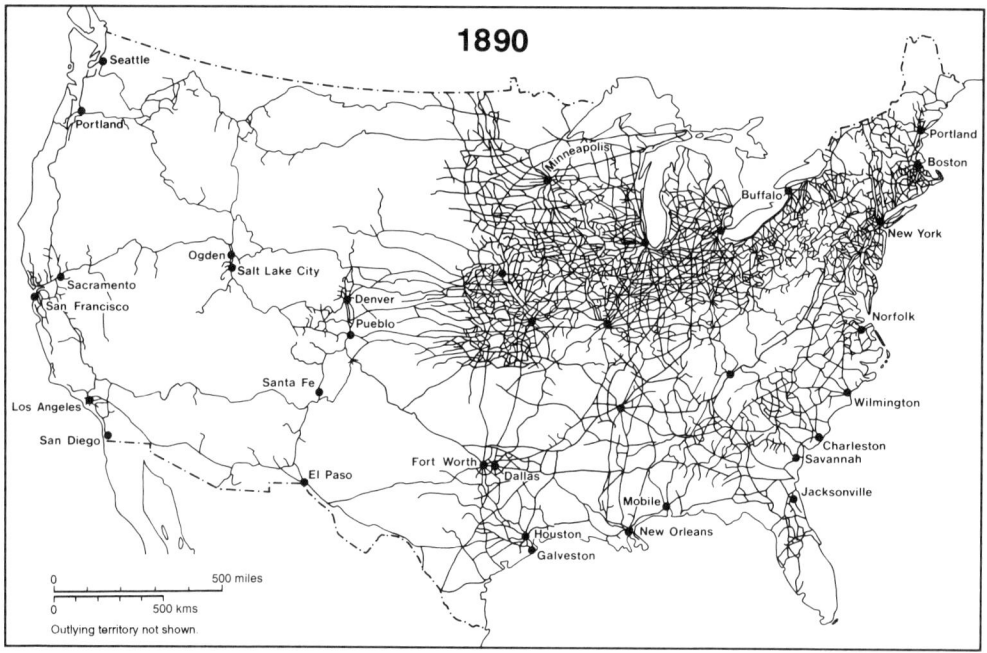

Figure 13 Railroad expansion in the United States, 1870–1890.

six months after the Golden Spike ceremony. The concept of 'America's railroad to the Orient' soon became symbolic, even nostalgic. Walt Whitman's *Passage to India*, written in 1870, depicted a dream and a West which had already largely disappeared. As far as the United States was concerned, interest in the Pacific, the Spanish imperial outposts, the Hawaiian Islands and the Asian Rim had become more strategic than commercial, and it was left to artists, writers, and showmen to foster the romantic image, and sometimes the myth, of a pre-railroad West.

Strengthening the foundations

> **The design of BASES and FOUNDATIONS can materially affect the performance of the whole building . . .**
> **The 'raft' foundation consists of a flat slab covering the whole area of the superstructure. It serves to tie the structure together as well as spreading the loads placed on it.**
>
> (A.G. Smyrell, *Design of Structural Elements*)

Basic structural work had proceeded rapidly after the Civil War, when the United States launched a major new program of exploration across the trans-Mississippi West. Following Josiah Whitney's surveys of California in 1860–68, the four great Federal Government surveys between 1867 and 1879 carried the work forward, and represented an outstanding achievement in geological and topographical mapping, resource evaluation, and scientific data-collection. These were the King Surveys along the 40th parallel (1867–72); the Hayden Surveys of Nebraska, the Yellowstone region, and Colorado (1867–78); the Wheeler Surveys West of the One-Hundredth Meridian (1867–79); and the Powell Surveys of the Colorado River and the Colorado Plateau region (1869–79)—all of which paved the way for the creation in 1879 of the United States Geological Survey.

The population of the United States west of 96°W more than doubled in the 1870s. In the 1880s, it nearly doubled again, as did Western railroad construction, in a decade of phenomenal expansion.

Strong growth in parts of the trans-Mississippi West was a component of the record levels of immigration into the United States in the late nineteenth and early twentieth centuries. The country's total population rose from 39.9 millions in 1870, to over 76 millions in 1900, and by 1924 it would be more than 114 millions. About half the emigrants settling beyond the 96°W meridian after the Civil War came from the Eastern States, and about half of them directly from Europe. "We may well ask—and with special reference to the West," wrote Josiah Strong somewhat anxiously in 1885, "whether this in-sweeping immigration is to foreignize us, or we are to Americanize it."[87] In the event, the extension of the full, two-tiered United States' tension structure across the West was to become one of the most "Americanizing" building periods of all.

The strength and variety of Eastern influence upon the West increased, not only through Federal agencies and economic controls but through **the trusses, cable-stays, and stiffening girders of cultural and social connections**—schools, colleges, churches, stores, national newspapers, magazines, and the spread of mail-order. Many Yankees saw the speed of growth in the West (and the retreat of the Indian) as the clearest, least complicated image they could find of the post-Civil War renaissance of American spirit and purpose, and a ripe new field of operation for Eastern enterprise and investment. If this was thinly-disguised neo-colonialism, the mandate was the "westward course of empire". In any event, the imperial analogy had more long-term economic than political application here; it was obvious that the West was already engaged on its own vast building program and would in time complete the Federal tension structure's two-tiered span with the addition of new States between the Great Plains and the Pacific Ocean.

Alongside the expansion of the Midwest (and, most notably, the spectacular growth of Chicago), the north Atlantic seaboard cities and the Manufacturing Belt had greatly strengthened their own support and financing of the Federal tension structure, while at the same time coping with a huge increase in tensile stress and strain, and strong buffeting. The country's total 'live load' had expanded and diversified at an unprecedented rate, particularly during the peak immigration years between 1880 and 1924.

Washington, D.C. had successfully fought off the post-Civil War demands from the Midwest to shift the Federal capital closer to the centre of the United States, but with the growth of the trans-Mississippi West, **the 'raft' foundation of the Federal**

Government and the Federal Government deck were now to be greatly strengthened in order to tie the structure more firmly, and to control and spread the load. A landmark piece of basal construction was introduced in 1887 with the Interstate Commerce Act, which authorized Congressional control of interstate railroad rates. **It was the start of increasing intervention, and increasing assistance, by the Federal government in the strengthening, repair and maintenance of the whole of the tension structure—its support towers under compression, its suspension system, cable stays, decks, and foundations.** The works program would expand and in time include business regulation, natural resources management, power supply, irrigation, flood control, farm financing, crime prevention, urban renewal, interstate highways, the aptly-named Works Progress Administration Projects, and much else besides.

Nevertheless, the increasing participation of *Federal* government in the country's structural engineering was not simply an urgent response to the needs of farms and cities in the West, the East, and the South. Nor was it always at the expense of *State* government. Enlarged Federal authority was also the inevitable result of the United States' growing involvement in world affairs, and in the expansion of foreign policy and national defence, both of which were designated areas of *Federal* government responsibility. Even so, the interpretation of States' rights, and of the reserve of power held by the States under the Tenth Amendment to the Constitution, have continued to be an integral (and normal) part of the action of, and reaction to, the tension forces present between the span's twin decks, and within the main hangers and suspension cables.

2. The Structural Significance of the Word 'Transcontinental'

> Americans have not only a right to adopt new words, but are obliged to modify the language to suit the novelty of the circumstances, geographical and political, in which they are placed.
>
> (Noah Webster, compiler of the first *American Dictionary of the English Language*, 1828)

Western settlers were already known as 'trans-Alleghanians' by the 1770s and the term 'trans-Atlantic' was introduced in 1782. At this period the prefix usually meant 'beyond' rather than 'across', but in the mid-nineteenth century this meaning was to change with the coming of the word 'trans-continental'—an American introduction that slipped into the language with impeccable timing and unmistakable force. It was born and bred in the United States, born of the railroad and bred in a new phase of Federal expansion and national identity after the Civil War. It had a strong economic and technological accent, but, above all, 'transcontinental' was a word of great structural significance.[88]

Its meaning was so obvious, its adoption so rapid, that the importance of the word itself escaped further notice. Despite the huge literature on American railroads, and the endless fascination with transport history and railway lore shown by professionals and amateurs alike around the world, none subsequently appears to have given any thought to the introduction of one of the most indispensable words the Americans have ever produced. 'Transcontinental' appears in none of the early reports on the U.P.–C.P. Railroad, none of the advance publicity, and none of the Golden Spike ceremonial. The 'Pacific Railroad' was still the universal term. Yet immediately after the joining of the rails at the 'Great Event' in May 1869, 'transcontinental' was suddenly the word that everyone needed to describe, not simply the railroad, but the United States' huge tension structure as a whole: its capacity, accomplishment, and the accelerating movement of its 'live load'. Statesmen and businessmen, journalists and advertisers, geographers and historians, teachers and novelists, all found the word compelling—the newest Americanism, and a vivid encapsulation of distance, vision, and achievement.

Ironically, the word 'transcontinental' gained such immediate popularity *after* the opening of the first 'Pacific Railroad' in 1869 that writers began to insert it into the vocabularies of a much earlier period, confident that no President or diplomat, Congressman or editor, could possibly have managed without the word 'transcontinental' when discussing Westward expansion. From studies of Thomas Jefferson to those on John Quincy Adams, from 'statements' by Lewis and Clark to the naming of the U.S.–Spanish treaty in 1819, from the 'personal accounts' of Oregon boosters to those of California forty-niners, the word 'transcontinental' has since been inserted into reported speech with utter certainty, and total error. Seldom can any word have been wrongly put into so many mouths by subsequent commentators. It is a unique compliment to the *mot juste*.

Yet the assumption was reasonable. Although the word 'transcontinental' spread like wildfire through the language (and round the world) in 1869—largely through the initial efforts of one individual[89]—the movement it described in the United States was already old. Coast-to-coast linkage by overland means, summarized so neatly by the word 'transcontinental', had become familiar in everything but name. With the continental perspective already scaled and measured by the Mississippi 'coast', and by New England's early sweep into the Pacific, Americans had quickly thrown a variety of temporary bridges, cables and stays across the trans-Mississippi West during the first half of the nineteenth century to connect Oregon and California to the Mississippi Valley. Segments of experience, *building* experience, had been pieced together so effectively that the new rail transport technology could now promote a new awareness of the huge *interior* continental land-span by exploiting the railroad's greater speed, greater safety and much greater economy. In 1869–70, travelling time over the 1,800 miles between Omaha and San Francisco had been cut to three-and-a-half days, and the entire coast-to-coast journey from California to New York to about six days. The 'Pacific Railroad' across the trans-Mississippi West, now connected to the Eastern networks, had at once become 'transcontinental' in form and function. For the first time in the Americas, 'interoceanic' linkage was focused on the land tie and its great internal developmental role.

Thus the word coined in the East and first applied in the West had been defined by them both. Trade directories show the influence of this one word by recording the increasing use of Transcontinental, Transcon, Transco, or simply Continental for company and brand names after the Great Event of 1869. The word 'overland' fell noticeably out of favour save as an evocative or nostalgic link with the past. But while the term 'overland' declined, greater use of the words 'transatlantic', 'trans-State', 'trans-America' (all meaning *across* not *beyond*) owed as much to the imagery and popularity of the word 'transcontinental' as to the country's spectacular developments in transport and communication.

The word itself had become an essential component in the tying of the United States' tension structure. It belonged to the period of post-Civil War construction which involved expansion, infilling, and increased standardization. **No single word ever more effectively closed the gap in the national mind between territorial scale and structural achievement.**

Samuel Bowles of New England reflected the new American mood after his first transcontinental journey:

> The continent spanned, the national breadth measured. There is no such knowledge of the nation as comes of traveling it, of seeing eye to eye its vast extent . . .
>
> Whatever we go out to see, whatever pleasures we enjoy, whatever disappointments suffer, this, at least, will be our gain,—a new conception of the magnitude, the variety and the wealth, in nature and resource, in realization and in promise, of the American Republic— and a new idea of what it is to be an American citizen.[90]

Indeed, no region was more acutely aware of the transcontinental achievement than New England, nor more responsive to the opportunities it offered, as the Boston Board of Trade was quick to demonstrate in 1870:

> *OUR TRANS-CONTINENTAL JOURNEY!!*
> *From the Atlantic to the Pacific and Back!!!*
>
> All agree that the excursion has been a splendid success; and that it has done much to annihilate the idea of distance and separation, and to bind together the East and the West in indissoluble bonds. The great valley of the Mississippi . . . Chicago . . . Omaha . . . Cheyenne are, in comparison, close by.
>
> Thank God that we have a Massachusetts, a Maine, and a California . . . Thank God for all the States; but thank Him more than all, that our State pride is lost in the admiration and love which we bear to our country at large . . . The trans-continental railroad has literally blended all the States into *one nation*.[91]

17

Afterword and Conclusions
Design and Construction
in the New World

> There is only one world, and although we speak of the Old World and the New, this is because the latter was lately discovered by us, and not because there are two.
>
> (Garcilaso de la Vega, *Royal Commentaries*, i, 9; Córdoba, Spain, 1609)

Spanish initiatives had indeed been global. Far in advance of its time, Spain saw the Old World and New World as One World, enfolded by the State and by the Church—a 'Oneness' in vision and polity that based its unity on Spain's own perception of sovereignty, and on the wider medieval concept of Christendom. Spain's New World was always structurally part of the Old, a scaled-up Castilian model—extended, adjusted, but basically unchanged.

The United States on the other hand saw Two Worlds from the start. The more varied origins and independent style of colonization in Anglo-America, and the perpetual need to accommodate dissent, helped to emphasize the contrasts at an early stage between the Old World and the New. Despite the links, new Americans were never in any doubt that there were Two Worlds, and that Old World and New were strikingly different—not just in their physical and human geographies, for creole and peninsular Spaniards were also well aware of this, but in the fundamental structural break from Old World design that would be required in the future organization of the New World.

After independence, this 'Two World' reality would soon be placed within a One World setting as the United States quickly developed that global involvement in both the Atlantic and Pacific spheres which is part of the glorious opportunity of the American continent. But the United States had initially identified Two

Worlds. Whatever the ties to Europe and Africa, the Americas were a world apart, and in the Americas, only the design and construction of the United States would ever fully reflect that fact.

1. Contrasts in Interpretation: Responses to Risk

> **THE FUNDAMENTAL PRINCIPLES OF ARCHITECTURE**
>
> **Architecture depends on Order, Arrangement, Harmony, Symmetry, Propriety, and Economy.**
>
> (Vitruvius, *De Architectura*
> [*The Ten Books on Architecture*])

It is not the rules, only the *interpretation* of the rules that can change, observed Vitruvius, the Roman architect-master builder whose rediscovery had such a profound influence on Renaissance design. Spain and the United States interpreted the rules and approached their task from opposite directions. In the Spanish power structure, building initiatives flowed from the top down, those in the United States from the bottom up.

Spain

Spain's demand for certainty in an uncertain world could make little allowance for the *political* handling of dissent. While the weight of formality and procedural delay exhausted some of the tensile force, the imperial structure remained vulnerable to a huge range of tensional stresses and strains, despite its formidable strength under compression. This was what lay behind Francis Bacon's seventeenth-century assessment of "the ticklish and brittle state of the greatnesse of Spaine." For the Spanish empire possessed many of the engineering characteristics of a **'brittle solid'**—strong in compression, weak in tension. For centuries, the great rhythms of prescribed procedure flowed safely through the structure. The avoidance as far as possible of sudden, uncontrolled movement characterized imperial Spain once the brief early turbulence of exploration was ended. Standing still in a changing world was *policy*, not inertia.

The most successful, and therefore the most dangerous challenge to such policy was mounted by the world of commerce. Although Mexico City was something of an exception, and a small entrepreneurial elite developed in scattered parts of the empire during the Bourbon reforms, Hispanic institutions designed to encourage business venture were for the most part rudimentary and poorly financed. As is well documented, the vast majority of Spanish Americans did not regard membership of a creole merchant class as a desirable ambition, certainly not in comparison with an ecclesiastical, military, or bureaucratic career. Even large land-owning enterprises did not normally reach high levels of profitability, and their wealth was to a great extent put to non-economic use. Investment, by and large, was not attracted to productive business enterprise. Late-eighteenth-century achievements were often remarkable only by comparison with what little had gone before.

State control stamped every structural component, revealing as it did so Spain's hardened resistance to change. As John Campbell emphasized in the 1740s:

> The *Spaniards*, who from being very active and vigorous as they were when they first settled in this country, are now become slow, cautious, and so wedded to their own Opinions, that Custom is always a stronger Argument with them than Reason.[92]

Even where economic activity was left in private hands, Spain subjected it to minute and often stultifying regulation—"forever fixing their Commerce by Constraint," as Campbell put it. This is not to say that originality was completely suppressed by Spain's risk-avoidance policies. Hindrance, even prohibition, of innovation and experiment will not necessarily stop them, but it does *slow them down*, restricting in the end the number and variety of new ideas and new opportunities that will emerge. Although the effects of the Crown's restrictions on unauthorized movement can be exaggerated, over time they undoubtedly hampered the development of many linkages and initiatives that could have blossomed given official encouragement. Spain's instinct to over-regulate trade and industry, like everything else, removed much of the decision-making away from local technicians, away also from the local conditions which shaped local needs—as was intended.

The United States

Centralized policy on the Spanish scale contrasted strongly in its actions and its legacy with United States philosophy, which fostered innovation—"Do not simply look for opportunities to experiment," wrote one American, "*create* them. Aggressively pursue change." The pursuit of change as well as happiness, was an early Yankee characteristic.

> Strangers are welcome.
>
> (Benjamin Franklin, *Information to those who would remove to America*, 1782)

The priority given by the United States to increasing its 'live load' did not diminish the country's awareness of the risks involved. Many remained conscious of the difficulties of achieving strength and stability in such a huge, innovative tension structure. Spanish certainties were never characteristic of the United States. The advance into space vacated by the retreating European empires in North America, as well as by the powerful thrust of the United States into Indian and Mexican territories, was sharpened by an early sense of opportunity and 'destiny', and produced bold strokes in the United States' imperial ground-plan. But such enlargement, whether by purchase or conquest, was never without its critics, most of whom continued to look not at the ethics of expansion, but at the enormous distances and the tensions involved.

With all the risks however, the increasing energy and heterogeneity of the 'live load' was to be extraordinarily well supported and accommodated by the United States' tension structure. Individual mobility, the constant emphasis on improving transportation and promoting commerce, the wealth of economic resources—all these accelerated the early spread of Statehood (commonly paired North and South) between the Tidewater and the Mississippi. It was this rapid construction of the *two*-tiered deck that stabilized the structure and, particularly in the North and West, confirmed the building skills and self-confidence of the Union's construction workers.

As the span extended and the dynamics of the 'live load' introduced fresh risk, the Federal components were strengthened throughout the structure—the huge supporting towers, the end-fittings and anchorages, the main suspension cables, the cable-stays, the deck, and the foundations. There was no roof; there has never been a roof on this great tension

structure. It has remained open to cross winds, to the elements, to geological hazards, to traffic surges, and to heavy wear and tear. Its protection is its foundation, its suspension system, its regular inspection and repair, and its maintenance of continuous, adjustable compressive force on which all successful tension depends. In this remarkable piece of late-eighteenth-century engineering, the Americans had not, as one historian has asserted, "erected their constitutional roof before they put up the national walls"[93]—a difficult exercise at the best of times. On the contrary, there is no cover over this Federal tension structure; it has no protection from above. It has boundaries, but no walls. Its visible working components are the essence of its design, and it rests on a magnificent foundation.

2. Contrasts on the Peripheries of Empire

The durability of Spanish America's mining economy as the major structural component of empire

The fringes of Spain's American empire were largely zones of disappointment. The real treasure of empire—silver, and the sedentary Indian societies—remained lodged in the Mexican and Peruvian core regions; the isolated growth points which emerged in the later phases of imperial reform did little to modify the long-standing social and economic importance of the core in relation to the periphery. This represented an extraordinary survival of the *initial* attractions of empire, of medieval quest. It gave Mexico and Peru enduring advantages over all other regions; the rest—California, New Mexico, La Plata, Venezuela, Chile, even New Granada—remained peripheral to the main structure even though they were at different stages of development.[94] 'Peripheries' were as much the product of perception as of geographical location.

In many ways, Spanish America as a whole remained in the 'mining frontier' stage. Conquest, exploration, settlement, and exploitation of Spanish America were all spurred on by the prospect of mining, and for more than 300 years, mining determined to a remarkable degree the colonies' hierarchical relationship with the metropolitan core as well the design of their internal political and administrative structure. Such stringency of purpose gave impressive coherence to Spain's architectural design.

The contrasted frontier dynamics of the eighteenth- and nineteenth-century United States' periphery is well documented—a generally outward expansion and infilling that offered high levels of risk, growth and opportunity as well as failure and disappointment, but which retained a vigorous and evolving relationship with central government based on the periphery's political and economic needs for increased population, markets, transport, and advance to Statehood.

In the Spanish empire therefore, the maintenance of strong thrust lines depended primarily on the maintenance of strong 'central' core structures; in engineering terms, the edges *as edges* were not vital to structural integrity. Indeed, they were often zones of neglect where strain energy could if necessary become fracture energy without inflicting serious damage. They could be broken off.

In the United States' tension structure, development of the edges of the structure was essential to the design—to the balance of the overall compressive and tensile forces, to the continued safe construction and extension of the spans, and to the increased economic range and political integration of the 'live load'.

*Edge to Edge: The Crucial Juxtaposition
of the United States and the Viceroyalty of New Spain*

This was the primary contact zone between the Spanish and American empires, and brought two such highly contrasted engineering styles into close proximity that it produced one of the most dynamic, as well as one of the most discordant junctions in the whole of the Americas. It was also the only region where the United States made direct contact with Spain's mining frontier, a frontier which was reviving strongly in the Bourbon period.

The contact was not confined to Mexico. Eastward, the junction of the United States and the Viceroyalty of New Spain had included the lower Mississippi River and New Orleans at an early stage, and the contact zone remained significant in the Gulf of Mexico and the Caribbean, for it was the changes in the Caribbean power balance in the 1600s that had exposed the vulnerability of the archipelago to structural chipping and breakaway. While Spain's huge mainland empire remained intact, the Caribbean islands became the setting for a European presence and a European challenge to Spain's exclusivity in the New World. In many respects, however, those most profoundly influenced by the challenge were the Anglo-Americans.

So far as Spain was concerned, the Caribbean islands and the Guianas had always formed a potentially dangerous Shatter Belt on the threshold of empire. Nevertheless for the most part, it was a manageable zone of strain, even fracture, provided Spain still retained the key ports and sea-lanes in the region. The real significance of the Shatter Belt was its proximity to the Anglo-American colonies. Here was the colonists' closest view of the Spanish empire, at least among those colonists in the business of looking out. For planters in England's southern Tidewater colonies, the Caribbean basin represented the outer rim of another sub-tropical, slave-owning, agrarian society which was nonetheless different (in some ways) from that of Virginia, the Carolinas, or Georgia. Anglo-Americans farther north saw the Caribbean's Shatter Belt as a golden opportunity for trade, including contraband trade, with Spanish as well as other imperial markets, for the Caribbean cul-de-sac was a varied and highly rewarding hunting-ground.

Spain itself rarely had the desire, or the experience, to cope with trading competition, whether this occurred in Europe, the Americas, or Asia. On the west Pacific rim, Macao, not Manila, was the risk-taker. Even in the 1580–1640 period, when Spain incorporated Portugal and all its overseas possessions into the Spanish empire, the Castilians failed to exploit the trading potential of Brazil. The Portuguese on the other hand penetrated every part of Spain's imperial world with outstanding success at this time, not least the lucrative market of Potosí. Two hundred years later, United States traders doing business on the Spanish/Mexican perimeter in the 1780s–1840s—in New Orleans, Vera Cruz, Santa Fe, or Monterey for example—were still astonished by the Spanish perception of ports as passive "revenue factories" for the government exchequer, rather than as local or regional growth points promoting Spanish trade and industry.

For Anglo-American colonists transformed into United States traders, Mexico and Cuba were prime targets, since Mexico was the most advanced, and Havana the most accessible and receptive foreign market for early American enterprise. In the late eighteenth century, the Mexican silver peso was equal in value to the American dollar and trade was crucial because, as one Baltimore merchant put it, "*from Spain alone* we can get specie in return." Between 1795 and 1801, U.S. exports to Mexico and the Caribbean had increased six-fold (to nearly $11 million), and four-fold to Spanish America as a whole.

The Viceroy in Mexico City reported to Spain in 1793 that the new American Republic was presenting creoles with both a highly visible model of prosperity and much competition. In 1790 (when the United States recorded 3.9 millions at its First Census), New Spain's population had reached 6–7 millions, some forty-four per cent of Spanish America's total population, with Mexico City alone containing 113,000. South America was empty by comparison; even the Andean centres together comprised only *c.*twenty-five per cent of the Spanish American total.[95]

New Spain in fact possessed the most diverse economy in Hispanic America, and achieved greater recovery under the Bourbon reforms than any other imperial region. By 1798 Mexico was producing sixty-seven per cent of the Americas' entire output of silver, and Cuba's tobacco and sugar exports were expanding dramatically.[96] As noted earlier, New Spain also contained a more vigorous frontier society in sections of its northern borderlands than anywhere else on the fringes of empire. Despite all the excesses of Spanish imperialism that Mexico presented to American eyes, especially the unacceptable wealth and dominance of the Church and the oligarchy, New Spain's silver resources and market potential rendered it both the nearest and the most stimulating of all the Spanish imperial peripheries for the United States. It was a juxtaposition of lasting significance to both. Here, the supreme risk-takers of the New World were face to face with Spain. The doorstep combination of high demand and still relatively low overall performance in the Mexican and Cuban economies (despite the reform) were an irresistible challenge. British and French merchants would not always be allowed to have the final word.

3. Cross-Bracing

The most striking feature about the geography of settlement in Hispanic America at the end of empire was the lack of any fundamental change in the early population distribution patterns. With few exceptions, a total population of some fifteen million continued to cluster around the pre-Columbian centres, or centres which had been established in the first fifty years of empire. Such population clusters as there were around the coasts and in the cordilleras formed islands in the wilderness, widely separated from

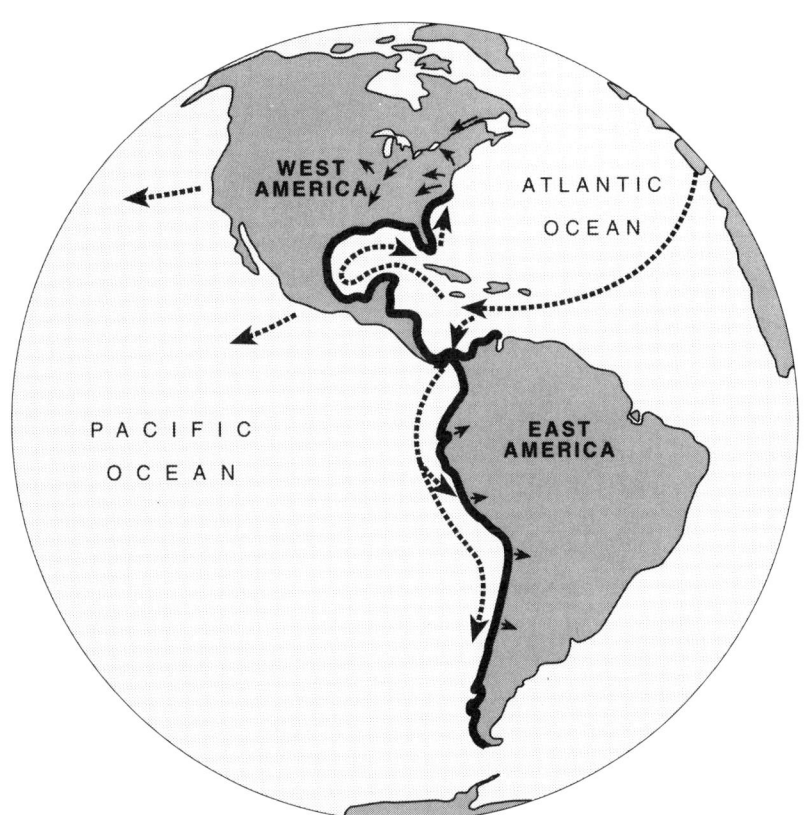

RELATIVE LOCATION IN THE NEW WORLD : WEST AND EAST AMERICA

The geographical fact that North and South America are also West and East America is rarely noted, yet it was to be of lasting significance in the differing imperial patterns of development in the New World.

The early discovery of the Middle Seas and the Panama Isthmus allowed Spain in effect to 'sail past' South America. *The west coast of South America became the western rim of the Atlantic rather than the eastern rim of the Pacific.* There lay the true western margin of Spain's Atlantic world, and the baseline for Spain's eastward, 'reverse' penetration of the Andes.

The role of South America's west coast as an *Atlantic*, not a Pacific, coast was further emphasized by the extreme isolation of this stretch of the Pacific rim. South (i.e. East) America provided a remote and difficult baseline from which to start any voyage across the Pacific. North (i.e. West) America by contrast, already closer to Europe, and offering a number of western land corridors from the Atlantic seaboard into the continental interior, also presented a more serviceable Pacific frontage for trans-Pacific connection, mainly because of the relatively closer proximity of the Asian and American continents in this region, and the more favourable island, wind and current distributions in the north Pacific.

Figure 14

each other, and marginal in relation to the continental land-mass as a whole.

Linkages between these clusters were not encouraged. Spain of course was not alone as an imperial power in organizing its colonies to serve imperial needs in general, and the metropolitan core region in particular. Nor was it alone in neglecting internal linkages between colonies where no military or economic purpose was to be served by such interconnection. But, with the exception of Tsarist Russia, no other European empire failed to cross-brace its structure overland so consistently and for such an enormous span of time as did Spain.

The United States on the other hand became the first to recognize and to exploit the unique dual potential of the New World's 'double ocean' setting in both the Atlantic and the Pacific—two trading seaboards consolidated by strong overland cross-linkage and the development of transcontinental land power.

Like Spain, the United States had also experienced the lasting effects of early encounter. At the very moment American colonists along the Atlantic seaboard were declaring their Independence in July 1776, Spain was building the San Francisco mission and *presidio* 3,000 miles to the west. But when George Washington was being sworn in as the first President of the United States in April 1789, Boston seamen had already entered the Pacific.

The United States was never in doubt about its imperial role. The term EMPIRE was applied to the new country immediately after the end of the Revolutionary War, and became well established during the 1780s–90s. At the same time, the United States knew what it meant by empire—an American not a European structure, an empire defined by territorial scale and expanding trade, not by colonialism (however much 'neocolonialism' would be discernible during some stages of westward expansion).

The virtually simultaneous acquisition of Texas, Oregon, California and New Mexico represented a huge extension to the ground-plan, greater than any that had previously occurred. Yet it was the territorial acquisition for which the United States was most prepared—a filling out to a Pacific coast that was already part of the American maritime trading sphere.

Paradoxically, for a country that was so soon to display a mastery of transcontinental connection, the scale of the early Gold Rush to California in 1849–50 forced Congress to turn immediately to Spain's old basic principle of *interoceánico*. Various canal projects which had followed the 1846 transit agreement with Colombia were shelved; instead, a concession was obtained by the United States for the 46-mile Panama Railroad, built between 1850 and 1855 close to the old Spanish trail. This highly profitable line was linked to scheduled steamship services and used by the U.S. Mail, the army, and for official government business of all kinds. But while the Panama Canal would later play an indispensable role in the United States' 'double ocean' circulation, the Panama Railroad was no more than a temporary tie between New York and San Francisco. Indeed, it accelerated the onset of the transcontinental age.

Styles of Survival

The SPANISH EMPIRE operated for more than three centuries on the American continental mainland; elsewhere, substantial imperial remnants survived for another 100 years. Everywhere in the successor states, to varying degrees, the architectural style and structural mechanics of Spain's New World remain in evidence—from the survival of the early ground-plan to the continued dominance of the early urban hierarchies; from the extreme isolation of much of the interior to the still wholly inadequate cross-bracing overland (both within the state boundaries and especially across international frontiers); and from the durability of a more centralized, more theoretical, approach to structural form, rather than a construction policy combining both philosophical and practical considerations.

After independence, the official adoption of a federal, or quasi-federal, structure by some of the Hispanic successor states has always in practice revealed the structural strength of the surviving imperial compression components, together with the general unsuitability of these old compression components for conversion to the new support towers of a genuine tension structure. Not least, the structural legacy of Spain's imperial design is evident, with only rare exceptions, in the successor states' greater ease in maintaining continuity than in the productive handling of change.

The UNITED STATES EMPIRE, designed and built on site, was always to be more closely associated with the land and with the demands of the environment. While *historical imagery* and *legal framework* dominated Spain's imperial construction, *geographical imagery* had a powerful influence on the United States' perception of empire, on the strategy of expansion, and on the *physical frame-*

work of a new national identity. Sectionalism itself placed major regional social, economic, and political differences in a geographical setting. Moreover, the early emphasis on land survey and mapping, land ownership, land settlement, and land improvement was fundamental to America's entire building program. The empire's original, stunningly radical design has been the key to its survival, since this particular piece of late-eighteenth-century engineering possessed one enormous advantage—it proved to be capable, without major alteration, of handling the transition to the organization of a modern industrialized society of great size and ever-increasing diversity.

This does not mean that the structure is perfect, nor that it cannot be damaged or violated by the careless or the corrupt. Even so, basic design principles involving the continuous interaction of tension and compression, together with the promotion and productive management of risk, were to develop skills in maintaining balance (or retrieving equilibrium), in stimulating and exploiting innovation, and in responding rapidly to change. At the same time, the United States was continuing to hone its own definition of an American 'empire' in terms of territorial scale, integrated transportation, economic productivity, commercial expansion, and political and military power.

Whatever the claims by the United States for a non-European style of empire however, the USA's swift replacement of parts of the British, French, Spanish and Russian empires across much of North America was consciously imperialistic. "No Empire without a mission, and no Empire without a profit—in reality or in imagination" was also true of the United States. The desire to project and bring 'American civilization' to new lands and peoples, the determination to increase national power and strategic advantage, and the brief, overt political imperialism of overseas expansion in 1898–1900, were all the stuff of empire. But by then, the United States, with its huge internal market, had also evolved into a vast and expanding unit of economic production, and it was to be economic imperialism that would most sharply define the United States empire among the other great powers. By the early years of the twentieth century, the USA was poised to present this new and formidable imperial phenomenon to what was, by comparison, a much more slowly modernizing world.

4. Maintaining and Strengthening the United States' Tension Structure

Let every man praise the bridge that carries him over.

(Seventeenth-century English proverb)

> **THE NEED FOR BRIDGE MAINTENANCE**
>
> "People take bridges for granted."
>
> "The danger is always in the lack of maintenance. Once you build a bridge, you have to maintain it to keep it safe."
>
> "The cause of collapse is often traced to poor or delayed maintenance."
>
> "If you do not maintain a bridge, you reduce its life cycle substantially . . . You cannot leave it unattended."
>
> (Extracts from reports and comment on the U.S. Department of Transportation's *Report on the Nation's Highway Bridges and National Bridge Inventory*, (1994–5)

In scale and complexity, the United States is both the largest and the oldest tension structure in the world. It has also been, so far, the most successful.

The early and continued dual policy of increasing the 'live load' *and* facilitating its dispersal demanded sustained levels of risk-management by democratic means on a scale completely unknown up to that time—risk-management that was simultaneously required to expand territorially and to become more coherent. The United States structure was therefore to depend on the *creative* use of tension.

As a solution to inherent complexity, Federalism is always a difficult structure to maintain. Faced with a range of historical, geographical, or cultural variations (or with all three), legislators over the years in all five continents have clutched at Federalism (or at looser Confederation) as the 'obvious' structural solution for the problems of diversity. But Federalism is not a universal political panacea for the discordant human condition, and it is certainly not a political catch-all into which all the regional, ethnic, or racial conflicts in any given area can be conveniently stowed, and then tidily contained.

The United States not only invented Federalism but also made its construction and maintenance look deceptively easy to the superficial observer. 'Unity in Diversity' became a popular slogan for nineteenth- and twentieth-century federations and confederations modelled ostensibly on the United States' blueprint. But although the accompanying tenet 'Diversity is Strength' sounds attractive, it is structurally unsound as a building principle unless matched by sophisticated levels of engineering and design. Wherever increased diversity and increased tensile force are introduced, these have to be balanced (i.e. 'resisted') by increased centralizing or compressive force if the system is to operate and the structure to stand.

The immense importance of the *early* stylists of the United States' tension structure struck De Tocqueville forcibly in the 1830s. While many visitors commented on the blend of idealism and pragmatism that characterized the United States, De Tocqueville also emphasized the vital contribution of the early New Englanders who, unlike the slave-owning planters of Virginia, were "more conversant with the notions of right and the true freedom." The Calvinist tradition of thrift, perseverance, and the belief that to labour industriously was one of God's commands, is an inextricable part of the USA's maintenance manual.

* * *

STRUCTURAL ANALYSIS

Structural Analysis is for the most part concerned with finding the structural response to the LIVE LOAD . . . While the dead load or weight of a structure should be known accurately to its designer, the engineer frequently does not know precisely the uses to which the structure will be put during its lifetime – the *traffic* which will use his bridge, the *lateral deflection* of his building under wind load, and the *randomness* of heavy snowfall and earthquake shock.

(W.R. Spillers, *Introduction to Structures*)

The problem of load estimation, and the effects such loads will have on a structure, is probably one of the hardest with which engineers have to deal.

(H.J. Collins, *The Structural Engineer*)

"No sooner do you set foot upon American soil than you are stunned by a kind of tumult." De Tocqueville's experience is still relevant; the need to cope with the problems of expansion and diversification of the 'live load' has remained intrinsic to the design.

Structural Analysis: basic principles in the United States. Increased Carrying-Capacity dependent on Assimilation

Despite the severe shocks and vibration caused to the structure at the time, heavy bursts of immigration into the United States have for the most part in the past successfully demonstrated the creative use of tension. The "in-sweeping" has always been accompanied by a natural anxiety, and a continuous questioning, among the existing population as to whether the millions of new arrivals "will foreignize us or we will Americanize them." In the past however, *Americanization* by both formal and informal means has always been recognized by the newcomers, whether with joy or reluctance, as an essential design feature of U.S. construction, not as an optional extra. As early as 1797, John Jay had stressed: "I wish to see our people more *Americanized*, if I may use that expression," thereby sparking the adoption and rapid spread of the term. "It means," wrote Noah Webster in 1806, "*to render American.*"

Those would-be immigrants who disliked the prospect of assimilation were advised to emigrate elsewhere. Nineteenth-century German *auswanderer* wishing to preserve their national identity intact were warned by Johann Wappäus of Leipzig, for example, to settle "amongst any other people than the Americans, because of their prodigious power of assimilation."[97] In the event, the bulk of German immigrants went to the United States. In the nineteenth and early twentieth centuries, nearly six million Germans emigrated to America, over ninety per cent of the total German migration, and together with Austrians, German-Swiss, and Russian-Germans, comprised the largest single 'national' group entering the United States.[98] Today, those recording German ancestry still represent the largest single element in the U.S. population. This vital contribution has provided an indispensable strengthening of the 'live load' (both urban and rural), a dynamic reinforcement of all the country's major structural components, and a powerful example of the meaning and purpose of assimilation in American society.

* * *

STRESS AND SAFETY

Safety means that no point of the structure is stressed above a value called the ALLOWABLE or WORKING STRESS. . . . In any structure there are innumerable regions of stress concentration in which it becomes impractical, or even impossible, to analyze the stresses. In such cases we often tend just to overlook the stress peak and let the material fend for itself; this is particularly true in the vicinity of connections.

Stress raisers are unavoidable in structures. In many cases there is no obvious reason why the attainment of a critical stress at some point of the structure should necessarily coincide with the exhaustion of the safe carrying capacity of the structure. If the material is a *ductile* one, a phenomenon called *redistribution of stresses* occurs which will tend to relieve overstressed portions of the structure, and throw a fair share of the load to the understressed portions.

PREDICTABILITY OF LOADS. In some structures, *unexpected loads or overloads may be routine*, and provision must be made for their occurrence, since SAFETY means sufficient strength to resist applied loads without danger of collapse.

(K.H. Gerstle, *Basic Structural Design*)

CRITICAL LOAD

The strength of a structure is its capacity to support the expected and the unexpected loads without distress. There is always a CRITICAL LOAD, however: that is, the maximum load the structure can carry without buckling, suffering permanent deformation, or failure.

(A.J. Francis, *Introducing Structures*)

Despite its appeal as the land of opportunity, the United States was never meant to be "all things to all men" any more than Spain was in the New World.

Not all tension can be accommodated, even in the most spectacular and skilfully constructed tension structure. There is a critical load. It is still sometimes forgotten that any increase in tensile forces must be 'resisted' in structural terms by an increase in compressive force. As the deck weight is increased, and as more tensile and torsional stress and strain are introduced into the suspension system, so the foundations and support towers, among other components, must increase their own compressive thrust into the bedrock—and be enlarged and toughened in order to do so. Ultimately, the people must decide what loading the structure can bear, and legislate accordingly. And in making this decision, it is always the compression components—their strength, their stability and the cost of their upkeep—that will be the critical factor. They support the tension members; without them, the cables collapse, the decks fall.

Unlike any massive compression structure, sections of which can remain standing, even usable, after a major collapse, the collapse of any part of a tension structure destroys both its form and its function. The design itself of course anticipates heavy use. Group tensions and the tumult of the 'live load' are part of the structural dynamics of the bridge. But the structural dynamics and critical loading of a suspension bridge also involve reliable working estimates of the tolerable weight, as well as the control, and the self-discipline, of the traffic.

Americanization

America is not an "idea" that can be interpreted in unlimited ways. **America is a structure intended, like all structures, to sustain loads, accommodate services, work efficiently, and stay up**. The United States does not need "reinventing", whatever that is supposed to mean. Maintenance, repair, renewal, and strengthening are not reinvention, nor are they un-American. Indeed, the opportunity for repair work on the structure using Constitutional tools made a strong impression on De Tocqueville: "The great privilege of the Americans does not simply consist in their being more enlightened than other nations, but in their being able to repair the faults they may commit."

The design of the structure, and the origins of the 'live load', are sometimes confused however. The support towers, decks, suspension system, end-fittings and anchorages of the United States' tension structure were never located in Europe, never in Africa, in Asia, in Australasia, nor anywhere else in the Americas— and they are not located there now. The structural components have always been positioned entirely within the United States, designed and made there, to be shifted and strengthened where necessary as the span was extended. The richly varied *origins* of the 'live load' are indisputably multinational, multiracial, and multicultural, but once legally part of the structure, the 'live load' citizenry must become identified, sooner or later, by only *one* word—American. This is not a sentimental cliché nor a modern-day irrelevance. It is neither crude stereotyping nor outdated technology. It remains part of the permanent building code for maximizing the total weight of the 'live load', safely and efficiently, on this particular tension structure. Those few who cannot accept this still basic principle, for whatever reason, are neither maintaining nor strengthening the structure, or its load.

To be a temporarily 'hyphenated American' has been a long-established entrance to United States society, an early staging-post for new traffic on the bridge. But its continued use as a necessary form of identification for any individual or group among the 'live load' is a sign of weakness, individual or collective, however vociferously this is denied. *Valid* adjectival ethnic labels do not last long in the United States. For some who still need the added identity of a permanently hyphenated existence, this identity is often romanticized; the complexities of history can readily be rejected in favour of the agreeably softer focus of legend. For some, the need for a 'cause' or a political lobby within the USA will fan a few selected embers in the fire of memory which, in reality, bear little resemblance to the 'old country' they purport to represent. An American's sentimental journey 'home' after two or three generations, however congenial, emphasizes many more fundamental differences than similarities between the two environments. This basic building principle applies to all the builders, whatever the source or size of the original work force—be it British or French, German or Scandinavian, Irish or Italian, Russian or Czech, Polish or Greek, Chinese or Japanese, Malay or Moroccan. Moreover, if all those who cling to the term 'African' American could go to that continent, the overwhelming majority would discover for themselves how very little African there is about an 'African' American. The true power and potential of every black American is sapped whenever the label is applied or adopted. Of course, the inclusive term 'black' is as inaccurate as the inclusive term 'white'; both are simply the least unsatisfactory.

By the same token, to call American Indians 'Native Americans' as an exclusive, distinguishing identification merely replaces a late-fifteenth-century error with a late-twentieth-century error. The former was the more excusable. There are currently some 240 million native Americans in the United States, and fidgeting with capitalization—native and Native, or with the tautologous 'native-born', makes no difference to the true meaning of the word. If the tribal name, like the tribal land, is still a genuinely distinguishing feature, then, if wished, it should be used. Other American citizens, however, can accurately claim no more than Indian descent (or a specific tribal or linguistic-group descent) as part of their contribution to the hugely diversified origins of American society. For the terms 'American' and 'Americanization' already represent a new and necessary creation from countless strong and varied ingredients.

'Multiculturalism', by contrast, is a policy of giving equal attention, and often special emphasis, to the diverse cultural backgrounds and characteristics of the different 'groups' in American society in order to promote the differences, and to ensure their consolidation and preservation. If accurately defined, and not used merely as a loose synonym for the diversity of origin and viewpoint within the American population, 'multiculturalism' is a debilitating exercise. Indeed, the myth of 'multiculturalism' as a permanent and desirable characteristic of the United States' 'live load' is structurally unsound, a permanent crutch offered to wounded (or classified wounded) individuals which has been disguised, sometimes unintentionally, as a helping hand. Only the weak, whether on the giving or receiving end, will eventually be left with it, dependent on it, and further weakened by it. Movements which originate as a fight against arrant discrimination, or to correct the balance in too narrow or distorted a view of history and society, are long overdue and are of great value, provided that in correcting the imbalance they introduce no new inaccuracies or distortions. But the challenge to every member of the legal 'live load' remains that of being or becoming an American citizen in an American society that is intrinsically diversified but not cellular. It must still be the opportunity for individual development and self-reliance, not the palsy of an exclusive racial or ethnic group identity, in many cases no more than a short step from censorship, error, bigotry, and renewed discrimination or racism. Such burying of the individual in the mass is in fact a *medieval throw-back* for those in the New World, since it not only stifles true diversity and freedom of expression but also revives the inquisitorial style, rather than the more productive adversarial style, in the ordering and management of society.

For every U.S. citizen, the past—the most relevant past—is linked only to the United States, and to the citizen's future within it. This is not rootlessness, merely an individual's relaxing of his or her grip on a more distant history, and the shedding of history's grip on the individual. As Zbigniew Brzezinski observed, combining ethnic, racial, and geographical perspectives:

> For most Americans, the 200-year history of the United States is not a personally intimate engagement with the past. Indeed, if most Americans were deeply involved with their personal national pasts, they could not be united, as they are, as a people. It is their shared commitment to the future that defines them as Americans ... Fascination with the past is not compatible with the dominant American outlook. Unity focused on the future, not derived from an emotionally shared past, creates the American consciousness.[99]

Ethnic subcultures, wrote Schlesinger, if they have genuine vitality, will be sufficiently instilled in children by family, church, and community. Part of the role of the public school, on the other hand, is to encourage children to become contributors to a common American culture.[100]

This emphasizes the responsibilities of the education system when calculating critical load. In the design and performance of the tension structure, maximum benefit and efficiency depends on each structural component and every member of the legal 'live load' being used to its fullest capacity. While this now involves addressing problems that are by no means confined to the United States, the realization of 'fullest capacity' in the huge American tension structure requires a better educated population and improved American standards: higher expectations, higher demands, and better teaching (not, as a rule, more teachers) in many of the public schools. The drive to achieve higher standards of education for a large percentage of the United States' legal 'live load' has become an urgent priority in the maintenance program; it is the only means of invigorating and releasing individual talent, and, at the same time, of enabling the tension structure as a whole to sustain its role in the modern world.

The United States education system has a further specific responsibility—that is to ensure that all members of the legal 'live load' have a sound knowledge of the methods of construction and operation of their great support framework. In this sense, *every American citizen must become a structural engineer*, since active, informed participation by the 'live load' in the workings of the various compression and tension components at local, State, and Federal levels has always been an integral part of the overall design. As well as communicating knowledge and understanding of United States history and geography, clear, systematic teaching of the United States Constitution and of United States Government is a basic essential for all American schools. Builders and repairers must know how the structure works.

The English Language

In checking and carrying out America's regular maintenance and repair program, it is dangerous to ignore the basic principle that English is the only structural language in the United States. English-language classes justify public expenditure. Bilingual programs are almost always counter-productive and should be abandoned; they isolate and often hobble those they are intended to help, and certainly delay the rapid acquisition of standard English. Supporters of bilingual teaching, which in some cases is spread over many years, are noticeably reluctant to set up genuine control experiments showing the results that can be obtained from equivalent, or reduced, funding and resources invested in intensive English-language classes over a much shorter term. For the most part, individuals learn a foreign language as fast as they have to, and only that fast. Indeed, the vast majority of mankind will never make the effort to learn a foreign language unless it is essential first for their survival, and then for their material progress.

The requirement to learn English in order to live and work in the United States, and to gain citizenship, should not be overturned or side-stepped. Where this has occurred, urgent restoration work is required. Foreign-language notices, instructions, and services are for new arrivals and visitors—in ports, depots, and hotels; they should not be permanent and ubiquitous props for those anxious to be part of the United States' structure but unwilling to learn its one structural language. Specific language challenges have changed over the centuries, but structural imperatives have not. The English language remains one of the essential support and distributive mechanisms throughout the structure as a whole.

Changing Immigration Patterns

It must be said that the United States' own policies on both immigration and language have been conflicting, and often uncertain in recent years, during a period of rapidly changing global politics and domestic pressures. Three major pieces of legislation on immigration in the last thirty years will, unless modified or selectively repealed, continue to have more immediate and long-term impact on the United States' tension structure than any of the country's earlier historical surges of immigration—an impact not only on the composition of the 'live load' but also on the associated structural costs of maintaining and strengthening the suspension system.

Whatever support it attracted at the time, the 1965 legislation known as the Immigration and Nationality Act Amendments, and its proponents, failed to present any competent overall analysis, or any convincing evidence that detailed calculations had been undertaken (and costs worked out) concerning the possible major shifts in the weight and balance of the future 'live load' that could result from the Act. It abolished the national-origins quota system and favoured the principles of "family-reunification", "refugee" status, and "asylum-seekers" at the expense, in practice, of immigration linked to employment skills and the needs of the economy. The 1965 Act triggered a new, thirty-year period of mass immigration, heavily weighted in its implementation towards a few developing (Third World) states in Latin America and Asia, while also initiating new immigration from Africa and the Caribbean.

The far-reaching consequences of the 1965 Act may have been unintended (as some have already acknowledged), but the possibility of such consequences, matched against a full range of other variables, could and should have been foreseen, and made available for serious prior discussion by the people, *whatever decision was eventually reached*. Only the unskilled, the slipshod, and the devious, along with the uninformed, offer "the wisdom of hindsight" as a substitute for lack of foresight and accountability.

In the mid-1960s, immigration had been allowed to become part of the Civil Rights movement, a guise which ignored the fact that immigration to the United States is no one's civil right, and which blurred the real focus and true justice of the Civil Rights reform.

After the Immigration and Nationality Act Amendments of 1965, two further pieces of related legislation have increased both the weight and the imbalance of the 'live load'. In 1986, the Immigration Reform and Control Act legalized, on a scale unparalleled in America's history, *illegal* aliens who had been living in the United States since before 1982, as well as numbers of illegal agricultural labourers working in the USA in 1986 on perishable goods. In all, nearly three million illegal entrants to the United States have been legalized since 1989, a despairing recognition both of the difficulties and of the failure of the United States to control illegal immigration.

The third major piece of legislation, the 1990 Immigration Act, increased total annual immigration substantially once more under a flexible (and "pierceable") cap, while maintaining preferential treatment for "family reunification" under a range of different provisions whose application had widened considerably following the 1986 legalization process. Totals continued to dwarf the numbers admitted on the basis of "employment-based" skills.

So far as the late-twentieth-century loading of the United States' tension structure is concerned, the result has been that in the decade 1984–1993, 9.3 million immigrants have been granted permanent residence in the USA—a figure greater than any previous census decade in America's history, including the earlier record entries of 5.2 million in 1881–90, 8.7 million in 1901–10, and 5.7 million in 1911–20. In these three massive waves of immigration, over ninety per cent of the immigrants were European in origin, augmented by those entering from Canada. The ratio of immigrants to total population was of course much higher at the turn of the century, but the needs of the country were also very different—settlement expansion and infilling was still underway in the Midwest and the Far West, while most of the East's mining, manufacturing, and construction industries, as well as urban and commercial services, were still labour-intensive.

Perhaps no other area of the United States' structural analysis attracts so much spurious argument and so little calm, objective investigation as does current United States immigration policy. Indeed, vested interests of one sort or another appear to abhor such analysis. The financial arguments and the economic implications for the U.S. suspension system and its existing 'live load' in the modern world of current immigration patterns may be dismissed by some as "narrow", "hysterical", or even "racist", but they will always have to be calculated in the end. And only after such calculations have been presented to the people can any informed decisions be taken by them—the legal 'live load'—to expand, or to reduce, or to otherwise adjust the loading process.

The 1994 population of 261.7 million is estimated, on current trends, to reach 300 million by the year 2011, and about 350 million by 2040. In addition to the unprecedented growth in legal immigration, alien border crossings have continued to increase, and much illegal immigration remains uncontrolled. Control is difficult, but would not be impossible. Whether by individuals or by governments, tolerance of illegal immigration is not compassion. It is a betrayal of the rights of, and the obligations to, the legal 'live load'. The U.S. Immigration and Naturalization Service estimates net illegal entry at between 300,000 and 500,000 annually; the Census Bureau uses an official estimate of 200,000 annually, and for the 1990s as a whole, estimates a combined legal and illegal immigrant entry into the United States of 12–13 million. Under existing legislation, some place the estimate at nearer 15–18 million.

Mexico far outstrips all other countries in the world as the greatest source of both legal and illegal immigrants to the United States. Illegal Mexican immigrants in fact comprise about seventy per cent of the USA's estimated 4 million illegal residents. At the same time, Cuban "refugees" acquired a special fast-track legal admission to the United States' 'live load' under the Cuban Adjustment Act of 1966. The scale of immigration into the United States over the last twenty years or so has now brought the country's foreign-born population to nearly 23 million, more than forty-five per cent of them Hispanic, and with the heaviest concentrations of Hispanic immigration in California, Florida, Texas, and New York.

Immigration and Language

Given the size and acceleration of Latin American immigration into the United States in recent years, the sheer weight of numbers has been compounded by the continuing high proportion of Spanish--only speakers. The USA's Hispanic population comprise the highest percentage in the total population regularly using a language other than English at home, and by far the highest proportion recorded in the 1990 Census who do not speak English "very well". The question on the ability to speak English was asked by the U.S. Bureau of the Census for the first time in the country's history in 1980. Spanish speakers (based on those using Spanish at home) make up the largest number of "linguistically isolated households" in the United States, i.e. those households in which no person aged 14 years or over speaks only English, and no person aged 14 years or over who speaks a language other than English speaks English "very well".

The weight problem has been further aggravated by the fact that, while not ignoring special circumstances, Spanish-speaking Latin American immigrants *as a group* have rarely shown the same passion for learning English as quickly as possible that many other struggling waves of immigrants to the United States have traditionally displayed, and still do. New legislation on language in the 1960s once again became associated with the Civil Rights movement, and although broadly based, was strongly geared in practice to the demands of the monolingual Hispanic immigrants. The Voting Rights Act of 1965, so central to black Civil Rights and to the need to eradicate tactics still used in some southern States to disfranchise black voters, also prohibited any requirement for the voter to be able to read, write, and understand English. In 1975, reinforcing legislation under the Voting Rights Act Amendment stipulated that all forms, instructions, ballot papers and so forth were to be provided in the language of the minority group as well as in English. This ruling was to apply wherever more than five per cent of the citizens of voting age in the State (or the political subdivision) were members of a single language minority, and wherever the illiteracy rate of such persons as a group was higher than the national illiteracy rate.

Meanwhile, accompanying these 'Bilingual Election Requirements' came the Bilingual Education Programs sponsored by the Bilingual Education Act of 1968, in which Congress addressed itself to the "millions of children of limited English-speaking ability," whose problem is caused by the fact that [the Finding stated] "they come from environments where the dominant language is other than English." Since over the centuries, the arrival of millions of immigrants and their children who were quite unable initially to speak any English at all has been an intrinsic characteristic of the United States, the 1968 legislation exposed a new and serious structural flaw, but introduced a misguided policy for dealing with it. The Bilingual Education Programs quickly became a huge and highly expensive growth industry, time-consuming and limitless—a nursery for 'multiculturalism', and one of the least efficient methods known for teaching a basic knowledge of English.

Once in place however, the comfort and convenience of a bilingual environment are not relinquished without a struggle. Before long, group lobbyists and vested interests come to insist upon a *permanent* alteration to the official single-language component in the United States' structure, rather than accept the fact that the need for alteration in this case lies not in the structural framework but in the unreasonable assumptions made by certain of the minority groups within the 'live load'. Those Hispanics (by no means all) who demand ever-increasing bilingual programs, and bilingual services, together with those who seek in practice to maintain and extend permanent enclaves of *Spanish-only* speakers within the United States, are damaging the structure, however much this is disputed. Some assert that the traditional 'Americanization' process will be fully achieved in time, an assertion made perhaps more in hope than from close comparative study of past and present methods of defining 'Americanization', and achieving it. Others contend that the claims for evidence of gradual 'Americanization' and ethnic convergence, particularly within the United States' southern periphery and the southwest are unconvincing, and unsubstantiated by trends and by fact.[101] The modern dynamics of this old juxtaposition of the Spanish and United States empires has been dominated in recent years by the constant stream of new legal and illegal immigrants into urban areas with high concentrations of Hispanic population. Studies have shown that this continued spatial and cultural reinforcement by the new arrivals over several decades keeps the Spanish language alive and retards the acquisition of English.

In May 1993, Florida's Dade County Commissioners repealed the 'English-only' ordinance which had been passed in 1980 in response to the rapid increase in Cuban immigration. At that period, Dade County population (which includes Miami) was about one-third Hispanic. By 1993, well over half the County's population was Hispanic, fashioning a new requirement that all local government documents and information be printed in both English and Spanish. It is sometimes claimed that bilingualism is increasing in the existing areas of Spanish monolingualism in the United States, and that "over the long term" a growing familiarity with English will be seen to be advantageous. In practice, however, there are many well-established Hispanic immigrants working in shops, offices, transport, and manufacturing, who have no facility in English, do not intend to acquire any, and have no need to do so. Whatever contribution they may make to the economy, Spanish-only speakers will always be part of the weakness rather than the strength of America's 'live load'.

Language will remain an essential element in the assessment of permissible stress and strain concentrations within

the tension framework, since the use of English as the only official language is no more of an optional extra in the American structure today than it has ever been in the past; it is an indispensable structural component. Breaching of what until recent years had been a *de facto* requirement indicates that English should now be declared, *de jure*, to be the United States' only official language.[102]

* * *

Meaning well is not the same as doing well. The naive philosophy that 'meaning well' excuses everything and is in itself enough, is untenable. No strong society, and no permanent structure of any sort, has ever been built on such a principle. The vast majority of the 'live load' must be maintainers and repairers of the bridge as well as users. They must be supports as well as merely sources of weight and tension.

Within even the strongest and most ingenious tension structure, not all tension is creative; some is destructive. Engineering skills and engineering experience have always enabled America's great army of on-site builders to distinguish the two. Innumerable joints and junctions—social, economic, historical, geographic—articulate American society, and every generation has had to calculate the critical load, and the margins of tolerance, in order to maintain structural safety. Limits must be set, and within these limits, assimilation and integration remain fundamental to the design.

Engineering is a practical as well as a theoretical science. The United States invented, and has constructed, a huge tension structure of great openness, elegance, beauty, and utility. It is a structure that, well ahead of its time, adopted the functionalist philosophy that "Structural action should be evident to the layman." There is no superfluous decoration on this great suspension bridge; its structural lines are both form and decoration combined. The people use it, abuse it, care about it, complain about it, flock to it, and hang on to it, while going about their business.

Risk promotion is a risky strategy however. The United States is already an enormously visible and accommodating structure, but its capacity to absorb stress and strain can still be overestimated, and its innate flexibility, though stiffened, can still be overstretched and destroyed. There is never any permanent guarantee that a structure will survive, and there is certainly no automatic guarantee that the United States' tension structure will survive. It is a remarkable construction but it is not immune to disaster. Demolition is an unskilled exercise compared with the ability required to construct and maintain an exceptionally long-spanned, heavily used, tension framework—a framework, moreover, that is still required to meet the three age-old conditions of "well-building"— **Commoditie, Firmenes, and Delight**. Nevertheless, if the basic building principles and guidelines are strictly followed, the United States possesses the originality of design, the resources, and the experience to become the most durable imperial structure the world has ever seen. It is the only remaining empire on earth with global reach and global power.

There will always be the need for checks and balances, for maintenance, repair, reinforcement, adjustment, and expanded opportunity. But not for fundamental change. Continuity of purpose, discipline and sacrifice in construction, and faithfulness in design, still remain the United States' greatest contribution to both the Old World and the New, to the past and to the future:

> In 1780, while the House of Representatives of the State of Connecticut was in session, the noonday sky was so strangely darkened that some members, anticipating the approach of Judgment Day, called on the Speaker to adjourn the session so that they might prepare to meet their God. The Speaker ruled: "Gentlemen, either this is the end of the world or it is not. If it is not, our business should proceed. If it is, I prefer to be found doing my duty. Let lights be brought."[103]

Notes

Abbreviations:

CHLA The Cambridge History of Latin America
HAHR The Hispanic American Historical Review
JLAS Journal of Latin American Studies

Part I: Spain's Compression Structure

1. *The Journal of Christopher Columbus*, trs. C. Jane, rev. and annotated L.A. Vigneras, London and New York, 1960, p. 2; also *The Log of Christopher Columbus*, trs. R.H. Fuson, Camden, Maine and Southampton, UK, 1987, p. 52.
2. G. Jackson, *The Making of Medieval Spain*, London, 1972, p. 54.
3. J. Klein, *The Mesta: a study in Spanish Economic History, 1273–1836*, Harvard Univ. Press, 1920. See also R. Aitken, 'Routes of Transhumance on the Spanish Meseta', *Geographical Journal*, 106 (1945), pp. 59–69; C.J. Bishko, 'The Castilian as Plainsman: the medieval ranching frontier in La Mancha and Extremadura', in A.R. Lewis and T.F. McGann (eds), *The New World looks at its History*, Univ. of Texas Press, 1963, pp. 47–69; D.E. Vassberg, *Land and Society in Golden Age Castile*, Cambridge Univ. Press, 1984, pp. 79–83.
4. C.J. Bishko, 'The Peninsular background of Latin American cattle ranching', *HAHR*, 32 (1952), pp. 491–515. See also K.W. Butzer, 'Cattle and sheep from Old to New Spain: historical antecedents', *Annals of the Association of American Geographers*, 78 (1988), p. 43.
5. Klein, *The Mesta*, pp. 22–3; D.R. Ringrose, 'Carting in the Hispanic World: an example of divergent development', *HAHR*, 50 (1970), pp. 33–5.
6. L. Suárez Fernández, 'The Kingdom of Castile in the Fifteenth Century', in R. Highfield (ed.) *Spain in the Fifteenth Century, 1369–1516*, London, 1972, pp. 84–5.
7. *Ibid.*
8. Among the many biographies of Christopher Columbus, see S.E. Morison, *Admiral of the Ocean Sea*, 2 vols, Boston, 1942. See also Ferdinand Columbus, *The Life of Christopher Columbus by his son, Ferdinand*, trs. B. Keen, Rutgers Univ. Press, 1959. Successive editions of the four voyages, and other readings, are found in R.H. Major (ed.), *Select Letters of Christopher Columbus, with other original documents, relating to his Four Voyages to the New World*, Hakluyt Society, London, 1870; C. Jane (ed.), *Select Documents illustrating the Four Voyages of Columbus*, 2 vols, Hakluyt Society, London,

1930, 1933; O. Dunn and J.E. Kelley, Jr. (trs. and eds), *The Diario of Christopher Columbus's First Voyage to America, 1492–1493*, Univ. of Oklahoma Press, 1989; B.W. Ife (trs. and ed.), *Journal of the First Voyage*, Warminster, UK, 1990, and *Letters from America: Columbus's First Accounts of the 1492 Voyage*, King's College, London, 1992; M. Zamora, *Reading Columbus*, Univ. of California Press, 1993. Also *supra*, n. 1.

9. L. Weckmann, 'The Middle Ages in the Conquest of America', in L. Hanke (ed.) *History of Latin American Civilization*, Boston, 1967, I, p. 11.

10. "Sábese la concesión del Papa Alejandro; la división del mundo como una naranja." Letter of Alonso de Zuazo to Charles V, 22 January 1518.
In neither the Papal Bull (1493) nor the Treaty of Tordesillas (1494) was there any specific reference to an extension of the Demarcation Line right around the globe. The suggestion, and then the assumption, that it did so followed the European discovery of the Pacific Ocean. It is then that we first come across the belief that the Pope had in fact divided the whole world between Spain and Portugal. (See E.G. Bourne's Introduction in E.H. Blair and J.A. Robertson (eds), *The Philippine Islands, 1493–1803–1898*, Cleveland, Ohio, 1903–9, I, p. 25.)

11. Columbus's Letter on his First Voyage, 15 February 1493, on board the caravel *Niña*, off the Azores, during his return. Addressed to the Crown official Santángel, for transmission to the Spanish Monarchs, Isabella and Ferdinand. (See, *inter alia*, S.E. Morison, *Christopher Columbus, Mariner*, New York, 1955, pp. 149–55; and Jane/Vigneras, *The Journal*, pp. 191–202.)

12. Estimates of the size of the native population on the eve of the European invasions vary widely and continue to be debated. S.F. Cook and W. Borah favoured high estimates (e.g. Central Mexico, 25 million), A. Rosenblat a much lower figure (Central Mexico, 4.5 million). See W.M. Denevan (ed.), *The Native Population of the Americas in 1492*, Univ. of Wisconsin Press, 1976, 2nd ed. 1992; also L. Bethell's Note in *CHLA*, I, 1984, pp. 145–6. For a later commentary, see W.M. Denevan, 'The Pristine Myth: the landscape of the Americas in 1492', in K.W. Butzer (ed.), 'The Americas before and after 1492: current geographical research', *Annals of the Association of American Geographers*, 82 (1992), pp. 370–1. Estimates here include 17.2 million for Mexico, 5.6 million for Central America, 3 million for the Caribbean, 15.7 million for the Andes, and 8.6 million for lowland South America. Given perhaps 3–4 million in the remainder of North America (and a margin of error of *c*.twenty per cent), a New World aboriginal population of between 43 and 65 million is proposed.

13. *Cortés: the Life of the Conqueror by his Secretary, Francisco López de Gómara*, trs. and ed. L.B. Simpson, Univ. of California Press, 1964, pp. 321–2, 334, 396–404. Also *Hernán Cortés: Letters from Mexico*, trs. and ed. A.R. Pagden, Oxford Univ. Press, 1972; The Fourth Letter to Charles V, pp. 320–1; see also pp. 277, 286, 328.

14. Antonio Pigafetta, *Magellan's Voyage: a narrative account of the First Circumnavigation*, trs. and ed. R.A. Skelton, Yale Univ. Press, 1969.
The exact date of the first printed edition of Pigafetta's journal is unknown, but scholars place its publication soon after 1525.

15. An indispensable study on the development of the Galleon's trans-Pacific trade is that of W.L. Schurz, *The Manila Galleon*, New York, 1939.
16. Between one and four ships annually comprised the Manila Galleon until 1593, when Philip II restricted it to two ships of no more than 300 tons. But in fact, the restriction on the size of the galleons was never enforced. See Schurz, *The Manila Galleon*, pp. 193–6, 251.
17. For a comprehensive survey of Spain and the Pacific see O.H.K. Spate, *The Spanish Lake* (1979), *Monopolists and Freebooters* (1983), and *Paradise Found and Lost* (1988), an important trilogy entitled *The Pacific since Magellan*, Australian National Univ. Press, Canberra and London. See also Blair and Robertson, *The Philippine Islands*; K.R. Andrews, *Drake's Voyages: a reassessment of their place in Elizabethan maritime expansion*, London, 1967, pp. 40–80; E.G.R. Taylor, *Tudor Geography, 1485–1583*, London, 1930, pp. 110–19; and *Late Tudor and Early Stuart Geography, 1583–1650*, London, 1934.
18. Padre Casimiro Díaz, *Conquistas de las Islas Filipinas*, Madrid, 1698. For other accounts of the dangers and hardships endured by those on the eastbound voyages, see Schurz, *The Manila Galleon*, pp. 251–74.
19. E. Schäfer, *El Consejo Real y Supremo de las Indias*, 2 vols, Seville, 1935–47; C.H. Haring, *The Spanish Empire in America*, Oxford Univ. Press, New York, rev. edn 1952. (Chap. 6 'The Council of the Indies', forms part of a wide-ranging institutional history of the Spanish American empire.) See also J.H. Parry, *The Spanish Seaborne Empire*, London, 1966, pp. 63–4, 194–8.
20. J.H. Parry, *The Spanish Theory of Empire in the Sixteenth Century*, Cambridge Univ. Press, 1940, provides a clear, comprehensive introduction. A detailed study of the administrative divisions of empire is contained in Haring, *Spanish Empire in America*, chaps 4, 5, 7–9. See also Parry, *Spanish Seaborne Empire*, pp. 204–11; C. Gibson, *Spain in America*, New York, 1966, pp. 90–100; J. Lynch, *Spain under the Habsburgs*, II, *Spain and America, 1598–1700*, Oxford, 1969, 2nd edn 1981, pp. 19–25; J.H. Elliott, 'Spain and America in the Sixteenth and Seventeenth Centuries', in *CHLA*, I, 1984, pp. 287–300. For a comprehensive and masterly study of the age of Philip II, see F. Braudel, *The Mediterranean and the Mediterranean World in the age of Philip II* (trs.), 2 vols; 1st publ. Paris, 1949, 1966; London, 1972–3. On a selected office, see R.S. Chamberlain, 'The *Corregidor* in Castile in the Sixteenth Century and the *Residencia* as applied to the *Corregidor*', *HAHR*, 23 (1943), pp. 222–57; and J.H. Parry, *The Audiencia of New Galicia in the Sixteenth Century*, Cambridge Univ. Press, 1948.
21. Elliott, 'Spain and America in the Sixteenth and Seventeenth Centuries', pp. 299–300.
22. P.W. Powell, *Soldiers, Indians, and Silver: the northward advance of New Spain, 1550–1600*, Univ. of California Press, 1952, pp. 8, 28–31.
23. J.V. Fifer, *Bolivia: Land, Location, and Politics since 1825*, Cambridge Univ. Press. 1972, pp. 164–6, 175.
24. There is a huge literature on the role of the Church in Spanish America, both general and specialized. Among the former, see Haring, *Spanish Empire in America*, chap. 10; J.H. Elliott, *Imperial Spain, 1469–1716*, London, 1963, Pelican edn 1970, pp. 99–110; Parry, *Spanish Seaborne*

Empire, pp. 152–72; Gibson, *Spain in America*, pp. 68–89. Also J. M. Barnadas, 'The Catholic Church in colonial Spanish America', *CHLA*, I, 1984, pp. 511–40.

25. See, for example, the discussion by L. Hanke, *The Spanish struggle for justice in the conquest of America*, Univ. of Pennsylvania Press, 1949; and his *Aristotle and the American Indians*, London, 1959. In contrast to the debate about the treatment of the Indians, the *legitimacy* of African slavery was not questioned, although conditions and concern for the slaves' 'spiritual needs' varied widely. Until their expulsion in 1767, the Jesuits had long been the largest slaveholders in the western hemisphere. See F. P. Bowser, 'Africans in Spanish American colonial society', in *CHLA*, II, 1984, pp. 371–2.
26. Thomas Gage, *The English-American, his Travail by Sea and Land; or, a New Survey of the West Indias containing a journall of three thousand and three hundred miles within the main land of America*, London, 1648. Later edns include A.P. Newton (ed.), London, 1928; and J.E.S. Thompson (ed.), London, 1958.
27. D.A. Brading, 'Bourbon Spain and its American empire', in *CHLA*, I, 1984, pp. 421, 428; M.M. Swann, *Migrants in the Mexican North: Mobility, Economy, and Society in a Colonial World*, Boulder, Colorado, 1989.
28. Haring, *Spanish Empire in America*, p. 178.
29. N. Pevsner, *An Outline of European Architecture*, Pelican Books, 5th edn, 1957, p. 190.
30. H.E. Bolton, 'The Mission as a Frontier Institution in the Spanish–American Colonies', *American Historical Review*, 23 (1917), pp. 48–9. See also A. Ogden (ed.), *Greater America: essays in honor of Herbert Eugene Bolton*, Univ. of California Press, 1945, pp. 105–242, where seven individual studies of the work of Jesuit missionaries on the frontiers of New Spain are included.
31. M. Mörner, *The Political and Economic Activities of the Jesuits in the La Plata region: the Hapsburg era*, Stockholm, 1953; A. Hennessy, *The Frontier in Latin American History*, London, 1978, pp. 54–60.
32. The literature on Spanish colonial urban development is extensive. See particularly: R.M. Morse, 'Some characteristics of Latin American urban history', *American Historical Review*, 67 (1962), pp. 317–38; and 'The urban development of colonial Spanish America', in *CHLA*, II, 1984, pp. 67–104. See also J.M. Houston, 'The foundation of colonial towns in Hispanic America', in R.P. Beckinsale and J.M. Houston (eds), *Urbanization and its problems*, Oxford Univ. Press, 1968, pp. 352–90.
The Institute of Hispanic Culture in Seville records that "By 1630, there already existed 296 cities in the Americas listed by the chronicler of the Council of the Indies, Vázquez de Espinosa."
33. L. Hanke, *The Imperial City of Potosí: an unwritten chapter in the history of Spanish America*, The Hague, 1956.
34. P. Boyd-Bowman, *Patterns of Spanish Emigration to the New World (1493–1580)*, Buffalo, N.Y., 1973, p. 2; and 'Patterns of Spanish Emigration to the Indies until 1600', *HAHR*, 56 (1976), pp. 580–604.
35. Elliott, 'Spain and America in the Sixteenth and Seventeenth Centuries', in *CHLA*, I, 1984, p. 298.
36. Royal instruction to Pedrarias Dávila, 1513: 'Ynstrucción para el gover-

nador de Tierra Firme, la qual se le entregó 4 de agosto MDXIII', in M. Serrano y Sanz (ed.), *Orígenes de la dominación española en América*, Madrid, 1918, pp. cclxx-xci.
37. 'Ordenanzas de descubrimiento, nueva población y pacificación de la Indias, dadas por Felipe II en 1573'; see Z. Nuttall, 'Royal Ordinances concerning the laying out of New Towns', *HAHR*, 4 (1921), pp. 743-53, and *HAHR*, 5 (1922), pp. 249-54.
38. Elliott, *Imperial Spain*, 1970 edn, pp. 305-8; Lynch, *Spain under the Habsburgs*, II, 2nd edn, pp. 46, 51.
39. Boyd-Bowman, 'Patterns of Spanish Emigration . . .', *HAHR*, 56 (1976), pp. 596-601; A. Lavrin, 'Women in Spanish American colonial society', *CHLA*, II, 1984, p. 322.
40. J. Lockhart, 'Social Organization and Social Change in Colonial Spanish America', in *CHLA*, II, 1984, p. 306. For general surveys of Spanish migration to the New World during the colonial period, see also N. Sánchez-Albornoz, 'The population of colonial Spanish America', *ibid.*, pp. 15-19; and M. Mörner, 'Spanish migration to the New World prior to 1810: a report on the state of research', in F. Chiappelli (ed.), *First Images of America*, Univ. of California Press, II, 1976, pp. 737-82.
41. Lavrin, 'Women in Spanish American Colonial Society', in *CHLA*, II, 1984, p. 323.
42. See Mörner, 'Spanish migration . . . prior to 1810'.
43. Sánchez-Albornoz, 'The population of colonial Spanish America', p. 31.
44. J. Campbell, *A Concise History of the Spanish America*, London, 1741, p. 279.
45. Quoted by J.H. Elliott, *The Old World and the New, 1492-1650*, Cambridge Univ. Press, 1980, p. 73.
46. D. Defoe, *Review of the State of the British Nation*, London, 30 June 1711.
47. Still well over eighty per cent by value in the 1750s, by 1778, the proportion of foreign goods in Spain's exports to its American colonies by value had been reduced to sixty-two per cent. For a general survey of Spain's colonial trade and commerce, see, *inter alia*, Haring, *The Spanish Empire in America*, chap. 16; see also J.R. Fisher, *Commercial Relations between Spain and Spanish America in the Era of Free Trade, 1778-1796*, Univ. of Liverpool, 1985.
48. Analyses of the various aspects of Spain's imperial trade, and its protection, include: C.H. Haring, *Trade and Navigation between Spain and the Indies in the time of the Hapsburgs*, Harvard Univ. Press, 1918, repr. 1964; J.H. Parry, *Trade and Dominion: the European Oversea Empires in the Eighteenth Century*, London, 1971, pp. 17-28, 91-112; and *Spanish Seaborne Empire*, pp. 117-35, 251-71; Lynch, *Spain under the Habsburgs*, II, 2nd edn, pp. 187-93; Spate, *Monopolists and Freebooters*, pp. 131-59, and *passim*; I.A.A. Thompson, *War and Government in Habsburg Spain, 1560-1620*, London, 1976; M.J. MacLeod, 'Spain and America: the Atlantic trade, 1492-1720', in *CHLA*, I, pp. 341-88. The greatest single source of detailed documentation and analysis remains P. and H. Chaunu, *Séville et l'Atlantique, 1504-1650*, 8 vols, Paris, 1955-60.
49. J. Juan and A. de Ulloa, *A Voyage to South America: describing at large the Spanish cities, towns, provinces, etc., on that extensive continent*, 2 vols, 2nd edn London, 1760, pp. 78-81, 101-2. The experiences and shrewd

observation of these two Spanish naval officers, travelling between 1735 and 1746, were originally published in Madrid in 1748. The work aroused great interest, and a 5th edn was published in London in 1807. Ulloa, born in Seville, wrote most of it. See A.P. Whitaker, 'Antonio de Ulloa', *HAHR*, 15 (1935), pp. 155–94.

50. W. Borah, *Early Colonial Trade and Navigation between Mexico and Peru*, Univ. of California Press, 1954. See also the general discussion by Spate in *The Spanish Lake*, 'Seville and the Pacific', pp. 204–28; and L.A. Clayton, 'Trade and Navigation in the seventeenth-century Viceroyalty of Peru', *JLAS*, 7 (1975), pp. 1–21.

51. Juan and Ulloa, *A Voyage to South America*, pp. 206, 208.

52. *Ibid.*, p. 211.

53. An excellent display of early carts and wagons used on the *pampas*, including the traditional *carreta* and *carro*, is to be found at the *Museo del Transporte* in Luján, Buenos Aires province.

54. Concolorcorvo (Alonso Carrió de la Vandera), *El Lazarillo: a guide for inexperienced travellers between Buenos Aires and Lima*, Lima, 1773, trs. and ed. by W.D. Kline, Indiana Univ. Press, 1965. See also Ringrose, 'Carting in the Hispanic World', pp. 33–4, 40–5.

55. G.B. Cobb, 'Supply and Transportation for the Potosí Mines, 1545–1640', *HAHR*, 20 (1949), pp. 25–45; P.J. Bakewell, 'Mining in colonial Spanish America', in *CHLA*, II, pp. 124–6; and *Miners of the Red Mountain: Indian Labor in Potosí, 1545–1650*, Univ. of New Mexico Press, 1984; G.A. Cole, *The Potosí Mita, 1573–1700*, Stanford Univ. Press, 1985; E. Tandeter, *Coercion and Market: Silver Mining in Colonial Potosí, 1692–1826*, Univ. of New Mexico Press, 1993.

56. G.B. Cobb, 'Potosí, a South American Mining Frontier', in Ogden (ed.), *Greater America*, pp. 39–58; and 'Supply and Transportation . . . Potosí', pp. 26–8, 44–5; Hanke, *Imperial City of Potosí*.

57. A valuable account of the extent of this trade by the end of the colonial period is contained in *Report on Bolivia, 1827, by Joseph Barclay Pentland*, ed. J.V. Fifer, in *Camden Miscellany*, 25, Royal Historical Society, London, 1974.

58. Concolorcorvo. *El Lazarillo*, pp. 106–61; G.M. Wrigley, 'Salta, an early commercial centre of Argentina', *Geographical Review*, 2 (1916), pp. 116–33; and 'Fairs of the Central Andes', *ibid.*, 7 (1919), pp. 65–80; Fifer, *Bolivia: Land, Location, and Politics*, pp. 168–8. Spain transferred customs collection from Córdoba to Salta and Jujuy in 1676 in an attempt to bring the livestock trade revenues closer to Lima's authority, as well as to control illegal foreign imports and illegal silver exports more effectively.

59. *Report on Bolivia, 1827*, pp. 217–34. See also M. Mörner, 'The rural economy and society of colonial Spanish South America', in *CHLA*, II, pp. 213–14; M.J. MacLeod, 'Aspects of the internal economy of colonial Spanish America: labour, taxation, distribution and exchange', *ibid.*, pp. 254–9.

60. Morse, 'The urban development of colonial Spanish America', in *CHLA*, II, p. 96.

61. P.W. Rees, 'Origins of colonial transportation in Mexico', *Geographical Review*, 65 (1975), p. 334.

62. Lockhart, 'Social Organization and Social Change in colonial Spanish America', in *CHLA*, II, p. 315.
63. (i) The Treaty of London (1604) ended the long-running conflict during the Elizabethan age between Spain and England. Spain was forced to accept the principle of "effective occupation" as the legal justification for non-Spanish colonization in parts of North America (mostly English, French, and Dutch). However, permission for foreign trade with Spanish America was not included in the treaty, and officially remained illegal.
   (ii) Already angered in 1803 by France's willingness to sell Louisiana, Spain continued to regard the Floridas (which had been retrieved in 1783) as a vital component in the imperial structure. Faced with the cession of Florida to the United States under the U.S.–Spanish (Adams-Onís) Treaty of 1819, Madrid rejected the proposal, and refused to ratify the treaty until 1821. But by that stage, much of the Spanish American empire had already been lost in the wars of independence.
64. The Bourbon administrative reforms are examined, *inter alia*, in Haring, *Spanish Empire in America*, chap. 17; Parry, *Spanish Seaborne Empire*, pp. 281–91, 307–26; J. Lynch, *Spanish Colonial Administration, 1782–1810: the Intendant System in the Viceroyalty of the Río de la Plata*, London, 1958; J.R. Fisher, *Government and Society in colonial Peru, the Intendant System, 1784–1814*, London, 1970; D.A. Brading, 'Bourbon Spain and its American Empire', in *CHLA*, I, pp. 389–439.
65. Fisher, *Commercial Relations . . . 1778–1796*, p. 14.
66. Brading, 'Bourbon Spain and its American Empire', p. 406.
67. D.M. Dozer, *Latin America: an interpretive history*, New York, 1962, pp. 168–73. Lynch, *Spanish Colonial Administration, 1782–1810*, pp. 291–301, shows that of the twenty-five intendants in La Plata whose birthplace he had traced, just one was American-born. See also, Haring, *Spanish Empire in America*, pp. 175, 194–7; Parry, *Spanish Seaborne Empire*, pp. 327–43; Fisher, *Government and Society*, passim.
68. M.A. Burkholder, 'The Council of the Indies in the Late Eighteenth Century: a new perspective', *HAHR*, 56 (1976), p. 422.
69. Elliott, *Imperial Spain, 1469–1716*, 1970 edn, p. 367.
70. Haring, *Spanish Empire in America*, p. 257.
71. Brading, 'Bourbon Spain and its American Empire', pp. 416–17; Fisher, *Commercial Relations . . . 1778–1796*, pp. 71, 77–8; and *Trade, War and Revolution: Exports from Spain to Spanish America, 1797–1820*, Univ. of Liverpool, 1992.
72. Elliott, *Imperial Spain, 1469–1716*, pp. 123–4; Lynch, *Spain under the Habsburgs*, II, p. 160.
73. Thus we can distinguish the immediate event in 1808 which triggered the start of revolution, from the various existing social and economic disparities in colonial Spanish America, together with the gradual but growing creole support for independence, that emerged once the revolutionary movements had begun. For a discussion of the influences and interests involved, see A.P. Whitaker (ed.), *Latin America and the Enlightenment*, Cornell Univ. Press, 2nd ed. 1961, including C.C. Griffin, 'The Enlightenment and Latin American Independence', pp. 119–43; and J. Lynch (ed.), *Latin American Revolutions, 1808–1826: Old and New World Origins*, Univ. of Oklahoma Press, 1994. Introduction by Lynch, pp. 5–38.

Part II: The United States' Tension Structure

1. J.P. Greene, 'Changing interpretations of early American politics', and 'The role of the Lower Houses of Assembly', in P. Goodman (ed.), *Essays on American Colonial History*, New York, 2nd edn 1972, pp. 287–311 and 330–42. See also J.P. Greene, *The Quest for Power: the Lower Houses of Assembly in the Southern Royal Colonies, 1689–1776*, Univ. of North Carolina Press, 1963; J.T. Main, *The Social Structure of Revolutionary America*, Princeton Univ. Press, 1965; and J.P. Greene and J.R. Pole (eds), *Colonial British America: Essays in the new history of the early modern era*, Johns Hopkins Univ. Press, 1984.
2. M. Kraus, *Intercolonial Aspects of American Culture on the Eve of Revolution, with special reference to the Northern Towns*, Columbia Univ. Press, 1928, pp. 91–105. On related themes, see also Main, *Social Structure of Revolutionary America*, and R.L. Merritt, *Symbols of American Community, 1735–1775*, Yale Univ. Press, 1966.
3. J.V. Fifer, 'Unity by Inclusion: Core Area and Federal State at American Independence', *Geographical Journal*, 142 (1976), pp. 463–6.
4. W.H. Riker, *Democracy in the United States*, New York, 2nd edn, 1965, p. 290.
5. In both the Declaration of Independence and the new Federal Constitution, the legal justification for action rested collectively in the hands of *The People*, a point clearly and succinctly restated and analysed by John Adams' son, John Quincy Adams, in *The Jubilee of the Constitution*, New York, 1839.
6. George Washington to Colonel David Humphreys, Mount Vernon, 10 Oct. 1787, in *The Writings of George Washington*, (ed. W.C. Ford), New York, 1889–93, XI, pp. 166–7.
7. J.T. Main, *The Antifederalists: Critics of the Constitution, 1781–1788*, Univ. of North Carolina Press, 1961.
8. P.L. Ford, *Bibliography and Reference List of the History and Literature relating to the Adoption of the Constitution of the United States, 1787–8*, Brooklyn, N.Y., 1888; and *Essays on the Constitution of the United States, published during its discussion by the people, 1787–1788*, Brooklyn, N.Y., 1892.
9. Thomas Jefferson to Jean Pierre Brissot de Warville, Paris, 16 Aug. 1786, in *The Writings of Thomas Jefferson, 1760—1826*, (ed. P.L. Ford), New York, 1893—9, IV, p. 281.
10. Main, in *The Antifederalists*, pp. 263, 270–2, emphasized that not only did the overwhelming majority of merchants (wherever located) support the Federal Constitution, but that the 'mercantile interest', in its broad sense, did the same, i.e. rural suppliers, freighters, skilled artisans, seamen, shipowners, newspaper editors, and several providing professional services such as doctors and lawyers.
11. C.M. Green, *Washington: A History of the Capital, 1800–1950*, 2 vols, Princeton Univ. Press, 1962–3, provides a classic study of the origins and specialized development of Washington, D.C. See also W.M. Maury, *Washington, D.C.: Past and Present*, United States Capitol Historical Society, 1975; and J.V. Fifer, 'Washington, D.C.: the political geography of a Federal Capital', *Journal of American Studies*, 15 (1981), pp. 5–26.

12. Quoted by A.P. Whitaker in *The Mississippi Question, 1795–1803: a study in trade, politics, and diplomacy*, New York, 1934, p. 32.
13. John Jay, 3–15 Sept. 1780, in *Correspondence and Public Papers of John Jay, 1763–1826*, (ed. H.P. Johnston), New York, 1890–93, I, p. 395.
14. George Washington to Benjamin Harrison, Mount Vernon, 10 Oct. 1784, in *Writings*, X, pp. 407–9.
15. A.P. Whitaker, *The Spanish American Frontier, 1783–1795: the westward movement and the Spanish retreat in the Mississippi Valley*, New York and Boston, 1927, pp. 92–102; also *The Mississippi Question*, pp. 28–9, 83–4.
16. Thomas Jefferson to James Madison, Paris, 30 Jan. 1787, in *Writings*, IV, pp. 363–4.
17. *Archivo General de Indias*, Seville; *Mapas y Planos*, Manuscript Collection, div. *Florida y Luisiana*.
18. Alexander Hamilton to George Washington, New York, 15 Sept. 1790, in *The Works of Alexander Hamilton*, (ed. H.C. Lodge), New York, 1885–6, IV, p. 43. Hamilton's general argument on the principle of free navigation, and the importance to the United States of its application to the Mississippi, is recorded in pp. 5–49, *passim*, and pp. 434–5.
19. Whitaker, *The Spanish American Frontier, 1783–1795*, p. 32.
20. W.E. Hulings to U.S. Secretary of State, New Orleans, Louisiana Province, Spain, 15 May 1801 and 7 May 1802, in *Despatches from U.S. Consuls in New Orleans, Spain; General Records of the Dept. of State, Record Group 59*, Washington, D.C.
21. George Washington to Charles M. Thruston, Philadelphia, 10 Aug. 1794, in *Writings*, XII, pp. 450–3.
22. Alexander Hamilton to Charles C. Pinckney, Grange, N.Y., 29 Dec. 1802, in *Works*, VIII, p. 606.
23. Thomas Jefferson to Robert R. Livingston, Washington, D.C., 18 Apr. 1802, in *Writings*, VIII, p. 144; and Thomas Jefferson to John C. Breckenridge, Monticello, 12 Aug. 1803, *ibid.*, p. 243.
24. John Breckenridge, *Annals of Congress*, 8th Congress, 1st Session, 1803–4, Senate, p. 60.
25. Baron Louis A.F. de Beaujour, *Sketch of the United States of North America . . . from 1800–1810*, Paris, 1814, trs. W. Walton, London, 1814, p. 231.
26. A. Mackenzie, *Voyages from Montreal, on the River St. Laurence, through the Continent of North America, to the Frozen and Pacific Oceans, in the years 1789 and 1793*, London, 1801; Philadelphia, 1802.
27. See above Part I, n. 63 (ii). See also C.C. Griffin, *The United States and the Disruption of the Spanish Empire, 1810—1822*, Columbia Univ. Press, 1937; and P.C. Brooks, *Diplomacy and the Borderlands: the Adams-Onís Treaty of 1819*, Univ. of California Press, 1939.
28. S.E. Morison, *The Maritime History of Massachusetts, 1783–1860*, Boston and New York, 1921, p. 17. See also H. Bernstein, *Origins of Inter-American Interest, 1700–1812*, Univ. of Pennsylvania Press, 1945.
29. B. Bailyn, *The New England Merchants in the Seventeenth Century*, Harvard Univ. Press, 1955.
30. J. Campbell, *A Concise History of the Spanish America*, London, 1741, pp. 154–5.
31. C.L. Chandler, 'United States Merchant Ships in the Río de la Plata

(1801–1808), as shown by early newspapers', *HAHR*, 2 (1919), pp. 26–54; A.P. Whitaker, 'Early commercial relations between the United States and Spanish America', in R.A. Humphreys and J. Lynch (eds), *The Origins of the Latin American Revolutions, 1808–1826*, New York, 1965, pp. 84–93. See also J.A. Barbier and A.J. Kuethe (eds), *The North American role in the Spanish imperial economy, 1760–1819*, Manchester Univ. Press, 1984; and P. Gleijeses, 'The Limits of Sympathy: the United States and the Independence of Spanish America', *JLAS*, 24 (1992), pp. 481–505.

32. Reply from the Spanish Governor of Cuba received by J.W. Morton, U.S. Consul in Havana, and transmitted to the U.S. Secretary of State, 17 Mar. 1802, in *Despatches from U.S. Consuls in Havana, Cuba, Spain; General Records of the Dept. of State, Record Group 59*, Washington, D.C.
33. Henry Hill to U.S. Secretary of State, Havana, Cuba, 1 Nov. 1805, *ibid*.
34. Returns from these three Cuban ports were usually included in the despatches from the U.S. Consul in Havana, although a U.S. Consul was appointed (without Spanish approval) at Santiago de Cuba in 1799, after which more detailed despatches were sent direct to the U.S. Secretary of State.
35. Beaujour, *Sketch of the United States . . . 1800–1810*, pp. 174, 216, 239. See also R.H. Brown, *Mirror for Americans: Likeness of the Eastern Seaboard, 1810*, American Geographical Society Special Publication No. 27, New York, 1943, pp. 103–23, for an excellent survey of the growing range and enterprise of America's Atlantic seaboard commerce at this time.
36. See *Columbian Centinel*, Boston, 11 Aug. 1790; *Independent Chronicle*, Boston, 12 Aug. 1790; *The Boston Gazette*, 16 Aug. 1790. There was an exchange of gun salutes in the harbour, "which a great concourse of citizens, assembled on the several wharfs, returned with three huzzas, and a hearty welcome." Much was made in the press of the circumnavigation, and its significance for expanded commerce.
37. See 'John Boit's Log of the *Columbia*, 1790–1793', in *The Quarterly of the Oregon Historical Society*, 22 (1921), pp. 257–351; and 'Remnant of the Official Log of the *Columbia* . . . containing the account of her entrance into Gray's Harbor and the Columbia River', *ibid.*, pp. 352–6. Also 'Letters relating to the Second Voyage of the *Columbia*', *ibid.*, 24 (1923), pp. 132–52.
38. Morison, *The Maritime History of Massachusetts*, p. 84. See also Brown, *Mirror for Americans . . . 1810*, pp. 112–13, 121–3.
39. See *Despatches from U.S. Consuls in Manila, Philippine Islands, Spain, 1817–1856–1868*, in *General Records of the Dept. of State, Record Group 59*, Washington, D.C., *passim*. The first U.S. Consul to Manila was appointed in Jan. 1801.
40. C. Nordhoff, *Whaling and Fishing*, New York, 1855; Cincinnati, 1856; and *Nine Years a Sailor*, New York and Cincinnati, 1857. Also W.H. Thomas, *The Whaleman's Adventures in the Sandwich Islands and California*, Boston, 1872.
41. John C. Jones to U.S. Secretary of State, Oahu, Sandwich Islands, 1 July 1827, in *Despatches from U.S. Consuls in Honolulu, Oahu; General Records of the Dept. of State, Record Group 59*, Washington, D.C.
42. J. Turrill to U.S. Secretary of State, Oahu, Sandwich Islands, 25 Jan. 1848, *ibid*.

43. W.M. Hooper to U.S. Secretary of State, Honolulu, Oahu, 30 June 1843, *ibid.*
44. F. Warriner, *Cruise of the United States Frigate 'Potomac' round the world, during the Years 1831–34*, New York and Boston, 1835, p. 224. See also the wide-ranging survey by R.A. Rydell, *Cape Horn to the Pacific: the rise and decline of an ocean highway*, Univ. of California Press, 1952.
45. J.M. Gilliss, USN, *The U.S. Naval Astronomical Expedition to the Southern Hemisphere during the Years 1849–'50–'51–'52*, Washington, D.C., I, p. 240.
46. Alexander Forbes, *California: A History of Upper and Lower California*, London, 1839, p. 298. See also *Despatches from U.S. Consuls in San Blas, Mexico (1837–92)*, and *in Acapulco, Mexico (1823–55)*, in *Despatches from U.S. Consuls, General Records of the Dept of State, Record Group 59*, Washington, D.C., *passim.*
47. José San Martín, *Memorial and Proposals of Señor Don José San Martín on the Californias*, Mexico City, 23 March 1822, trs. H.R. Wagner, San Marino, California, 1945, pp. 22–3.
48. A. Robinson, *Life in California*, New York, 1846; San Francisco, 1897. See also A. Ogden, 'New England Traders in Spanish and Mexican California', in A. Ogden (ed.), *Greater America*, pp. 395–413.
49. R.H. Dana, *Two Years Before the Mast*, Boston, 1840, p. 83.
50. J.B. Alvarado, *Historia de California*, Monterey, 1876 (a series of historical sketches and reminiscences; Alvarado was born in Monterey in 1809). See also T.H. Hittell, *History of California*, San Francisco, 1885, 'Juan Bautista Alvarado', II, pp. 236–314; p. 289.
51. Thomas O. Larkin to U.S. Secretary of State, Monterey, Upper California, Mexico, 4 Jan. 1846, in *Despatches from U.S. Consuls in Monterey, Upper California, Record Group 59*, Washington, D.C.
52. R.G. Cleland, 'The Early Sentiment for the Annexation of California: an account of the growth of American interest in California from 1835 to 1846', *Southwestern Historical Quarterly*, 18 (1914–15), pp. 1–40, 121–61, 231–60. (Repr. as a separate, pp. 1 111.)
53. Larkin to U.S. Secretary of State, Monterey, Upper California, Mexico, 13 Aug. 1844 and 1 May 1847, in *Despatches from U.S. Consuls in Monterey, Upper California, Record Group 59*, Washington, D.C.
54. Daniel Webster, *Congressional Globe*, 31st Congress, 1st Session, Part I, Dec. 1849–May 1850, Senate, p. 483.
55. Beaujour, *Sketch of the United States of North America . . . 1800–1810*, p. 35.
56. G. Taylor and I. Neu, *The American Railroad Network, 1861–1890*, Harvard Univ. Pres, 1956, p. 41.
57. *Ibid.*, pp. 43–4, 47–8.
58. H.R. Helper, *The Impending Crisis of the South: How to Meet It*, New York, 1857, p. 22.
59. F.L. Olmsted, *Journeys and Explorations in the Cotton Kingdom*, London, 1861, I, pp. 12, 8.
60. *Ibid.*, pp. 20–1.
61. Helper, *Impending Crisis of the South*, pp. 45, 122.
62. D.R. Goodloe, *Is it Expedient to Introduce Slavery into Kanzas?*, Boston, 1855, p. 40.

63. W. Turrentine Jackson, *Wagon Roads West*, Univ. of California Press, 1952, repr. Yale Univ. Press, 1965, p. 284.
64. John J. Hardin, *Appendix to the Congressional Globe*, XIV, 28th Congress, 2nd Session, Dec. 1844–Apr. 1845, House of Reps., p. 277.
65. Daniel Webster, *Congressional Globe*, XXI, 31st Congress, 1st Session, Part I, Dec. 1849–May 1850, Senate, p. 483.
66. William Taylor to U.S. Secretary of State, Vera Cruz, Mexico, 8 Jan. 1826, in *Despatches from U.S. Consuls in Vera Cruz, Mexico; General Records of the Dept. of State, Record Group 59*, Washington, D.C. Similar anxieties about the catastrophic decline of U.S.–Mexican and U.S.–Texan trade in the face of British and French competition were reported to the State Department by U.S. Consuls in Galveston, Texas during both the Mexican and the Republican periods.
67. J. Gregg, *Commerce of the Prairies*, New York and London, 1844, I, p. 25. See also Augustus Storrs, *Santa Fe Trail: First Reports to Congress*, 1825; 18th Congress, 2nd Session, Senate Documents 7 and 79. (Repr. Houston, Texas, 1960). And *Answers of Augustus Storrs, of Missouri, to certain queries upon the origin, present state, and future prospect, of trade and intercourse, between Missouri and the internal provinces of Mexico, propounded by the Hon. Mr. Benton, January 3, 1825*. Printed by order of the Senate of the United States, Washington, D.C., 1825. The Santa Fe Trail was made an authorized road by Congress in 1825.
68. Gregg, *Commerce of the Prairies*, I, p. 113.
69. *Ibid.*, II, p. 195. The head of steamboat navigation on the Missouri River was Fort Benton, Montana, just below Great Falls, and 3,000 miles above the Missouri's confluence with the Mississippi near St. Louis.
70. B.P. Tilden, *Notes on the Upper Rio Grande; Explored in the months of October and November, 1846, on board the U.S. Steamer 'Major Brown'*, Philadelphia, 1847.
71. *Ibid.*, p. 31.
72. Manuel Alvarez to U.S. Secretary of State, Independence, Missouri, 1 July 1843, in *Despatches from U.S. Consuls in Santa Fe, Mexico; General Records of the Dept. of State, Record Group 59*, Washington, D.C.
73. Charles Bent to Manuel Alvarez, Taos, 20 April 1843, *ibid.*
74. James J. Webb, *Adventures in the Santa Fe Trade, 1844–1847*, Glendale, California, 1931. See also Lieut. J.W. Abert's 'Report on the Santa Fe Trail, 1846–1847', *Senate Executive Document 23*, 30th Congress, 1st Session; S.S. Magoffin, *Down the Santa Fe Trail and into Mexico: the diary of Susan Shelby Magoffin, 1846–1847*, (ed. S.M. Drumm), Yale Univ. Press, 1926; repr. 1962; H.R. Lamar, *The Far Southwest, 1846–1912: A Territorial History*, Yale Univ. Press. 1966, pp. 36–82.
75. Freighters continued to favour the Santa Fe Trail (known later also as the Arkansas Trail) during the Gold Rush to Pike's Peak in the late 1850s–60s when they turned off at Bent's Old Fort to head for Colorado: "It is the best natural road in the world; grass plenty all seasons of the year . . . and not one 'hard pull' on the whole route from Council Grove to Pike's Peak." See J.V. Fifer, *American Progress*, Chester, Connecticut, 1988, pp. 85–6.
76. An edited form of 'Cooke's Journal of the March of the Mormon Battalion, 1846–1847' is contained in R.P. Bieber and A.B. Bender (eds), *Exploring*

Southwestern Trails, 1846–1854, Glendale, California, 1938, pp. 22–5. Reports by the military expedition leaders at this period were normally published by Congress as House or Senate Executive Documents. See also Jackson, *Wagon Roads West*, pp. 19–22; and W.H. Goetzmann's survey of the Wagon Road Program in *Army Exploration in the American West, 1803–1863*, Yale Univ. Press, 1959, pp. 341–74.
77. J.J. Hill, 'The Old Spanish Trail: a study of Spanish and Mexican trade and exploration northwest from New Mexico to the Great Basin and California', *HAHR*, 4 (1921), pp. 444–73; and E. Lawrence, 'Mexican Trade between Santa Fe and Los Angeles, 1830–1848', *California Historical Society Quarterly*, 10 (1931), pp. 27–39.
78. Jackson, *Wagon Roads West*, p. 44.
79. 'Protection Across the Continent', *House Executive Document 23*, 39th Congress, 2nd Session, 1866–7, pp. 20–1.
80. Report of Capt. S.G. French, Quartermaster's Corps. 21 Dec. 1849, *Senate Executive Document 64*, 31st Congress, 1st Session, 1849–50, p. 50.
81. H.L. Lamar, *Texas Crossings: the Lone Star State and the American Far West, 1836–1986*, Univ. of Texas Press, 1991, p. 14.
82. Lieut. F.T. Bryan to Colonel John J. Abert, 10 Dec. 1857, *House Executive Document 2*, 35th Congress, 1st Session, 1857–8.
83. J. King, 'John Plumbe, Originator of the Pacific Railroad', *Annals of Iowa*, 6 (1904), pp. 289–96. In fact, Plumbe was an early supporter of the need for a Pacific Railroad, but not the originator of the proposal.
84. Memorial of Asa Whitney, 28 Jan. 1845, *Congressional Globe*, XIV, 28th Congress, 2nd Session, Dec. 1844–Apr. 1845, House of Reps., pp. 218–9.
85. William H. Seward, 19 Feb. 1855, *Congressional Globe*, XXX, 33rd Congress, 2nd Session, Dec. 1854–Mar. 1855, Senate, p. 809.
86. G.M. Dodge, 'How We Built the Union Pacific Railway', *Senate Documents, LIX, Serial No. 5658*, 61st Congress, 2nd Session, 1910; E.L. Sabin, *Building the Pacific Railway*, Philadelphia and London, 1919; R.R. Russel, *Improvement of Communication with the Pacific Coast as an issue in American politics, 1783–1864*, Cedar Rapids, Iowa, 1948; W.H. Goetzmann, *Exploration and Empire: the Explorer and the Scientist in the Winning of the American West, 1805–1900*, New York, 1966, pp. 265–302.
87. J. Strong, *Our Country: its possible future and its present crisis*, New York, 1885, p. 45.
88. J.V. Fifer, 'Transcontinental: the political word', *Geographical Journal*, 144 (1978), pp. 438–49.
89. This was George A. Crofutt, originally from Connecticut, who began pioneering in the trans-Mississippi West in 1860. He travelled to the Golden Spike ceremony in Utah in May 1869, and immediately decided to write and publish the first guidebook to the line, calling it the 'Great Trans-Continental Railroad'. The book came out a few weeks later in Chicago, and was an instant success. (The word 'trans-continental' had been invented in 1853 by a group of New York businessmen promoting a New York-San Francisco railroad as a private venture. But neither the speculation nor the word attracted attention). See J.V. Fifer, *American Progress*, pp. 16–20, 145–90.
90. S. Bowles, *Across the Continent*, Springfield, Mass. and New York, 1865, pp. 1–2; and *The Pacific Railroad . . . Open*, Boston, 1869, p. 116.

91. Extracts from the *Trans-Continental*, "the first newspaper ever to be compiled, printed and published on a railway train." Now collectors' items, twelve issues were published during the journey, recording the Boston Board of Trade's *Trans-Continental Excursion* to San Francisco, May–July 1870.
92. J. Campbell, *A Concise History of the Spanish America*, p. 147.
93. J.M. Murrin, 'A Roof Without Walls', in R. Beeman, S. Botein and E.C. Carter (eds), *Beyond Confederation: Origins of the Constitution and American National Identity*, Univ. of North Carolina Press, 1987, p. 347.
94. J. Lockhart, 'Social Organization and Social Change in colonial Spanish America', in *CHLA*, II, pp. 313–4.
95. N. Sánchez-Albornoz, 'The population of colonial Spanish America', *ibid.*, pp. 34–5. Population figures are for the period 'around 1800'.
96. D.A. Brading, 'Bourbon Spain and its American empire', in *CHLA*, I, pp. 417, 420–1. Although "the showpiece of the Bourbon age was undoubtedly the Mexican silver-mining industry," (overall, silver accounted for 75.4% of New Spain's exports by value in 1796–1820), by 1815–19 exports of Cuban tobacco and sugar were averaging a total value equal to the silver exports of New Spain.
97. J.E. Wappäus, *Deutsche Auswanderung und Colonisation*, Leipzig, 1846, p. 74.
98. M. Walker, *Germany and the Emigration, 1816–1885*, Harvard Univ. Press, 1964, pp. 119–20.
99. Z. Brzezinski, 'American Assessments', *The Times*, London, 21 March 1987.
100. A.M. Schlesinger, Jr., *The Disuniting of America: reflections on a multicultural society*, New York and London, 1991, p. 90.
101. For a review of the language issue, see *inter alia*: D. Baron, *The English-Only Question: an official language for Americans?*, Yale Univ. Press, 1990; K.L. Adams and D.T. Brink (eds), *Perspectives on Official English: the campaign for English as the Official Language of the USA*, Berlin and New York, 1990; J. Crawford (ed.), *Language Loyalties: a Source Book on the Official English controversy*, Univ. of Chicago Press, 1992. See also K. McHugh, 'Hispanic Migration and Population Redistribution in the United States', *Professional Geographer*, 41 (1989), pp. 429–39, a survey made before the effects of the 1986 Immigration Reform and Control Act became apparent. Reliance on out-dated statistics, and a somewhat superficial analysis, undermine the forecasts in C. Veltman's 'The Status of the Spanish Language in the United States at the beginning of the 21st Century', *International Migration Review*, 24 (1990), pp. 108–23.
102. In February 1995, a Bill was introduced into the House of Representatives "to declare English as the official language of the Government of the United States, and for other purposes." This 'National Language Act of 1995' requires the Government to conduct its official business in English, including publications, income tax forms, and informational materials.
(i) The Act does not apply to the use of a language other than English for religious purposes, for training in foreign languages for international communication, to programs in schools designed to encourage students to learn foreign languages, or by persons over the age of 62. It permits the Government to provide interpreters for persons over the age of 62.

(ii) The Act repeals the Bilingual Education Act, and terminates the Office of Bilingual Education and Minority Languages Affairs in the Department of Education.

(iii) The Act repeals provisions of the Voting Rights Act of 1965 regarding bilingual election requirements and regarding Congressional findings of voting discrimination against language minorities, prohibition of English-only elections, and other remedial measures.

(iv) The Act amends the Immigration and Nationality Act so as to require that all public ceremonies in which the Oath of Allegiance is administered pursuant to such Act be conducted solely in English.

The Bill was referred to committee.
103. Quoted by G. Vickers, 'Making institutions work', *Wharton Quarterly*, Univ. of Pennsylvania, Spring 1971; London, 1973, p. 33.

Bibliography

A selected bibliography on Structures is placed separately at the end.

Abert, Lieut. James W. 'Report on the Santa Fe Trail, 1846–1847', *Senate Executive Document No. 23*, 30th Congress, 1st Session, Annual Report of the Secretary of War, Washington, D.C., 1847–8.

Adams, John Quincy. *The Jubilee of the Constitution*, New York, 1839.

Adams, Karen L. and Brink, Daniel T. (eds). *Perspectives on Official English: the Campaign for English as the Official Language of the USA*, Berlin and New York, 1990.

Aiken, Charles S. 'The Evolution of Cotton Ginning in the Southeastern United States', *Geographical Review*, 63 (1973), pp. 196–224.

Aitken, Robert. 'Routes of Transhumance on the Spanish Meseta', *Geographical Journal*, 106 (1945), pp. 59–69.

Albion, Robert G. *The Rise of New York Port, 1815–1860*, New York, 1939, repr. 1961.

Alvarado, Juan B. *Historia de California*, 5 vols, Monterey, Calif., 1876.

Andrews, Kenneth R. *Elizabethan Privateering: English privateering during the Spanish War, 1585–1603*, Cambridge Univ. Press, 1964.

Andrews, Kenneth R. *Drake's Voyages: a re-assessment of their place in Elizabethan maritime expansion*, London, 1967.

Andrews, Kenneth R. *The Spanish Caribbean: Trade and Plunder, 1580–1630*, Yale Univ. Press, 1978.

Ault, Phil. *Wires West*, New York, 1974.

Bailyn, Bernard. *The New England Merchants in the Seventeenth Century*, Harvard Univ. Press, 1955.

Bailyn, Bernard. *The Peopling of America*, New York, 1986.

Bailyn, Bernard and Bailyn, Lotte. *Massachusetts Shipping, 1697–1714: a statistical study*, Harvard Univ. Press. 1959.

Bakewell, Peter J. 'Mining in Colonial Spanish America', in *The Cambridge History of Latin America*, II, 1984, pp. 105–51.

Bakewell, Peter J. *Miners of the Red Mountain: Indian Labor in Potosí, 1545–1650*, Univ. of New Mexico Press, 1985.

Bancroft, Hubert H. *The Works of Hubert Howe Bancroft*, 39 vols, San Francisco and New York, 1874–90. Includes History of Mexico (6 vols); History of Central America (3 vols); California (6 vols); Pacific Northwest and U.S. Mountain West (8 vols).

Bannon, John F. *The Spanish Borderlands Frontier, 1513–1821*, New York, 1970.

Bannon, John F. (ed). *Bolton and the Spanish Borderlands*, Univ. of Oklahoma Press, 1964.

Barbier, Jacques A. 'The Culmination of the Bourbon Reforms, 1787–1792', *Hispanic American Historical Review*, 57 (1977), pp. 51–68.

Barbier, J.A. and Kuethe, A.J. (eds). *The North American Role in the Spanish Imperial Economy, 1760–1819*, Manchester Univ. Press, 1984.

Barnadas, Josep M. 'The Catholic Church in Colonial Spanish America', in *The Cambridge History of Latin America*, I, pp. 511–40.

Baron, Dennis. *The English-Only Question: An Official Language for Americans?*, Yale Univ. Press, 1990.

Batman, Richard. *The Outer Coast*, New York, 1985.

Beaujour, Louis A.F. de. *Sketch of the United States of North America at the commencement of the nineteenth century, from 1800 to 1810; with statistical tables, and a new map*, Paris, 1814. Trs. William Walton, London, 1814.

Beeman, R., Botein, S. and Carter II, E.C. (eds). *Beyond Confederation: Origins of the Constitution and American National Identity*, Univ. of North Carolina Press, 1987.

Beloff, Max. 'American Independence in its Constitutional Aspects', in *The New Cambridge Modern History*, VIII, 1965, pp. 448–79.

Benton, Thomas Hart. *The North American Road to India*, St Louis, Missouri, 1819.

Bercovitch, Sacvan. *The Puritan Origins of the American Self*, Yale Univ. Press. 1975.

Bernstein, Harold. *Origins of Inter-American Interest, 1700–1812*, Univ. of Pennsylvania Press, 1945.

Bethell, Leslie (ed.). *The Cambridge History of Latin America*, 11 vols, Cambridge Univ. Press. 1984–95.

Bidwell, John. *Echoes of the Past About California*, 1st publ. in *The Century Magazine*, New York, 1890; Chicago, 1928.

Bieber, Ralph P. and Bender, Averam B. (eds). *Exploring Southwestern Trails, 1846–1854*, Glendale, Calif., 1938.

Billington, Ray A. *Westward Expansion: a History of the American Frontier*, New York and London, 1949, 4th edn 1974.

Billington, Ray A. *The Far Western Frontier, 1830–1860*, New York, 1956, repr. 1962.

Billington, Ray A. *America's Frontier Heritage*, New York, 1966.

Bishko, Charles J. 'The Peninsular Background of Latin American Cattle Ranching', *Hispanic American Historical Review*, 32 (1952), pp. 491–515.

Bishko, Charles J. 'The Iberian Background of Latin American History: recent progress and continuing problems', *Hispanic American Historical Review*, 36 (1956), pp. 50–80.

Bishko, Charles J. 'The Castilian as Plainsman: the Medieval Ranching Frontier in La Mancha and Extremadura', in *The New World Looks at its History*, A.R. Lewis and T.F. McGann (eds), Univ. of Texas Press, 1963, pp. 47–69.

Blair, Emma H. and Robertson, James A. (eds). *The Philippine Islands*, 1493–1803–1898, 55 vols, Cleveland, Ohio, 1903–9.

Bloom, Allan. *The Closing of the American Mind*, New York, 1987.

Bolton, Herbert E. 'The Mission as a Frontier Institution in the Spanish-American Colonies', *American Historical Review*, 23 (1917), pp. 42–61.

Bonnycastle, Capt. Richard H. *Spanish America; or, A Descriptive, Historical, and Geographical Account of the Dominions of Spain in the Western Hemisphere, Continental and Insular*, 2 vols, London, 1818.

Boorstin, Daniel J. *The Genius of American Politics*, Univ. of Chicago Press, 1953.

Boorstin, Daniel J. *The Americans: 1. The Colonial Experience*, New York, 1958; *2. The National Experience*, New York, 1965.

Borah, Woodrow. *New Spain's Century of Depression*, Univ. of California Press, 1951.

Borah, Woodrow. *Early Colonial Trade and Navigation between Mexico and Peru*, Univ. of California Press, 1954.

Borah, Woodrow. 'The Mixing of Populations', in *First Images of America*, F. Chiappelli (ed.), Univ. of California Press, 1976, II, pp. 707–22.

Borchert, John R. 'American Metropolitan Evolution', *Geographical Review*, 57 (1967), pp. 301–32.

Bowditch, Nathaniel. *Early American Philippine Trade: the Journal of Nathaniel Bowditch in Manila, 1796*, R.R. and M.C. McHale (eds), Yale Univ. Pres, 1962.

Bowles, Samuel. *Across the Continent*, Springfield, Mass. and New York, 1865.

Bowles, Samuel. *Our New West*, Hartford, Conn., 1869.

Bowles, Samuel. *The Pacific Railroad—Open*, Boston, 1869.

Bowser, Frederick P. 'Africans in Spanish American Colonial Society', in *The Cambridge History of Latin America*, II, 1984, pp. 357–79.

Boyd-Bowman, Peter. *Patterns of Spanish Emigration to the New World (1493–1580)*, Buffalo, N.Y., 1973.

Boyd-Bowman, Peter. 'Patterns of Spanish Emigration to the Indies until 1600', *Hispanic American Historical Review*, 56 (1976), pp. 580–604.

Bradford, Governor William. *History of Plymouth Plantation, 1606–1646*, ms. pub. by the Massachusetts Historical Society, 1856.

Brading, David A. *Miners and Merchants in Bourbon Mexico, 1763—1810*, Cambridge Univ. Press, 1971.

Brading, David A. 'Bourbon Spain and its American Empire', in *The Cambridge History of Latin America*, I, 1984, pp. 389–439.

Brading, David A. and Cross, H.E. 'Colonial Silver Mining: Mexico and Peru', *Hispanic American Historical Review*, 52 (1972), pp. 545–79.

Bradley, Harold W. *The American Frontier in Hawaii: the pioneers, 1789–1843*, Stanford Univ. Press, 1942.

Braudel, Fernand. *The Mediterranean and the Mediterranean World in the Age of Philip II*, 2 vols, Paris, 1949, 1966; London, 1972–3.

Braudel, Fernand. *The Structure of Everyday Life: Civilization and Capitalism, 15th–18th Centuries*, 3 vols, Paris and New York, 1979–84.

Bremner, Charles. 'Still a Promised Land', *The Times*, London, 15 May 1992.

Brimelow, Peter. *Alien Nation: Common Sense About America's Immigration Disaster*, New York, 1995.

Brooks, Philip Coolidge. *Diplomacy and the Borderlands: the Adams-Onís Treaty of 1819*, Univ. of California Press. 1939.

Brown, Jonathan C. *A Socioeconomic History of Argentina, 1776–1860*, Cambridge Univ. Press, 1979.

Brown, Ralph H. *Mirror for Americans: Likeness of the Eastern Seaboard, 1810*, American Geographical Society, Special Publication No. 27, New York, 1943.

Brown, Ralph H. *Historical Geography of the United States*, New York, 1948.

Brown, Vera L. 'Contraband Trade: a factor in the decline of Spain's empire in America', *Hispanic American Historical Review*, 8 (1928), pp. 178–89.

Bruchey, Stuart. *The Roots of American Economic Growth, 1607–1861: an essay in social causation*, London, 1965.

Bryce, James. *The American Commonwealth*, 3 vols, London and New York, 1st publ. 1888.

Brzezinski, Zbigniew. 'American Assessments', *The Times*, London, 21 March 1987.

Burkholder, Mark A. 'The Council of the Indies in the Late Eighteenth Century: a New Perspective', *Hispanic American Historical Review*, 56 (1976), pp. 404–23.

Burkholder, Mark A. and Johnson, Lyman L. *Colonial Latin America*, Oxford Univ. Press, 1990.

Bushman, Richard. *From Puritan to Yankee*, Harvard Univ. Press, 1967.

Butzer, Karl W. 'Cattle and Sheep from Old to New Spain: Historical Antecedents', *Annals of the Association of American Geographers*, 78 (1988), pp. 29–56.

Butzer, Karl W. (ed.). 'The Americas Before and After 1492: current geographical research', *Annals of the Association of American Geographers*, 82 (1992).

Cabeza de Vaca, Alvar Núñez. *Cabeza de Vaca's Adventures in the Unknown Interior of America*, trs. and ed. C. Covey, New York, 1961.

Campbell, John. *A Concise History of the Spanish America*, London, 1741.

Campbell, John. *An Account of the Spanish Settlements in America*, Edinburgh, 1762.

Cash, Wilbur J. *The Mind of the South*, New York, 1941.

Chamberlain, Robert S. 'The *Corregidor* in Castile in the Sixteenth Century and the Residencia as applied to the *Corregidor*', *Hispanic American Historical Review*, 23 (1943), pp. 222–57.

Chandler, Charles L. 'United States Merchant Ships in the Río de la Plata (1801–1808), as shown by Early Newspapers', *Hispanic American Historical Review*, 2 (1919), pp. 26–54.

Chapman, Charles E. *A History of California: the Spanish Period*, New York, 1921.

Chaunu, Pierre and Huguette. *Séville et l'Atlantique, 1504–1650*, 8 vols, Paris, 1955–9.

Chiappelli, Fredi (ed.). *First Images of America: the Impact of the New World on the Old*, 2 vols, Univ. of California Press, 1976.

Cipolla, Carlo. *Guns, Sails and Empires: technological innovation and the early phases of European expansion, 1400–1700*, New York, 1966.

Cipolla, Carlo. *The Economic Decline of Empires*, London, 1970.

Clark, Arthur H. *The Clipper Ship Era; . . . 1843–1869*, New York and London, 1910.

Clayton, L.A. 'Trade and Navigation in the Seventeenth-Century Viceroyalty of Peru', *Journal of Latin American Studies*, 7 (1975), pp. 1–21.

Cleland, Robert G. 'The Early Sentiment for the Annexation of California: An Account of the Growth of American Interest in California from 1835 to 1846', *The Southwestern Historical Quarterly*, 18 (1914–15), pp. 1–40, 121–61, 231–60. (Repr. as a separate, pp. 1–111).

Cleland, Robert G. *From Wilderness to Empire; A History of California, 1542–1900*, New York, 1944.

Cline, Gloria G. *Exploring the Great Basin*, Univ. of Oklahoma Press, 1963.

Cobb, Gwendoline B. 'Potosí, a South American Mining Frontier', in *Greater America: Essays in honor of Herbert Eugene Bolton*, A. Ogden (ed.), Univ. of California Press, 1945, pp. 39–58.

Cobb, Gwendoline B. 'Supply and Transportation for the Potosí Mines, 1545–1640', *Hispanic American Historical Review*, 29 (1949), pp. 24–45.

Cole, Geoffrey A. *The Potosí Mita, 1573–1700: Compulsory Indian Labor in the Andes*, Stanford Univ. Press, 1985.

Columbus, Christopher. *The Journal of Christopher Columbus*, trs. C. Jane, rev. and annotated L.A. Vigneras, London and New York, 1960.

Columbus, Christopher. *The Log of Christopher Columbus*, trs. R.H. Fuson, Camden, Maine and Southampton, UK, 1987.

Columbus, Christopher. *The 'Diario' of Christopher Columbus's First Voyage to America, 1492–1493*, trs. and ed. O. Dunn and J.E. Kelley, Jr, Univ. of Oklahoma Press, 1989.

Columbus, Christopher. *Journal of the First Voyage of Christopher Columbus*, trs. and ed. B.W. Ife, Warminster, UK, 1990.

Columbus, Christopher. *Letters from America; Columbus's First Accounts of the 1492 Voyage*, trs. and ed. B.W. Ife, King's College, London, 1992.

Columbus, Ferdinand. *The Life of the Admiral Christopher Columbus by his son, Ferdinand*, trs. and annotated B. Keen, Rutgers Univ. Press, 1959.

Commager, Henry S. (ed.). *Documents of American History, 1493–1949*, New York, 5th edn 1949.

Commager, Henry S. *The American Mind: an Interpretation of American Thought and Character since the 1880s*, Oxford Univ. Press, 1950.

Concolorcorvo, *pseud.* (Alonso Carrió de la Vandera). *El Lazarillo: A Guide for Inexperienced Travellers between Buenos Aires and Lima*, Lima, 1773, trs. and ed. W.D. Kline, Indiana Univ. Press. 1965.

Connell-Smith, Gordon. 'English Merchants trading to the New World in the Early Sixteenth Century', *Bulletin of the Institute of Historical Research*, 23 (1950), pp. 53–67.

Connell-Smith, Gordon. *Forerunners of Drake: a study of English trade with Spain in the early Tudor period*, London, 1954; repr. Westport, Connecticut, 1975.

Connell-Smith, Gordon. *The United States and Latin America: an historical analysis of Inter-American Relations*, London, 1974.

Conzen, Michael P. (ed.). *The Making of the American Landscape*, Boston, 1990.

Cook, Sherburne F. and Borah, Woodrow. *The Aboriginal Population of Central Mexico on the eve of the Spanish Conquest*, Univ. of California Press, 1963.

Cook, Sherburne F. *Essays in Population History: Mexico and the Caribbean*, 3 vols, Univ. of California Press, 1971–9.

Cook, Warren L. *Flood Tide of Empire: Spain and the Pacific Northwest, 1543–1819*, Yale Univ. Press, 1973.

Cortés, Hernán. *Hernán Cortés: Letters from Mexico*, trs. and ed. A.R. Pagden, Oxford Univ. Press, 1972.

Cortés: The Life of the Conqueror by his Secretary, Francisco López de Gómara, trs. and ed. L.B. Simpson, Univ. of California Press, 1964.

Costeloe, Michael P. *Response to Revolution: Imperial Spain and the Spanish American Revolutions, 1810–1840*, Cambridge Univ. Press, 1986.

Crawford, James (ed.). *Language Loyalties: a Source Book on the Official English Controversy*, Univ. of Chicago Press, 1992.

Cruz, Gilbert R. *Let There Be Towns: Spanish Municipal Origins in the American Southwest, 1610–1810*, Texas A & M Univ. Press, 1988.

Cumming, W.P., Skelton, R.A. and Quinn, D.B. *The Discovery of North America*, London, 1971.

Cumming, W.P., Hillier, S.E., Quinn, D.B. and Williams G. *The Exploration of North America, 1630–1776*, London, 1974.

Dana, Richard Henry. *Two Years Before the Mast*, Boston, 1840.

Davenport, Francis G. (ed.). *European Treaties bearing on the History of the United States and its Dependencies to 1648*, Washington, D.C., 1917.

Davis, Ralph. *The Rise of the Atlantic Economies*, Cornell Univ. Press, 1973.

Davis, William H. *Seventy-five Years in California*, San Francisco, 1929.

Day, A. Grove. *Coronado's Quest: the discovery of the southwestern States*, Univ. of California Press, 1940, repr. 1986.

Denevan, William M. (ed.). *The Native Population of the Americas in 1492*, Univ. of Wisconsin Press, 1976, 2nd edn 1992.

Denevan, William M. 'The Pristine Myth: The Landscape of the Americas in 1492', *Annals of the Association of American Geographers*, 82 (1992), pp. 369–85.

Depons, Francois. (Also recorded as Pons, Francois R.J. de). *Travels in South America during the years 1801–1804*, 3 vols, Paris and New York, 1806; London, 1807.

Díaz, Padre Casimiro. *Conquistas de las Islas Filipinas*, Madrid, 1698.

Dodge, Grenville M. 'How We Built the Union Pacific Railway', *Senate Documents*, 61st Congress, 2nd Session, 59, Serial No. 5658, Washington, D.C., 1910.

Dozer, Donald M. *Latin America: an interpretive history*, New York, 1962.

Dunbar, Seymour. *A History of Travel in America*, 4 vols, Indianapolis, 1915.

Dusenberry, William H. *The Mexican Mesta*, Univ. of Illinois Press, 1963.

Dwight, Timothy. *Travels; in New-England and New-York*, 4 vols, New Haven, Conn., 1821–22.

Earle, Carville. 'Pioneers of Providence: The Anglo-American Experience, 1492–1792', *Annals of the Association of American Geographers*, 82 (1992), pp. 478–99.

Edmonston, B. and Passel, J.S. (eds). *Immigration and Ethnicity: the Integration of America's Newest Arrivals*, Washington, D.C., 1994.

Elazar, Daniel J. *American Federalism: A View from the States*, New York, 1966, 2nd edn 1972; 3rd edn 1984.

Elazar, Daniel J. (ed.). *Federalism as grand design: political philosophies and the Federal principle*, Lanham: Univ. Press of America, 1987.

Elazar, Daniel J. *The American Mosaic: the Impact of Space, Time, and Culture on American Politics*, Boulder, Colo., 1994.

Ellicott, Andrew. *The Journal of Andrew Ellicott, Late Commissioner on behalf of the United States during part of the Year 1796, the Years 1797, 1798, 1799, and part of the Year 1800; for Determining the Boundary between the United States and the Possessions of His Catholic Majesty in America*, 2 vols, Philadelphia, 1803.

Elliott, John H. *Imperial Spain, 1469–1716*, London, 1963; Pelican edn 1970.

Elliott, John H. *The Old World and the New, 1492–1650*, Cambridge Univ. Press, 1970.

Elliott, John H. 'The Spanish Conquest and Settlement of America', in *The Cambridge History of Latin America*, I, 1984, pp. 149–206.

Elliot, John H. 'Spain and America in the Sixteenth and Seventeenth Centuries', in *The Cambridge History of Latin America*, I, 1984, pp. 287–339.

Elliott, John H. *Spain and its World, 1500–1700*, Yale Univ. Press, 1989.

Falkner, Father Thomas. *A Description of Patagonia and the Adjoining Parts of South America*, Hereford, England, 1774.

Farmer, Charles J. *In the Absence of Towns: Settlement and Country Trade in Southside Virginia, 1730–1800*, Lanham, Maryland, 1993.

Fernández-Armesto, Felipe. *Columbus*, Oxford Univ. Press, 1991.

Fifer, J. Valerie. *Bolivia: Land, Location, and Politics since 1825*, Cambridge Univ. Press, 1972.

Fifer, J. Valerie (ed.). 'Report on Bolivia, 1827, by Joseph Barclay Pentland', Royal Historical Society, *Camden Miscellany*, 25 (1974), pp. 169–267.

Fifer, J. Valerie. 'Unity by Inclusion: Core Area and Federal State at American Independence', *Geographical Journal*, 142 (1976), pp. 462–70.

Fifer, J. Valerie. 'Transcontinental: the political word', *Geographical Journal*, 144 (1978), pp. 438–49.

Fifer, J. Valerie. 'Washington, D.C.: the political geography of a federal capital', *Journal of American Studies*, 15 (1981), pp. 5–26.

Fifer, J. Valerie. *American Progress: the Growth of the Transport, Tourist, and Information Industries in the Nineteenth-Century West*, Chester, Connecticut, 1988.

Fifer, J. Valerie. *United States perceptions of Latin America, 1850—1930: A 'New West' south of Capricorn?*, Manchester Univ. Press and New York, 1991.

Fisher, John R. *Government and Society in Colonial Peru: the Intendant System, 1784—1814*, London, 1970.

Fisher, John R. *Commercial Relations between Spain and Spanish America in the Era of Free Trade, 1778–1796*, Centre for Latin American Studies, Univ. of Liverpool, 1985.

Fisher, John R. *Trade, War and Revolution: Exports from Spain to Spanish America, 1797–1820*, Institute of Latin American Studies, Univ. of Liverpool, Monograph Series No. 16, 1992.

Fishlow, Albert. *American Railroads and the Transformation of the Ante-bellum Economy*, Harvard Univ. Press, 1965.

Florescano, Enrique. 'The Formation and Economic Structure of the Hacienda in New Spain', in *The Cambridge History of Latin America*, II, 1984, pp. 153–88.

Fogel, Robert W. *Railroads and American Economic Growth: Essays on Econometric History*, Johns Hopkins Univ. Press, 1964.

Forbes, Alexander. *California: A History of Upper and Lower California*, London, 1839.

Forbes, Robert B. *Personal Reminiscences*, Boston, 2nd edn 1882.

Ford, Paul L. *Bibliography and Reference List of the History and Literature relating to the Adoption of the Constitution of the United States, 1787–8*, Brooklyn, N.Y., 1888.

Ford, Paul L. *Essays on the Constitution of the United States, published during its discussion by the people, 1787–1788*, Brooklyn, N.Y., 1892.

Frémont, John Charles. *A Report of an Exploration of the Country lying between the Missouri River and the Rocky Mountains on the line of the Kansas and Great Platte Rivers*, Washington, D.C., 1843.

Frémont, John Charles. *Report of the Exploring Expedition to the Rocky Mountains in the Year 1842, and to Oregon and North California in the Years 1843–'44*, Washington, D.C., 1845. Also, *Narratives of Exploration and Adventure*, ed. A. Nevins (incl. the first three expeditions and Frémont's "Geographical Memoir upon Upper California"), New York, 1956.

Gage, Thomas. *The English-American, his Travail by Sea and Land; or, A New Survey of the West Indias, containing a Journall of Three Thousand and Three Hundred Miles within the Main Land of America . . . By the true and painfull endevours of Thomas Gage*, London, 1648. (Ed.) A.P. Newton, London, 1928; (Ed.) J.E.S. Thompson, London, 1958.

Gallatin, Albert. *Report of the Secretary of the Treasury, on the Subject of Public Roads and Canals; Made in Pursuance of a Resolution of Senate of March 2, 1807*; presented to the Senate by Gallatin, April 1808, and printed by Order of the Senate, Washington, D.C., 1808.

Gibson, Charles. *Spain in America*, New York, 1966.

Gibson, Charles. 'Indian Societies under Spanish rule', in *The Cambridge History of Latin America*, II, 1984, pp. 381–419.

Gilchrist, David T. (ed.). *The Growth of the Seaport Cities, 1790–1825*, Univ. Press of Virginia, 1967.

Gilliss, James M., USN. *The U.S. Naval Astronomical Expedition to the Southern Hemisphere during the Years 1849–'50–'51–'52*, 6 vols, Washington, D.C., 1855.

Glade, William P. *Latin American Economies: a study of their institutional evolution*, New York, 1969.

Gleijeses, Piero. 'The Limits of Sympathy: The United States and the Independence of Spanish America', *Journal of Latin American Studies*, 24 (1992), pp. 481–505.

Goetzmann, William H. *Army Exploration in the American West, 1803–1863*, Yale Univ. Press, 1959.

Goetzmann, William H. *Exploration and Empire. The Explorer and the Scientist in the Winning of the American West, 1805–1900*, New York, 1966.

Goetzmann, William H. *New Lands, New Men: America and the Second Great Age of Discovery*, New York, 1986.

Goodloe, Daniel R. *Is It Expedient to Introduce Slavery into Kanzas?*, Boston, 1855.

Goodloe, Daniel R. *The Southern Platform*, Boston, 1858.

Goodman, Paul (ed.). *Essays on American Colonial History*, New York, 1967, 2nd edn 1972.

Goodrich, Carter. *Government Promotion of American Canals and Railroads, 1800–1890*, New York, 1960.

Green, Constance M. *Washington: A History of the Capital, 1800–1950*, 2 vols, Princeton Univ. Press, 1962–3

Green, Fletcher M. *The Role of the Yankee in the Old South*, Univ. of Georgia Press, 1972.

Greene, Jack P. *The Quest for Power: the Lower Houses of Assembly in the Southern Royal Colonies, 1689–1776*, Univ. of North Carolina Press, 1963.

Greene, Jack P. 'Changing interpretations of early American politics', and 'The role of the Lower Houses of Assembly', in *Essays on American Colonial History*, P. Goodman (ed.), New York, 1972, pp. 287–311, 330–42.

Greene, Jack P. and Pole, J.R. (eds). *Colonial British America: Essays in the new history of the early modern era*, Johns Hopkins Univ. Press, 1984.

Gregg, Josiah. *Commerce of the Prairies; or, the Journal of a Santa Fe Trader during Eight Expeditions across the Great Western Prairies, and a Residence of nearly Nine Years in Northern Mexico*, 2 vols, New York and London, 1844.

Gregg, Josiah. *Diary and Letters of Josiah Gregg: Southwestern Enterprises, 1840–1847*, Univ. of Oklahoma Press, 1941; and *Excursions in Mexico and California, 1847–1850*, Univ. of Oklahoma Press, 1944.

Gregg, Kate L. *The Road to Santa Fe: the surveying and marking of a road from the Missouri frontier to the settlements of New Mexico, 1825–27*, Univ. of New Mexico Press, 1952.

Griffin, Charles C. *The United States and the Disruption of the Spanish Empire, 1800–1822: a study in the relations of the United States with Spain and with the rebel Spanish Colonies*, Columbia Univ. Press, 1937.

Griffin, Charles C. 'The Enlightenment and Latin American Independence', in

Latin America and the Enlightenment, A.P. Whitaker (ed.), 2nd edn 1961, pp. 119–43.

Hall, Thomas D. *Social Change in the Southwest, 1850—1880*, Univ. of Kansas Press, 1989.

Hamilton, Alexander. *The Works of Alexander Hamilton*, ed. H.C. Lodge, 9 vols, New York, 1885–6.

Hamilton, Alexander, Madison, James and Jay, John. *The Federalist Papers*, New York, 1787–8.

Hamilton, Earl J. *American Treasure and the Price Revolution in Spain, 1501–1650*, Harvard Univ. Press, 1934.

Hamilton, Earl J. 'The Decline of Spain', *Economic History Review*, 8 (1937–8), pp. 168–79.

Hanke, Lewis. *The Spanish Struggle for Justice in the Conquest of America*, Univ. of Pennsylvania Press, 1949.

Hanke, Lewis. *The Imperial City of Potosí: an unwritten chapter in the history of Spanish America*, The Hague, 1956.

Hanke, Lewis. *Aristotle and the American Indians*, London, 1959.

Hanke, Lewis (ed.). *History of Latin American Civilization: sources and interpretations*, 2 vols, Boston, 1967, 1973.

Hardoy, Jorge (ed.). *Urbanization in Latin America: approaches and issues*, New York, 1975.

Hargreaves-Mawdsley, W.N. *Spain under the Bourbons, 1700–1833*, London, 1973.

Haring, Clarence H. *Trade and Navigation between Spain and the Indies in the time of the Hapsburgs*, Harvard Univ. Press, 1918, repr. 1964.

Haring, Clarence H. *The Spanish Empire in America*, New York, 1947; rev. edn 1952.

Harris, R. Cole. 'The Simplification of Europe Overseas', *Annals of the Association of American Geographers*, 67 (1977), pp. 469–83.

Helper, Hinton R. *The Impending Crisis of the South: How to Meet It*, New York, 1857.

Hennessy, Alistair. *The Fronter in Latin American History*, London, 1978.

Higginbotham, Sanford W. 'Philadelphia Commerce with Latin America, 1820–1830', *Pennsylvania History*, 9 (1942), pp. 252–66.

Highfield, Roger (ed.). *Spain in the Fifteenth Century, 1369–1516*, London, 1972.

Hill, Joseph J. 'The Old Spanish Trail: a study of Spanish and Mexican trade and exploration northwest from New Mexico to the Great Basin and California', *Hispanic American Historical Review*, 4 (1921), pp. 444–73.

Hillgarth, Jocelyn N. *The Spanish Kingdoms, 1250–1516*, 2 vols, Oxford Univ. Press; *I. 1250–1410: Precarious Balance*, 1976; *II. 1410–1516: Castilian Hegemony*, 1978.

Hittell, Theodore H. *History of California*, 4 vols, San Francisco, 1885, 1897.

Horgan, Paul. *Great River: the Rio Grande in North American History*, 2 vols, New York, 1954; Univ. Press of New England, 1984.

Houston, James M. *The Western Mediterranean World*, London, 1964.

Houston, James M. 'The Foundation of Colonial Towns in Hispanic America', in *Urbanization and its problems*, R.P. Beckinsale and J.M. Houston (eds), Oxford, 1968, pp. 352–90.

Humboldt, Alexander von. *Political Essay on the Kingdom of New Spain*, 4 vols, Paris, 1807–11; trs. from the original French, London, 1811–14.

Humboldt, Alexander von and Bonpland, Aimé. *Personal Narrative of Travels to the Equinoctial Regions of the New Continent during the Years 1799–1804*, 7 vols, Paris, 1807–17; trs. from the original French, London, 1814–29.

Humphreys, Robert A. 'The Development of the American Communities outside British Rule', in *The New Cambridge Modern History*, VIII, 1965, pp. 397–420.

Humphreys, Robert A. and Lynch, John (eds). *The Origins of the Latin American Revolutions, 1808–1826*, New York, 1965.

Hussey, Roland D. 'Spanish reaction to foreign aggression in the Caribbean to about 1680', *Hispanic American Historical Review*, 9 (1929), pp. 286–302.

Jackson, Gabriel. *The Making of Medieval Spain*, London, 1972.

Jackson, W. Turrentine. *Wagon Roads West: a study of Federal Road Surveys and Construction in the Trans-Mississippi West, 1846–1869*, Univ. of California Press, 1952.

Janson, Charles W. *The Stranger in America: Containing Observations made during a Long Residence in that Country, on the Genius, Manners, and Customs of the People of the United States*, London, 1807.

Jay, John. *The Correspondence and Public Papers of John Jay, 1763–1826*, ed. H.P. Johnston, 4 vols, New York, 1890–3.

Jefferson, Thomas. *The Writings of Thomas Jefferson*, ed. P.L. Ford, 10 vols, New York, 1893–99.

Jefferson, Thomas. *A Summary View of the Rights of British America*, Williamsburg, Virginia, 1774.

Jefferson, Thomas. *Notes on the State of Virginia*, London, 1787; Philadelphia, 1788.

Jeffrey, Julie R. *Frontier Women: the Trans-Mississippi West, 1840-1880*, New York, 1979.

'John Boit's Log of the *Columbia*, 1790–1793', *Quarterly of the Oregon Historical Society*, 22 (1921), pp. 257–351; Also 'Remnant of Official Log of the *Columbia*, containing the account of her entrance into Gray's Harbor and the Columbia River', pp. 352–6.

Jones, Howard M. *O Strange New World. American Culture: The Formative Years*, New York, 1967.

Jones, Richard C. 'Immigration Reform and Migrant Flows: compositional and spatial changes in Mexican migration after the Immigration Reform Act of 1986', *Annals of the Association of American Geographers*, 85 (1995), pp. 715–30.

Jordan, Terry G. *North American Cattle-Ranching Frontiers: Origins, Diffusion and Differentiation*, Univ. of New Mexico Press, 1993.

Juan, Jorge and Ulloa, Antonio de. *A Voyage to South America: describing at large the Spanish cities, towns, provinces, etc., on that extensive continent*, 2 vols, London, 1758; 2nd edn rev. 1760; 5th edn 1807.

Kammen, Michael G. *People of Paradox: an inquiry concerning the origins of American civilization*, New York, 1972.

Kendall, Edward A. *Travels through the Northern Parts of the United States in the Years 1807 and 1808*, 3 vols, New York, 1809.

Kennedy, Paul M. *The Rise and Fall of the Great Powers: economic change and military conflict from 1500 to 2000*, London, 1988.

Key, Jr., Valdimer O. *Southern Politics in State and Nation*, New York, 1949.

King, John. 'John Plumbe, originator of the Pacific Railroad', *Annals of Iowa*, 6 (1904), pp. 289–96.

Kirkland, Edward C. *Men, Cities, and Transportation: a study of New England History, 1820–1900*, 2 vols, Harvard Univ. Press, 1948.

Klein, Julius. *The Mesta: a Study in Spanish Economic History, 1273–1836*, Harvard Univ. Press, 1920.

Knight, Franklin W. and Liss, Peggy K. (eds). *Atlantic Port Cities: Economy, Culture, and Society in the Atlantic World, 1650–1850*, Univ. of Tennessee Press, 1991.

Kraus, Michael. *International Aspects of American Culture on the Eve of Revolution, with special reference to the Northern Towns*, Columbia Univ. Press, 1928.

Lafaye, Jacques. 'Literature and Intellectual Life in Colonial Spanish America', in *The Cambridge History of Latin America*, II, 1984, pp. 663–704.

Lamar, Howard R. *The Far Southwest, 1846–1912: A Territorial History*, Yale Univ. Press, 1966.

Lamar, Howard R. *Texas Crossings: the Lone Star State and the American Far West, 1836–1986*, Univ. of Texas Press, 1991.

Lavrin, Asunción. 'Women in Spanish American Colonial Society', in *The Cambridge History of Latin America*, II, 1984, pp. 321–55.

Lawrence, Eleanor. 'Mexican Trade between Santa Fe and Los Angeles, 1830–1848', *California Historical Society Quarterly*, 10 (1931), pp. 27–39.

Lemon, James T. *The Best Poor Man's Country: a geographical study of early southeastern Pennsylvania*, Johns Hopkins Univ. Press, 1972.

Leonard, Irving A. *Baroque Times in Old Mexico: Seventeenth-Century Persons, Places, and Practices*, Univ. of Michigan Press, 1959.

Lerner, Max. *America as a Civilization*, London, 1958.

Lewis, Archibald R. and McGann, Thomas F. (eds). *The New World Looks at its History*, Univ. of Texas Press, 1963.

Lewis, Meriwether and Clark, William. *History of the Expedition under the command of Captains Lewis and Clark to the sources of the Missouri, thence across the Rocky Mountains, and down the river Columbia to the Pacific Ocean. Performed during the years 1804–5–6*, 2 vols. (Based on manuscript material of Lewis and Clark, and oral information of Clark), Philadelphia, 1814. A copy of the official report of the expedition was also publ. in London, 1814.

Liss, Peggy K. *Atlantic Empires: the Network of Trade and Revolution, 1713–1826*, Johns Hopkins Univ. Press, 1983.

Lockhart, James. 'Social Organization and Social Change in Colonial Spanish America', in *The Cambridge History of Latin America*, II, 1984, pp. 265–319.

Lockhart, James and Schwartz, Stuart B. *Early Latin America: a history of colonial Spanish America and Brazil*, Cambridge Univ. Press, 1983.

Long, Stephen H. *Account of an Expedition from Pittsburgh to the Rocky Mountains, performed in the years 1819 and 1820, . . . under the command of Major Stephen H. Long. Compiled from the Notes of Major Long (et al.) by Edwin James, . . .* 2 vols, Philadelphia, 1822–3.

Lubbock, Basil. *The China Clippers*, Glasgow, 2nd edn 1914.

Lynch, John. *Spanish Colonial Administration, 1782–1810: the Intendant System in the Viceroyalty of the Río de la Plata*, London, 1958.

Lynch, John. *Spain under the Habsburgs: I, Empire and Absolutism, 1516–1598*, Oxford, 1964, 2nd edn 1981; *II, Spain and America, 1598–1700*, Oxford, 1969, 2nd edn 1981.

Lynch, John. *The Spanish American Revolutions, 1808–1826*, London, 1972; 2nd edn 1986.

Lynch, John. 'The Institutional Framework of Colonial Spanish America', *Journal of Latin American Studies*, 24 (1992), Quincentenary Supplement, pp. 69–81.

Lynch, John (ed.). *Latin American Revolutions, 1808–1826: Old and New World Origins*, Univ. of Oklahoma Press, 1994.

McFarlane, Anthony. *The British in the Americas, 1480–1815*, London, 1994.

McHugh, Kevin E. 'Hispanic Migration and Population Redistribution in the United States', *Professional Geographer*, 41 (1989), pp. 429–39.

MacKay, Angus. *Spain in the Middle Ages: From Frontier to Empire, 1000–1500*, London, 1977.

Mackenzie, Alexander. *Voyages from Montreal, on the River St Laurence, through the continent of North America, to the Frozen and Pacific Oceans, in the years 1789 and 1793*, London, 1801; Philadelphia, 1802.

MacLachlan, Colin M. *Spain's Empire in the New World: the role of ideas in institutional and social change*, Univ. of California Press, 1988.

MacLeod, Murdo J. *Spanish Central America: a socioeconomic history, 1520–1720*, Univ. of California Press, 1973.

MacLeod, Murdo J. 'Spain and America: the Atlantic Trade, 1492–1720', in *The Cambridge History of Latin America*, I, 1984, pp. 341–88.

MacLeod, Murdo J. 'Aspects of the internal economy of Colonial Spanish America: labour; taxation; distribution and exchange', in *The Cambridge History of Latin America*, II, 1984, pp. 219–64.

Magoffin, Susan S. *Down the Santa Fe Trail and into Mexico: the diary of Susan Shelby Magoffin, 1846–1847*, ed. Stella M. Drumm, Yale Univ. Press, 1926. Repr. 1962.

Mahan, Alfred T., USN. *The Influence of Sea Power upon History, 1660–1783*, London and Cambridge, Mass., 1890.

Main, Jackson T. *The Antifederalists: Critics of the Constitution, 1781–1788*, Univ. of North Carolina Press, 1961.

Main, Jackson T. *The Social Structure of Revolutionary America*, Princeton Univ. Press, 1965.

Mathews, Lois K. *The Expansion of New England, 1620–1865*, Boston, 1909.

Maw, William H. and Dredge, James. *Modern Examples of Road and Railway Bridges; illustrating the most recent practice of leading engineers in Europe and America*, London, 1872.

Meinig, Donald W. 'American Wests: preface to a geographical interpretation', *Annals of the Association of American Geographers*, 62 (1972), pp. 159–84.

Meinig, Donald W. *The Shaping of America: a geographical perspective on 500 years of history, I. Atlantic America, 1492–1800*, Yale Univ. Press, 1986; *II. Continental America, 1800–1867*, Yale Univ. Press, 1993.

Merk, Frederick. *Manifest Destiny and Mission in American History: a reinterpretation*, New York, 1963.

Merk, Frederick. *History of the Westward Movement*, New York, 1978.

Merriman, Roger B. *The Rise of the Spanish Empire in the Old World and the New*, 4 vols, New York, 1918–34, repr. 1962.

Merritt, Richard L. *Symbols of American Community, 1735–1775*, Yale Univ. Press, 1966.

Michaux, François A. *Travels to the West of the Alleghany Mountains*, London, 1805.

Mitchell, Robert D. (ed.). *Appalachian Frontiers: Settlement, Society, and Development in the Preindustrial Era*, Univ. Press of Kentucky, 1991.

Modelski, George and Thompson, William R. *Seapower in Global Politics, 1494–1993*, Univ. of Washington Press, Seattle, 1987.

Morison, Samuel E. *The Maritime History of Massachusetts, 1783–1860*, Boston and New York, 1921.

Morison, Samuel E. *Admiral of the Ocean Sea*, 2 vols, Boston, 1942.

Morison, Samuel E. *By Land and By Sea: essays and addresses by Samuel Eliot Morison*, New York, 1953.

Morison, Samuel E. *The European Discovery of America: I. The Northern Voyages, 500–1600; II. The Southern Voyages, 1492–1616*, New York, Oxford Univ. Press, 1971, 1974.

Mörner, Magnus. 'Spanish Migration to the New World prior to 1810: A Report on the State of Research', in *First Images of America*, F. Chiappelli (ed.), Univ. of California Press, 1976; II, pp. 737–82.

Mörner, Magnus. 'The Rural Economy and Society of Colonial Spanish South America', in *The Cambridge History of Latin America*, II, 1984, pp. 189–217.

Morse, Jedidiah. *The American Geography*, 1st publ. Elizabeth-Town, N.J., 1789, repr. Boston. Successive edns, rev. and enlarged, Boston, New York, Philadelphia.

Morse, Jedidiah. *A Geographical and Historical View of the World*, Boston, 1811.

Morse, Richard M. 'Some characteristics of Latin American Urban History', *American Historical Review*, 67 (1962), pp. 317–38.

Morse, Richard M. 'The Urban Development of Colonial Spanish America', in *The Cambridge History of Latin America*, II, 1984, pp. 67–104.

Murrin, John M. 'A Roof Without Walls: the dilemma of American national identity', in *Beyond Confederation: Origins of the Constitution and American National Identity*, R. Beeman, S. Botein and E.C. Carter II (eds), Univ. of North Carolina Press, 1987, pp. 333–48.

Nasatir, Abraham P. *Spanish War Vessels on the Mississippi, 1792—1796*, Yale Univ. Press, 1968.

Newton, Arthur P. *The European Nations in the West Indies, 1493–1688*, London, 1933; repr. 1966.

Nordhoff, Charles. *Whaling and Fishing*, New York, 1855; Cincinnati, 1856.

Nordhoff, Charles. *Nine Years a Sailor*, New York and Cincinnati, 1857.

Nordhoff, Charles. *California: for Health, Pleasure and Residence*, New York, 1872.

Nordhoff, Charles. *Northern California, Oregon, and the Sandwich Islands*, New York, 1874.

North, Douglass C. *The Economic Growth of the United States, 1790–1860*, Englewood Cliffs, N.J., 1961.

Nuhn, Ferner R. *The Wind Blew from the East: a study in the orientation of American culture*, New York, 1940; repr. 1967.

Nuttall, Zelia. 'Royal Ordinances concerning the Laying Out of New Towns', *Hispanic American Historical Review*, 4 (1921), pp. 743–53; 5 (1922), pp. 249–54.

Ogden, Adele. *The California Sea Otter Trade, 1784–1848*, Univ. of California Press, 1941.

Ogden, Adele (ed.). *Greater America: Essays in Honor of Herbert Eugene Bolton*, Univ. of California Press, 1945.

Ogden, Adele. 'New England Traders in Spanish and Mexican California', in *Greater America*, pp. 395–413.

Ogilby, John. *America: Being the Latest, and Most Accurate Description of the New World*, London, 1671.

O'Gorman, Edmundo. *The Invention of America: an inquiry into the historical nature of the New World and the meaning of its history*, Indiana Univ. Press, 1961.

Olmsted, Frederick L. *Journeys and Explorations in the Cotton Kingdom*, 2 vols, London, 1861.

Pagden, Anthony R. *European Encounters with the New World*, Yale Univ. Press, 1993.

Paine, Ralph. *Ships and Sailors of Old Salem*, New York, 1910.

Pares, Richard. *Yankees and Creoles: the trade between North America and the West Indies before the American Revolution*, London, 1956.

Parry, John H. *The Spanish Theory of Empire in the Sixteenth Century*, Cambridge Univ. Press, 1940.

Parry, John H. *The Audiencia of New Galicia in the Sixteenth Century*, Cambridge Univ. Press, 1948.

Parry, John H. *Europe and a Wider World, 1415–1715*, London, 1949; 3rd edn rev., 1966.

Parry, John H. *The Sale of Public Office in the Spanish Indies under the Hapsburgs*, Univ. of California Press, 1953.

Parry, John H. *The Age of Reconnaissance: Discovery, Exploration and Settlement, 1450–1650*, London, 1963.

Parry, John H. *The Spanish Seaborne Empire*, London, 1966.

Parry, John H. *Trade and Dominion: the European Oversea Empires in the Eighteenth Century*, London, 1971.

Parry, John H. *The Discovery of the Sea*, New York, 1974; London, 1975; Univ. of California Press, 1981.

Parry, John H. *The Discovery of South America*, London, 1979.

Pattie, James Ohio. *The Personal Narrative of James O. Pattie, of Kentucky, during an expedition from St. Louis, through the vast regions between that place and the Pacific Ocean, and thence back through the City of Mexico to Vera Cruz, during Journeyings of Six Years*, ed. T. Flint, Cincinnati, 1831; 2nd edn 1833.

Paul, Rodman W. *Mining Frontiers of the Far West, 1848–1880*, New York, 1963.

Pereira Salas, Eugenio. *Los Primeros Contactos entre Chile y los Estados Unidos, 1778–1809*, Santiago de Chile, 1st publ. 1936; repr. 1940 and 1971. (Minor title variations).

Pevsner, Nikolaus. *An Outline of European Architecture*, Pelican Books, 1943; 5th edn 1957.

Phillips, James D. *Salem and the Indies: the story of the great commercial era of the city*, Boston, 1947.

Pigafetta, Antonio. *Journal of the Voyage of Magellan and the First Circumnavigation*, trs. and ed. R.A. Skelton, Yale Univ. Press, 1969.

Pike, Zebulon Montgomery. *Exploratory Travels through the western territories of North America; comprising a voyage from St. Louis, on the Mississippi, to the source of that river, and a journey through the interior of Louisiana, and the north-eastern provinces of New Spain. Performed in the years 1805, 1806, 1807, by order of the Government of the United States*, London, 1811. (Pike's Journal 1st publ. Philadelphia, 1810; title begins *An Account of Expeditions* . . .).

Pomeroy, Earl S. *The Territories and the United States, 1861–1890*, Univ. of Pennsylvania Press and Oxford Univ. Press, 1947.

Pomeroy, Earl S. *The Pacific Slope: A History of California, Washington, Idaho, Utah, and Nevada*, New York, 1965.

Pope, Thomas. *A Treatise on Bridge Building*, New York, 1811.

Powell, Philip W. *Soldiers, Indians, and Silver: the northward advance of New Spain, 1550—1600*, Univ. of California Press, 1952.

Pownall, Thomas. *The Administration of the Colonies, wherein their Rights and Constitution are Discussed and Stated*, London, 1768.

Price, A. Grenfell. *The Western Invasions of the Pacific and its Continents: A Survey of Moving Frontiers and Changing Landscapes, 1513–1958*, Oxford, 1963.

Quinn, David B. 'Some Spanish reactions to Elizabethan colonial enterprises', *Transactions of the Royal Historical Society*, 5th Series, 1 (1951), pp. 1–23.

Rees, Peter W. 'Origins of Colonial Transportation in Mexico', *Geographical Review*, 65 (1975), pp. 323–34.

Reynolds, Clark G. *Command of the Sea: the history and strategy of maritime empires*, New York, 1974.

Richman, Irving B. *California under Spain and Mexico, 1535–1847*, Boston and New York, 1911.

Riker, William H. *Federalism: Origin, Operation, Significance*, Boston, 1964.

Riker, William H. *Democracy in the United States*, New York, 2nd edn 1965.

Riker, William H. *The Development of American Federalism*, Norwell, Mass., 1987.

Riley, Major Bennet and Cooke, Lieut. Philip St. George. *The First Military Escort on the Santa Fe Trail, 1829*; Journal and Reports, ed. O.E. Young, Glendale, Calif., 1952.

Ringrose, David R. 'Carting in the Hispanic World: an example of divergent development', *Hispanic American Historical Review*, 50 (1970), pp. 30–51.

Ringrose, David R. *Transportation and Economic Stagnation in Spain, 1750–1850*, Durham, N.C., 1970.

Robinson, Alfred. *Life in California*, New York, 1846; San Francisco, 1897.

Robinson, David J. 'Trade and Trading Links in Western Argentina during the Viceroyalty', *Geographical Journal*, 136 (1970), pp. 24–41.

Robinson, David J. (ed.). *Studies in Spanish Population History*, Boulder, Colo., 1981.

Robinson, David J. (ed.). *Migration in Colonial Spanish America*, Cambridge Univ. Press, 1990.

Robinson, David J. and Thomas, Teresa. 'New Towns in Eighteenth Century Northwest Argentina', *Journal of Latin American Studies*, 6 (1974), pp. 1–33.

Robinson, William Davis. *A Cursory View of Spanish America, particularly the Neighboring Vice-Royalties of Mexico and New Granada, chiefly intended to elucidate the policy of an Early Connection between the United States and Those Countries*, Georgetown, D.C., 1815.

Robinson, William Davis. *Memoirs of the Mexican Revolution; including a Narrative of the Expedition of General Xavier Mina. With Some Observations on the Practicability of Opening a Commerce between the Pacific and Atlantic Oceans, . . . and on the Future Importance of Such Commerce to the Civilized World, and more especially to the United States*, 2 vols, Philadelphia, 1820, London, 1821.

Russel, Robert R. *Improvement of Communication with the Pacific Coast as an issue in American Politics, 1783–1864*, Cedar Rapids, Iowa, 1948.

Rydell, Raymond A. *Cape Horn to the Pacific: the rise and decline of an ocean highway*, Univ. of California Press, 1952.

Sánchez-Albornoz, Nicolás. *The Population of Latin America: a history*, trs. W.A.R. Richardson, Univ. of California Press, 1974.

Sánchez-Albornoz, Nicolás. 'The population of Colonial Spanish America', in *The Cambridge History of Latin America*, II, 1984, pp. 3–35.

San Martín, José. *Memorial and Proposals of Señor Don José San Martín on the Californias*, Mexico City, 1822; trs. with an Introduction, H.R. Wagner, San Marino, Calif., 1945.

Sauer, Carl O. *The Early Spanish Main*, Univ. of California Press, 1966.

Sauer, Carl O. *Sixteenth Century North America: the Land and the People as seen by the Europeans*, Univ. of California Press, 1971.

Savelle, Max. *Empires to Nations: Expansion in America, 1713–1824*, Univ. of Minnesota Press, 1974.

Scammell, Geoffrey V. *The World Encompassed: the first European Maritime Empires, c.800–1650*, Univ. of California Press, 1980, London and New York, 1981.

Scammell, Geoffrey V. *The First Imperial Age: European Overseas Expansion c.1400–1715*, London, 1989.

Schäfer, Ernesto. *El Consejo Real y Supremo de las Indias: Su historia, organización, y labor administrativa hasta la terminación de la Casa de Austria*, 2 vols, Seville, 1935–47.

Schlesinger, Jr., Arthur M. *The Disuniting of America: reflections on a multicultural society*, New York and London, 1991.

Schurz, William L. *The Manila Galleon*, New York, 1939.

Sempat Assadourian, Carlos. 'The Colonial Economy: the transfer of the European System of Production to New Spain and Peru', *Journal of Latin American Studies*, 24 (1992), Quincentenary Supplement, pp. 55–68.

Shiels, William E. *King and Church: the rise and fall of the Patronato Real*, Chicago: Loyola Univ. Press, 1961.

Sluiter, Engel. 'Dutch-Spanish Rivalry in the Caribbean Area, 1594–1609', *Hispanic American Historical Review*, 28 (1948), pp. 165–96.

Smith, Henry Nash. *Virgin Land: the American West as Symbol and Myth*, Harvard Univ. Press, 1950.

Smyth, John Ferdinand D. *A Tour in the United States of America; Containing an Account of the Present Situation of that Country: the Population, Agriculture, Commerce, Customs, and Manners of the Inhabitants*, 2 vols, London, 1784.

Socolow, Susan M. *The Merchants of Buenos Aires, 1778–1810: Family and Commerce*, Cambridge Univ. Press, 1978.

Socolow, Susan M. and Johnson, Lyman L. 'Urbanization in Colonial Latin America', *Journal of Urban History*, 8 (1981), pp. 27–59.

Spanish America and the United States; or, Views on the Actual Commerce of the United States with the Spanish Colonies. By a Merchant of Philadelphia, Philadelphia, 1818.

Spate, Oskar H.K. *The Pacific since Magellan: I. The Spanish Lake*, Australian National Univ. Press, Canberra and London (1979); *II. Monopolists and Freebooters* (1983); *III. Paradise Found and Lost* (1988).

Spicer, Edward H. *Cycles of Conquest: the Impact of Spain, Mexico, and the United States on the Indians of the Southwest, 1533–1960*, Univ. of Arizona Press, 1962.

Stanislawski, Dan. 'Early Spanish Town Planning in the New World', *Geographical Review*, 37 (1947), pp. 94–105.

Starbuck, Alexander. *History of the American Whale Fishery*, Waltham, Mass., 1878.

Stein, Stanley J. and Barbara H. *The Colonial Heritage of Latin America: essays on economic dependence in historical perspective*, New York, 1970.

Stilgoe, John R. *Common Landscape of America, 1580–1845*, Yale Univ. Press, 1982.

Storrs, Augustus. *Answers of Augustus Storrs, of Missouri, to certain queries upon the origin, present state, and future prospect of trade and intercourse, between Missouri and the internal provinces of Mexico, propounded by the Hon. Mr. Benton*; January 3, 1825. Printed by Order of the Senate of the United States, Washington, D.C., 1825.

Storrs, Augustus. 'Santa Fe Trail; first reports, 1825', *Senate Documents Nos. 7 and 79*, 18th Congress, 2nd Session, Washington, D.C., 1825–6. (Repr. Houston, Texas, 1960).

Stover, John F. *American Railroads*, Univ. of Chicago Press, 1961.

Strong, Josiah. *Our Country: its possible future and its present crisis*, New York, 1885.

Suárez-Fernández, Luís. 'The Kingdom of Castile in the Fifteenth Century', in R. Highfield (ed.), *Spain in the Fifteenth Century, 1369–1516*, London, 1972, pp. 80–113.

Swann, Michael M. *Migrants in the Mexican North: Mobility, Economy, and Society in a Colonial World*, Boulder, Colo., 1989.

Symcox, Geoffrey W. 'The Battle of the Atlantic, 1500–1700', in F. Chiappelli (ed.), *First Images of America: the Impact of the New World on the Old*, 1976, I, pp. 265–77.

Tandeter, Enrique. *Coercion and Market: Silver Mining in Colonial Potosí, 1692–1826*, Univ. of Mexico Press, 1993.

Taylor, Eva G.R. *Tudor Geography, 1485—1583*, London, 1930.

Taylor, Eva G.R. *Late Tudor and Early Stuart Geography, 1583–1650*, London, 1934.

Taylor, George R. *The Transportation Revolution, 1815–1860*, New York, 1951.

Taylor, George R. and Neu, Irene D. *The American Railroad Network, 1861–1890*, Harvard Univ. Press. 1956.

Taylor, William R. *Cavalier and Yankee: the Old South and American National Character*, New York, 1961.

Thomas, Hugh. *The Conquest of Mexico*, London, 1993.

Thomas, William H. *The Whaleman's Adventures in the Sandwich Islands and California*, Boston, 1872.

Thompson, I.A.A. *War and Government in Habsburg Spain, 1560—1620*, London, 1976.

Thwaites, Reuben G. (ed.). *Early Western Travels, 1748–1846*, 32 vols, Cleveland, Ohio, 1904–07.

Tilden, Bryant Parrot. *Notes on the Upper Rio Grande, explored in the months of October and November, 1846, on board the U.S. Steamer 'Major Brown', commanded by Capt. Mark Sterling, of Pittsburgh. By Order of Major General Patterson, U.S. Army, commanding the Second Division, Army of Occupation, Mexico*, Philadelphia, 1847.

Tocqueville, Alexis de. *Democracy in America*, 2 vols, Paris 1835; London, 1835; New York, 1836; 3rd American edn 1839.

Turner, Frederick Jackson. 'The Significance of the Frontier in American History', *Annual Report of the American Historical Association for 1893*, Washington, D.C., 1894.

Turner, Frederick Jackson. *Rise of the New West, 1819–1829*, New York and London, 1906.

Turner, Frederick Jackson. 'Greater New England in the Middle of the Nineteenth Century', *Proceedings of the American Antiquarian Society*, 29 (1919), pp. 222–41.

Turner, Frederick Jackson. *The Frontier in American History*, New York, 1920.

Turner, Frederick Jackson. *The Significance of Sections in American History*, New York, 1932.

Ulloa, Antonio de. See Juan, Jorge.

Vance, Jr., James E. *The Merchant's World: the geography of wholesaling*, Englewood Cliffs, N.J., 1970.

Vance, Jr., James E. *Capturing the Horizon: the historical geography of transportation*, New York, 1986.

Varg, Paul A. *New England and Foreign Relations, 1789–1850*, Univ. Press of New England, 1983.

Vassberg, David E. *Land and Society in Golden Age Castile*, Cambridge Univ. Press, 1984.

Vatter, Harold G. *The Drive to Industrial Maturity: the U.S. Economy, 1860–1914*, Westport, Connecticut, 1976.

Veltman, Calvin. 'The Status of the Spanish Language in the United States at the Beginning of the 21st Century', *International Migration Review*, 24 (1990), pp. 108–23.

Verlinden, Charles. *The Beginnings of Modern Colonization*, Cornell Univ. Press. 1970.

Vevier, Charles. 'American Continentalism: an Idea of Expansion, 1845–1910', *American Historical Review*, 65 (1960), pp. 323–35.

Vicens Vives, Jaime. *An Economic History of Spain*, Princeton Univ. Press, 1969.

Vickers, Geoffrey. 'Making Institutions Work', *Wharton Quarterly*, Univ. of Pennsylvania, Spring 1971; London, 1973.

Wachtel, Nathan. 'The Indian and the Spanish Conquest', in *The Cambridge History of Latin America*, I, 1984, pp. 207–48.

Walker, Geoffrey J. *Spanish Politics and Imperial Trade, 1700–1789*, London, 1979.

Walker, Henry P. *The Wagonmaster: High Plains Freighting from the earliest days of the Santa Fe Trail to 1880*, Univ. of Oklahoma Press, 1966.

Walker, Mack. *Germany and the Emigration, 1816–1885*, Harvard Univ. Press, 1964.

Walton, William. *Present State of the Spanish Colonies . . . with a general survey of the settlements on the South Continent of America, as relates to History, Trade, Population, Customs, Manners, etc., with a concise statement of the sentiments of the people on their relative situation to the Mother Country, etc.*, 2 vols, London, 1810.

Wappäus, Johann E. *Deutsche Auswanderung und Colonisation*, Leipzig, 1846.

Warriner, Francis. *Cruise of the United States Frigate 'Potomac' round the world, during the Years 1831–34*, New York and Boston, 1835.

Washburn, Wilcomb E. 'The Meaning of "Discovery" in the Fifteenth and Sixteenth Centuries', *American Historical Review*, 68 (1962), pp. 1–21.

Washington, George. *The Writings of George Washington*, ed. W.C. Ford, 14 vols, New York, 1889–93.

Webb, James Josiah. *Adventures in the Santa Fe Trade, 1844–1847*, Glendale, Calif., 1931.

Webb, Walter Prescott. *The Great Plains*, Boston, 1931.

Webb, Walter Prescott. *The Great Frontier*, Harvard Univ. Press, 1952.

Weber, David J. *The Mexican Frontier, 1821–1846: the American Southwest under Mexico*, Univ. of New Mexico Press, 1982.

Weber, David J. *The Spanish Frontier in North America*, Yale Univ. Press, 1992.

Weber, David J. and Rausch, Jane M. (eds). *Where Cultures Meet: the Frontier in Latin American History*, Wilmington, 1994.

Weckmann, Luis. 'The Middle Ages in the Conquest of America', in *History of Latin American Civilization*, L. Hanke (ed.), Boston, 1967; *I. The Colonial Experience*, pp. 10–22.

West, Robert C. and Augelli, John. *Middle America: Its Lands and Peoples*, Englewood Cliffs, N.J., 1966; 2nd edn 1976.

Whigham, Thomas. 'Cattle Raising in the Argentine Northeast: Corrientes, c.1750–1870', *Journal of Latin American Studies*, 20 (1988), pp. 313–35.

Whitaker, Arthur P. *The Spanish American Frontier, 1783–1795: the westward movement and the Spanish retreat in the Mississippi Valley*, New York and Boston, 1927.

Whitaker, Arthur P. *The Mississippi Question, 1795–1803: a study in trade, politics, and diplomacy*, New York, 1934.

Whitaker, Arthur P. 'Antonio de Ulloa', *Hispanic American Historical Review*, 15 (1935), pp. 155–94.

Whitaker, Arthur P. *The United States and the Independence of Latin America, 1800–1830*, Johns Hopkins Univ. Press, 1941; New York, 1954.

Whitaker, Arthur P. (ed.). *Latin America and the Enlightenment*, Cornell Univ. Press, 2nd edn 1961.

Whitaker, Arthur P. 'Early Commercial Relations between the United States and Spanish America', in *The Origins of the Latin American Revolutions, 1808–1826*, R.A. Humphreys and J. Lynch (eds), New York, 1965, pp. 84–93.

Wilkes, Charles, USN. *Narrative of the United States' Exploring Expedition during the Years 1838, 1839, 1840, 1841, 1842*, 5 vols, Philadelphia, 1844.

Williams, Jerry M. and Lewis, Robert E. (eds). *Early Images of the Americas: Transfer and Invention*, Univ. of Arizona Press, 1993.

Williams, William A. *The Roots of the Modern American Empire*, New York, 1969.

Williamson, Harold F. *The Growth of the American Economy*, New York, 1944.

Winther, Oscar O. *The Transportation Frontier: Trans-Mississippi West, 1865–1890*, New York, 1964.

Wood, Gordon. *The Creation of the American Republic, 1776–1787*, Univ. of North Carolina Press, 1969.

Woodruff, William. *America's Impact on the World: a study of the United States in the world economy, 1750–1970*, New York and London, 1975.

Wright, Esmond. 'American Independence in its American context; Social and Political Aspects; Western Expansion', in *The New Cambridge Modern History*, VIII, 1965, pp. 509–36.

Wrigley, Gladys M. 'Salta, an early commercial centre of Argentina', *Geographical Review*, 2 (1916), pp. 116–33.

Wrigley, Gladys M. 'Fairs of the Central Andes', *Geographical Review*, 7 (1919), pp. 65—80.

Zamora, Margarita. *Reading Columbus*, Univ. of California Press, 1993.

Zavala, Silvio. 'The Frontiers of Hispanic America', in *The Frontier in Perspective*, W.D. Wyman and C.B. Kroeber (eds), Univ. of Wisconsin Press, 1957, pp. 35-58.

Zelinsky, Wilbur. *The Cultural Geography of the United States*, Englewood Cliffs, N.J., 1973.

STRUCTURES: A SELECTED BIBLIOGRAPHY

Addis, W. *Structural Engineering: the nature of theory and design*, Chichester and New York, 1990.

Cox, H.L. *The Design of Structures of Least Weight*, Oxford, 1965.

Francis, A.J. *Introducing Structures*, Oxford, 1980.

Gerstle, K.H. *Basic Structural Design*, New York, 1967.

Gordon, J.E. *Structures; or Why Things Don't Fall Down*, Penguin Books, Harmondsworth, England, 1978.

Holgate, A. *The Art in Structural Design*, Oxford, 1986.

Marshall, W.T. and Nelson, H.M. *Structures*, London, 2nd edn 1977.

Morgan, W. *The Elements of Structure*, London, 1964, 2nd edn (ed. I.G. Buckle), 1977.

Rosenthal, H.W. *Structure*, London, 1972.

Salvadori, M. and Heller, R. *Structure in Architecture: the building of buildings*, Englewood Cliffs, N.J., 2nd edn 1975.

Salvadori, M. *Why Buildings Stand Up: the strength of architecture*, New York, 1980.

Schodek, D.L. *Structures*, Englewood Cliffs, N.J., 2nd edn 1975.

Smyrell, A.G. *Design of Structural Elements*, London and New York, 1982.

Spillers, W.R. *Introduction to Structures*, Chichester and New York, 1985.

Acknowledgements

Quotations and extracts are reproduced by kind permission of the following:

Addison-Wesley Longman for extracts from W. Morgan, *The Elements of Structure* (Pitman, 1977), and from A.G. Smyrell, *Design of Structural Elements* (Longman, 1982).

Alfred A. Knopf, Inc., New York for one map based on Hubert Herring with Helen Baldwin Herring, *A History of Latin America* (Jonathan Cape, 1968). Copyright c 1968 by Helen Baldwin Herring, Executrix of the Estate of Hubert Herring. Copyright c 1955, 1961 by Hubert Herring.

American Geographical Society, New York for one map based on J.R. Borchert in *The Geographical Review*, vol. 57.

Cambridge University Press for one map based on M.J. MacLeod in *The Cambridge History of Latin America*, I, 1984.

Professor A.J. Francis, University of Melbourne, Australia for extracts from *Introducing Structures* (Pergamon Press, 1980; Ellis Horwood, 1989).

Professor K.H. Gerstle, University of Colorado at Boulder for extracts from *Basic Structural Design* (McGraw-Hill, 1967).

The Institution of Structural Engineers, London for extracts by H.E. Brooke-Bradley and H.J. Collins in *The Structural Engineer*, vol. 16.

John Wiley & Sons for the extract from W.R. Spillers, *Introduction to Structures* (Ellis Horwood, 1985).

Oxford University Press for the extract from A. Holgate, *The Art in Structural Design* (Clarendon Press, 1986).

Penguin Books UK for extracts from J.E. Gordon, *Structures*, 1978.

Random House, Inc., New York for the extract from Robinson Jeffers, *The Eye*, from *Selected Poems* by Robinson Jeffers. Copyright c 1941, 1944; Renewed 1969, 1972 by Donnan Jeffers and Garth Jeffers.

Routledge for one map based on M. Gilbert, *American History Atlas* (Weidenfeld & Nicolson, 1968).

Royal Geographical Society, London for two of my maps, with accompanying text, in *The Geographical Journal*, vols 142 and 144.

Simon & Schuster, New York for the extract from Vachel Lindsay, *Bryan, Bryan, Bryan, Bryan*, from *The Collected Poems of Vachel Lindsay*. Copyright c 1920 by Macmillan Publishing Company; Renewed 1948 by Elizabeth C. Lindsay.

Louis Simpson for the extract from his poem *To the Western World*.

I also wish to thank the Institution of Civil Engineers, London for allowing me the use of the library.

Index

Acapulco, Mexico, 62–3, 111, 122
Adams, John, 147, 153
Adams, John Quincy, 171, 181
Allegheny Mts, USA, *see* trans-Alleghany (Allegheny) region
Almagro, Diego de, 45, 47
Alvarado, Juan Bautista, 186
Amazon (river), 31, 34, 48, 51
 and Orellana's exploration (1541–2), 52–3
Americanization, 238, 257–8, 260–4
Andalusia (al-Andalus), Spain, 9, 12, 16, 23, 26, 56, 92, 135
Antifederalists, USA, 154–8 *passim*, 165, 207
Aragón, 9–10, 14, 16–17, 23, 26–7, 135
 and Muslim, *morisco* explusions, 92–3
Arica, official port for Potosí (Upper Peru), 118, 119, 122
Armada: de Barlovento; de la Mar del Sur; del Mar Océano; 103
Armada de la Carrera, 105–6
Articles of Confederation (USA, 1777–87), 149–50, 163, 164
asiento, 108
Atlantic Ocean: its early political allocation (1493), 30–1; (1494), 31–2
 Spain's subsequent perception of its western margin, 123, 251; *see also* trade
Azores (Port.), 30

Balboa, Nuñez de, 36, 123
beams and **tie-beams**: 18
 in Iberian peninsula, 19–25 *passim*
 role of Church as, 76
 Spanish imperial sea lanes as, 102–8
 their landward extension in Spanish America, 117–24, 129
 Mississippi River as, 165;
 in USA, 145, 192–3, 198, 211, 216, 217

cantilever beams, 76, 80–3, 129
Bent, Charles (of Bent, St Vrain & Co.), 221, 222, 223
Benton, Thomas Hart, 230–2
Bilingual Education Act (1968), 268;
 proposed repeal of (1995), 267n. 102(ii)
Bilingual Election Requirements (1965, 1975), *see* Voting Rights Act USA, and Amendment
Bogotá (Santa Fe de Bogotá), capital of Viceroyalty of New Granada, 72, 114
Boston, Massachusetts, 142, 145, 174, 178–80, 183–4, 198, 201
 as synonym for the United States, 188
 controls California's seaborne trade, 185–90; *see also* New England
Bourbon reforms, imperial Spain (18th century), 126–36
bridges: suspension, 151, 169, 215
 trussed, 203–5, 215
Buenos Aires, 87, 116, 118, 122
 as capital of Viceroyalty of Rio de la Plata (*q.v.*), 119, 121, 129

Cádiz, Spain, 26, 96–8, 105, 127
California, Upper:
 Spain's first coastal exploration of (1542–3), 46
 Spanish settlement in (after 1769), 130, 227
 its isolation from Mexican administration (after 1821), 185
 increased immigration to (1840s), 188, 252
 acquires US Statehood (1850), 208; *see also* Monterey *and* New England *and* San Francisco
canal transport, USA, 192–3, 201
Canary Islands (Spain), 28, 31, 39, 40, 97

Cape Verde Islands (Port.), 30–1
Caribbean Sea:
    Spain's exploration of, 30–7
    its early Spanish settlement and organization, 39–42, 85
Carrera de Indias, see trade
Cartagena (Caribbean), as official imperial trading port, 101, 105–6, 108
Casa de la Contratación de las Indias (Board of Trade, 1503–1790), 96, 99, 111, 131
    transferred from Seville to Cádiz (1717), 96, 127
Castile, Spain:
    expands and consolidates, 11–28
    expels Jews (1492) and Muslims (1502), 92, and remaining *moriscos* (1609–14), 93
    economic depression in, 94–5; *see also* empire *and* trade
cattle ranching:
    in medieval Spain, 22–3
    on *pampas* of Paraná-Plata, 118–19
Charleston, South Carolina, 145, 147, 198
Chile:
    explored by Valdivia, 47
    audiencia of, 72
    captaincy-general of (1778), 73, 130
    its official overland link to Buenos Aires (late 18th century), 129
Church, its role and relationship with Spanish Crown, 27, 77–83
Cimarron (river), 219
Clark, George Rogers, 162
Clark, William, 170
clipper ships, 184–5
Colorado (river):
    explored by Spain (1539–41), 46, 54–5
    (1687–1711), 226
    explored and surveyed by USA, 237
Columbia (river), named by Capt. Gray (1792), 179; 189, 231
Columbus, Christopher (*Span.* Cristóbal Colón; *Ital.* Cristoforo Colombo):
    his preparation and first transatlantic voyage, 5–7, 27–8
    his four voyages, 5, 32–3, 41

compression structures in Castile and Spanish America, general principles, 14–15, 67, 76, 78, 99–100
Confederate States of America (1861–5), *see* South, USA
Córdoba, Spain, 8, 11, 17, 26, 49, 97
Coronado, Francisco Vásquez de, 54–5
Cortés, Hernán:
    invades Mexico (1519), 44
    organizes early Pacific fleet, 44, 60
    promotes Mexico-Peru trade, 110
    his reward, 57
critical load, 259–60, 266
Crofutt, George A., triggers adoption of word 'transcontinental', 285n. 89
Cuba:
    Columbus's discovery of, 32–3
    new Captaincy-general at (1764), 130
    Intendancy of (1765), 127
    its trade with Anglo-America, 175–7, 249–50, 286n. 96
    Cuban Adjustment Act, USA (1966), 267; *see also* Havana

De Soto, Hernando, explores lower Mississippi and south-east region (1539–death May 1542), 53, 54
De Vaca, Alvar Núñez Cabeza:
    sights mouth of Mississippi River (1528), 49
    extends exploration westward, 53–4, and in South America (1540–2), 46
Domínguez, Father Francisco Athanasio: with Escalante seeks overland route New Mexico-Upper California (1776–7), 227
Drake, Francis, 63

El Camino Real, 116, 118, 219
El Dorado, 52, 170
empire:
    Spanish perceptions and policies of, 39–42, 56–7, 65–8, 74–5, 86, 90, 100, 116–17, 126, 132, 135–6, 243–5, 247–51, 253
    financial costs of, 133–4
    English style of, in American colonies, 141, 143, 146

United States' perceptions and policies of, 168, 192, 217, 238, 246–7, 252–4, 271
encomienda, 39–40, 79
English language:
  in American colonies, 140
  in USA, after independence, 158
  in late 20th century, 264, 267–70
Escalante, Father Silvestre Vélez de, *see* Domínguez

Federalism and Federal Constitution, USA, 152–7, 255–6, 280n. 5
  distribution of support for (1787–90), 154, 155–6
  Federal development initiatives, 224, 234–5, 237–9; *see also* Gallatin *and* railroads *and* roads
Finley, James, 151, 215
flexibility, 141, 149
flota, 103–8, 131
Fort Ross, California, 185, 188
foundations, 29, 225, 237, 238–9
Franciscans:
  in New Spain, 71, 227
  expand into Florida and Texas, 83
  into Upper (Alta) California, 129, 130
Frémont, John Charles, 226

Gadsden Purchase (1853), 232, 233
Gage, Thomas, 78–9, 107
galeones, 103–8, 131
Gallatin, Albert (Secretary of the Treasury): his *Report on Public Roads and Canals* presented to US Senate (1808), 230
Gálvez, José de, 132
Gray, Capt. Robert, 178–9, 180
Guadalquivir (river), Spain, 16, 17, 22–3
  navigation of, 49, 59, 97–8
Guayaquil, 52, 112, 115, 120

Hamilton, Alexander, 155, 166, 168
Havana, Cuba (founded 1515): as official imperial trading port, 101, 102–3, 127, 175
  made responsible for Spain's defence of the Caribbean (1793), 176; *see also* Cuba
Hawaiian Islands, 64, 178–90 *passim*;
  first European discovery (Capt. James Cook, 1778), 178
  as base for US whaling industry, 180–2
  first New England Congregational mission in (1820), 182–3
  US strategic interests in, 183, 237
Houses of Assembly, Anglo-American colonies, 143, 146

immigration: Spanish, to New World, 91–5
  to Anglo-American colonies (17th-18th centuries), 140–7
  to USA (19th-20th centuries), 238, 265–70
imperialism, *see* empire
Indians:
  population estimates (1492), 274n. 12
  Spain's conflicting attitudes to, 39–40, 77–8, 79
  Araucanian, 73, 89
  Aztec (Mexica), 44, 71, 79, 87
  Chibcha (Muisca), 47
  Chichimeca, 71
  Chiquito, 82
  Guaraní, 81
  Inca, 45, 79, 87
  Maya, 55
  Mojo, 82
  Pueblo, 72, 83
  Toba, 73
  Zuñi, 54
Intendancies, introduced in Spanish America, 127, 129, 131–2, 279n. 67
interoceánico, Spain's concept of overland connection, 121–4

Jay, John, 155, 163
Jefferson, Thomas, 147, 155, 156, 164, 195;
  and the Ordinances (1784–7), 223
  and the Louisiana Purchase (1803), 168, 170
  and the Embargo Act (1807–9), 177

Jesuits:
  on northern frontier of New Spain (16th century), 71
  in Paraguay, 81–3
  in Lower California and in Sonora/Arizona, Gila, lower Colorado region (17th-18th centuries), 226
joints and **jointing**, 100

Kino, Father Eusebio, 226

Larkin, Thomas Oliver, US Consul in Upper California, Mexico (1844–8), 187, 189
Lewis, Meriwether, 170
Lima, Peru (founded by Pizarro 1535), 45;
  audiencia of, 72
  as viceregal capital, 80, 85, 111, 121; *see also* Viceroyalty of Peru
Lincoln, Abraham, 208, 209, 211
Louisiana: name originally given by La Salle to entire Mississippi Valley (1682), 83
  territory west of Mississippi ceded by France to Spain (1762), Spain's policies in, 161–8
  ceded by Spain to France (1800) and purchased by USA (1803), 168–70

Madison, James, 155, 156, 170
Magdalena (river), 51, 114
Magellan, Ferdinand, crosses Pacific (1520–1), 59
Magellan Strait, 35, 36, 107
Manila, Philippine Islands, 62, 64, 101, 111, 127, 130, 180;
  audiencia of, 70
  US Consuls at (first appt. 1801), 180; *see also* Manila Galleon *and* Philippine Islands
Manila Galleon, 61–4
Mesta, Spain, 19–22, 26
Mexico City, 44, 69–70, 85, 111; *see also* Viceroyalty of New Spain
Mississippi (river):
  sighted by De Vaca (1528), 49
  crossed by De Soto (1541), 53
  its extensive exploration by France leads to La Salle's designation of Valley as Louisiana (1682), 83
  and US-Spanish relations (1783–1800), 161–8
  its structural and geographical significance to USA, 161–72, 211–12
  first steamboat service on Mississippi-Ohio Rivers (1811), 171
Missouri (river and State):
  departure point for Santa Fe Trail and overland trade to Mexico, 219
  and for Oregon and California Trails, 229–30
  steam navigation on, 284n. 69
mita, 79, 117
Monterey, Upper California (mission founded 1770): official entry port and customs point under Mexico (1821–48), 185–7
mortar, 65, 78, 100
multiculturalism, 262–3, 268
Muslim invasion and organization of Iberian peninsula, 8–12, 49

Natchez (Mississippi river port, founded by French 1716), 162, 165, 167;
  ceded by Spain to USA (1795), 166–7
National Language Act, USA (proposed 1995), 286n. 102
New England:
  in colonial period, 141–8
  expands seaborne trade after independence, 174–8
  enters Pacific, 173, 178–90, 252
  expands manufacturing, 178, 193
  and the whaling industry, 180–2
  and California, 185–90, 242
New Mexico:
  Spanish colonization of (1598, 1693–6), 71–2, 83
  part of reorganized Internal Provinces (late 18th century), 130; *see also* Santa Fe *and* Santa Fe Trail
New Orleans:
  founded by French (1718), 83
  ceded to Spain (1762–1800), 162–5
  as key port for trans-Alleghany country, 162–8, 177

sold to USA as part of Louisiana Purchase (1803), 168
challenged by New York, 197–8, and by growth of Northern markets, 201–2, 212; *see also* Mississippi river

New Spain, *see* Viceroyalty of

New York (city and State), 145, 156–7, 174, 176, 197–8, 201

'Old Spanish Trail', 218, 227
Oregon Trail, 188, 211, 217, 218
Orellana, Francisco de, 52–3
Orinoco (river), its discovery and exploration by Spain, 32, 49, 50–1

Pacific Ocean:
 Spain's discovery of (1513), 36; crossed by Magellan (1520–1), 59
 early transpacific exploration and trade (by Spain), 60–4
 (by New England), 178–90;
 official US exploration of (Wilkes, 1838–42), 181–2
Pacific Railroad, *see* railroad transport, USA *and* transcontinental
Panama City (founded 1519), 86, 107, 114
 audiencia of, 72
Panama Isthmus, 36–7, 123
Panama Railroad, 184, 232, 253
Paraguay (river and region):
 explored by Spain, 46, 49–50
 Jesuit missions in, 81–3
 as part of the San Ildefonso treaty line (1777), 82–3, 128
peninsulares (Spaniards born in Spain), 74–5, 94, 131–3
Philadelphia, Pennsylvania, 145, 146, 152, 176, 177, 193, 198, 201
Philippine Islands, 59–64 *passim*, 69, 93, 111; *see also* Manila *and* Manila Galleon
Pigafetta, Antonio, 59
Pike, Zebulon Montgomery, 170, 217
Pizarro, Francisco, 45, 72
population:
 in Americas (estim. 1492), 274n. 12;
 (in 1790s): Spanish America, 250, USA, 144, 250

its 19th century growth and westward expansion in USA, 201–2, 237–8
late 20th century USA, 267; *see also* immigration

Portugal:
 its independence from Spain, 17–18
 incorporated under Spanish Crown (1580–1640), 249; *see also* Treaty of Tordesillas, of Madrid, and of San Ildefonso
Potosí, Upper Peru (later Bolivia):
 Spain's silver discoveries at (1545), 52, 72
 its population growth, 85
 its influence on imperial structural design, the 'port' of Potosí, 117–22
prestressed components, 73–5, 78, 90, 129, 131–3
Puerto Bello (Portobello), Caribbean port, Panama Isthmus: replaces Nombre de Dios as imperial trading port (1598), 101; 106–8, 114

Quesada, Gonzalo, 47, 51

railroad transport, USA:
 in North, 193, 196
 in South, 195–6
 across West: early proposals for, 229–32
 construction of (1869–93), 235–6
 Pacific Railroad Act (1862), 210, 234
 Pacific Railroad Surveys (1853–4), 232–3; *see also* transcontinental
Reconquista, 11, 12, 15–18, 84
repartimiento, 39–40
resilience, 109, 126
Río de la Plata (river), discovery of, 34, 48; *see also* Viceroyalty of
Río Grande (river), 54, 72, 220–1
road transport, incl. trails and wagon roads: in medieval Spain, 23–6
 in colonial Spanish America, 113–24
 in USA, National Road (authorized 1806), 192, 225
 Federal wagon roads (1840s–50s), 225–9

stage lines, 218, 232–4; *see also El Camino Real and* Gallatin
Roebling, John Augustus, 215
Royal Council of the Indies, Spain, 66–7, 74, 77, 99, 133, 165

Saavedra, Álvaro de, 60
'safe cracks', 109, 125, 126, 207–8
safety in structures, 259
St Louis (Mississippi river port, founded 1764), 165, 230–4 *passim; see also* Missouri
Salem, Massachusetts, 179, 183–4
Salta, Andean foothill town, 87, 116, 119
Salvatierra, Father Juan, 226
San Blas, Mexico, 185, 186
San Diego, Upper California (mission founded 1769):
 involved in New England-Mexican hide trade, 187–9
 terminus of US Federal wagon road from Santa Fe (1847), 226, 227
San Francisco, Upper California:
 Spain's overland exploration (1769) and mission construction (1776), 226, 252
 under Mexico, 187–9 *passim*
 as US coastwise trade centre, 184, 202
 as Pacific Railroad terminus, 182, 231, 241; *see also* California
Santa Fe, New Mexico:
 founded (1610), 72
 as base for Spanish exploration of the south-west, 227
 first US Consul at (1825), 221
 and the 'Old Spanish Trail', 227
 its first wagon road to California (1847), 226; *see also* Santa Fe Trail
Santa Fe Trail:
 authorized by Congress (1825), 284n. 67
 and the Mexican trade, 217–23
 its continued popularity (1850s–60s), 284n. 75
Santiago de Chile (founded 1541), *see* Chile
Santiago de Compostela, Spain, 24–5

Seville, Spain:
 recaptured from Moors (1248), 17
 as river port and regional centre of Andalusia, 26, 96–8
 dominates Spain's transatlantic trade, 98–9; *see also* Cádiz *and* trade
slavery and slave trade:
 in Spanish America, 40, 81, 91, 108, 131, 276n. 25
 in USA, 140, 145, 194, 199–201, 206–10
South, USA:
 its growing structural contrast with North and West, 194–214
 cotton production in, 197–200
 and the Confederate States of America (1861–5), 208–14
stress and **strain**, defined, 2
structural analysis, 257, 266
Sutter, John, 188

tension structures, basic principles and components, 151, 152, 158, 159–60, 210, 213–14, 246–7, 248, 260
Texas:
 Spanish missions establ. in, 83
 its annexation by USA (1845), 212, 227
 in 1850s, 228; *see also* road transport/stage lines *and* Santa Fe Trail
Tilden, Bryant Parrot, explores and reports on Río Grande (1846), 220–1
Tordesillas Line, *see* Treaty of
towns:
 their role in colonial Spanish America, 84–90
 in northern Anglo-American colonies, 141–5
 their limited development in the South, 145, 195, 212; *see also* population
trade (Spanish):
 in medieval Spain, 23–6, 134–5
 and Spanish imperial controls, 96–112; transatlantic convoys (*Carrera de Indias*), 102–8, 127
 via Cape Horn (legalized 1740), 107, 127; in Pacific, 110–12
 overland to Potosí, 118–20

and 'Free Trade' legislation (1765 and after), 130–5
contraband, 99, 108, 111, 118, 131, 177, 185, 187, 249
trans-Alleghany (Allegheny) region, USA:
  its early settlement and trade, 161–72, 192, 201, 212
transcontinental:
  defined in contrast to 'interoceanic' connection, 121
  Spanish perceptions of, 121–4
  USA's rapid adoption of word (1869) and its structural significance, 239–42, 285n. 89
trans-Mississippi region (US Federal initiatives in): 210–11, 221, 224, 225–9
  railroad surveys and construction, 232–5
  govt. topographic and resource surveys (1867–79), 237
transport, *see* canal *and* railroad *and* road
Treaty of:
  Tordesillas (1494), and the Tordesillas Line, *Spain-Portugal*, 31–2, 46, 59, 81, 173, 274n. 10
  London (1604), *England-Spain*, 279n. 63 (i)
  Utrecht (1713/14), *Great Britain/ Holland/Austria et al. – Spain/France*, 108, 127
  Madrid (1750), *Spain-Portugal*, 81–2
  San Ildefonso (1777), *Spain-Portugal*, 82–3
  Paris (1783), *Great Britain-USA*, 162
  Paris (1783), *Great Britain-Spain*, 130, 162
  San Lorenzo (1795, the Pinckney Treaty), *Spain-USA*, 166–7
  Florida and Western Boundaries, (1819, Adams/Onís), *Spain-USA*, 171, 279n. 63 (ii)
  Amity, Commerce, and Navigation (1831–2), *USA-Mexico*, 222
  Guadalupe Hidalgo (1848), *USA-Mexico*, 228
trussing, 18, 99, 203–5

Ulloa, Antonio de, 106–7, 114–15, 277n. 49
Upper Peru:
  transferred to Viceroyalty of Río de la Plata (1776), 129
  Intendancies introduced (1782), 132; *see also* Potosí
Urdaneta, Andrés de, 61

Valdivia, Pedro de, 47
Venezuela (prov. of New Granada), 72–3, 112, 127
Vera Cruz, Mexico:
  founded (1519), 44
  as official imperial trading port, 101, 108
  US Consul at (first appt. 1822/3), and trade competition, 219, 220
Vespucci, Amerigo, 34, 48
Viceroyalties (Spanish):
  in Europe, 68–9
  Viceroyalty of New Granada, 72, 127
  Viceroyalty of New Spain, 69–72, 110–12
  its silver production, 134, 286n. 96
  reorganization of northern frontier into Internal Provinces (18th century), 130
  its juxtaposition with Anglo-America, 248–50;
  Viceroyalty of Peru, 72, 110–12, 121; *see also* Lima
  Viceroyalty of Río de la Plata, 119, 128; *see also* Buenos Aires
Voting Rights Act, USA (1965), and Amendment (1975), 268
  proposed repeal of (1995), 287n. 102 (iii)

Washington, District of Columbia, 157, 193, 238
Washington, George:
  on new Federal Constitution, 155
  on importance of trans-Alleghany West, 163, 168
  sworn in as President (New York, 1789), 157, 252
Webster, Daniel, 157, 190, 212

Whitney, Asa, 231–2
Whitney, Eli, 197
Whitney, Josiah, 237
Wilkes, Charles, and Pacific exploration (1838–42), 181–2

Zacatecas, New Spain/Mexico:
  silver strike at (1546), 70, 71
  served by merchants from Santa Fe, New Mexico, 219
  and from Texas, 228